Reforming the Soviet Economy

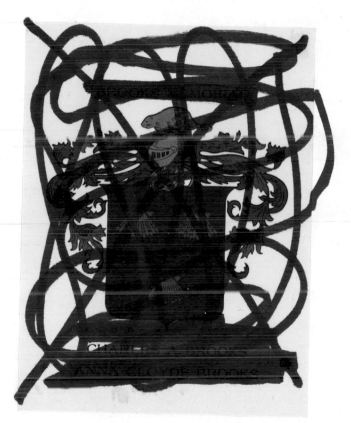

ED A. HEWETT

Reforming the Soviet Economy

Equality versus Efficiency

THE BROOKINGS INSTITUTION
Washington, D.C.

Library of Congress Cataloging-in-Publication data:

Hewett, Edward A.
   Reforming the Soviet economy: equality versus efficiency / Ed A. Hewett.
      p.   cm.
   Includes index.
   ISBN 0-8157-3604-5   ISBN 0-8157-3603-7 (pbk.)
   1. Soviet Union—Economic policy—1981–   2. Soviet Union—Economic
conditions—1976–   I. Title.
   HC336.25.H48   1988
   338.947—dc19   87-29500
                                                             CIP

9 8 7 6 5 4 3 2

THE BROOKINGS INSTITUTION is an independent organization devoted to nonpartisan research, education, and publication in economics, government, foreign policy, and the social sciences generally. Its principal purposes are to aid in the development of sound public policies and to promote public understanding of issues of national importance.

The Institution was founded on December 8, 1927, to merge the activities of the Institute for Government Research, founded in 1916, the Institute of Economics, founded in 1922, and the Robert Brookings Graduate School of Economics and Government, founded in 1924.

The Board of Trustees is responsible for the general administration of the Institution, while the immediate direction of the policies, program, and staff is vested in the President, assisted by an advisory committee of the officers and staff. The by-laws of the Institution state: "It is the function of the Trustees to make possible the conduct of scientific research, and publication, under the most favorable conditions, and to safeguard the independence of the research staff in the pursuit of their studies and in the publication of the results of such studies. It is not a part of their function to determine, control, or influence the conduct of particular investigations or the conclusions reached."

The President bears final responsibility for the decision to publish a manuscript as a Brookings book. In reaching his judgment on the competence, accuracy, and objectivity of each study, the President is advised by the director of the appropriate research program and weighs the views of a panel of expert outside readers who report to him in confidence on the quality of the work. Publication of a work signifies that it is deemed a competent treatment worthy of public consideration but does not imply endorsement of conclusions or recommendations.

The Institution maintains its position of neutrality on issues of public policy in order to safeguard the intellectual freedom of the staff. Hence interpretations or conclusions in Brookings publications should be understood to be solely those of the authors and should not be attributed to the Institution, to its trustees, officers, or other staff members, or to the organizations that support its research.

For my parents

Foreword

RUSSIA began this century as a primarily rural and poor country, militarily weak, in political decay. As the century draws to a close, the USSR, with Russia at its core, has emerged as one of the world's two superpowers with the unquestioned capability to destroy the human race. In between lie Lenin's revolution and Stalin's industrialization, which together transformed Russia and profoundly affected the entire globe.

But the transformation was an uneven one in which military power and improved living standards were purchased through a brute-force industrialization controlled centrally by a party and a government committed to the management of even the smallest details of economic life. Human rights, and even human material needs, were given second priority behind the needs of the nation's, and the party's, security. The USSR's enormously rich endowments in material resources provided the huge quantities of "fuel" required to run this industrialization machine. The result was an economy run by and for bureaucrats, biased toward heavy industry and geared to focus on quantity, not quality.

In March 1985, when Mikhail Gorbachev assumed the post of general secretary, he inherited an economy overripe for reform and a population eager for change. He has set himself to the task with an enthusiasm and a vision that have captured the attention of the world. Gorbachev understands the narrow, primarily military, foundations on which Soviet superpower status rests, and he is clearly concerned about the long-term viability of such a posture. His response is a program for military, economic, political, and social reform that—if it is fully implemented— will match Lenin's revolution in its implications for the USSR, and possibly for the world. It is too early to judge Gorbachev's chances for success or failure. What is important now is to understand what he must do, in order to gauge his progress.

Economic reform lies at the core of Gorbachev's approach; it is his first priority and the focus of much of his attention. In this book Ed A. Hewett, a senior fellow in the Brookings Foreign Policy Studies program, analyzes the challenge facing Gorbachev in his efforts to reform the economic system. The first half of the book examines the strengths and weaknesses of the current system, and the institutions that allow it to function as well as it does. The second half analyzes efforts to reform the system, discussing previous reforms in the post-Stalin era, and then focusing on Gorbachev's current reform program. The final chapter considers what the Gorbachev reforms will mean for the West.

In preparing the study the author benefited from the advice of many scholars in the United States, Europe, and the Soviet Union. He is particularly grateful to John D. Steinbruner, Jerry F. Hough, and Joseph R. Berliner for their comments on early drafts of the whole manuscript. In addition, Thane Gustafson, Philip Hanson, Gertrude E. Schroeder, and Vladimir G. Treml provided helpful advice on selected chapters. The Washington Forum on Soviet Affairs (WAFSA) and many other scholarly forums provided the author with valuable opportunities to try out his ideas. During his several visits to the USSR while he was writing the book, Soviet economists gave generously of their time to discuss some of the material.

The author thanks Christine L. Potts and Mark R. Thibault for research assistance; Caroline Lalire and Venka Macintyre for editing the manuscript; and Stephen K. Wegren and Amy Waychoff for verifying it. He is also grateful to Ruth E. Conrad, Kathryn Ho, Louise F. Skillings, and Susan L. Woollen for typing the various drafts of the manuscript. Max Franke prepared the index.

Funding for this project was provided by the Carnegie Corporation of New York, the Andrew W. Mellon Foundation, the John D. and Catherine T. MacArthur Foundation, the U.S. Department of Energy, the National Council for Soviet and East Europe Research, the Rockefeller Foundation, and the German Marshall Fund of the United States. Brookings is very grateful for this support.

The views in this book are those of the author and should not be ascribed to the persons whose assistance is acknowledged above, to the sources of funding support, or to the trustees, officers, or other staff members of the Brookings Institution.

November 1987   BRUCE K. MAC LAURY
Washington, D.C.   *President*

Contents

Tables

Figures

CHAPTER ONE

The Analytical Framework

Accounting and control—these are the principal *things that are necessary for the "setting up" and correct functioning of the* first phase *of communist society. . . . All citizens become employees and workers of a* single *national state "syndicate." All that is required is that they should work equally—do their proper share of work—and get paid equally. The accounting and control necessary for this have been so utterly* simplified *by capitalism that they have become the extraordinarily simple operations of checking, recording and issuing receipts, which anyone who can read and write and who knows the first four rules of arithmetic can perform.*

—V. I. Lenin [1]

LENIN'S vision of the first, socialist, phase of communism was powerful in its simplicity. He foresaw a system in which workers, having taken control of the capital that was rightfully theirs, would enthusiastically pitch in to produce for each other, distributing the fruits of their labor fairly and equally. The management of that system, although necessary, would not prove an onerous burden, given the educational level of the labor force and the smooth operation of systems inherited from capitalism. Socialism, for Lenin, was the marriage of the efficiency of capitalism and the equity so fervently sought by generations of socialists.

Now, seven decades after the Russian Revolution, Soviet leaders are still searching for a formula that will make that "marriage" work. They have a system that can boast many successes, most notably in achieving some of the equity goals of fundamental importance to Lenin and his Bolshevik party. The state, virtually the sole employer, has a tremendous appetite for labor. Thus the USSR has almost no involuntary unemploy-

1. From V. I. Lenin, *The State and Revolution* (1917), quoted in Henry M. Christman, ed., *Essential Works of Lenin* (Bantam, 1966), p. 348.

1

ment, still one of the main sources of waste and human misery in much of the capitalist world. This guarantee of universal state employment insulates jobs from the vagaries of economic cycles, effectively socializing what in capitalist societies are the individualized costs of business cycles. An egalitarian wage system, combined with subsidized prices for most necessities, fills out the USSR's institutionalized cushion of economic security, which is unmatched in capitalist countries.

This is the ultimate "welfare state." The individual enjoys entitlements to job, income, housing, and necessities guaranteed by the state and—more important—by the Communist party of the Soviet Union. In reality there are serious gaps—both qualitative and quantitative—in the government's fulfillment of those implied commitments, but they should not be allowed to obscure the massive economic security enjoyed by Soviet citizens.

It is the efficiency side of the marriage that has not gone at all well. The system that Josef Stalin imposed in the late 1920s and 1930s—an edifice whose basic outlines are clear in the modern Soviet economy—proved adept at industrializing the economy. But it is now quite clear to Soviet leaders that the management of an industrialized economy, far from being "utterly simple," is enormously complex, and the Stalinist command economy is particularly ill-suited to the task. The system has come into conflict with the level of the economy's development and is creating pressures for reform that grow stronger as the economy matures and becomes more complex.

The logic of those pressures points to a decentralization of the decisionmaking authority toward those with information and thus implies a substantial reduction in the reliance on central administration of the economy. The inevitable implication of such a reduction is a greatly increased reliance on markets, which—when they are working well—are unmatched in their ability to coordinate the complex interactions of firms and individuals in a mature industrial society.

These pressures for reform present Soviet leaders with a dilemma concerning the essence of socialism. The strength of well-functioning markets is the constant, unforgiving, and impersonal pressure they put on all of society for maximum efficiency and maximum efforts to satisfy customers. If left to their own devices, markets are ruthless in punishing individuals and enterprises that do not measure up to pure efficiency criteria. Furthermore, markets can be unfair by rewarding some undeserving individuals who are simply lucky and penalizing others who are unlucky. Those are the costs of the efficiency gains that are the hallmark of markets. Because the rules are clear and their enforcement unforgiving, individuals and enterprises are strongly motivated to do their best to survive, and to prosper. Insert an extensive set of entitlements into this system and the incentives for greater efficiency are diluted, or—in an extreme case such as the USSR—virtually eliminated.

This trade-off between equality and efficiency is what Soviet leaders in the post-Stalin era have struggled with, although not in those precise terms, nor in the stark extremes suggested by a contrast between "pure" markets and "pure" central planning. Rather, the debate has been about particular questions. Under what conditions should enterprises fail? Under what conditions should workers be fired? How should necessities be priced? What is the socially acceptable spread among incomes? Overall, however, the debate is about the trade-off between equality and efficiency. The central issue, still unresolved, is the large one that has occupied intellectuals and politicians for much of the twentieth century: is a socialist state, which values equality more than capitalist states have done, nevertheless an economically viable entity in the modern industrial world? On a more practical plane, the issue for Soviet leaders is whether there is a politically acceptable way that they can dilute the egalitarian bias of this system in favor of more efficiency without jeopardizing the very foundations of the party's legitimacy in the system.

This book analyzes the search for an answer to that question in the oldest socialist state. The main period under consideration is the post-Stalin era. Soviet leaders' dissatisfaction with the system bequeathed to them by Stalin has led to four efforts at reform—Nikita S. Khrushchev's 1957 *sovnarkhoz* reforms, Aleksei N. Kosygin's 1965 reforms, Leonid I. Brezhnev's merger decree of 1973, and a July 1979 decree, all of which have proved disappointing. Now Mikhail S. Gorbachev is in the midst of a fifth reform cycle in which the issues of equality and efficiency are clearer than ever before.

It is too early to assess the results of this latest effort. What is possible, however, and what this book does do, is to provide a sound framework for analyzing the reform process as it unfolds and for speculating on the likely consequences of economic reform in the USSR. The foundations for such a framework can be drawn from the USSR's previous experience with reform, that of other centrally planned economies, and a careful analysis of the particular reform package now emerging.

Previous reform efforts provide a rich store of information on what does and does not work, what is difficult to implement and not so difficult to implement. Because Soviet leaders are no less prone than politicians

elsewhere to repeat past mistakes, a knowledge of their past miscalculations may help observers to identify a weakness in a new reform
program early on, well before it becomes apparent in the performance
statistics or in accounts of problems in implementing the reform.

Reform programs in Eastern Europe and China may suggest not only
pitfalls that similar programs in the Soviet Union might encounter, but
also possible outcomes in the Soviet context. However, such information
will at best be suggestive, since no reform program introduced in one
country can automatically be transferred to another; there are no
certainties in the analysis of reforms in any event, although suggestive
experiences can be a source of interesting hypotheses.

A study of the system itself, how it operates, and the ultimate source
of its performance problems provides powerful tools for analyzing reform
programs and judging the likelihood of their success. In other words, a
clear understanding of the logic of the existing system—the way in which
its constituent parts fit together and function as a whole—and of how
that logic is linked to performance will make it possible to see how well
the design of a reform program respects existing interconnections and,
where it fails in that regard, what the consequences might be for the
reform and for economic performance.

Strengths and Weaknesses of Analysis by an Outside Observer

Any outside observer seeking to analyze developments in a country
such as the USSR brings to the task some definite advantages. Most
notably, the outside observer has the potential to maintain an intellectual
distance from his subject that allows for an impartial analysis of the
operation of the system and efforts to reform it. Economists writing in
the Soviet Union find it more difficult to assume an air of impartiality.
Not only are they very close to their problems and thus may have
difficulty seeing them in a broader context, but various pressures work
against questioning the basic assumptions that underlie the system. The
outsider is not so constrained, and if he can bring himself to view the
system without preconceived notions or conclusions, it can work to his
advantage.

Outsiders with training in Western economics also have a certain
advantage in approaching the economy from a somewhat different

perspective from Soviet-trained economists. The point is not that formal Soviet education in economics is inadequate; it seems to be quite adequate for training economists and planners to operate within the traditional system. Rather, the logic of Soviet economic reform is pointing in the direction of greater use of markets in allocating resources, which involves a series of concepts far more well developed in Western economic theory than in economic theories taught in the Soviet Union.

The handicaps for an outsider, on the other hand, are formidable. Along with intellectual distance comes a dangerously partial view of the important actors in the system and of the relative influence of various factions in the debates about how the system is to change. Distance provides a clarity of vision that can be totally wrong. Debates in the USSR about the system can be quite far-reaching and frank in private (although even there limits exist concerning what an individual can say without jeopardizing his job, and possibly much more), whereas public discussion is severely constrained. What outsiders can read and hear is at best but a faint reflection of what is being discussed in private, and hardly a random sample of the range of opinions expressed. Although the limits on public discussion are loosening under Mikhail Gorbachev, they remain in place on important issues (such as the role of the party). Those in the Soviet Union who push at the edge of limitations on free intellectual inquiry and discourse frequently resort to Aesopian language and faint hints to argue in public about the large issues facing their system.[2]

The outsider watching the debate from afar must develop intellectual capabilities analogous to the power of those very large dishes that scientists use to capture faint signals from outer space. Even the most skilled interpreter of Soviet developments must frequently conjecture about what an author wishes to convey. This technique, which is frequently called Kremlinology, can provide indispensable information on debates that are going on behind the scene but that cannot be discussed publicly.[3]

2. For an excellent example of a work in that genre, see Jerry F. Hough, *The Struggle for the Third World: Soviet Debates and American Options* (Brookings, 1986).

3. Of course Kremlinology can also go too far. Not all weak signals are in fact signals. An excellent discussion of the origins, strengths, and limitations of Kremlinology is included in the collection of articles on the state of Soviet studies in *Survey*, no. 50 (January 1964), pp. 41–194. See, in particular, Arthur E. Adams, "The Hybrid Art of Sovietology," pp. 154–62; and T. H. Rigby, "Crypto-Politics," pp. 183–94. I am grateful to Stephen Wegren for calling my attention to these sources.

The outsider is also handicapped by the quantity and quality of the information available. The sheer volume of information is overwhelming. Newspapers, articles in scientific journals, books, leadership speeches, decrees, and personal interviews all provide potentially useful material for the outside analyst. Furthermore, the diversity as well as the frankly critical nature of much of the information would probably surprise someone who has not come in contact with the Soviet popular press and scientific journals. But the quality varies and there are large lacunae where nothing is available.

Newspapers, Journals, Books, and Personal Interviews

Soviet newspapers provide a good example of the useful information that is available. Each of the hundreds of newspapers published in the Soviet Union is on the whole tedious reading. They are replete with stories praising the operation of the system under the current leader and mocking the capitalist system. Yet those same newspapers carry letters to the editor, results of reader surveys, special investigative reports by the newspaper's staff, and articles from factory managers, academics, party officials, government bureaucrats, and workers—all of which can prove an invaluable source of anecdotal information on the workings of the system. Here one finds a deputy editor of the party's daily paper on industrial issues writing a scathing account of why shoe manufacturers persist in producing shoes in inadequate numbers and of low quality;[4] or the director of a research institute reporting on a survey of 10,150 citizens of employable age in an effort to understand why some people want to work, and others do not;[5] or an economist and a member of the management staff of one of the Soviet Union's largest truck manufacturers documenting the incredibly complex and irrational constraints under which their factory operates, which make it unprofitable to shift output toward more efficient and modern truck production.[6] This sort of information is always available in the Soviet press, although the quality (in terms of frank analysis) seems best during times of debate about the

4. L. Biriukova, "Za shirmoi korrektirovok" (Behind the screen of corrections), *Sotsialisticheskaia industriia*, January 22, 1985. (Hereafter *Sots. ind.*)
5. Interview with V. Ivanov, director of the USSR Academy of Sciences Institute of Social Research, *Izvestiia*, May 3, 1985.
6. G. Popov and V. Shcherbakov, "Podriad dlia zavoda" (Contract for a factory), *Pravda*, June 8, 1985.

system (the current period being an example). However, it is anecdotal and therefore illustrates much but proves little. If one were to rely exclusively on anecdotes in the Soviet press, the system would appear to be on the verge of collapse. That may be true, but it has been the case for a very long time.

The difficult job for an outsider is to show not that the system is on the verge of collapse, but to show how a system in which all of this anecdotal information is true has nevertheless performed as well as it has for so long. Some of the more general information needed for this task can be found in scholarly journals and books that, presumably because they are read by a much more limited audience, cover somewhat broader and—at times—more controversial issues. It is in the journals and books that one can find in-depth, and now and then highly informative, discussions of various components of the economic system, their interactions with other parts of the system, and the workings of the system as a whole. Data not otherwise available are published in journal articles, which may analyze the results of surveys or assess the progress in implementing new experimental programs.

Newspapers, books, and journals together constitute the major sources of the factual information in this book. In addition personal interviews with Soviet economists have been used to fill in some of the gaps. Although much of the information gained from such interviews is nonspecific, it provides a "feel" for the context of a particular article. Few interviews will provide startling new information of lasting and fundamental importance to one's research. Indeed under current law a Soviet citizen is forbidden to pass on anything other than published information to a foreigner, which means that unless one's interviewee is reckless or very sure of himself, he will give out no more than can be found in a careful search of the literature and available statistical sources.[7]

Statistical Data

Other major sources of information include the statistical yearbooks for the economy as a whole, the reports of economic plans and their fulfillment, and Western estimates of Soviet economic performance

7. To be sure, even hints to existing published sources can be very helpful given the mass of available material.

statistics. This is the information that allows the outsider to test his own hypotheses, by supplementing—and possibly going far beyond—the work of Soviet economists.[8]

The quality of official Soviet data is the subject of some dispute among Western specialists working on the Soviet economy. For such a large mass of data as the Soviets publish, few generalizations will hold universally. The general consensus is that there is little evidence of an effort to use statistics to mislead the outside world by putting direct lies out in the form of false data. These data are all that are available to most Soviet researchers, and lies would mislead Soviet economists and distort research results that Soviet leaders use in devising strategies to change policy and reform the system. There is ample evidence that when the regime does not like a number, it stops publishing it.[9]

The much more serious problem for the researcher trying to judge Soviet economic performance is that documentation for Soviet official statistics is almost always inadequate—and frequently nonexistent. Moreover, the quality of documentation has deteriorated since the 1960s. Therefore in many cases we cannot be sure that statistics on important variables provide an acceptable indication of movements in those variables.[10] In sum, gaps in knowledge concerning Soviet statistical methodologies, and not outright lies, are the major impediment to research and the source of controversy over the reliability of Soviet official statistics.

Western reconstructions of Soviet data are sometimes a useful supplement to official data, mainly because they reaggregate Soviet data in

8. The econometric modeling of the Soviet economy is a good example of how western economists have blended Soviet official data with western reconstructions to build a model of the system beyond anything attempted by Soviet economists. See, for example, Donald W. Green and Christopher I. Higgins, *SOVMOD I: A Macroeconomic Model of the Soviet Union* (Crane-Russak, 1977).

9. When, for example, the Soviet grain harvest fell dramatically in 1981, the Central Statistical Administration simply discontinued publication of those data, a policy continued through the 1985 data. Similarly, as infant mortality began to rise in the mid-1970s, those data disappeared from the public record. For a brief account of this practice, and the signs that the policy may be changing under Gorbachev, see Vladimir G. Treml, "A Turning Point in Availability of Soviet Economic Statistics?" *Soviet Economy*, vol. 2 (July–September 1986), pp. 277–82.

10. For example, the fixed-price series for national income, investment, and other macroeconomic aggregates may be so constructed that they overstate real growth. Of course Soviet leaders have very little incentive to encourage the Central Statistical Administration to improve its estimates, which amounts to publishing misleading statistics through a failure to revise procedures known to be inadequate.

a form closer to Western concepts and thus facilitate comparison with Western economies. Abram Bergson's pioneering reconstruction of Soviet national income accounts for the period from 1928 to 1940 set the standard for objective and high-quality estimates of variables familiar to Western economists, but with Soviet data as raw material.[11] The U.S. Central Intelligence Agency's estimates of Soviet gross national product and its components are the prime example of a useful reconstruction.[12] Vladimir Treml and his research team have assembled extremely useful reconstructions of Soviet input-output tables.[13]

In these and other cases, the reconstruction is based primarily on official Soviet data organized in a different way and on guesses concerning the appropriate adjustments for known or suspected biases and for missing data. Consequently the reliability of the Western reconstructions may also be questioned, not only because some of the guesses may be wrong, but also because underlying problems in Soviet data may pass through to the reconstruction.

Nonetheless, the general point is clear: outsiders know, or can find out, a great deal about the Soviet economy, how it performs, and how it operates. Much of this information is useful, because it is candid and critical where it should be. However, it is skewed, and—most important of all—is determined by Soviet leaders, more specifically, by the censors. We know what they allow us to know. As a result, the outsider studying the Soviet economy must do his best to exploit the available data without in any way permitting these data to determine the direction of his inquiry.

Guiding Principles

From the advantages and drawbacks of being an outside observer studying the process of economic reform in the Soviet Union there emerge several guiding principles, which I have followed in this study.

11. Bergson's work dates back to the 1960s and spawned the work of many other scholars, much of it at the Rand Corporation. See, for example, Abram Bergson, *The Real National Income of Soviet Russia since 1928* (Harvard University Press, 1961). For a sampling of the work of others related to Bergson's framework, see U.S. Congress, Joint Economic Committee, *USSR: Measures of Economic Growth and Development, 1950–1980,* Joint Committee Print, 97 Cong. 2 sess. (Government Printing Office, 1982), note 3 on p. 11.

12. See, for example, Joint Economic Committee, *USSR.*

13. Vladimir Treml and others, "The Soviet 1966 and 1972 Input-Output Tables," in U.S. Congress, Joint Economic Committee, *Soviet Economy in a New Perspective,* Joint Committee Print, 94 Cong. 2 sess. (GPO, 1979), pp. 322–76.

First, the primary goal of such studies should be to move a step beyond mere reporting of events and to construct a framework in which the reform process can be analyzed as it unfolds. Second, such a framework, however well constructed, cannot be expected to provide more than fairly broad qualitative predictions of how a reform process will develop. Nevertheless, it should be possible to judge whether a particular reform package has a high or low probability of being implemented and to provide some notion of how such a package, if implemented, will affect economic performance in a broad sense. Going beyond that to put dates on the implementation phase or on the failure of the package is expecting too much. Too many variables—political and economic—are involved to make such judgments a priori.

More important, although it may be possible to achieve an understanding of how and why reform proposals emerge in the Soviet Union, that does not automatically translate into an ability to predict when new reforms will actually be introduced and implemented. To have a decent chance at predicting reforms, one requires a good theory of the politics of economic reform. Such a theory cannot be formulated without a detailed knowledge of the reform proposals initiated within the central bureaucracy that never made it to the stage of a decree. Because outsiders know so little about the reform decrees that never advanced beyond the internal draft stage and so much more about those that were announced, they have a biased picture of the politics of reform in the Soviet Union, too biased to permit serious predictive efforts.

An outside observer is obviously not equipped to advocate a particular reform program, that is, to become part of the debate. Most outsiders simply cannot know enough to go beyond general principles and comment on specifics. More to the point, economic reform is ultimately a domestic political issue, and a recommendation for a particular reform strategy is ultimately a political recommendation. If an outside analyst can at least understand the intricate political considerations that go into a reform process, that in itself is a major accomplishment. To try to go beyond that and advocate a particular path for the process surely exceeds the bounds of what an outside observer can confidently discuss, and in addition interferes with the very important need to remain impartial.

The Concept of Economic Reform

The concept of economic reform is far from an ideal vehicle for studying the way Soviet leaders are dealing with the economy. The term itself is so vague that different people may use it to mean entirely different things and thus may rest their analyses and possibly debates on nothing more than an ambiguity. Also, political leaders do not think, or make policy, in terms of whether or not they should introduce economic reforms. They debate various measures and eventually implement some combination of the alternatives. Some of the measures may qualify as reforms, whereas some may be only policy changes. To add to the possible confusion, politicians have a habit of using, or avoiding the use of, the word *reform* when it suits their political needs, irrespective of what is actually being done. In the 1960s the word *reform* was constantly used by Soviet and Eastern European leaders to describe the policies they were implementing even though in many cases they had no real intention of reforming the economy. Then, for most of the 1970s and early 1980s, the word was dead in the Soviet and Eastern European political lexicon, having been replaced by such euphemisms as *restructuring, further perfection,* and *improvement.* Although now Mikhail Gorbachev has resurrected the term *radical reform* to describe his reforms, it is too early to conclude that the actual reforms emerging will live up to that ambitious term.

Even when an analyst has managed to sort out what is reform and what is not, there is still the danger of defining the field of vision too narrowly by focusing only on "true" instances of economic reforms. A myopic preoccupation with whether or not a particular reform package meets the litmus test of "radical" or "comprehensive" reforms can easily lead one to ignore the real possibilities for improvement by "muddling through," which is, after all, the traditional response of political elites throughout the world to the problems they face.[14] If the analysis of a reform package shows that it is far from comprehensive, or radical, that should not be the end of the story. It is still necessary to ascertain if the measures contemplated have a chance of being implemented, and if so, what their effect might be on performance. Not all partial reform packages are automatically doomed to failure because they ignore some interconnections in the system; and not all policy changes come to naught. The question is how to sort out the possible from the impossible, both in partial reforms and in policy changes.

This is precisely the issue brought to light by developments in the Soviet economic system. The Soviet Union does not appear to be poised on the edge of an era of great comprehensive reforms that will quickly

14. On this point, see Thane Gustafson, *Reform in Soviet Politics: Lessons of Recent Policies on Land and Water* (Cambridge University Press, 1981), pp. 6–8.

liberalize the economy and society at large. At the same time, generational change in the leadership and the growing contradiction between the old system and the requirements of a modern economy in a nation enjoying superpower status are coming together to stimulate significant reforms and policy changes. The result will be "economic reform," and at times it will probably be quite exciting. However, it is unlikely to be "the" comprehensive reform that some think is the ultimate option for a Soviet leadership wanting to retain power.

On Distinguishing between Reforms and Everything Else

To reform an economic system means just that: to reform the institutional arrangements constituting the system by which resources are allocated. All systems consist of a set of institutions that somehow decide what will be produced, in what quantities, who will produce it, what techniques and factor combinations will be used, and who will receive the product. Economic reforms alter the way those decisions are made in an effort to improve performance in areas of importance to political leaders.

Economists' concerns with reforms touch on only a part of the problem of interest to the political scientists and historians who have written on the great reforms in history. When, for example, Samuel Huntington offered his seminal analysis of reform, he was referring to the transformation of an entire traditional system with a weak center and localized pockets of authority into a system with a much stronger center, with a national identity, national goals, and the authority to carry them out.[15] For Huntington the prototypical reform effort was Mustafa Kemal's reforms in Turkey in the 1920s, in which he skillfully united the nation, then reformed political institutions by eliminating the Sultanate, then undertook religious reform, and then finally moved to economic reform.[16] The Soviet Union and Eastern Europe have already experienced those reforms, including—in Huntington's definition—economic reform (unified budget, national currency and banking system, and so on). Economists working on Eastern Europe and the Soviet Union are primarily interested in economic reforms beyond those first great reforms. Other reforms unrelated to the economy are of secondary interest, as are the

15. Samuel P. Huntington, *Political Order in Changing Societies* (Yale University Press, 1968).
16. Ibid., pp. 346–57.

potential political consequences of an economic reform. That is not in any way meant to denigrate the importance of those topics, but merely to distinguish between economic research on the reform of the system and more general inquiries into reform in societies.

Those who write on the Soviet and Eastern European economies generally associate the concept of reform with a decentralization of the resource-allocation authority either to lower echelons of the hierarchy (say, industrial associations in the German Democratic Republic or the Soviet Union) or to enterprises, and with increased reliance on markets to guide resource allocation. Typically the decentralization to lower echelons is referred to as "administrative decentralization"; and the increased reliance on markets "economic decentralization."[17] This focus on decentralization is understandable in that the feasible systemic solutions to the performance expectations that Soviet and Eastern European leaders have set for their economies are probably only consistent with further decentralization. Still, recentralization is also reform, and economic reforms in the Soviet Union could move in that direction.[18]

In this regard it is important to keep in mind a distinction between reforms that recentralize formal authority over resource allocation and those that recentralize effective control over the economy. Reforms that recentralize authority over the resource allocation may, for example, take away from enterprises the authority they previously had to decide on investments, product lines, staffing, and so on, and may move that authority up the hierarchical line to ministries. However, such a move may so overburden the information-gathering and decisionmaking capabilities of ministries that they will lose some of the actual control they had over the operation of enterprises and effectively *decentralize* decisionmaking power.

The converse may also occur. Administrative or economic decentralization may enhance control over the economy in the variables of most importance to the center (the rate of savings and investment,

17. Morris Bornstein, "Economic Reform in Eastern Europe," in U.S. Congress, Joint Economic Committee, *East European Economies Post-Helsinki*, Joint Committee Print, 95 Cong. 1 sess. (GPO, 1977), pp. 102–34.

18. Such a move would probably be a mistake, but there are still many in the USSR who advocate it. For a plausible set of alternative reform scenarios, including both decentralizing and recentralizing reforms, see Joseph S. Berliner, "Planning and Management," in Abram Bergson and Herbert S. Levine, eds., *The Soviet Economy: Toward the Year 2000* (London: Allen and Unwin, 1983), pp. 362–80.

industrial structure, the balance of payments, and so on). This is precisely what the Hungarians said they were trying to do; and they have had some success. When Gorbachev says, as he does frequently, that he wishes to restructure the economy in order to enhance central control and at the same time to strengthen enterprise autonomy, he is—nominally at least—outlining two potentially consistent goals.

Even economic reform, narrow as its scope may be within the context of great reform efforts, still covers a very large set of alternative measures open to Soviet leaders. First there is the issue just discussed: does the reform intend to move authority down the hierarchy or up? A second issue is whether the reform is comprehensive or partial in its design: does it affect all major economic institutions, or just some of them?

Comprehensive Reforms

The distinction between comprehensive and partial reforms implies that economic systems can be separated into discrete parts and that some can be changed while others are not. Of course systems do seem to break down into identifiable "parts": the price system, the wage system, and central planning organs being just three examples. In order to analyze economic reforms, whether comprehensive or partial—indeed to distinguish between the two—it is necessary to define those parts in a way that makes analytical sense. In this book I rely on a fairly simple partitioning of the economic system, which I sketch out only briefly here to facilitate a definition of comprehensive and partial reforms. Later chapters develop the concepts further.

Economic systems are composed of a large number of actors brought together to produce and consume goods and services. How that process operates is the heart of what is called an economic system. Any system can be categorized according to three characteristics of its institutions: the decisionmaking hierarchy that defines the rights and responsibilities of the various actors, the information system that links those actors to each other, and the incentive mechanism that motivates those actors to function within the system.

In the Soviet economic system the major actors are the party, planners, central administrators, enterprise managers, and households. All individuals enter into more than one of these categories, but the distinction is nevertheless an important one since individuals in different capacities have different interests and may behave differently.

Planners include those individuals and institutions that issue obligatory plans, decrees, and instructions designed to control the way the economy currently operates and to specify additions to the economy's productive capacity (through control over new investments). Central administrators are those individuals and institutions (ministries, state committees) charged with overseeing the implementation of plans; their task is to supervise enterprises. Enterprise managers are in charge of the basic economic unit in the system; their task is to manage workers and their capital stock in such a way as to fulfill plans. Households are at the center of the entire process: they supply labor and are the ultimate destination for national product.

The planning process is central to the Soviet economic system, performing many of the functions that markets perform in Western economies. It passes information on production possibilities and consumer preferences among the various actors. It organizes negotiations among the actors—primarily the planners, central administrators, and enterprise managers—whose final goal is to arrive at an internally consistent plan that maximizes goals set by central political authorities. It searches for potential disequilibriums between supplies and demands and seeks to eliminate them; chooses the savings, and therefore the investment, rate; guides the flow of new investment to various sectors; and makes decisions on specialization and trade. This is the heart of the resource allocation mechanism in the USSR, but not all of it.

The wage system plays an important role in managing relations between workers and enterprises, allocating labor among sectors, and it is a critical (although not perfect) instrument for controlling aggregate consumption. The price system is actually several loosely connected price systems serving different functions, mostly of an accounting nature. Prices follow, rather than lead, plans. The financial system plays a small role in this economy, reinforcing, but not interfering with, planned allocations of capital. Investments financed with state funds go through the banking system, but that is primarily a formality; the planning system, and not interest rates, determines the level and structure of investment.

The legal system as it pertains to the economy specifies the rights and responsibilities of the various actors and the mechanism for adjudicating disagreements that arise among them. It manages relations among planners, central administrators, managers, workers, and consumers as well as relations among enterprises. It is the detailed implementation of the general principles of the planned economy.

The party is both actor and institution, and very important in both capacities, with influence throughout the system. Top echelons of the party in the Politburo and Central Committee set the major directions for economic policy, including policy on the system itself. The bottom rungs of the party in factory committees are charged with seeing that their individual units function in ways consistent with those policies. As an actor, the party influences what all other actors do, and in that capacity it is also one of the important institutions in the economic system, influencing how smoothly the economy operates and how well it responds to centrally determined policy changes. It is also one of the center's most important sources of information on problems in the system and on the potential political consequences of dealing with those problems, or ignoring them.

The incentives that motivate actors in this system are to some extent political and reflect the broad influence of the party. However, the primary incentive mechanisms operate on the desire to gain access to goods and services, which means a desire to earn ruble incomes. The difference between the Soviet economy and a market economy in this regard is not so much in the motives as in the fact that in the USSR it is planners, not markets, that manipulate the incentives in an effort to induce actors farther down the hierarchy to do what the planners wish them to do.

A truly comprehensive reform of this system would affect all the institutions simultaneously: the hierarchy, the information system, and the incentive mechanism. A comprehensive reform designed to enhance the role of markets and increase the autonomy of enterprises would simultaneously change the price system so that prices could move more freely to reflect shifts in supply and demand; change the financial system to give more authority to banks to decide on competing applications for funds to finance working capital and investment needs; change the wage system to enable enterprises to compete more freely for labor and to allow wage rates to reflect more accurately the supply of, and demand for, various kinds of labor; and change the role of the party so that enterprises could operate in search of higher profits without party interference. The legal system would require a massive overhaul in which much of the law on enterprise rights and obligations would be totally changed; the very knotty issue of bankruptcy laws would have to be resolved; and an entire new section of the law relating to monopolies, unfair competition, price gouging, and so on would have to be developed.

This exhausting, but not exhaustive, list of requirements for a truly comprehensive reform illustrates the magnitude of the effort involved. It emphasizes the very strong interdependence among institutions in the economy and the consequent need to respect those interconnections in designing a reform package. As stated, even in this incomplete form, every reform ever introduced in the Soviet Union and Eastern Europe would clearly fail the test of being comprehensive. Even the Hungarian reforms of 1968 would probably not "pass," although the intention of those reforms may well have been as broad as the "comprehensivity" discussed here.

As a practical matter, a somewhat weaker definition of "comprehensiveness" of a reform seems to make more sense. A reform would be sufficiently comprehensive if it recognized vital interconnections and sought to deal with them in a way that seems a priori to have a chance of succeeding. Consider a reform that seeks to give enterprises more autonomy to make decisions on their own guided by profits. At the very least it can be judged sufficiently comprehensive if it simultaneously limits the power of central administrators and planners to issue obligatory plans, revises the prices for key inputs in the economy (fuels and raw materials) to reflect relative scarcities more adequately (even if the reform of the price mechanism as a whole is postponed), and implements temporary provisions to override those parts of the law obviously not applicable to the new system. Many reforms in the financial system could be put off since they relate more to investment allocation than to current operations, and it is quite feasible to have a reformed economy in which control over new investments remains centralized (although it is not at all advisable to do that).

This less strict concept of comprehensive reforms is the one I use in this study. It is not at all precisely defined, and the judgment about comprehensivity is just that, a judgment. Nevertheless, it is much more useful than the first, pure, definition. No reform is likely to satisfy the criterion of strict comprehensiveness, but many reforms meeting the looser test of comprehensiveness can have a real and lasting impact on performance in a system. Certainly the Hungarian reforms of 1968 pass the test in their design, as did the Czech reforms. The Kosygin reforms of 1965 would not pass the test (they failed to change the functions of planners and central administrators in a way consistent with new enterprise rights and duties, thus setting up an unavoidable conflict among the actors), but they were the closest to a comprehensive reform of any Soviet reforms in the postwar period.

Partial Reforms

Partial reforms affect only one, or a few, of the key economic institutions in the system, leaving the remainder intact. This might involve a reform of the wage system, or the price system, without changing the remainder of the system. All reforms in the Soviet Union's postwar economic history have been partial in nature, as have most reforms in Eastern Europe and China. Indeed, for the analyst dealing with reforms in centrally planned economies, the major problem is devising an analytical scheme that makes it possible to judge which partial reforms have a chance of successfully achieving their goals and which are likely to fail. If, for example, the rules for setting prices are changed in an effort to encourage economizing on resources, but nothing else changes, will that new price system by itself change enterprise behavior, given how the remainder of the system functions? And will the introduction of the new price system create new conflicts among the actors so that either some actors' functions will have to change or the old price system will have to be reinstituted?

Any partial reform must be scrutinized in this fashion to reach a judgment on how well it will fit into the existing system, or, to put it another way, what the probability is that the old system will "reject" this "implant." Although not all partial reforms are doomed to fail, probably a good starting assumption is that partial reforms will create tensions that will lead Soviet leaders either to reverse the reforms or to introduce further reforms.

Policy Changes

In their fairly constant search for ways to improve the performance of their system, Soviet leaders most often turn not to reforms, whether partial or comprehensive, but to policy changes that use the existing system to implement new policies designed to improve performance. These could involve any of a myriad of new measures ranging from something as minor as a wage increase for coal miners, in an effort to increase their productivity, to something as major as a restructuring of the allocation of investments. In the Soviet Union such policy changes are a constant part of the environment of the economy, as they are in any nation.

The sheer number of policy changes introduced in any particular year is enormous, and in general their effect is minor. They are usually intended as fine-tuning and are not meant to represent a major change of course for the system. That is one reason why analysts regard policy changes as a generally ineffective response to performance problems; they tend to deal with symptoms, not causes. Still, some policy changes can have far-reaching consequences for the system's operation, and quite possibly for its performance.

One of the areas in which major policy changes occur most frequently is investment. Planners have very tight control over the structure of investment, and it is one of the key determinants of the direction of economic development. In the 1970s Brezhnev responded to poor performance in agriculture with an impressive array of new programs supported by a substantial increase in investment funds allocated to agriculture. This was a major policy change in which Brezhnev required five years simply to build up a coalition in the Politburo to support it, and another ten years to implement it.[19] During 1978–80 the leadership responded to emerging problems in the petroleum industry with a significant reallocation of investment funds away from other sectors. In the Twelfth Five-Year Plan, for 1986–90, Mikhail Gorbachev introduced another investment maneuver by shifting funds from other sectors into manufacturing.

These three examples illustrate a general point. Policy changes, although they may not be reforms, can nevertheless constitute a major shift in the system that is capable of generating significant internal opposition and that requires careful political work to garner support. At the same time such policy changes can conceivably affect the performance of the system without running into the difficulties posed by partial reforms. They are not changing the system, but rather are using the existing system to do different things.

Any study of economic reform in the USSR must also be a study of the most important aspects of economic policy in that country. Economic policy changes always accompany economic reform, and sometimes are meant as a substitute for it. Indeed it is the range of policy alternatives open to Soviet leaders, as yet untried, that in part explains the infrequency with which they set out to undertake economic reforms.

That said, it still is sensible to structure the book around economic reforms and not the more general topics of economic policy or the

19. Gustafson, *Reform in Soviet Politics*, pp. 16–33.

management of the economy. The experience of the Soviets with economic policy changes clearly shows that economic reforms are a far more promising way to deal with the problems they face. To be sure, economic policy changes must be part of any reform package if it is to be effective, but the economic reforms themselves will be driving the agenda. By focusing on economic reforms one is focusing on the core of the problem as it exists, and as Soviet leaders have come to understand it. Only by comprehending the pressures for economic reforms and the impediments to undertaking them will it be possible to form a view of economic performance prospects for the Soviet economy in the future.

Stages of Economic Reform

Economic reforms are a process, not an event. The process typically commences with debate, much of which occurs in private, so that outsiders have difficulty following it, but some of which may be public. The debate culminates in a draft of the reform decree (or decrees), which, after public debate, may be modified and then becomes law. Then there is a long period of implementation in which the detailed decrees, regulations, and instructions are issued and brought into force. In most reforms implementation meets resistance, and there is at least a partial retrenchment. After a period of time, during which the old economic performance problems continue (or reemerge), discussions about another reform effort may occur.

Unfortunately it has become general practice to identify a reform by the particular date (Hungary in 1968, or the Kosygin reforms of 1965) associated with the reform decree. This takes attention away from the process, particularly the critical implementation stage in which most reforms die a quiet death. It would be more accurate to identify reforms by lifespans (the Kosygin reforms of 1965–70; the Hungarian reforms of 1968–; and so on) in order to indicate the period of time over which their implementation occurred. In some cases that would coincide with their death, in others with their partially or totally successful implementation. Putting on those end dates is potentially a subject of debate in itself, and never an easy matter, so the practice of identifying reforms with one point in time is probably here to stay.

The reform experience of the Soviet Union, Eastern Europe, and China indicates that although reforms have their peculiar features, they do tend to follow a set of stages that conform with what one would expect of a bureaucracy seeking ways to reform itself. That general pattern is what is being described here. The details, as they apply to either the Soviet Union or Eastern Europe and China, will be left to later chapters.

The Stage Leading to a Decree

Reform cycles begin with an indication by the leadership that a problem or set of problems is sufficiently serious to merit attention. The leadership then gathers information on the nature of the problem and takes readings on possible and politically feasible solutions. The publicly available writings of economists already contain much of the requisite information. Debates about the system are a fairly constant feature of the post-Stalin writings of economists in the Soviet Union and Eastern Europe. However, when the leadership publicly undertakes a search for a new set of system arrangements, what has been merely a smoldering debate can burst into a full-blown argument about what is wrong with the current system and how it could be changed. The result is a substantial addition to existing information on the operation of the system, as well as some sense of the range of options under active consideration.

In recent Soviet economic history two such debates have occurred. During 1962–64 a debate about new bonus schemes blossomed into a full-scale debate on the system, which was followed in 1965 by the Kosygin reforms.[20] Since 1982 a similarly wide-ranging debate has been going on concerning the current reforms. The debate had its genesis in the selection of Iurii V. Andropov as general secretary, and—more important—in the speeches in which he indicated a clear dissatisfaction with economic performance, without any strong suggestion as to what might be done to rectify the situation. The debate continued under Konstatin U. Chernenko and blossomed fully under Gorbachev.

The public debate is typically a muted sampling of the internal debate that precedes any reform. Some of the participants in the public debate are also involved in the internal debate, but certainly not all. Many academic economists, for example, may write about their reform ideas, yet have no opportunity to defend them in the party- and government-

20. Eugene Zaleski, *Planning Reforms in the Soviet Union, 1962–1966: An Analysis of Recent Trends in Economic Organization and Management* (University of North Carolina Press, 1967), pp. 67–102.

sponsored debates. Conversely, many participants in the internal debate say nothing on the outside.[21]

The internal debate is probably much franker than the public one, treating more openly the problems, as well as the possible solutions and impediments to reaching them. Not enough is known about the internal debates in the USSR preceding reforms to generalize on how accurately the publicly available information reflects the range of opinions expressed about what the problems are and what should be done about them. It is plausible to suppose that there are two main ingredients missing from the public record: detailed information on the nature of economic problems (from surveys, classified economic records, from party and security organs on signs of discontent and unrest), and the strongly expressed opinions of the key leadership, undiluted by any effort to present a public illusion of unanimity and harmony within the leadership. Although outside observers must engage in intricate detective work to surmise from faint clues the differences among the leadership, it is highly unlikely that an outsider privileged to observe internal debates would need those finely honed detective skills.

If this is an accurate picture of that part of the internal debates not reflected in public, or to put it another way, if the public debates are a fair, if muted, indication of the substance of the internal debates, then the public record is a useful indicator of the range of possible strategies under consideration. That is my working assumption in this book: we know, or can find out, in general what is being discussed in internal debates, but it is sometimes extremely difficult to be sure who is taking what position, what the coalitions are, and so on.

How do the debates influence, if at all, the final reform decrees? The role of economic debates in the USSR is in some ways analogous to the role of debates in the United States concerning tax reforms. Economists are deeply involved in the public debate and have strong opinions on the issue. However, the ultimate decision on what position the president or particular members of Congress may take is as much a political as an economic one, and here economists have little influence. The same seems to be the case in the Soviet Union. Economists can put forth compelling arguments in favor of one or another reform package, but ultimately party leaders must reach a judgment on the politics of the

21. Many ministers and their staff, Politburo members, the central committee staff, and the regional party secretaries are all involved in the internal debate to one extent or another, yet may not express their views publicly.

various alternatives. Both the internal and external debates may clarify those issues for the leaders but are unlikely to resolve them. The leaders may come away from the debates with a sense of where the major opposition lies and what measures might command the greatest support in the party and the government. Nonetheless, the draft of the decree is still theirs to write. Even though a clear consensus favoring a particular strategy may emerge out of debates among economists, it is quite possible that the decrees and their implementation will take a different approach.

The decree that comes at the end of these debates may not stop further debate, but it certainly will put a damper on it for a time. The decree represents the party leadership's consensus on what should be done, and democratic centralism dictates that the time to argue over that matter has passed. The issue now turns to implementing the reform and assessing its effect on performance.

Implementation

A reform decree constitutes a statement of intent to reform the system, but says little about the strength of the intent within the leadership or the strength of opposition within the system itself. That all becomes evident in the implementation stage. Typically the reform is destroyed in this stage, a victim of bureaucratic guerrilla warfare, or of its own poor design.

The vulnerability of a reform program during implementation arises from three sets of factors. First, there are the potential consequences of poor design, which, early in the implementation stage, may create sufficient chaos to force a retrenchment. Second, there is opposition from the hierarchy itself, namely, the planners and central administrators who are losing power as a consequence of the reform program and who will resort to various tactics in an effort to sabotage the reform. Third, there are the enterprises themselves, which, although they may voice support for the reform, engage in a determined effort to except themselves from the very pressures to improve performance that the reform is designed to generate.

Within each of these three groups of factors there are forces capable of destroying a reform; and the combination of the three is usually fatal. The impact of the factors depends greatly on the political will behind the reform program and the degree of consensus within the population on the necessity of the reform. A leadership committed to reform and a population prepared for it (Hungary) can make significant headway, even in the face of opposition. Without that commitment, even well-designed reforms will fail during implementation.

DESIGN FLAWS. Design flaws refer primarily to inconsistencies that, wittingly or unwittingly, are built into the reform decree. Most of these stem from the partial nature of the reform package. Any set of partial reforms runs the risk of building in contradictions that can be resolved only by retreating from the reforms or moving ahead; and only the most carefully designed partial reforms can minimize that risk (it can never be eliminated). Virtually every reform program actually introduced in the Soviet Union and Eastern Europe has had significant flaws in design. Several of the more common design flaws of reform programs illustrate the nature of the problem.

If enterprises are given more autonomy in their operational decisions and told to rely on profits as a guide to their decisionmaking, but if prices are not reformed in a way to make them a useful guide to the supply and demand conditions for various products, then the design of the reform has set up an inherent contradiction that will show up when enterprises make decisions that are consistent with individual profitability but are unprofitable for society. As that contradiction emerges during the implementation stage, authorities will be under increasing pressure to reassert central control over enterprises in order to prevent further damage to the economy. If the center goes that route instead of moving ahead with price reform, then the retrenchment phase has begun.

Another example of a design flaw that is virtually universal in previous reforms introduced in the Soviet Union and Eastern Europe is that enterprises are given increased autonomy whereas central administrators and planners are expected to do what they have done before—most notably, guarantee the supply of key products to the economy. That sets up a contradiction between the new rights of enterprises and the continuing rights and responsibilities of higher levels in the hierarchy. Unless something is done to alter the responsibilities and rights of higher-level authorities, the logic of the system combines with the distribution of power to take back the temporarily enhanced decisionmaking autonomy of enterprises.

It is interesting to speculate on the reason that flaws are so common in reform designs. In some cases it may be inadvertent. Soviet leaders may be able to convince themselves, for example, that ministries can and will reduce their interference in enterprise affairs and that they will still be able to fulfill central requirements as effectively as they had before. The more common reason for design flaws, however, is probably political, stemming from a natural desire to minimize the chaos associated with reforms and to minimize the intrabureaucratic conflict associated with implementing reforms. Putting off price reform until later is a natural political instinct, albeit bad economics; and delaying a ministerial reorganization may seem to be good bureaucratic politics, even if it turns out to be a fatal error.

The most interesting aspect of design flaws is that they recur so frequently, even though the problems created are well known from earlier experience in the reforming country or in other countries. The problems with ministerial interference in the activities of enterprises was one of the hallmarks of the implementation of the Kosygin reforms, yet precisely the same type of design reappeared in the 1984 industrial experiments that were a prelude to the Gorbachev reforms. The persistence of these design flaws indicates in part how short politicians' memories can be, and how great is their capacity for wishful thinking. The more important contributing factor is simply the strength of opposition to reforms within the party and the bureaucracy that forces political leaders to focus first on the easiest parts of the reform, hoping that somehow they will ride over the rough spots and create a groundswell of support on which they can do the harder things. For whatever reasons these design flaws are built in, the consequences they have for economic performance form a major source of support for the opponents who are out to sabotage the reform.

RESISTANCE FROM PLANNERS AND CENTRAL ADMINISTRATORS. It is natural that any reform program will, as it is being implemented, generate resistance, if in fact it is reforming anything. Planners and central administrators are losing power, and they will fight the reform as best they can, in many cases because they are genuinely convinced that the economy will dissolve in chaos if their particular position or institution is abolished. The only time this resistance can be fairly open is during the debate stage, where it is possible to state a conservative position without fear of contradicting a final leadership position.

After the reform decree is issued, the opposition must go "underground." The decree represents a decision of the top leadership, and the task of the day is to implement it. However, even at this stage there is an opportunity for bureaucratic guerrilla warfare because the actual character of the reform is determined by the implementing decrees, and not by the initial decree. The first line of defense is to delay issuing the decrees. After Brezhnev's 1973 decree on the merger of enterprises into production associations and a shift of some ministerial powers to those associations and intermediate authorities, the ministries delayed the implementing regulations until Brezhnev openly criticized them for their delay and ordered them to proceed. Similarly, in July 1983 Andropov announced experiments with expanded autonomy for enterprises in five ministries and ordered the ministries to prepare to introduce the reforms by January 1, 1984. In December 1983 the Politburo called in the ministers involved to criticize them for dragging their feet, ordering them to speed up the issuance of implementing regulations. In some cases the central administrators never issue the regulations, and they get away with it, the July 1979 decree being a good case in point.

The second line of defense is in the content of the implementing regulations themselves. There is ample evidence that the ministries and planning authorities are not above designing an implementing decree that at the very least "bends" the meaning of the reform in the direction of the old system. In some cases they may simply ignore part of the decree and do things as they have done them in the past.[22]

The third line of defense is to interpret whatever regulations have been issued in such a way as to minimize the actual effect of the reforms. In the case of the 1973 reforms, for example, the ministries finally did, under prodding from Brezhnev, issue decrees on the mergers and shifts of power. But the final result was no more than a formalistic shift to a new version of the old system. The ministries conformed to the letter of the law in the new reform, but ignored the spirit. In 1984, after the drubbing Andropov gave the all-union ministries for dragging their feet on the experiments, they did issue the required decrees. Then the ministries proceeded to interpret them in such a way that in fact they retained much of their old power and old operating procedures.

This third line of defense is virtually impossible for an outsider to follow contemporaneously, and not much easier for the Soviet leadership. The ministries have enormous leverage over enterprise manage-

22. Consider, for example, the complaint of a doctor of law from Moscow writing about this problem. He notes that several decrees of the state, from the 1979 reform and since, have given enterprises the right to make their own decision on how large their capital expenditures will be for housing financed from funds set aside within the enterprise for that purpose. Yet, contrary to the law, the banks and Gosplan have maintained limits on those expenditures. See A. Vengerov, "Uvlechenie ogranichen-iiami" (A passion for limitations), *Sots. ind.,* July 30, 1985.

ment flowing from the power to appoint managers, promote or demote them, and set their salaries and bonuses. Thus, even if a decree formally states that a ministry can no longer instruct a manager on, say, investments for renovating a factory, the fact is that if the ministry informally pressures the enterprise manager to take a certain decision, he has every reason to respond to that pressure and to ignore the formal decree.

The result of these three lines of defense is that reform decrees take considerable time to implement and are seldom fully implemented as intended. The latter point is important because it is not fully appreciated in the West. Given the fact that the information available about a reform is skewed toward the public information— decrees, some anecdotes, and some of the implementing regulations—there is a temptation to confuse the decrees with the reform as it was actually implemented. Thus one can easily find analyses of the effect of "the" Hungarian reform on economic performance in Hungary, where "the" reform is associated with the 1968 decree. In fact the reform as it was actually implemented in Hungary fell far short of the decree, and whatever changes did occur in Hungarian economic performance can be attributed not to that decree, but to what actually occurred. The general lesson is that in order to assess what effect any reform has on performance, it is first necessary to ascertain carefully the de facto content of the actual reform.

The final line of defense for the opponents comes as implementing regulations are put into place and problems in performance begin to arise, because of either design flaws or simply the difficulties of moving from one system to another. Inflationary pressures may surface as enterprises exercise their new-found autonomy at a rate exceeding what the economy can manage; balance of payments problems may arise as import demand surges; interruptions in supplies of key products may develop—those are just three of a large number of potential difficulties. Such difficulties are to be expected even of a well-designed reform package; a poorly designed package makes matters worse. All the while, the opposition is searching for support for its case against the reform, and it will latch onto performance problems to strengthen its case, irrespective of whether those performance problems are in fact attributable to the reform.

In this sense design flaws play into the hands of the opposition, but they may also simply reflect the influence of the opposition during the debate stage. In an effort to minimize the extent of the reform, the opposition may manage to—consciously or unconsciously—build in design flaws that will make its job easier during the implementation stage.

OPPOSITION FROM THE ENTERPRISES AND WORKERS. Even a well-designed reform, with support from the planners and central administrators, will run into opposition from enterprises in the form of a battle for exceptions. Reforms are an effort to dismantle the particularized network of subsidies and taxes negotiated between each enterprise and its ministry, reflecting a deal in which the enterprise obtains funds and the ministry has the most important plan indicators fulfilled. In place of this maze of special deals, the reform seeks to introduce simple, universal criteria for determining winners and losers, based on a set of meaningful prices.

At the new prices, and in the new environment in which the power of customers is enhanced, many enterprises will lose money unless they make drastic alterations in their operations, which may include firing some workers; some enterprises with old capital and outmoded products may simply have to close down. As implementation begins, enterprises will argue for a temporary exception in their own case, in the form of a subsidy sufficient to buy time to make the necessary adjustments to higher input prices, higher capital prices, and a more demanding set of customers. Typically the manager will find allies in the local party and government officials who are easily convinced that without the subsidy the enterprise will have to lay off workers.

This is the conflict between equality and efficiency in its raw, and most political, form. If a system of well-defined rules for winners and losers is to be credible, then there must actually be winners and losers. Yet Soviet society has grown accustomed to the socialization of all losses, and a move to de-socialize those losses can create political problems of a sort any sensible Soviet leader will seek to minimize. Hence the temptation is to grant exceptions, with the expectation that, over time, the rules can be enforced universally.

This battle for exceptions is much harder to follow than the decrees, indeed almost impossible to follow contemporaneously. Newspapers do not publish lists of enterprises that have been granted exceptions; ministers naturally do not brag about them; political leaders do not discuss them and many times may not even know about them. Frequently it is not until some years into the implementation stage that the extent of exceptions becomes known, either during a postmortem explaining the failure of the reform or during the debate leading up to the beginning of the next reform cycle. Nevertheless, the battle for exceptions is a critical, if not the critical, factor determining the ultimate fate of a reform program. Well-intentioned and well-designed programs can easily fall prey to a liberal policy of exceptions granted by central administrators, where no single exception is important, yet collectively they destroy the reform.

A LOSS OF POLITICAL WILL. The problems in economic performance flowing from the difficulty of transition and design flaws will combine with the opposition forces to put tremendous pressure on leaders to retreat from the reform. There are several ways in which the will of the leadership to implement the reforms—assuming it was there in the first place—can be eroded during the implementation stage.

First of all, the problems in performance may come to genuinely threaten the economic, and therefore the political, stability of the system. At least that is the way it may seem to a leadership moving into uncharted waters. If inflation accelerates, the balance of payments deteriorates, or market disruptions increase, the natural fear will be that this could get out of hand and that as a consequence the party's control over the entire society could be threatened. That is a powerful argument for the opposition (which probably warned of such problems during the debates), particularly if the performance problems are emerging, as they probably are. Only a very strong and confident leadership, with an economy strong enough to take a period of shocks, would be able to sustain the reform course in the face of such criticism.

An even more difficult issue during the implementation phase arises in the form of various dilemmas regarding equality. Guaranteed full employment, a relatively flat income distribution, and stable prices will be threatened during the implementation stage of a reform, particularly if it is a comprehensive reform that decentralizes economic decision-making to the enterprise level. As the reform is implemented, some people will make enormous incomes by past standards as they cash in on the rents accruing to scarce factors (including entrepreneurship), and others will be in danger of losing their jobs. Even a program to retrain workers threatened by the reform is not likely to mollify those faced suddenly, for the first time in their lives, with the possibility of involuntary unemployment.

The reduction in economic security is the first half of a shift toward somewhat less equality in an effort to bring about an increase in the efficiency with which the economy operates. What makes it particularly difficult for the leadership is that there is a lag between cause and effect and a great deal of uncertainty about the exact nature of the links. During the interim, when the population is feeling the cold impersonal effect of the new rules without seeing any dramatic improvement in its economic situation, the pressures will grow rapidly for a retreat. The result is a test of political will that few leaders in the Soviet Union or Eastern Europe have ever passed.

Retrenchment

The typical response is a retrenchment. It may come early, in the failure to implement a reform; in midstream if the leadership allows the bureaucracy to get away with sabotage; or later, in new decrees that have the effect of neutralizing the reform. When, if, and how the retrenchment comes depends on the interplay of a number of factors already discussed: most notably, the design of the reform, the strength of the resistance, the degree of unity in the leadership concerning the reform, and therefore the strength of political will the leadership brings to the inevitable battle.

Each reform has its particular array of forces, factors, and personalities that are critical to determining the final outcome. A study of the reform efforts from Khrushchev to Brezhnev provides information on four reform cycles in which the combination of critical components was fatal to the reform and the outcome was virtually complete retrenchment. Whether Gorbachev's reforms are likely to suffer the same fate cannot be adequately addressed without analyzing the nature of the system, the history of previous reform efforts, and the design of his emerging reform.

CHAPTER TWO

Soviet Economic Performance: Strengths and Weaknesses

In general, comrades, there are many pressing problems in the economy. I have, to be sure, no prepared prescriptions for their resolution. But it falls to all of us—the Central Committee of the Party—to find answers. . . . I wish to emphasize that these questions are of the highest order and of vital importance for the country. By deciding them successfully, the economy will continue to advance, and the welfare of the population will increase. —Iurii V. Andropov, November 22, 1982[1]

The historic fate of the country, the position of socialism in the modern world in large part depends on how we proceed from here. . . . We must achieve a significant acceleration in social-economic progress. There simply is no other path.
—Mikhail S. Gorbachev, April 23, 1985[2]

There has been a tendency for some Government spokesmen to describe the Soviet economy as one in crisis, a basket case in danger of collapse. My view is that this exaggerates the seriousness of Soviet economic problems, which are serious enough without exaggeration. I do not think it serves a useful purpose to magnify their economic difficulties out of proportion, and I think it is counterproductive to deceive ourselves about the strength as well as the weakness of the Soviet Economy.
—Senator William Proxmire, June 28, 1983[3]

1. "Rech' General'nogo sekretaria TsK KPSS Iu. V. Andropova na Plenume TsK KPSS 22 Noiabria 1982 goda" (Speech of the general secretary of the CC of the CPSU Iu. V. Andropov at the Plenum of the CC of the CPSU, 22 November 1982), *Kommunist*, no. 17 (November 1982), p. 16.

2. "O sozyve ocherednogo XXVII s"ezda KPSS i zadachakh, sviazannykh s ego podgotovkoi i provedeniem. Doklad General'nogo sekretaria TsK KPSS M. S. Gorbacheva na Plenume TsK KPSS 23 Aprelia 1985 goda" (On the convocation of the regular XXVII Congress of the CPSU and the tasks connected with its preparation and execution. The report of the general secretary of the CC of the CPSU, M. S. Gorbachev at the Plenum of the CC of the CPSU, 23 April 1985), *Kommunist*, no. 7 (May 1985), p. 6.

3. U.S. Joint Economic Committee, *Allocation of Resources in the Soviet Union*

31

FOR SOME TIME many in the West have taken for granted that the USSR is in an economic crisis. The primary evidence supporting that conviction comes from the most authoritative of sources: the Soviet economic press and economic journals, official Soviet economic statistics, and Soviet leaders themselves. Even a casual reading of the economic literature over any of the past four decades turns up an abundant supply of stories that add up to an economy in which obsolete, unreliable products are the norm, not the exception. Official statistics provide further support in their documentation of a slowdown in economic growth seemingly impervious to the almost constant efforts of Soviet planners to stabilize the situation through policy changes and economic reforms.

Soviet economic leaders have traditionally been more circumspect than Soviet publications in their public comments on the country's economic performance. Since the death of Brezhnev, however, top Soviet political leaders have joined the ranks of the economy's harshest critics. Mikhail Gorbachev, picking up on a theme introduced forcefully by Iurii Andropov, leaves no doubt that he regards the resolution of Soviet economic problems as his top priority. "The . . . fate of the country, the position of socialism" rest, he tells us, on the leadership's ability to turn this economy around.

As if all this were not enough, a visit to the USSR provides even more evidence of an economy in deep difficulty. The service sector is incredibly primitive by Western standards, indeed by world standards. Consumer durables are scarce; the selection is modest; the underlying technology dates from the early postwar years; and the quality is frequently poor. This economy seems unable to produce a cheap, reliable, automatic washing machine, radio, or phonograph, and cheap, powerful hand calculators and personal computers are still no more than a distant hope. Decent fruits and vegetables available throughout the country in quantity at reasonable prices are seemingly out of reach even though 20 percent of the labor force works in agriculture.

Yet this same economy produces a titanium-hulled "alpha-class" submarine that goes faster and deeper than any submarine in the world. It has also managed to build one of the world's largest natural gas distribution systems by relying primarily on domestically produced compressors and turbines, and all of this realized ahead of schedule,

and China—1983, Hearings before the Subcommittee on International Trade, Finance, and Security Economics, 98 Cong. I sess. (Government Printing Office, 1984), pt. 9, p. 2.

despite the U.S. administration's best efforts to delay construction. With its own technology the Soviet Union has sent remote-operated machinery to the moon, established and maintained a working space station, drilled the deepest oil wells in the world, and developed a technology for producing continuous cast aluminum that U.S. defense contractors have purchased. More important, over the last quarter century, it has moved from a position of distinct strategic inferiority vis-à-vis the United States to one of at least parity, if not superiority.

The manual washing machine—which may not work anyway—the titanium-hulled submarine, the abacus a Soviet clerk uses to add up a customer's bill in the bookstore, and the world's largest-capacity, long-distance power lines are symbols of the vast range of Soviet economic capabilities. An adequate description of Soviet economic performance must accommodate all of them.

On the Need for a Balanced Picture

It is dangerous, as Senator Proxmire so rightly points out, to either under- or overestimate Soviet economic capabilities. To underestimate them—for example, to believe that the Soviet economy is incapable of an adequate response to President Ronald Reagan's Strategic Defense Initiative—is self-delusion, which at best could lead the United States to engage in a very expensive round of the arms race and could result in far less than the anticipated improvement in U.S. national security. To overestimate Soviet economic capabilities, particularly as they relate to defense technologies, could lead to unnecessarily large defense expenditures, efforts at embargo or export restrictions, and other measures that in fact are unnecessary. The only sensible way to assess Soviet economic performance is to draw up a balance sheet that captures both the strengths and weaknesses of performance and to relate those to specific capabilities, for example, in the area of national security.

There are compelling reasons to begin a study of the dynamics of economic reform in the Soviet Union by drawing up such a balance sheet. It is possible, without much effort at all, to list performance problems associated with Soviet central planning that add up to a clear justification for immediate and far-reaching economic reforms. Indeed, the problems are so serious, and the solutions seem so obvious, that many despair of finding a rational explanation for the persistence of the old system. The plausible explanations seem to boil down to the leadership's desire to retain power at virtually all costs, supported by the ideological blinders that automatically exclude the more effective responses to Soviet economic problems.

Although those considerations surely capture part of the explanation, they do not tell the entire story. Soviet leaders are neither as irrational nor as blind as a superficial familiarity with the system might suggest. There have been, and still are, some strong points in the performance of the Soviet economic system that distinguish it from Western economies and are valued by both the leadership and the population. In the past, Soviet leaders have encountered tremendous difficulties in devising and implementing reforms that adequately address economic performance problems because they have sought a compromise that preserves the strengths in the old system while eliminating, or reducing, the weaknesses. Because the strengths and the weaknesses are intertwined, they have not yet succeeded. But they have not yet exhausted the options they think they have. Only by understanding this point is it possible to make sense of the reforms that have *not* been introduced, as well as those that have.

This chapter considers Soviet economic performance, focusing first on the strengths, and then on the weaknesses. The data used in the analysis span the quarter century from 1960 to 1985. These are the years that form the immediate backdrop to the efforts to improve the system, including the ongoing Gorbachev reforms. The more recent data available for 1986–87 already show, or can be used to test for, the consequences of Gorbachev's early policy measures. Those issues and the data necessary to explore them are discussed in chapters 7 and 8.

Assessing Soviet Economic Performance

Any analysis of the strengths and weaknesses of Soviet economic performance is complicated by the fact that there is no universal norm to which one can refer in labeling a particular aspect of Soviet economic performance as "strong" or "weak." Different social groups in the USSR naturally have different viewpoints about a particular aspect of the system: Soviet leaders regard the defense buildup as a strong point of Soviet economic performance; Soviet consumers may—with justification—regard that as one reason they have such a poor selection of consumer goods. Soviet workers value highly the job security in the

USSR, whereas Soviet leaders are coming to regard job security as one of the causal factors behind low labor productivity. These are just two instances in which the preferences of the leadership and the population diverge. It is important, therefore, to be clear on whose preferences are being used to measure performance.

The Norms Used

The preferences of Soviet leaders—defined for convenience as encompassing the Central Committee of the Communist Party of the Soviet Union (CPSU), but giving heavy weight to the Politburo—obviously matter the most. If the leaders judge economic performance to be satisfactory, then there is little reason to expect actions to change it. In theory, whether or not the population at large concurs in that assessment is not, or at least need not be, of great concern. If, on the other hand, the leaders are dissatisfied with performance, then they are likely to seek improvement, either through changes in policy or through changes in the system itself.

Although Soviet leaders can ignore societal preferences concerning the economy, they do so at their own peril. Economic performance is an important source of whatever support may exist for government policies, and, ultimately, for the party's control over society. Consequently political leaders pay close attention to the population's concerns regarding the economy and make an obvious, constant effort to show that they understand the population's concerns and are doing their best to respond to them.

Nevertheless, Soviet leaders' preferences count most. Soviet leaders are the "gatekeepers" defining which problems are sufficiently serious to merit attention and what policy and reform measures are acceptable responses to those problems. The preferences of the population can change the leadership calculus only when the political risks of not changing are judged high enough to require remedial action. These considerations all suggest that leadership preferences and perceptions are the ones to focus on in discussing the strengths and weaknesses of Soviet economic performance.

A Brief Note on Statistics

The aggregate data used in this chapter to evaluate the strengths and weaknesses of Soviet economic performance are drawn primarily from

official Soviet statistics, supplemented by data from the CIA and other
sources wherever the latter sources tell a different story or fill a gap left
by Soviet data. There are many reasons to be very careful about basing
judgments solely on Soviet data. Soviet official data tend to be poorly
documented, if documented at all; and what we do know suggests that
many of the data sets have limited validity as indicators of the underlying
processes to which they refer. Even CIA data should be approached
with great care since they derive primarily from Soviet micro data.

Soviet data seem least reliable in the area of national income statistics.
One obvious problem is that official statistics are limited to output of
material branches, excluding all services (legal or, of course, illegal), so
that the government publishes no comprehensive measure of aggregate
economic activity. But more important is the growing conviction, shared
by Soviet and Western economists, that Soviet macroeconomic statistics
overstate the rate of real growth and understate the true rate of inflation.[4]
The strongest case has been made for high rates of hidden inflation in
the machinebuilding and metalworking sector, and therefore in the
investment statistics, with estimates in the range of 4–10 percent per
annum for recent years.[5] That may account for 10 percent of national
income.[6] The case has yet to be made for the remaining 90 percent, but
high rates of hidden inflation there are not excluded. To the extent that
there is hidden inflation, it probably increased in recent years.[7]

4. For arguments that Soviet real growth is less than official statistics claim, see
Alec Nove, "Has Soviet Growth Ceased?" paper presented to the Manchester Statistical
Society, November 15, 1983; and Michael Ellman, "Did Soviet Economic Growth End
in 1978?" in Jan Drewnowski, ed., *Crisis in the East European Economy: The Spread
of the Polish Disease* (London: St. Martins Press, 1982), pp. 131–41. For a Soviet
economist's argument in the same vein, see Vasilii Seliunin and Grigorii Khanin,
"Lukavaia tsifra" (Cunning figures), *Novyi mir*, no. 2 (February 1987), pp. 181–201.

5. For a general discussion of the literature on this, see Philip Hanson, "The CIA,
The TsSU and the Real Growth of Soviet Investment," *Soviet Studies*, vol. 36 (October
1984), pp. 571–81. Also see David Dyker, "More on Inflation in Soviet Investment
Statistics," *Radio Liberty Research Bulletin*, RL 104/85, April 2, 1985. The estimate of
a 10 percent rate of inflation for machinery and equipment is attributed to a Gossnab
official, V. Doronin; see Vasilii Seliunin, "Eksperiment" (Experiment), *Novyi mir*, no.
8 (August 1985), p. 186.

6. Machinery accounts for 40 percent of gross investment; and gross investment is
roughly one quarter of national income. That means investment works out at about 10
percent of national income.

7. See "Panel on Soviet Economic Performance: Perceptions on a Confusing Set of
Statistics," *Soviet Economy*, vol. 3 (January–March 1987), pp. 3–39.

At this point the doubts about Soviet data are not sufficiently grave, or at least those in the West and the USSR have not sufficiently documented their grave doubts, to justify ignoring Soviet national income accounts. In any event, they are generally acknowledged to accurately reflect—in general trends, although not in detail—the data available to the leadership. Nonetheless, care must be exercised in drawing conclusions from these data. My general rule in this chapter is to focus on general trends that are likely to survive a revision of Soviet data, which appears increasingly likely under Gorbachev.[8] Turning points in a particular year, or differences of only a few percentage points, are generally ignored, since they may in fact be an illusion.

Soviet Economic Performance: Strengths

From the point of view of Soviet leaders, the performance of the system has been strong, or positive, in three respects: historically, the growth rates of economic activity and living standards have been high; an extraordinarily high degree of economic security has been maintained throughout this growth process; and an egalitarian bias has been built into the system. Soviet leaders are obviously dissatisfied with some aspects of the performance in these areas, but on the whole they think the record here is good.

The Growth Record

Soviet leaders have good reason to be proud of their country's economic growth, which was particularly impressive during the first quarter century of Soviet power. Based on Soviet official data, growth rates for the period are simply unbelievable. But even Abram Bergson's meticulous efforts to eliminate the upward bias and construct a fair measure of Soviet GNP growth come up with very respectable rates for

8. There is an increasingly acrimonious debate about the Central Statistical Administration and the weaknesses of its data, symbolized by the publication of the Selunin and Khanin article in *Novyi mir*. Also the Politburo in its April 2, 1987, meeting reviewed the work of statistical organs and called for a major overhaul of the statistical system; a new decree on reforms in statistics is scheduled for the fall of 1987.

1928–55, which are in the range of 4.4–6.3 percent per annum.[9] These years witnessed the first and most important spurt of industrialization in the Soviet Union. Entire industries were created, along with millions of jobs that drew peasants away from the countryside and into higher-paying jobs and higher living standards. They were also higher-productivity jobs, a major source of the high growth rates.[10]

The postwar record, while less impressive, is still decent by world standards. Soviet statistical yearbooks indicate that by the mid-1980s the level of economic activity was ten times higher than in 1950 and that per capita consumption had increased fivefold. Simultaneously a massive and successful effort was under way to achieve rough parity with the United States in military capabilities.[11]

More conservative U.S. Central Intelligence Agency estimates of Soviet national income accounts still suggest a very good performance record, according to Western concepts. The CIA estimates that Soviet real GNP rose about 4.5 times between 1950 and the mid-1980s, an average of slightly under 4.5 percent per annum. Over roughly the same period, GNP in the United States rose 2.7 times, and in the United Kingdom it doubled. The remainder of Europe did better than that—real GNP in Germany, France, and Italy rose 4–4.5 times—but even by that standard, Soviet economic performance over the past third century is quite satisfactory.[12]

As for Soviet leaders' views of their performance, their own data probably have much more weight than CIA reestimates (although the latter are probably known to Soviet leaders and may carry some

9. Abram Bergson, *The Real National Income of Soviet Russia since 1928* (Harvard University Press, 1961), p. 261. The lower figure is an estimate of GNP growth, weighted by Bergson's estimate of 1937 ruble factor costs, for all years during the 1928–55 period. The upper figure is the result of a "composite" index that blends weights from 1928, 1937, and 1950, and, in addition, attempts to impute to the wartime years the growth rates that would have obtained if there had been no war over the entire period. There are other figures within the interval under different assumptions.

10. Ibid., p. 284.

11. Data are from Tsentral'noe statisticheskoe upravlenie SSSR, *Narodnoe kho-ziaistvo SSSR v 1984 g: Statisticheskii ezhegodnik* (Moscow: "Finansy i statistika"), p. 36. (Hereafter cited as *Narkhoz.*)

12. Central Intelligence Agency, *Handbook of Economic Statistics, 1985: A Reference Aid*, CPAS 85-10001 (Directorate of Intelligence, September 1985), p. 39; Joint Economic Committee, *USSR: Measures of Economic Growth and Development, 1950–1980*, Joint Committee Print, 97 Cong. 2 sess. (GPO, 1982) pp. 64–67; and U.S. Department of Commerce, Bureau of the Census, *Statistical Abstract of the United States, 1985*, 105th edition (GPO, 1984), p. 434.

weight).[13] They would like to continue that growth performance in the future and improve on it, if possible. Indeed, that is an important thrust of Mikhail Gorbachev's efforts to revitalize the Soviet economy. The motive behind this desire for sustained high growth rates is easily discernible: a preference for dividing a rapidly expanding pie among consumption, investment, and defense. There is also the perpetual goal to close the gap between Soviet living standards and those of developed Western countries, particularly the United States. Thus rapid economic growth is one of the major criteria by which leaders will judge the success or failure of new policies and economic reforms.

Economic Security

Possibly even more impressive to Soviet leaders, and to the population, is the economic security provided by the system. This is basically a fixed-price system with an internally generated excess demand for labor and a relatively flat income distribution. The result is something as close to full employment as any industrialized economy can hope to achieve, with a relatively low level of uncertainty about nominal and real incomes, both of which add up to a degree of personal economic security in the workplace virtually unparalleled in Western countries. In effect, the party and government in the USSR have issued workers as a whole an insurance policy against personal economic risk that no insurance company in the West could afford to offer, and that no government in the West has been inclined to offer.

FULL EMPLOYMENT. The official position of the Soviet government is, in effect, that involuntary unemployment is close to zero; if there is

13. An interesting question in itself is how carefully Soviet leaders, or at least their advisers, follow Western analyses of their economy and what conclusions they draw from divergences between their own data or analyses and Western data and analyses.

In recent years Soviet specialists in the West have encountered increasing interest in their work on the part of Soviet economists working on the Soviet economy. The U.S. Joint Economic Committee's collection of articles on the Soviet economy published every three years, which contains a number of pieces written primarily by Soviet specialists (including those working in the Central Intelligence Agency), is always ordered in significant quantities for direct shipment to the USSR. The volume *The Soviet Economy: Toward the Year 2000,* edited by Abram Bergson and Herbert Levine (George Allen and Unwin), has been translated into Russian, and was circulated in numbered copies, accompanied by a special introduction. These are a few of many indications that the work of Western specialists on the Soviet economy is followed in the USSR. How much of that filters to the top and is taken seriously is not known.

unemployment, it is transitional in nature (as individuals move from one job to another). As a consequence, there are no unemployment statistics, nor is there a well-developed network of institutions designed to help the unemployed find a new job. For both of these reasons it is difficult to say what the employment situation in the Soviet Union actually is.

In fact, unemployment does exist in the Soviet Union. By world standards, however, the level of unemployment appears to be low, and a high proportion of it is voluntary and not the result of a lack of jobs.

The existence of unemployment is documented in scattered surveys of workers who have either been dismissed or have left their jobs in particular factories or regions. Berliner cites a study of new workers in four Gorky factories in the mid-1960s that found that 28 percent of the workers had been out of work for at least twenty days, and 12 percent had been without a job for over a month. Another survey of workers who left their jobs voluntarily in Sverdlovsk in the mid-1960s concluded that the average length of unemployment for those individuals was twenty-three days.[14]

More recent studies suggest the length of unemployment is certainly no shorter in the 1980s, and may be considerably longer than it was in the 1960s. A 1981 survey of enterprises in Novosibirsk concluded that although half of the unemployed found a new job within a month, the average period of unemployment—excluding those who were out of work more than 180 days—was 40 days; when all the unemployed were included, the average rose to 53 days. This is not strictly comparable to the 1960s studies, since they covered only those who voluntarily left their jobs, whereas the later study covers workers unemployed for all reasons, including dismissal.[15]

There is also some circumstantial evidence of unemployment in small towns and in regions that receive only limited capital funds for new investments because they are of relatively low priority.[16] Speaking in

14. Joseph S. Berliner, *The Innovation Decision in Soviet Industry* (MIT Press, 1976), p. 168.

15. Z. V. Kupriianova, "Tekuchest' kadrov: perelomit' nezhelatel'nye tendentsii" (Turnover of cadre: reversing undesirable tendencies), *EKO*, no. 5 (May 1984), p. 23. Kupriianova notes that an important reason for the length of periods of unemployment in her Novosibirsk sample was that people coming into the region required a substantial amount of time to arrange permission to stay in the city, arrange for children, and so on. She also found a significant increase since 1964 in absences due to illness or the family situation, an important element of the latter being the unavailability of places in children's preschools, which forced a parent to stay home from work.

16. Berliner, *Innovation Decision*, p. 163. Both Gorbachev and Ryzhkov tacitly

broad terms, it is probably the case that most of the Asian republics, which account for the bulk of additions to the Soviet labor force, are sufficiently capital-poor to have significant pockets of unemployment.

The same surveys mentioned earlier, and others, provide some indications of why workers leave their jobs. Soviet enterprises have the theoretical right to fire workers for disciplinary reasons, but also when demand for their products falls. However, enterprise managers are required to help workers who are released because of staff reductions to find new jobs, either within the factory or within the area in which the factory is located.[17] The demand for labor is so high, particularly in the European USSR, that enterprise directors probably fire workers only if they cause disciplinary problems.[18]

Surveys at the Novosibirsk Institute of the Economics and Organization of Industrial Production for the years 1964, 1970, and 1981 provide useful information on the motives of those who voluntarily leave their jobs. The most important reason for leaving, and it is becoming increasingly important, has been living standards, which in 1981 accounted for 39 percent of resignations. Within this category the most important issue was housing; 10 percent of the workers who left voluntarily cited that as a reason in 1964, 16.5 percent in 1981. The second most important reason has been working conditions, which in 1981 accounted for 27 percent of the leavings.[19]

Housing is a major problem because enterprises provide housing for their workers and compete for workers through housing. In addition, however, economic motives probably play a role in voluntary departures. There is much money to be made in the second economy, and presumably some of the "unemployed" workers—we do not know how many—are in fact working quite hard in proscribed activities. For example, the director of an unnamed instrument-making factory in the Novosibirsk

---

admitted to these pockets of unemployment in their speeches to the Twenty-seventh Party Congress in which they supported the creation of small enterprises in part to create new employment opportunities in rural areas.

17. Ibid., p. 161.

18. Kupriianova implies that in the Novosibirsk enterprises she surveyed—which have higher labor turnover than in the USSR as a whole—about one-half of the job leavings are a result of workers being fired for disciplinary reasons. In the absence of other studies with comparable information, this proportion can only be taken as one piece of anecdotal information; my guess is that for the USSR as a whole involuntary leavings have in fact accounted for well under half of total job leavings, but that can only be a guess. Kupriianova, "Tekuchest' kadrov," pp. 19–20.

19. Ibid., p. 19.

region complains that about a third of his 600 workers "disappear" for three to four months in the summer months to sell vegetables from their kitchen gardens, for which they are apparently far better compensated than they would be if they stayed in the factory.[20]

In any case, these surveys do clearly indicate the existence of involuntary unemployment. However, the proportion of involuntary unemployment is probably low throughout the country, but lowest in large urban areas of the European USSR, where the demand for labor far exceeds supplies. It is probably higher in rural areas, and in the Asian republics, where the labor force is growing relatively rapidly and the capital-to-labor ratio is still far below what it is in European USSR.

Without systematic information, it is impossible to reach any precise conclusions regarding unemployment in the USSR. If the Soviet Central Statistical Administration were to collect and publish unemployment statistics in a fashion similar to that in the United States, the rate of unemployment would probably come out under 2 percent for the mid-1980s.[21] Western countries, and particularly Western workers, can only envy a society with such a consistently low level of unemployment.

CERTAINTY ABOUT INCOMES. The economic security provided in the USSR today is only partly a result of the relatively high demand for labor and the low level of unemployment. It is also related to certainty concerning the worth of income in real terms, which is much higher in the Soviet Union than in Western countries. To be sure, Soviet workers face uncertainties in all of these areas, but the relative security of job and real income combine to produce a high degree of personal economic security in the Soviet Union.

Nominal incomes. Workers' concerns about future income in any society are a combination of their expectations that they can find and hold a job, and that they will receive a certain income in that job. The most important difference between the Soviet Union and Western countries in this regard is in the area of job security. Individual workers in the Soviet Union know that the likelihood they will have to leave their job involuntarily is low, and for that reason alone Soviet workers enjoy

20. V. A. Aranovskii, "Obshchii poriadok i ditsiplina—zven'ia odnoi tsepi" (General order and discipline—links in one chain), *EKO*, no. 5 (May 1984), pp. 34–37.

21. If labor turnover in the Soviet Union is 20 percent, which is not out of line with what some studies indicate, and if the average duration of unemployment is in the range of 30 days, then that suggests a rate of unemployment of $30/365 \times .2 = 1.6$ percent, which is well below what many Western economists suggest is the minimal level of unemployment in a Western country consistent with price stability.

more certainty than their Western counterparts regarding their incomes from earnings. The main sources of this job security are the high demand for labor and the fact that the ministries—and ultimately the central planners—are willing to subsidize enterprises operating at a loss so that they can cover the wage liabilities.

What one might call "income security"—high certainty of what one's nominal income will be in a job—also seems to be the rule in the USSR, unlike the West. However, this is a more complicated issue, both because situations differ among various groups in the labor force, and because the data necessary to reach a conclusion are not all available.

For Soviet managers, who constitute a minority of the labor force, bonuses are a relatively high share of their income and may vary over time. According to the most recent data, unfortunately only for the early 1970s, reported bonuses of managerial and professional employees in all Soviet industry accounted for about one-quarter of their income; in the same year apparently one-third of high-level managers of all enterprises supervised by the Russian Republic office of the State Bank had total earnings at least twice the base salary for their post.[22] There are no published data on the degree of variability of managerial bonuses over time at the national level. But it is likely that the variation in bonus payments combined with their relatively high share in total compensation contributes to some uncertainty regarding managerial incomes in the USSR.

The remainder of the labor force would seem to enjoy somewhat greater predicability in their incomes. Bonuses for workers on a salary are a relatively small share of their income and are apparently fairly stable over time; hence the informal designation of these bonuses as the wage for the "thirteenth month." Workers on piece-rate systems, whose share has declined over time, enjoy less income security. Just how much less depends on how total wages from piece rates fluctuate over time, about which no data have been published.

Real incomes. In any society it is real, not nominal, incomes that are the ultimate concern of the population. Rising nominal incomes associated with high rates of inflation may, for a short time, create a "money illusion" that masks the modest or nonexistent rise in real incomes; but

22. David Granick, "Institutional Innovation and Economic Management: The Soviet Incentive System, 1921 to the Present," in Gregory Guroff and Fred V. Carstensen, eds., *Entrepreneurship in Imperial Russia and the Soviet Union* (Princeton University Press, 1983), p. 246.

that is unlikely to work for long. In Western countries the minority of workers employed under union contract are typically insured against inflation through escalator clauses, whereas other workers must negotiate with their employers and take their chances.

In the Soviet Union there are no escalator clauses built into labor contracts that guarantee some excess rate of growth of nominal wages over the rate of inflation. Instead there is an informal understanding between the leadership and the population to the effect that (1) rates of inflation will either be zero or very low, and when consumer prices rise they will do so in an orderly manner; (2) the prices of necessities will be low and stable; and (3) real incomes will rise continuously. In general, Soviet leaders have kept their side of the bargain, although the uneven quality of Soviet economic statistics leaves much room for doubt.

Official Soviet statistics on retail prices report rates of inflation averaging 0.3 percent in the 1970s and approximately 1 percent in the 1980s.[23] These figures do not include second economy transactions, part of the daily life of Soviet citizens, or the prices of imported consumer goods. Furthermore, the costs of forced substitution (which means accepting available products, even when they are not what the consumer intended to buy) are not captured in the index, and the costs of long queues are ignored.[24]

However, even if the rate of inflation reported for state retail prices understates by two, three, or even four times the actual rate of inflation that would show up in a properly estimated consumer price index (CPI), the figure is still quite low by Western standards, as is evident from the CPIs for the major industrialized countries shown in table 2-1. Even if the actual CPI in the USSR in the 1970s had not been the 0.3 percent implied in the state retail price index, but had been, say, 2–3 percent, it would still have been far below the 7.8 percent of the United States or the 13 percent plus in Italy and the United Kingdom.

It appears that necessities are relatively cheap in the Soviet Union. Consider, for example, data assembled by Abram Bergson on lira-dollar and ruble-dollar ratios for 1975 and 1976, respectively (see table 2-2).

23. *Narkhoz 1984*, p. 493. But there are ample reasons to be skeptical about this poorly documented index, and every reason to believe that it understates the true rate of inflation. See, for example, the discussion of Soviet price statistics in "1987 Panel on the Soviet Economic Outlook: Perceptions on a Confusing Set of Statistics," *Soviet Economy*, vol. 3 (January–March 1987), pp. 3–39.

24. Derived from data on nominal and real national income produced as reported in various issues of *Narkhoz*.

Table 2-1. *Consumer Price Indexes for Major Industrialized Countries, 1970–85*

Country	1970	1980	Percent annual change, 1970–80	1985	Percent annual change, 1980–85
United States	100	212	7.8	277	5.5
Canada	100	217	8.1	310	7.4
Japan	100	237	9.0	271	2.7
France	100	252	9.7	399	9.6
Italy	100	365	13.8	700	13.9
United Kingdom	100	360	13.7	510	7.2
West Germany	100	165	5.1	199	3.8

Source: U.S. Central Intelligence Agency, *Handbook of Economic Statistics, 1986* (Washington, D.C., 1986), p. 53.

Each figure in table 2-2 is a ratio, the numerator being the ruble-dollar, or lira-dollar, ratio of prices in the given product group; the denominator being the ruble-dollar, or lira-dollar, ratio for all household consumption. A number greater than (less than) unity indicates that prices in that product group are relatively higher (lower) in the USSR or Italy than in a comparable product group in the United States.

Compared with the United States, the USSR has relatively low prices for housing, transport, publications, and recreation, and relatively high

Table 2-2. *Ruble-Dollar and Lira-Dollar Ratios for Major Consumer Goods, Mid-1970s*

Consumer goods category	Ruble-dollar ratio (1976)	Lira-dollar ratio (1975)
All household consumption	1.00	1.00
Food	1.23	1.10
Beverages	1.42	1.11
Tobacco	1.66	1.09
Clothing, footwear	1.75	1.24
Gross rent, utilities	0.34	0.94
House furnishings	1.00	0.83
Transport, communications	0.52	0.81
Publications, school supplies	0.35	n.a.
Recreation	0.58	1.18

Source: Abram Bergson, "Income Inequality under Soviet Socialism," *Journal of Economic Literature*, vol. 22 (September 1984), p. 1060.
n.a. Not available.

Figure 2-1. *Growth Rate of Real Per Capita Income and Consumption, 1965–85*

Percent

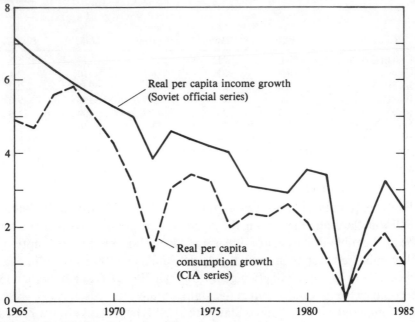

Sources: Soviet official data and sources in note 25.

prices for food, clothing and footwear, beverages, and tobacco. Within the food category, breads, cereals, and fish are relatively cheap. This certainly looks like a price structure that favors necessities, as is part of the contract. But it inevitably loads very high prices on luxuries, in comparison with the West. Italy's price structure seems closer to that of the United States than that of the USSR, which is further evidence of a particular slant in the Soviet price structure.

The third part of the contract—that real incomes will continuously rise—has also been kept, to judge from both official statistics on real per capita income growth and independent CIA estimates of real consumption growth rates. Figure 2-1 shows the record since the mid-1960s; the official data are from *Narkhoz*, and the CIA data are estimates by Schroeder and Denton for the CIA.[25] To be sure, real income growth

25. Gertrude E. Schroeder and M. Elizabeth Denton, "An Index of Consumption in the USSR," in Joint Economic Committee, *USSR: Measures of Economic Growth and Development*, Joint Committee Print, pp. 317–401. The Schroeder-Denton index is built up from the best available information (Soviet official) on consumption in individual

rates are falling, but they are falling from a high level, and the general downward trend is similar to one observed throughout the world. Even in recent years per capita personal incomes have been growing in the range of 2–3 percent, which is quite respectable by world standards.

Egalitarian Bias

Marx's central criticism of capitalism was that its inner logic automatically produced and perpetuated inequities in the distribution of wealth, income, and power. The reserve army of the unemployed was one important indicator of that system at work, but so was the fact that even most of those who were employed received a pittance for their work, while the few who owned the means of production received the bulk of society's income, and therefore its newly created wealth. In the half-century preceding the Russian revolution, socialists focused on the distribution of income and wealth as the critical issue; hence their preoccupation with socialization of the means of production. The Russian revolution was the first effective implementation of the idea in a nation-state, an implementation that took more than a decade to realize and was completed only after Stalin's brutal collectivization of the peasantry during 1929–31.

The result is a system in which—with insignificant exceptions—the state is the only legal owner of productive and financial capital, and in which what would otherwise be rents, dividends, and interest are state income collected primarily through confiscation of what the state determines to be excess enterprise profits. In theory the only way one can earn income in the Soviet Union is to be gainfully employed; income through lending money, owning income-producing assets, or enjoying economic rents from scarce assets (land, for example) are all legally excluded. Even with the second economy, there is probably relatively little income from nonlabor sources.[26]

---

categories, aggregated in a way to maximize conformity with techniques used to estimate consumption in Western national income accounts. The index only goes to 1980; subsequent years were estimated using estimates of the growth of real consumption in the Central Intelligence Agency *Handbook*, 1985, and Soviet data on population growth.

26. The anecdotal information suggests that much of the economic activity in the second economy consists of *labor* in proscribed goods- or service-producing activities, although it is certainly true that returns to risk-bearing activities and economic rents also occur in this portion of the economy.

The mere fact that wages and salaries are the major source of personal income in the Soviet Union should have a leveling influence on the distribution of personal income in the Soviet Union. Additional flattening comes from the low rate of unemployment and the implicit income protection offered workers in enterprises that are unprofitable. The tendency to equalize wages in the same job, and even a tendency to hold down the variance among all wages, has also worked in the same direction. One further consideration applying to families is the high (by world standards) participation of women in the labor force, which should have a leveling influence on the distribution of income among consuming units. Thus, if a correction is made for the level of development, the income distribution among wage and salary workers in the Soviet Union is probably somewhat more equal than in most Western countries, and the income distribution among consuming units is far more equal than in some Western countries, such as the United States.[27]

An egalitarian bias is built into the system in several other ways. When there is a loss to the economy (for example, a crop failure or a decline in the terms of trade), the incidence of the loss is spread across society. When grain production falls way below trend as a result of poor weather conditions, the general effects on income in the agricultural sector are far less serious than they would be in a Western country. Workers on state farms receive their wages, irrespective of the size of the crop; and there is no accumulation of private debt flowing from the crop failure. The debt is socialized and shows up in the form of increased imports from the West, which are financed either with dollar debt, a drawdown in dollar reserves, or some other maneuver.

By the same token, when an explosion in oil prices, such as the one that occurred in the 1970s, provides windfall gains to the Soviet Union, these are automatically socialized, as the system captures the higher dollar revenues "at the border," diverting them from the balance sheets of individual enterprises and into the state budget. In a Western society, those people with control over oil-bearing formations reap large rents;

27. Abram Bergson, "Income Inequality under Soviet Socialism," *Journal of Economic Literature*, vol. 22 (September 1984), p. 1092. This is a very useful survey comparing research on income distribution in the USSR with results of similar research on Western countries. In both cases—the distribution of income among wage and salary workers and the distribution of income among consuming units—Bergson concludes that some Western countries are no less equal than the USSR. Sweden, Norway, and the United Kingdom, for example, exhibit distributions of income among consuming units that are either indistinguishable from or very close to the Soviet distribution.

in the Soviet Union the rents are no smaller, but the state captures them and in effect distributes them to society as a whole.

The fact that the distribution of wealth is so equal weakens any potential link between income or wealth and power. The shortage of goods is also to some extent an equalizer (rich and poor alike must stand in line).

Nevertheless, some parts of the system have developed an anti-egalitarian bias, most notably in the hierarchy of special privileges afforded the elite. Special stores, special service organizations, special health care facilities, and the right to travel are all available to the elite, but not to the population as a whole. In a society where goods are in short supply, the right to have access to them through a preferential network is itself worth the equivalent of some (possibly substantial) amount of income. In that sense the income distributions reported here understate somewhat the degree of inequality flowing from special access afforded those at the very top of the income distribution. But in view of the fact that we are talking of relatively few people and that—with the exception of the top leaders—the resulting differences in living standards are not huge, this element of inequality does not overwhelm the general egalitarian bias of the system.

Gains to Be Preserved

The three strengths of the system described here—high growth, economic security, and an egalitarian bias—are all regarded by the leadership, and probably by much of the population, as the gains of socialism that should be preserved as far as possible. Clearly they are desirable attributes of any economic system and understandably the pillars supporting the political leadership in a country so absorbed in its revolutionary roots. Any political leader introducing economic reforms will make every effort to minimize the impact of reforms in these three areas in order to secure popular support for the required measures.

Yet many of the weaknesses in the USSR's economic performance can be traced to this very framework of economic security and to the egalitarian bias. Consequently, any economic reform that is to address these performance problems at their roots must seek to redefine the meaning of economic security and egalitarianism under Soviet socialism. That is why economic reform in the Soviet Union is so difficult to carry

out and why previous efforts at reform have had such a checkered
history.

Soviet Economic Performance: Weaknesses

In recent years Soviet leaders have publicly expressed increasing
dissatisfaction with the performance of their economic system. Frequently in speeches on the economy a particular leader will provide a
long list of problems without singling out one or two as the most important
and without noting the interrelationships among the problems (for
example, between the low rates of technical change and the low rates of
labor productivity growth). By reviewing the recent leadership speeches
on the economy, however, particularly since Andropov assumed office,
it is possible to delineate the critical issues and to identify those that are
secondary.

The leadership's greatest concern is the inefficiency of the USSR's
economic system. In terms familiar to Western economists, the concern
is not so much with allocative inefficiency (the misallocation of resources
among sectors or subsectors), but with technical inefficiency (the misuse,
actually pure waste, of resources in the production of particular products). The anecdotal evidence that Soviet enterprises have a hunger for
all inputs—labor and material—is overwhelming. As a result, inputs are
used at far higher rates than are typical in the world economy, or even
necessary in the Soviet context.

Much of the effort at economic reforms in the postwar period has
been directed at forcing enterprises to economize on inputs, simply by
paying more attention to costs and by introducing innovations in production processes. The general failure of those reforms and the consequent slow rate of technological progress have assumed greater importance over time as input growth rates have fallen and thus have led to a
secular decline in national income growth rates.

In recent years falling growth rates have left Soviet leaders with less
room for maneuver in responding to the competing claims from the
military, consumers, and the investment needs of the economy itself.
"The acceleration of social-economic development of the country,"
said Mikhail Gorbachev at the Twenty-seventh Party Congress, "is the
key to all of our problems: near-term and long-term, economic and
social, political and ideological, internal and foreign. Only by such a

path is it possible and desirable to attain a qualitatively new situation in Soviet society."[28]

Gorbachev, in calling for a reversal in the downward decline in growth rates, is doing no more than expressing the general leadership view that this is essential for the future of the system. In their search for the causes of the decline, Soviet leaders have increasingly focused their attention on falling labor productivity growth rates and their underlying causes: the low level of mechanization in Soviet industry, lack of innovative activity, and labor discipline problems.

A second major concern of the Soviet leadership—separable from, but not unrelated to the concern over the growth slowdown—is that the system has had a chronic tendency to produce low-quality goods that fall far short of world standards and of the needs of Soviet users. This issue is also linked to technical efficiency in the sense that enterprises are using valuable resources to produce goods that many consumers find dissatisfying and some simply refuse to buy. The problem, outside the defense industry, is widespread, although not universal. It has adverse consequences for consumer welfare, economic performance, and hard currency export capacity. If Soviet leaders could manage to bring about a dramatic improvement in system performance in this area, then even if low growth rates were to persist, they would judge this to be an important achievement.

A third concern, also separable from, but not totally unrelated to, the growth slowdown, is the persistence of imbalances in the system. Some are macro imbalances, an excess demand for consumer goods or investment goods; some are imbalances among sectors, for example, a tendency for industrial development in certain areas to far outpace the development of infrastructure. Some are imbalances in the supply and demand for particular factors, including labor. If these imbalances could be reduced, then the leadership would value the mere reduction in chaos and improvement in the smooth running of the system, whether or not growth rates might rise.

Deteriorating Growth Performance

There are basically three issues here. First, what is the nature of the deterioration in performance? Second, what consequences has it had for

28. "Doklad General'nogo sekretaria TsK KPSS tovarishcha Gorbacheva M. S. 25 Fevralia 1986 goda" (Report of the general secretary of the Central Committee of the CPSU Comrade M. S. Gorbachev, February 25, 1986), *Pravda*, February 26, 1986.

Table 2-3. *Soviet Economic Performance Indicators, 1961–85, and Plans to 2000*
Average annual growth rate (percent)

Item	1961–65 FYP7	1961–65 Actual	1966–70 FYP8	1966–70 Actual	1971–75 FYP9	1971–75 Actual	1976–80 FYP10	1976–80 Actual	1981–85 FYP11	1981–85 Actual	1986–90 FYP12	1990–2000 Plan
Macroeconomic activity												
National income produced	n.a.	6.5	n.a.	7.8	n.a.	5.7	n.a.	4.4	n.a.	3.5	4.5	n.a.
National income utilized	7.3	6.0	6.9	7.1	6.7	5.1	4.7	3.9	3.4	2.7[a]	4.1	5.0
GNP (Western estimate)	n.a.	4.7	n.a.	5.0	n.a.	3.0	n.a.	2.3	n.a.	2.0	n.a.	n.a.
Sectoral output												
Industrial production	8.6	8.8	8.2	8.3	8.0	7.4	6.3	4.5	4.7	3.7	4.6	4.8
Machinebuilding and metalworking	n.a.	12.4	n.a.	11.8	11.4	11.6	n.a.	8.2	7.0	6.2	7.4	n.a.
Agricultural production	7.9	2.4	4.6	4.3	4.0	0.6	3.0	1.5	2.5	2.1	2.7	n.a.
Labor productivity												
In all material production	n.a.	5.5	n.a.	6.8	n.a.	4.6	n.a.	3.3	n.a.	3.1	4.2	6.5–7.4
In industry	5.7	4.5	6.0	5.6	6.8	6.0	5.5	3.1	3.6	3.2	4.6	n.a.
In agriculture	n.a.	3.3	7.3	6.2	6.7	1.4	n.a.	2.8	n.a.	2.7	4.1[b]	n.a.
In construction	n.a.	5.2	n.a.	4.1	6.5	5.2	n.a.	1.5	n.a.	2.7	3.9	n.a.
Capital formation												
Gross total investment	n.a.	6.3	8.0	7.5	6.7	7.0	n.a.	3.3	n.a.	3.5	4.3	n.a.
Gross state investment[c]	8.8	7.3	n.a.	7.2	6.2[d]	7.1	2.8	3.7	1.1	3.5	2.9[e]	n.a.
Real per capita income	4.9	3.9	5.4	5.9	5.5	4.4	3.9	3.3	3.1	2.1	2.7	3.4–4.7

Sources: GNP estimates are from CIA, *Handbook of Economic Statistics, 1986: A Reference Aid*, CPAS 86-10002 (Directorate of Intelligence, September 1986), p. 70. Plan data are from Ed A. Hewett, "Gorbachev's Economic Strategy: A Preliminary Assessment," *Soviet Economy*, vol. 1 (October–December 1985), p. 289; Ed A. Hewett, Bryan Roberts, and Jan Vanous, "On the Feasibility of Key Targets in the Soviet Twelfth Five Year Plan (1986–90)," in Joint Economic Committee, *Gorbachev's Economic Plans*, 100 Cong. 1 sess., vol. 1 (GPO, forthcoming); and the following plan documents: *Promyshlenno-ekonomicheskaia gazeta*, February 7, 1959; *Pravda*, April 10, 1966; *Gosudarstvennyi piatiletnii plan razvitiia narodnogo khoziaistva SSSR na 1971–1975 gody* (Moscow: Politizdat, 1972) (hereafter *Gosplan 1971–1975*); *Ekon. gaz.*, no. 51 (December 1975); *Ekon. gaz.*, no. 45 (November 1976); *Pravda*, November 20, 1981; *Pravda*, June 19, 1986; and *Sotsialisticheskaia industriia*, March 9, 1986 (hereafter *Sots. ind.*). Performance data are from Hewett, "Gorbachev's Economic Strategy"; Hewett and others, "On the Feasibility of Key Targets"; and Tsentral'noe statisticheskoe upravlenie SSSR, *Narodnoe khoziaistvo SSSR: Statisticheskii ezhegodnik* (Moscow: "Finansy i statistika," various years) (hereafter *Narkhoz*).
n.a. Not available.
a. *Narkhoz 1985* (p. 40) reports two figures for the growth of "National income utilized" in 1985: 3.1 percent and 0.8 percent (implied from p. 410 of *Narkhoz 1985* and p. 425 of *Narkhoz 1984*). The higher figure yields a growth rate for 1981–85 of 3.1 percent (*Narkhoz 1985*, p. 41). The lower figure yields a growth rate for 1981–85 of 2.7 percent (*Narkhoz 1984*, p. 425). The problem appears to be in the treatment of alcohol production. See "1987 Panel on the Soviet Economic Outlook: Perceptions on a Confusing Set of Statistics," *Soviet Economy*, vol. 3 (January–March 1987), pp. 3–39. I have tentatively accepted the lower figure as the best indicator of performance over that period.
b. Average from the draft of the Twelfth FYP. See *Sots. ind.*, November 9, 1985.
c. Excludes investments by collective farms and private individuals.
d. See *Gosplan 1971–1975*, p. 352; and *Narkhoz 1922–1972*, p. 321.
e. State "centralized" investment, which presumably excludes investments by state enterprises financed from their own funds.

the economy? And third, what are the apparent causes of the performance problems? The discussion of the second and third issues is necessarily brief, pending the discussion in chapters 3 and 4 of how the system works, but much can be said even though the focus is only on the performance of the system. Before these three issues are taken up, however, it is useful to review the economy's overall performance in order to provide the context for a discussion both of performance itself and of some of the major causal factors.

Table 2-3 summarizes the basic statistics for five-year periods over the last quarter century along with plans to the year 2000. The data refer to targets specified in the five-year plans for each period and to actual performance in the same period.

The first three rows of table 2-3 provide three different measures of macroeconomic performance. National income produced (or net material product; hereafter, NIPR) is value-added only in the production of material goods.[29] National income utilized (hereafter NIUT) is NIPR minus losses and the trade surplus (in domestic prices); it therefore measures the actual value, in domestic prices, of goods and those services related to material production purchased by the population.[30] Gross national product is a CIA estimate arrived at by using accounting conventions of developed Western countries. It differs from NIPR in several ways, most notably in that it includes all services in social product as well as gross investment, which includes depreciation.

Whichever measure of macro activity one uses, the downward trend in growth rates from a recent peak in 1966–70 is unmistakable. The CIA's estimate of GNP shows a lower growth rate; but the downward trend is virtually identical to that shown in the two official national income series. Moreover, actual growth since the 1970s has been lower than planners had hoped for. This does not necessarily mean they were "surprised" by the outcome. Five-year plans are not simply an effort to generate a best forecast; they are also meant to motivate producers to achieve maximal improvement in performance. But at the very least the decline was to some extent involuntary from the point of view of planners. The

29. Goods produced in industry, construction, agriculture and forestry, transport and communications, trade, and water, net of depreciation; this excludes all services produced in education, health, housing, and public administration sectors, but includes some services produced in the material goods sectors.

30. If, for example NIPR does not change, but the trade surplus or losses rise, then NIUT falls as the actual goods available for final use fell because of increased net exports or increased losses.

cornerstone of Mikhail Gorbachev's strategy is a turnaround in that downward trend, the hope being that by the 1990s growth will be back at the rates of the early 1970s.

The next three rows provide information on growth in sectoral outputs: industry, within that the subsector involved in machinebuilding, and agriculture. These are all gross output indexes where inputs can be counted multiple times as they move up the chain in the production process; therefore the series are not directly comparable to the two Soviet national income series based solely on value-added in material production. Still, the sectoral indexes have an interesting story to tell.

Growth rates in agriculture are erratic and in recent years have been quite low, which is one explanation for their slowdown. Not only does slow growth in agriculture directly affect national income growth rates, but it indirectly affects performance by pushing up the demand for food imports (which means either the energy sector requires more resources than it otherwise would to maintain exports, or available hard currency is spent on food at the expense of imports of intermediate and final products) and by constraining industrial output in sectors dependent on agricultural inputs.

The slowdown in the growth of industrial output has been somewhat more pronounced than for national income as a whole. The slowdown was clearly greater than planners had expected, the biggest apparent surprise coming in the latter half of the 1970s. Although some of this slowdown may be directly or indirectly related to agriculture's problems (indirectly, for example, in that bad weather exacerbates transport bottlenecks and thus reduces industrial production), industry has its own problems, which show up in the sharp declines in labor productivity.

The subsequent four rows report on labor productivity in the production of all material goods, and in three key sectors. These figures represent ratios of the growth of gross sectoral outputs to the employed labor force, and thus are not directly comparable to Western figures, which frequently relate value-added in a sector to hours worked. However, they are the figures on which Soviet leaders base their greatest dissatisfaction with the system's performance. Industry is the only sector for which plan data are consistently available, and they show underfulfilled labor productivity targets since the beginning of the 1970s, with—again—the greatest surprise in the latter half of the 1970s. As with national income growth rates, the most recent peak in labor productivity growth was in 1966–70; since then it has slid down to about half the rates of those years. It is here that Soviet targets for the 1990s are the most ambitious, calling for growth rates in labor productivity during the 1990s to surpass any in the last quarter century. Although the attainability of such targets is in doubt, they are the logical consequence of trying to accelerate growth while labor force growth rates fall to close to zero.

The next two rows report two separate, but closely related, investment series. "Total investment" is investment from all sources, including a small private investment component. "State investment" excludes private and cooperative investments. These latter two account for about 10 percent of total investment. Both total and state investments are reported here because sometimes the plan fulfillment reports give one, but not both.

Investment growth rates have fallen along with national income growth rates, but not by as much as planners had hoped. In each of the last three five-year plans the investment and national income targets combined implied a hoped-for improvement in investment efficiency that was unattainable. Thus planners were forced into a compromise in which investment grew faster than planned, whereas national income grew more slowly than planned. This was most notable in the last two five-year plans, covering the latter half of the 1970s and the first half of the 1980s. The decision for the 1976–80 plan was that investment growth could be halved without a proportionate effect on national income growth by decreasing the time required to finish investment projects. The rationale behind cutting investment was apparently the need to improve the supplies of consumer goods.[31] As it turned out, investment growth rates were cut—although not as far as the plan called for—but national income growth rates fell further than planned. During the Eleventh FYP planners sought to introduce even deeper cuts in investment growth, with no success at all. Gross investment grew slightly faster in 1981–85 than in 1976–80. Soviet plans for 1986–90 implicitly admit that the extraordinarily slow growth of investment called for in the Eleventh FYP is unattainable.

According to official Soviet data (bottom row of table 2-3), the growth of per capita personal income has fallen from the recent peak in 1966–70. Like total national income, it has grown more slowly than plan targets called for.

31. For an explicit statement to that effect, see B. Plyshevskii, "Nakoplenie i intensifikatsiia" (Accumulation and intensification), *Ekonomicheskaia gazeta,* no. 3 (January 1986). (Hereafter *Ekon. gaz.*)

The data in table 2-3 suggest several general observations that will prove important in understanding how Soviet leaders and their planners interpret the current state of the system. First, note that in the 1960s actual performance came reasonably close to medium-term plan targets, whereas in the 1970s actual performance was far inferior to planned performance. Planners in the 1970s must have felt that their control of the system was deteriorating, precisely as these data suggest.

Second, the best economic performance in recent years occurred in 1966–70, immediately after the introduction of the "Kosygin" reforms. Most of the five-year plan targets were fulfilled at the aggregate level; the growth rates of national income, labor productivity, and real personal incomes were all above plan.

Finally, there was a major break in the middle of the 1970s, after which performance was much worse than before. That break, coming on top of the general downward trend begun in the first half of the decade, has fed the reform debate.

A CLOSER LOOK AT ANNUAL DATA. In order to better understand how Soviet leaders and planners perceived and sought to deal with the deterioration in Soviet economic performance, it is necessary to analyze the annual data on planned and actual peformance. Although the five-year plans give some notion of planners' hopes, tempered by a sense of what is possible, annual plan data provide an annual reading on what planners think is possible, even if that differs significantly from five-year plan targets. The result provides interesting insights into the ways planners have resisted the growth slowdown, but with little success.

National income growth. The nature of the deterioration in the performance of the Soviet economy can be seen in figure 2-2, which reports data on planned and actual growth of Soviet national income since 1961. The solid black lines spanning five-year intervals are NIUT growth rate targets from five-year plan documents, or—for the 1961–65 period—the last five years of the seven-year plan, referred to as the Seventh Five-Year Plan.[32] The thin solid line is the actual growth rate

32. Macro data for the five-year plans are generally growth rates, but come in one of two forms. Drafts of the plans rely almost exclusively on the ratio between the macro aggregate in the upcoming plan period and that of the period just concluded (for example, national income during 1971–75 divided by national income during 1966–70). The actual plan law passed by the Supreme Soviet relies almost exclusively on growth rates relative to estimated actual performance in the last year of the previous plan period (for example, relating the level of national income in 1975—and all intervening years—to that of 1970).

Figure 2-2. *Growth Rate of National Income Utilized, 1961–90*

Percent

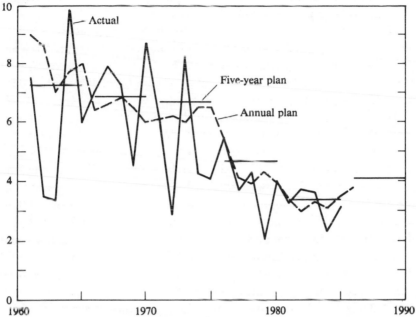

Source: Author's calculations using Soviet official and plan data.

for NIUT; the dashed line is annual plan targets for NIUT growth. These are all official Soviet data. Like the five-year data, CIA estimates of Soviet GNP tell a story of decline, the only difference being that the growth rates are somewhat lower.

The secular trend downward in growth rates is unmistakable. Clear also is the lower amplitude of fluctuations over time; by the early 1980s growth rates were in a narrow and low range. The mid-1970s break point stands out: performance in the period since 1974–75 is markedly worse than before. This abrupt decline in the middle of the last decade is what has deepened the concern of Soviet leaders.

Also clear in figure 2-2 is the reluctance of Soviet leaders to acquiesce

The latter format is clearly preferable for relating five-year plans to annual plans and to actual performance as it unfolds during the five-year plan. I have used data from the plan law where they are available, namely in the Ninth FYP (1971–75) through the Eleventh FYP (1981–85). The seven-year plan and the Eighth FYP were controversial and never passed into law. Where the law was not available, growth rates from the draft plans were used as an indication of what the plan law growth rates would be, but they may be off somewhat.

in the economy's tendency toward lower growth. The story implied in these data cannot be understood without some idea of the different functions of five-year and annual plan targets. Five-year plan targets, which are generally not even published in final form (that is, as a law) until the end of the first year of the new plan period, are not, in fact, what the planners use to control economic activity. Rather, five-year plans are meant to be a detailed and formal statement of what Soviet leaders hope they can accomplish over the ensuing five-year period.

The annual plans are the operational plans in the system. Although they are supposedly drawn up in the framework of the five-year plans, in fact the annual plans are—on the whole—a more realistic assessment of what planners judge to be possible. To be sure, even the annual plans represent a mixture of a hard-headed forecast and a fervent wish; but the weight in annual plans is probably more heavily on the forecast than it is in the five-year plans. The combination of five-year and annual plan data with data on actual performance provides three useful, and separable, bits of information: a reading on what planners wish they could do over a five-year period, tempered by a reluctant recognition of constraints; an annual update on targets for that five-year period, which is based on what planners are learning about the constraints under which they are working; and the actual outcome.

The patterns of the 1960s are fascinating, and somewhat puzzling. In the first half of the decade, NIUT growth targets were above the seven-year plan (SYP) target in all years save one, whereas actual performance fluctuated widely, and annual plan targets were significantly underfulfilled in four out of the five years. That may be one reason why planners set annual targets for 1966–70 significantly lower than those for 1961–65, and even consistently below the Eighth FYP target. They were surprised again, but in the other direction: national income growth rates were higher than the annual plans in four out of the five years, and they came out slightly higher than the five-year plan target.

In the 1970s the annual plans fluctuated in a range of 6–6.5 percent, which was consistent with targets of the late 1960s, but below the 6.7 percent of the five-year plan. The first major disappointments came in 1974–75 when NIUT growth rates fell way below targets, although not below rates that had been experienced in the previous fifteen years. To judge from the data, the two years of slow growth and the considerable underfulfillment of the NIUT target for the Ninth FYP led to a much more modest target for NIUT growth in the Tenth FYP.

The interesting point about the abrupt deterioration in performance in the mid–1970s is that the annual plans anticipated it, moving very quickly below the five-year plan targets. They were in general a decent predictor of actual outcomes, except in 1979, another bad year in agriculture. Either planners saw the slow growth of 1974–75 as signs of deeper problems, and therefore the annual plans were simply predicting the downturn, or there was a conscious decision to grow more slowly in an effort to regain control of the system.

The targeted national income growth for 1981–85 (Eleventh FYP) was still more modest, and both annual plans and performance were reasonably close to that target. At least during the last plan constructed under Brezhnev, planners managed to produce realistic plans. But they did so by choosing a target lower than one political leaders could ultimately accept.

The plan for 1986–90 seeks to raise growth rates to an average of 4.1 percent, which is still well below the high rates of the early 1970s, but a significant reversal of the downward trend since then.

Industry. The data for planned and actual output in industry indicate even greater frustrations for planners, but also some very strange behavior (see figure 2-3). In the 1960s the SYP and the Eighth FYP targets for industrial output were fulfilled, even though the annual plan targets were always lower than the medium-term targets, and therefore were generally overfulfilled. Since then the five-year plan targets for the growth rate of industrial output have been too ambitious. The targets in the annual plans, on the other hand, have continued to be far more conservative in a way that suggests they are hardly connected to the five-year plan targets. Until the mid-1970s the annual plans were over-fulfilled significantly in eleven of the fifteen years between 1961 and 1975. This may indeed mean that, for inexplicable reasons, planners tended to be very conservative in annual plans during this period. But it is equally likely that unplanned hidden inflation in actual performance figures is the culprit; therefore one should be careful not to read too much into the result.[33]

In the period after 1978, planned (annual) and actual industrial output growth rates diverged in a way unprecedented in the previous two

33. Since hidden inflation is most likely focused on manufactured goods and since planners are unlikely to build hidden inflation into the output plans, one would expect actual output in general to grow faster than planned. I am grateful to Douglas Diamond for pointing this out to me.

Figure 2-3. *Growth Rate of Industrial Output, 1961–90*

Percent

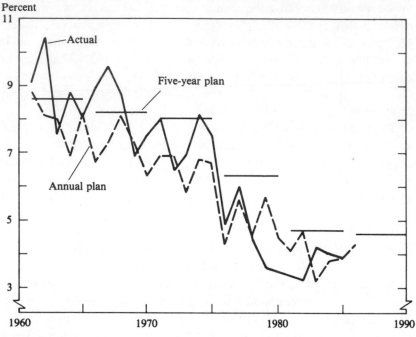

Source: See figure 2-2.

decades as planners resisted, but eventually acquiesced to, a precipitous decline in the growth of industrial production. Notice that if hidden inflation tends to push actual output above the plan, then something peculiar happened in the late 1970s and early 1980s. The most likely explanation would be unrealistic annual plans reflecting a reluctance to accept the precipitous decline in industrial output growth during that period. In 1986–90 planners hope to sustain the high growth of the last few years, but no more than that.

Agriculture. Figure 2-4 gives data on growth rates of agricultural output since 1961, which consist of a complete series on output, but an incomplete series on annual and five-year plans. Performance has been so erratic in agriculture that Soviet authorities have chosen not to commit themselves to a growth rate in many years, at least not in public. The scanty information available suggests that this is a sector over which planners have little control. Weather is surely an important variable here; in each of the years of negative growth poor weather conditions

Figure 2-4. *Growth Rate of Agricultural Output, 1961–90*

Percent

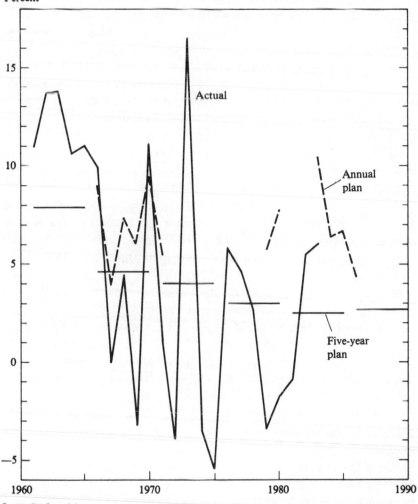

led to a sharp drop in harvests of grains. But the weak infrastructure in this sector and the incentives in the system itself provide weak defenses against the vagaries of weather.

CONCLUSIONS FROM THE OBSERVED INTERACTION BETWEEN PLANNED AND ACTUAL MACRO PERFORMANCE. Several implications emerge from these data on planned and actual macro performance. First, it is with great reluctance that planners have lowered plan targets and thus ratified the growth rate decline of the last quarter century. The five-year plans have indicated a persistent hope that the decline could be at least attenuated, and the plans for 1986–90 announce that the decline is over.

In the interaction of five-year and annual plans with actual perform-ance, the differences between the annual and five-year plans are clearest in the case of national income. The five-year plans contain a strong sense of hope; the annual plans are—with the exception of bad weather years—a decent predictor of annual growth, even when that prediction departs considerably from the five-year plan target for that period. In industry the relationship between the two plans themselves, and with actual performance, is more difficult to discern. This appears to be a sector in which planners' best efforts produce only modest predictive success. Agriculture has the characteristics of a lottery.

CONSEQUENCES OF THE GROWTH SLOWDOWN. With the slowdown in growth, Soviet leaders have had less room for maneuver in choosing among the competing demands of consumers, enterprises and ministries seeking investment resources, and government, most notably defense. The constraints on the first two categories of final demand can be analyzed by using official Soviet statistics; the constraints on defense spending are much more difficult to quantify.

Consumption. The impact of the growth slowdown on real per capita consumption is easy to see in figure 2-5, which presents official Soviet data on the growth of real per capita personal incomes and on annual and five-year plan targets for that measure. This is a measure of real incomes (including income in kind), not consumption, but it is the best one can do with Soviet statistics. As noted earlier, the CIA's estimate of real consumption shows slower growth, but otherwise a similar pattern of decline.

The story that figure 2-5 tells is striking, and unsettling for Soviet political leaders. First, the decline in the growth rate of real per capita incomes is rapid, and virtually unrelieved. During 1966–70 both annual plans and performance were above the five-year plan, but the growth of real per capita incomes fell steadily, from 7.1 percent in the beginning of the period to 5.3 percent at the end. The annual plans—with the odd exception of 1968—were somewhat more modest than actual perform-ance, but still close, and above the five-year plan.

The five-year plans in the 1970s were unrealistic, and the annual plans implicitly recognized that by setting targets consistently below the five-

Figure 2-5. *Growth Rate of Real Per Capita Income, 1961–90*

Percent

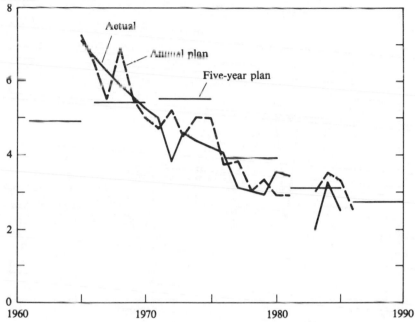

Source: See figure 2-2.

year plan target. Actual performance has generally run below even the annual plan targets. As with national income, so with real per capita incomes—planners resisted the growth slowdown in 1974–75 (which was presumably a direct consequence of the slowdown in national income growth); then in 1976–80 they seem to have accepted it, setting plan targets below the five-year target and reasonably close to actual.

Investment. Figure 2-6 provides data on actual and planned growth rates of total investment. The five-year plan data are for total investment where that target is available, and otherwise for state investment only. Plan targets for total capital investment are only available for 1966–70, 1971–75, and 1986–90. Targets for state investment were used for the other years. Where both targets have been published simultaneously, they are generally close to each other. However, for 1986–90, where the target for total investment is set at 4.3 percent, the target for state investment is 2.9 percent. The difference implies a predicted burst in investments by private individuals and *kolkhozy*.

Figure 2-6. *Growth Rate of Total Capital Expenditures, 1961–90*
Percent

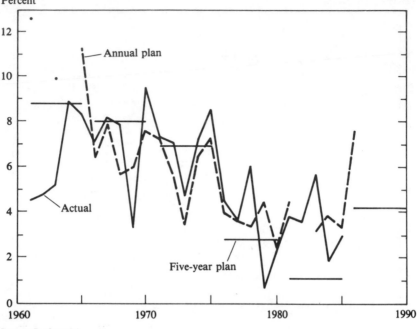

Source: See figure 2-2.

Although investment competes with consumption and defense in the use of national income, it is different because it is both output and input, simultaneously using national income and being put to use to sustain and expand productive capacity. The natural tendency for planners is to attempt to minimize the growth of investment required to attain national income growth targets. Because planners cannot know precisely how little investment will be sufficient to meet their goals, they must work by trial and error; in addition they must constantly choose between consumption now and investment (consumption later). Both of these factors were at work in the last several decades.

In figure 2-6, notice first that investment is much more volatile than consumption. Also, the five-year plan targets were fairly realistic until the second half of the 1970s, after which planners sought to significantly reduce investment growth, presumably to check the growth slowdown and to make room for consumption growth. The annual plan targets during the seven-year plan were pure fantasy, but after that during 1966–

75 they tracked fairly closely to actuals in a way that presaged the five-year investment cycles.

Like the other five-year plan targets in 1976–80, the investment targets were too ambitious, which in this case means they were too low if it is assumed that national income growth rate targets could be met with a lower investment growth rate than turned out to be feasible. At the same time, the annual plan targets were consistently set above the five-year target; this implies that the five-year target was regarded as unachievable from the beginning.

Nevertheless investment growth during 1976–80 was lower than in the previous five-year period, and planners, apparently deciding it could go even lower during 1981–85, set a target of 1.1 percent per annum. Yet the annual plans totally ignored that ambitious five-year plan, and actual investment grew at about the same pace as in 1976–80 (the average for 1976–80 was 3.3 percent for total investment; the average for 1981–85 was 3.5 percent). The plan for 1986–90 calls for a growth rate of 4.3 percent, approximately one percentage point above the average of actual growth over the preceding two five-year periods.

Priorities for investment versus consumption. One distinctive feature of the interaction between annual plan targets and actuals for NIUT, real per capita income, and investment is the reluctance of planners to give in quickly to downward trends, which thus led to unfulfilled targets. The interesting question, when national income grows more slowly than planned, is whether the practice is to protect investment or consumption. A casual glance at figures 2-5 and 2-6 suggests that investment is taking more than its share of the adjustments to below-plan growth in national income, and a simple econometric test corroborates that notion.

Table 2-4 reports the results of two equations that explore the correlation between deviations of NIUT growth from the annual plan target (NIUTPLFF, the independent variable in both, equal to actual NIUT growth minus planned NIUT growth, divided by planned) and deviations of actual and planned growth of, respectively, investment (TCEPLFF) and consumption (CTOTPLFF).[34] The numbers in the body

34. TCEPLFF and CTOTPLFF are calculated using formulas identical to that for NIUTPLFF. Soviet officials do not publish data on actual or planned growth of total consumption. I have estimated those variables here using the growth rate of planned and actual real per capita income summed, in each case, with the growth rate of the population. Thus, the estimated growth of total consumption (CTOTGR) equals the growth rate of real per capita income plus the growth rate of population.

Table 2-4. *Regressions Exploring the Implications for Consumption and Investment of Deviations of National Income Growth from Annual Plan Targets*[a]

Independent variable	Dependent variable	
	TCELFF	CTOTPLFF
Constant	0.056	−0.011
	(0.744)	(−0.489)
NIUTPLFF	0.642	0.121
	(20.634)	(1.700)
$\bar{R}^2$	0.205	0.076
Standard error	0.352	0.103
Durbin-Watson	2.368	1.961
Time period	1961–84	1965–84

Source: Author's calculations.
a. The numbers in parentheses are t-statistics.

of the table are coefficients, the numbers in parentheses are the t-statistics.

The correlation between deviations from plan in NIUT and deviations from plan in consumption and investment is surprisingly weak given the fact that investment and consumption account for most of the national income utilized. Either the plans as constructed are not interconnected via national income identities (for example $C + I + G + X − M = GNP$), in which case a deviation from plan in national income does not necessarily require a compensating deviation from plan in one of the final demand categories; or the final demand categories not accounted for are taking the brunt of the adjustments.[35] The only statistically significant coefficient is for investment; this suggests that a deviation in NIUT plan fulfillment of 1 percent is accompanied by a 0.64 percent deviation in the investment plan in the same direction. The coefficient on the consumption equation is statistically insignificant at the 0.05 level, and one cannot reject the hypothesis that deviations in the NIUT plan have no perceptible effect on fulfillment of the consumption plan.

35. The main items excluded are inventories and government spending, the latter including the important category of defense spending. Remember, though, that both variables used here are only proxies for consumption and investment. The consumption figure is actually based on the growth rate of real incomes, including income in kind, and may not correspond to the figure for material consumption embodied in NIUT. The figure for investment is gross, while NIUT only includes investment net of depreciation.

Therefore investment appears to carry the burden of the adjustment. Note, however, that neither category takes the full adjustment of NIUT (which would be indicated by a coefficient of unity). It seems that when NIUT falls below plan, consumption is protected relative to investment. But the opposite also appears to operate: overfulfillment of the planned growth for NIUT benefits investment more than consumption.

Government expenditures. The "silent partner" in this analysis is government expenditures, most notably those for defense. There is little useful official information on total defense expenditures. The only published figure comes from the state budget and is ludicrously low.[36] Therefore any analysis of the important role defense plays in the Soviet economy must rely for its statistical information on Western estimates, the most well known being those of the Central Intelligence Agency.

According to the CIA, defense in recent years has accounted for 15–17 percent of Soviet GNP, estimated in dollars; in contrast, the U.S. share is currently about 7 percent of GNP.[37] That share cannot be translated directly into an estimate of the share of defense in NIUT; differences in relative prices and in the proportion of services in total defense may be great enough to produce a considerably different number in rubles when Soviet national income accounting concepts are used. Nevertheless, defense clearly accounts for a significant share of NIUT, and fluctuations in national income could well influence defense expenditures. To what extent such fluctuations could affect defense would

36. In 1981–84 the defense figure in the state budget was an unchanged 17.1 billion rubles, which amounted to 3 percent of 1984 NIUT (*Narkhoz 1984*, pp. 424, 573). During 1985–86 plans call for an increase to 19.063 billion rubles (annual plan documents for 1985 and 1986, *Pravda*, November 18, 1986). The universal assumption among Western observers is that this figure includes part, but far from all, of the defense budget, and therefore that it is of little use for analytical purposes.

37. "Gorbachev's Modernization Program: A Status Report," joint CIA-DIA paper submitted to the Subcommittee on National Security Economics, Joint Economic Committee, March 19, 1987, p. 15. The figure of 15–17 percent is somewhat controversial; others believe it is considerably higher. Some of the difference of opinion can be traced to different underlying numbers; in other cases, those who favor a higher number favor a definition for Soviet defense that includes expenditures excluded on the U.S. side (the space program and security forces, for example). I am comfortable with the CIA's estimate as the best possible estimate of a defense burden similar in concept to the figure of 7 percent often cited for the United States. For a discussion of the full range of issues, see Abraham S. Becker, *Sitting on Bayonets: The Soviet Defense Burden and the Slowdown of Soviet Defense Spending*, JRS-01 (Santa Monica, Calif.: Rand Corp., and University of California, Los Angeles, 1985).

clearly depend on the priority given to defense and the ability of planners to push that priority if economic performance deteriorates.

The estimates of the growth of Soviet defense expenditures suggest that in fact there was a break downward in 1976, simultaneous with the general downturn in growth. Before 1976, CIA-estimated defense expenditures were increasing at approximately 4 percent per annum, which was close to the growth rate of GNP; from 1976 into the early 1980s, that figure was closer to 2 percent by CIA estimates. According to these estimates, military procurement stagnated during 1976–82.[38] The causes of the slowdown in defense are not fully understood, but certainly one of the leading candidates is the troubled economy. Despite the high priority accorded to the military, the economic difficulties, particularly in sectors such as transportation and metallurgy, spilled over into defense. However, the fact that the slowdown stretched out over at least seven years suggests policymakers consciously decided to reduce defense expenditure growth, possibly because they wanted to make room for consumption growth as national income growth fell or because they felt the USSR was approaching military parity with the United States, or both.[39] Without trying to resolve this complicated issue here, it seems fair to conclude that defense probably shared in the adjustments planners made in response to the growth slowdown of the mid-1970s.

The widespread repercussions of the growth slowdown for all of the Soviet economy affect, in a fundamental way, the options open to Soviet planners. Their search for the causes of the slowdown, which is now being led by Mikhail Gorbachev, has been vigorous and constant. What Soviet leaders and Soviet economists have considered to be the causes

38. CIA does not publish information on underlying details behind these calculations, but the general principles and basic findings are publicly available. For an excellent summary of the CIA's estimates, which represented a revision of previous estimates for the second half of the 1970s, see Richard F. Kaufman, "Causes of the Slowdown in Soviet Defense," *Soviet Economy*, vol. 1 (January–March 1985), pp. 9–31, with comments by John Steinbruner (pp. 32–36) and David Holloway (pp. 37–41). After some initial controversy between DIA and CIA over the estimates showing a growth slowdown from 1976 into the early 1980s, DIA now is in substantial, although far from complete, agreement. See Joint Economic Committee, *Allocation of Resources in the Soviet Union and China*, pt. 10, pp. 127–29.

39. John Steinbruner makes the case for a conscious decision related to strategic, rather than economic, considerations in *Soviet Economy*, vol. 1 (January–March 1985). For a discussion of the various possible explanations, see the articles by Kaufman, Steinbruner, and Holloway in ibid., and Joint Economic Committee, *Allocation of Resources*, pt. 10, pp. 52–53, 129–31.

of the slowdown and the remedies they have recommended to check it should be given close attention.

FACTORS BEHIND THE SLOWDOWN: SOVIET ANALYSES. Soviet economists tend to view growth rates in their country in terms of "extensive" and "intensive" patterns. Extensive growth occurs when inputs expand, whereas intensive growth occurs when increased factor productivity accounts for the bulk of national income growth. The working assumption of Soviet economic analysis today is that the Soviet Union has relied on extensive growth in the past, but that if the growth decline is now to be reversed, intensive factors will have to be emphasized.

The few Soviet economists who have made an effort to quantify the relative contribution of extensive and intensive factors have resorted to production function concepts familiar to Western economists, although they have used a different terminology and far inferior data sets.[40] Abel Aganbegian discusses this approach in an analysis of the sources of growth in the Soviet Union, an analysis made all the more interesting because of his apparent role as an economic adviser to General Secretary Gorbachev. Table 2-5 contains the basic concepts Aganbegian uses in his analysis, but relies on data taken directly from *Narkhoz* (which are very close to his) so that series can be constructed for periods both more recent and earlier than those in his table.[41] All the data are average annual growth rates for five-year plan periods from 1961 to 1980 and for 1981–84.

The first two rows report growth rates for NIUT and NIPR. The next three rows report the growth rate of inputs: productive capital stock (in

40. The production functions divide the forces influencing growth into two groups: factor inputs and factor productivity. Factor inputs include land (shorthand for natural resource endowments), labor effort, and the services of real capital (machinery, buildings, inventories). All of a society's national income, including intermediate products such as steel, can eventually be traced back to inputs from these three sources. An increase in one or more of these inputs will—other things being equal (most notably factor productivities)—cause national income to rise.

The productivity of these factors, measured as output per unit of input, may rise because of technical changes that introduce a new production process requiring fewer inputs. Productivity may rise simply because resources are moved from less, to more, efficient uses (for example, from low-productivity agricultural work to higher-productivity factory work). They may rise because of major improvements in the economic system itself.

41. A. G. Aganbegian, "Vazhnye pozitivnye sdvigi v ekonomicheskoi zhizni strany" (Important positive changes in the economic life of the country), *EKO*, no. 6 (June 1984), pp. 3–16. Table 2-5 uses the concepts behind Aganbegian's tables 1 and 2, pp. 9, 11.

Table 2-5. *Output, Input, and Efficiency Indicators for the Entire Economy*
Average annual growth rate (percent)

Item	1961–65	1966–70	1971–75	1976–80	1981–84	Weights
National income utilized (NIUT)	6.0	7.1	5.1	3.9	3.2	. . .
National income produced (NIPR)	6.5	7.8	5.7	4.4	3.6	. . .
Total productive inputs	4.5	3.9	3.8	2.6	2.1	. . .
Employment (material sectors)	1.8	1.5	1.4	1.0	0.6	0.5
Capital (*Proizvod. osnov. fondy*)	9.3	8.3	8.7	7.4	6.6	0.2
Material inputs	5.7	5.1	4.6	1.9	1.6	0.3
Total factor productivity	1.5	3.2	1.3	1.3	1.1	. . .
Capital productivity (*Fondootdacha*)	−2.6	−0.5	−2.8	−2.8	−2.8	. . .
Labor productivity	4.6	6.2	4.2	3.4	3.0	. . .
Intensive/extensive (ratio)	25.0	45.0	25.0	33.0	34.0	. . .

Source: Tsentral'noe statisticheskoe upravlenie SSSR, *Narodnoe khoziaistvo SSSR: Statisticheskii ezhegodnik* (Moscow: "Finansy i statistika," various years).

"comparable" prices, gross of depreciation; inventories are excluded, as are buildings and equipment associated with the nonproductive, or nonmaterial, sectors); the rate of growth of employment in material sectors; and the rate of growth in the output of extractive industries (an imperfect proxy for material inputs because it does not adjust for the growth of export-output ratios in extractive industries).

Aganbegian aggregates the three inputs into one aggregate input, the results here shown in the row labeled "total productive inputs," using unspecified weights, which through experimentation I have estimated to be those indicated in the last column of the table. The difference between NIPR and productive inputs is what is generally referred to in Western economic literature as total factor productivity growth, namely that part of national income growth not accounted for by input growth.[42] That row is also calculated in table 2-5, and it indicates that total factor productivity growth peaked in the second half of the 1960s, and then fell precipitously in the 1970s, hovering a little above 1 percent.

The growth of total factor productivity divided by NIUT growth

42. One of the puzzling aspects of Aganbegian's analysis, also found in the work of other Soviet economists using similar techniques, is his use of NIUT instead of NIPR. NIPR is what is actually produced with the factors; NIUT is only the part that is used and may include imports as well as losses. Possibly the rationale is that even though NIUT does include net imports, it still best approximates use values actually available to the population after losses and depreciation. Thus a decline in losses would increase NIUT and therefore show up quite rightly as an increase in factor productivity.

yields Aganbegian's measure of intensity. A ratio of 100 indicates that growth resulted entirely from intensive factors; a ratio of zero, that extensive factors were the sole source of growth.[43]

The figures in table 2-5 support the conventional wisdom in the Soviet Union that extensive factors have dominated Soviet growth in the past. Aganbegian's measure of intensity never rises above one-half, and is generally closer to one-third. He suggests it should be the reverse: intensive factors should account for two thirds of the growth of the economy, which, judging from the performance of Western economies, is rather optimistic.[44] Assuming that productive inputs can continue to sustain their growth at 2 percent per annum, total growth would then approach 6 percent, which is in the range of targets for the 1990s approved at the Twenty-seventh Party Congress.

The two rows of table 2-5 under total factor productivity show growth rates of NIPR relative to capital and labor, each of which are frequently discussed in Soviet economic analyses. According to these data, the productivity of capital has fallen at a fairly steady pace in the

43. Although he does not say so, Aganbegian is assuming that NIPR is linked to inputs via a Cobb-Douglas production function in which

(1) $$NIUT = e^{rt} \cdot K^a \cdot L^b \cdot M^c,$$

where $a + b + c = 1$, K = capital stock, L = labor, and M = materials. Taking the logs of both sides of equation 1, and the first derivative, yields

(2) $$niut = (ak + bl + cm) + r,$$

where $niut$, k, l, and m are the growth rates of NIUT, capital, labor, and materials. The coefficients "a, b, c" are Aganbegian's weights; the expression in brackets, his aggregate measure of productive inputs. In market economies conforming to a very stringent set of assumptions, these weights represent each factor's share in national income. In the real world, and in particular in the Soviet economy, it is best to think of these coefficients as no more than an estimate of the contribution of each factor to the growth of national income, in the form of an "elasticity" stating the percentage increase in NIUT that will result from a 1 percent increase in each of the productive factors. Given the growth rate of NIUT, the three weights, and the growth rate of each productive factor, r is a residual representing the change in total factor productivity. Aganbegian's measure of intensive growth is defined as $r/niut$.

44. Bosworth's data for the U.S. economy show "intensity" ratios of 0.5 during 1948–67, 0.36 for 1967–73, and -0.05 in 1973–80 (total factor productivity fell -0.1 percent per annum while output grew 2.1 percent per annum). But the data he quotes for other Western industrialized countries show total factor productivity accounting for two-fifths or more of total growth in most of those countries in the 1960s and 1970s. Barry P. Bosworth, *Tax Incentives and Economic Growth* (Brookings, 1984), tables 2-3 and 2-5 on pp. 26, 39.

last quarter century. Although disaggregated capital data are not available, other evidence indicates that capital productivities in extractive industries are plummeting, whereas those in manufacturing may be rising.[45] Labor productivity growth rates peaked during 1966–70 and have fallen since then. The fact that materials output has consistently grown more slowly than NIPR suggests that the "productivity" of materials has increased.

Table 2-5 points to four conclusions, which in some cases go beyond what Soviet economists have drawn from the data:

1. There was a burst in total factor productivity and in the individual factor productivities in 1966–70, immediately following the Kosygin reforms.

2. Total factor productivity growth dropped dramatically in the 1970s and fell off slightly more in the early 1980s.

3. The problem was compounded by a significant decline in total factor inputs during the second half of the 1970s, led by a sharp drop in the growth of material inputs.

4. Data on individual productivity factors suggest that labor productivity played a particularly important role in the productivity decline. Whereas capital productivities have fallen at a fairly steady pace (except during 1966–70), labor productivities fell dramatically during 1971–75, relative to the previous five-year period, and then fell again in 1976–80, and yet again during the first half of the 1980s.

FACTORS BEHIND THE SLOWDOWN: WESTERN ANALYSES. Although these data and the interpretation of them reported above reflect a broad consensus among Soviet economists, there are several good reasons to look more carefully at the factors behind the growth slowdown in the Soviet Union. While the data that underlie estimated production functions for any country are typically less than ideal for the purposes to which they are put, Soviet data are fraught with all those difficulties and more. The output data in table 2-5 are suspect since they are probably upwardly biased. The data on the labor input are for total employment, not hours worked. The capital stock data are undepreciated, which

45. For example, if constant price investments are taken as a proxy (admittedly a loose approximation) of increments to capital, the data suggest a dramatic shift in efficiencies. During 1971–75 investment grew at 92 percent the rate of output growth in industry as a whole; 81 percent in the MBMW sector; but 131 percent in fuels. During 1976–84 investment grew at 88 percent the rate of output in industry as a whole; 45 percent in the MBMW sector; and 333 percent the rate of output growth in fuels.

means that no account is taken of the deteriorating capabilities of older equipment in the capital stock; the utilization of capital is not taken into account, so that idle machines are counted as being in use; and the capital stock may also embody hidden inflation that overstates the growth of capital over time. All of these problems are compounded for the late 1970s and early 1980s, when hidden inflation may have grown worse, work stoppages may have increased (owing to bottlenecks), and therefore capital utilization rates may have fallen.

In addition, objections might be raised concerning the form of the production function assumed to underlie the link between inputs and outputs. The Cobb-Douglas production function assumes a particular relationship between capital and labor, the practical consequence of which is the constant weights Aganbegian uses to aggregate factor inputs over time.[46] A more general form of the production function, which attempts to draw information on how easily capital substitutes for labor directly from the data, allows for the possibility that the weights on factor inputs change over time, and thus implies that the weight of capital may fall over time. Since capital is the fastest growing input in the Soviet Union, a decline in the weight placed on its growth and a concomitant increase in the weight placed on much-slower-growing labor input would produce a lower rate of growth for total inputs. That in turn would lead to a higher estimate for total factor productivity growth; indeed, it could lead to a conclusion that total factor productivity growth has not fallen at all.

Western researchers have devoted considerable attention to the behavior of factor productivities in the Soviet economy, in the process correcting for some of the weaknesses noted above. But the results are mixed, and some important weaknesses in Soviet data cannot be rectified. As a result, the precise causes of the growth slowdown remain unclear.

Data issues. To address the data issues first, table 2-6 utilizes the Cobb-Douglas specification Aganbegian used, but CIA data on GNP and man-hours, instead of employment.[47] The capital stock data are official

46. The assumption is that as capital is substituted for (grows more rapidly than) labor, that capital's productivity will fall relative to labor's productivity at precisely the rate that maintains capital's and labor's respective shares in national income. In well-functioning market economies, those factor shares are the weights in the Cobb-Douglas production function.

47. CIA, *Handbook of Economic Statistics, 1985,* p. 68. The input and output data

Table 2-6. *Total Factor Productivity Calculations Using CIA Data*
Average annual growth rate (percent)

Item	1961–65	1966–70	1971–75	1976–80	1981–84	Weights
GNP	5.0	5.3	3.7	2.6	2.7	...
Total productive inputs	4.5	4.1	4.2	3.5	3.0	...
Man-hours	1.6	2.0	1.7	1.1	0.8	0.56
Capital	8.8	7.4	8.0	6.9	6.3	0.41
Land	0.6	−0.3	0.8	−0.1	−0.2	0.03
Total factor productivity	0.5	1.2	−0.5	−0.9	−0.3	...
Man-hours	3.4	3.2	2.0	1.5	1.9	...
Capital	−3.5	−2.0	−4.0	−4.0	−3.4	...
Land	4.4	5.6	2.9	2.7	2.8	...
Intensive/extensive	0.10	0.23	−0.14	−0.35	−0.11	...

Source: CIA, *Handbook of Economic Statistics, 1985: A Reference Aid*, CPAS 85-10001 (Directorate of Intelligence, September 1985), p. 68, which uses 1970 prices.

Soviet statistics; no adjustment has been made for capital utilization. The format is slightly different from Aganbegian's ("land" instead of "materials" is the third input), and the output and input data are not solely for material production, but for all value-added. Still, the comparison seems sufficiently close to judge roughly the impact of accepting the CIA's data as an adjustment for hidden inflation on the output side and of accepting the CIA estimate of man-hours to adjust for the bias of relying on total employment data.

The story in table 2-6 differs somewhat from that of table 2-5, but is also similar in several important respects. The burst in productivity growth during 1966–70 is still there, as is the decline in 1971–75 and beyond. The drop in input growth in the mid-1970s is still there. Finally, labor and capital productivities behave almost the same in the two tables, although the absolute numbers are different, as is to be expected.

The shape of the production function. The other question raised earlier is whether the Cobb-Douglas specification is the right one, or whether another specification that allows the growth weights to vary is superior. The economic issue here is, how easy is it to substitute capital for labor over time? If it is very difficult to do so, then when capital grows more rapidly than labor (in effect a "substitution" of capital for labor), capital productivities rapidly decline and consequently are blamed for any growth slowdown not attributable to a decline in factor inputs.

---

for the quinquennial from 1961–65 through 1976–80 are taken directly from table 41 on p. 68, while the data for 1981–84 are calculated from the annual data given for each of those years. The total factor productivity residual is calculated directly, and differs slightly from that reported in the *Handbook* (presumably because of rounding).

If, however, capital is relatively easy to substitute for labor, then the blame falls on whatever is affecting total factor productivity. The logical suspect in that case is the system itself, in view of its inability to handle the growing complexity of the economy. If, on the other hand, the explanation is the increasing difficulty of substituting capital for labor, then more technical or nonsystemic factors may be at work rather than factors specific to the Soviet system.

Numerous Western analysts have explored this issue, but the results have been inconclusive. With statistics like those in table 2-6, it is virtually impossible to choose between a Cobb-Douglas production function that presupposes constant weights and a more general constant elasticity of substitution (CES) production function (of which the Cobb-Douglas is a special case) that allows for the possibility that capital-labor substitution causes the weight of capital to fall and that of labor to rise. If the estimates associated with the more general CES function are accepted, then total factor productivity in the Soviet Union has not declined in the postwar period, and the growth slowdown reflects the combined effects of a falling growth rate for inputs and increasing difficulty in substituting capital for labor. If estimates associated with the more restrictive Cobb-Douglas are accepted, then the growth rate decline reflects the decline in total inputs, and some general factors leading to a decline in total factor productivity, but not increasing difficulties in substituting capital for labor.[48]

48. Martin L. Weitzman, "Industrial Production," in Abram Bergson and Herbert S. Levine, eds., *The Soviet Economy: Toward the Year 2000* (London: George Allen and Unwin, 1983), pp. 178–90, discusses the difficulty of distinguishing between the two types of production functions, using data only for industry. Despite Weitzman's convincing argument that it is, statistically speaking, too close a call to distinguish between the CES production function and its more restrictive Cobb-Douglas version, there are analysts on each side of the issue who are sure they are right.

Robert Whitesell has argued—using data just for Soviet industry—that the evidence tilts in favor of a CES production function with an elasticity of substitution of about one-half (indicating far more difficulty in substituting capital for labor than the unitary elasticity of the Cobb-Douglas function), implying a constant rate of growth of total factor productivity of 2.6 percent over 1950–80. However, he agrees with Weitzman that statistically it is a close call between this CES function and a Cobb-Douglas function. Robert S Whitesell, "The Influence of Central Planning on the Economic Slowdown in the Soviet Union and Eastern Europe: A Comparative Production Function Analysis," *Economica*, vol. 52 (May 1985), pp. 235–44.

Padma Desai explores a number of specifications for all of Soviet industry, and for ten subbranches, and concludes that the Cobb-Douglas function fits best, implying a falling growth rate for total factor productivity from about 1 percent during 1961–65 to

Remaining weaknesses in the data. In general Western studies have relied on CIA estimates of value-added in industry (although many also use the official Soviet series on industrial output), some estimate of man-hours, and the official Soviet series on capital stock. It is probably the weaknesses in these data, not further experiments with various statistical techniques, that can provide some insight into the Soviet growth slow-down. The hours-worked series for the labor input is actually an hours-paid figure, derived by multiplying the average legal workweek by the number of weeks in the year. That is very similar to data used to estimate production functions in Western countries, which use hours worked without allowance for downtime due to strikes, work stoppages, and the like. But in the Soviet case, the anecdotal evidence suggests significant downtime due to broken machinery, inadequate labor force, or unavailable inputs to such an extent that the official labor-hours series is of dubious value. More important, it is probably the case that work stoppages increased in the second half of the 1970s and that actual hours worked did not rise as much as the official data (or the CIA estimates) would indicate. That means labor productivity growth rates may not have fallen as far as the data suggest.[49]

---

about − 1 percent during 1976–80 (according to data similar to that in table 2-6). Padma Desai, "Total Factor Productivity in Postwar Soviet Industry and Its Branches," *Journal of Comparative Economics*, vol. 9 (March 1985), pp. 1–23. Abram Bergson has reviewed the various estimates and concludes that a Cobb-Douglas function would seem to make much more sense economically. Abram Bergson, "Notes on the Production Function in Soviet Postwar Industrial Growth," *Journal of Comparative Economics*, vol. 3 (June 1979), pp. 116–26; and Bergson, "Technological Progress," in Bergson and Levine, eds., *The Soviet Economy*, pp. 34–78.

49. It is easy to show that interruptions in production due to the lack of inputs, or of labor, are an important influence on economic activity in the Soviet Union, but it is somewhat more speculative to suggest that they have grown more important in the past decade. To give some flavor of the anecdotal evidence, note, for example, a statement by one Soviet economist that a survey of a number of enterprises and construction projects suggests that production interruptions take up 10 percent of the labor force's time. E. Rusanov, "Proizvoditel'nost truda i zarplata" (The productivity of labor and wages), *Sotsialisticheskaia industriia*, January 24, 1985. Another study analyzed more than forty factors contributing to variations in labor productivity among enterprises in one of the Soviet Union's major construction ministries. One of the most important factors identified was worker absence, including absences authorized by the factory. V. Balan, "Pofaktornyi analiz proizvoditel'nosti truda" (A factor analysis of labor productivity), *Ekon. gaz.*, no. 12 (March 1985).

The evidence supporting lower labor utilization rates in the last decade is circumstantial. As output growth rates fell in the second half of the 1970s and energy and transport shortages grew worse, it is likely that the incidence and length of work

The problems with capital stock are even worse. First, the data are gross, not net. Most production function estimates for Western countries can at least utilize an estimated net capital stock series to avoid that problem. The particular difficulty with Soviet data is that—again, according to anecdotal information—Soviet enterprises keep old equipment on the books far beyond the end of its useful life. Thus the gross capital stock series may be even more misleading in the Soviet case than they would be for a Western country.

Varying rates of capital utilization suggest a related concern. The proper capital input into a production function is capital services, not capital stock, gross or net.[50] If the ratio of capital services varies relative to capital, then estimates of total factor productivity using a production function with capital as an input may misstate the growth of total factor productivity. For the Soviet case, if the anecdotal evidence is to be believed, a significant, and possibly growing, portion of the capital stock stands idle, primarily because of problems in manning the new machines. If this is true, then the capital services–capital ratio may have fallen over time, and using capital as a proxy for capital services in the production functions has overstated both the growth of the capital input and the decline in the productivity of the capital.[51]

This is not to suggest that the considerable research Western economists have done on Soviet productivity should be treated lightly, but that caution should be exercised in reaching conclusions on the growth

stoppages grew, and hence that both capital and labor utilization rates grew. In an economy with a policy of full employment, output variations will fall almost totally on labor productivity since there will be virtually no layoffs for pure cyclical reasons. Thus a secular decline in output growth rates will automatically appear as a decline in labor productivity growth, even though in fact some of the decline is accounted for by decreased utilization of the labor force.

50. For an explicit treatment of the capital services–capital stock ratio for the U.S. economy, see Martin Neil Baily, "The Productivity Growth Slowdown and Capital Accumulation," *American Economic Review*, vol. 71 (May 1981), pp. 326–31; and Bosworth, *Tax Incentives*, pp. 35–37.

51. For example, V. V. Kazarezov, first secretary of the Novosibirsk Gorkom, notes that a growing labor shortage in the 1970s and 1980s has led to a reduction in capital utilization. He found in Novosibirsk that between 1972 and 1982 the number of machines rose 19.5 percent, whereas the number of machine operators fell 6.9 percent. As a result, the number of undermanned machines rose and stands now at 15 percent. Similarly, Gertrude E. Schroeder, "The Slowdown in Soviet Industry, 1976–1982," *Soviet Economy*, vol. 1 (January–March 1985), p. 52, quotes from a Soviet source that estimates capacity utilization increased in Soviet industry during the first half of the 1970s to somewhere in excess of 90 percent, but it fell during the remainder of the decade.

slowdown. It would appear that Westerners have a somewhat more reliable notion of the behavior of national income than of the dynamics of the inputs, particularly the dynamics of capital inputs. Until, and if, better input data can be constructed, it is unlikely that production function analysis will yield more than the ambiguous results obtained to date.

Even if the data problems were to be resolved, it is well to remember that analyses of the slowdown of total factor productivity growth rates in Western countries, which work with data generally superior to what is likely to ever be available for the USSR, usually can explain no more than half of that slowdown.[52] There is no reason to expect that Western or Soviet economists will be able, under the best of conditions, to better that record in their efforts to explain the productivity slowdown in the Soviet Union.

Persistent Problems in the Quality of Goods and Services

Soviet leaders have become concerned not only about the downward trend in growth rates, but also about the chronic and widespread problems with the quality of goods and services, which in some areas (particularly consumer goods) appear to be growing worse. Quality problems appear to be so severe that consumers are refusing to buy some goods, even though in general there is an excess demand for consumer goods. As a result, retail inventories seem to be growing much more rapidly than the supplies of consumer goods;[53] and dissatisfied customers are sending a constant stream of letters to the Soviet press complaining about the quality of manufactured goods. Moreover, enterprises in Western countries are reluctant to buy Soviet manufactures in any significant quantities.

These problems led Iurii Andropov to ask: "Can we really be satisfied, with the fact that . . . good-quality raw materials and other inputs are utilized to produce goods which will not find a market, which will lie in stocks, and later require markdowns?"[54] Obviously not. As

52. Bosworth, *Tax Incentives*, p. 30.

53. During 1971–80 retail sales grew at a rate of 5.4 percent per annum; total inventories grew at a rate of 3.9 percent. During 1981–84, retail sales growth fell to 2.8 percent per annum, while inventory growth averaged 8.7 percent per annum. *Narkhoz 1984*, pp. 473, 488.

54. "Tekst vystupleniia General'nogo sekretaria TsK KPSS tovarishcha Iu. V. Andropova" (Text of the address of the general secretary of the Central Committee of the CPSU, Comrade Iu. V. Andropov), *Kommunist*, no. 1 (January 1984), p. 9.

Nikolai Ryzhkov noted in his speech to the Twenty-seventh Party Congress, "This is not just an economic problem but also a political problem. . . . The economy is at such a point that without a dramatic improvement in the quality dimension we cannot resolve a single one of our major productive and social tasks "[55]

The "quality problem" in the Soviet Union has three dimensions. The economy produces an abundance of low-quality goods that consumers (private and enterprise) must nevertheless accept because in many cases no alternatives are available. Second, many goods, whatever their quality, are one or more "generations" behind the latest versions available in large quantities elsewhere in the developing world. Third, the services available to consumers and enterprises are generally of low quality. Each of these factors has consequences for the economy and, as Nikolai Ryzhkov noted, an increasing resonance within the population.

A discussion of these factors should begin, however, with a word of caution about making generalizations. The problem here is not that all Soviet-produced goods are of poor quality or that all the services embody outdated technology. Soviet defense industries and even enterprises in the civilian sector have invented and developed technologies and products competitive with the best available in the world.[56] Rather, the problem is that these products tend to be the exception, not the rule. Many are prototypes, not yet in serial production.[57] Others are produced in small quantities, which are saved for special stores accessible only to the elite and to foreign tourists.

55. "Ob osnovnykh napravleniiakh ekonomicheskogo i sotsial'nogo razvitiia SSSR na 1986–90 gody i na period do 2000 goda. Doklad Predsedatelia Soveta Ministrov SSSR tovarishcha Ryzhkova N.I. 3 Marta 1986 goda" (On the basic guidelines for the economic and social development of the USSR for 1986–1990 and the period through the year 2000. Report by the chairman of the Council of Ministers Comrade N.I. Ryzhkov, March 3, 1986), *Pravda,* March 4, 1986.

56. John W. Kiser III, "Tapping Eastern Bloc Technology," *Harvard Business Review,* vol. 60 (March–April 1982), pp. 85–94.

57. The general director of the ZIL Auto Factory registers a typical complaint when he tells of visiting an industrial exhibit: "The entire scientific-technical revolution stands there in prototypes. . . . Are they good? Sure. And can you take delivery of 100 units? It would seem not; those are prototypes. Who produces them? No one knows." "Zil: vozmozhnosti, zaboty, sversheniia. Beseda korrespondenta *EKO* s general'nym direktorom proizvodstvennogo ob"edineniia ZIL E.A. Brakovym" (Zil: possibilities, concerns, accomplishments. A conversation by *EKO*'s correspondent with E. A. Brakov, the general director of the ZIL production association), *EKO,* no. 10 (October 1986), p. 10.

Products in the same category that are much more readily available are of lower quality or embody technologies considered obsolete in the West. For example, Soviet enterprises find it difficult to obtain the few fourth- and fifth-generation computers now produced in the Soviet Union, but far less difficult to obtain second- and third-generation machines that are still produced today, even though they embody twenty-year-old technology and are generally no longer produced in the West.

This coexistence of the many obsolete products with a few embodying the latest technologies, of many low-quality products with a few high-quality products, considerably complicates any attempt to generalize about the problem of quality in the Soviet Union. In fact the problem is not one of quality in an absolute sense. The real problem is one of the *mix* of goods available. There are too many low-quality or obsolete goods and an insufficient supply of high-quality or up-to-date goods.

LOW QUALITY AND OBSOLESCENCE. The general impression in the West, and apparently among Soviet leaders, that Soviet manufactured goods are generally of low quality seems to touch on two dimensions of the quality problem. Many Soviet-manufactured goods are clearly unreliable and incapable of operating at designed capacity. At the same time, some goods are reliable enough, but embody obsolete technologies. On the one hand, the Soviet-produced Zhiguli, a car with rear-wheel drive, has a 1960s-technology engine and drive train, but it provides adequate transportation for the users; on the other hand, it lags far behind what can be obtained in any developed Western country. The Soviet turbines and compressors installed in gas pipelines work well enough, but the technology embodied in their design and the quality of materials are such that the equipment is far more expensive to operate and maintain than its Western counterparts.

Although it is natural to intermingle quality considerations with the issue of obsolescence, the two should be kept separate for purposes of analysis. To the extent that the problem with Soviet products is not quality, but obsolescence, Soviet enterprises appear to be capable of producing high-quality products faithful to the original designs, but do not seem motivated to search for, develop, and introduce new designs. If this is the crux of the problem, then the solution would focus on design bureaus and the innovative behavior of Soviet enterprises. To the extent that the problem is low quality because of carelessness in the production process, the solution would focus much more on the productive process within the enterprise.

Without trying to come up with an all-encompassing definition of what constitutes a low-quality product, one can identify several characteristics that would clearly fit into any definition. Unreliable products in need of frequent repair are of low quality. Products that easily break and that cannot be repaired also belong in this category. Finally, products that cannot perform up to purportedly designed capacities seem to be candidates for low-quality status.

Anecdotal evidence suggests that many such products are produced and sold in the Soviet economy, and that in the consumer goods sector in particular they are a quite widespread and persistent phenomenon. The problem is serious enough now for the leadership to talk openly about it. In his December 1983 speech to the Central Committee Plenum, Iurii Andropov lamented that the quality of many consumer goods—including TVs, radios, cameras, and watches—was so low that they simply could not be sold and instead sat in warehouses.[58] Even when consumers do purchase products, it may be owing not to satisfactory quality, but to the lack of other options. One survey of the Soviet ready-to-wear industry indicated that one-sixth to one-third of the knitted outerwear, clothing, and footwear purchased by the population were the subject of quality complaints.[59]

Countless anecdotes in the press embellish this story, but of course they cannot establish the relative importance of such products in the system. There are no aggregate data available, nor is it clear how one would design aggregate statistics that would test for the proposition that the USSR produces a large proportion of low-quality products. At best, all one can say is that the general impression of outsiders, and of the Soviet population, is that the quality of consumer goods is low, and that the quality of manufactured goods traded among enterprises in the civilian sectors is similarly low.

If one defines obsolete products as those still under production in the Soviet Union but superseded by a new technological generation in the West, then the examples of such products in the USSR are legion. The

58. Andropov listed 500,000 TVs, which were in stock because consumers would not buy them; 115,000 radios; 250,000 cameras; 1.5 million watches, and 160,000 refrigerators. On the basis of the reported production of these goods in 1983, these figures accounted for 1.2 to 8.4 percent of annual output of these various commodities. The Andropov figures are from "Tekst vystupleniia General'nogo sekretaria," p. 9. The ratios to output were calculated by the author using 1983 plan fulfillment figures.

59. O. Latsis, "Kak shagaet uskorenie?" (How goes the acceleration?), *Kommunist*, no. 4 (March 1987), p. 58.

Soviet Union is still producing computers embodying 1960s technologies whereas their counterparts in the West are either no longer produced or in general use.[60] Soviet communications satellites, although generally reliable, are designed with far fewer capabilities than their Western counterparts.[61] Many Soviet products have not made the transition from vacuum tube to transistor technology, let alone the transition to microprocessors.

These and countless other cases illustrate the point that the Soviet economy produces many goods of decent, if not high, quality that would, however, be difficult to market in the West at any but a very low price because they are obsolete. From the point of view of the Soviet economy, they are serviceable, albeit probably more expensive than their Western counterparts.

To go beyond these anecdotes is difficult; yet not to go further than they allow is frustrating. The extent of our ignorance here can be demonstrated by means of a two-dimensional graph. Along the horizontal axis is a measure of quality: zero is average quality; to the right of zero, above average; to the left of zero, below average. The vertical axis measures obsolescence; zero might represent products using technologies primarily introduced in quantity in at least one country in the early 1980s; above zero is for newer technologies; below zero for older technologies. It would be extraordinarily difficult to develop empirical versions of either of these measures, but as conceptual devices they are useful. Products in the northeast quadrant embody the latest technologies and are of high quality. Those in the southwest quadrant embody relatively old technologies and are of low quality. The northwest quadrant includes advanced, but low-quality products; the southeast quadrant, older, but high-quality products.

Now if it were possible to grade every product in the leading industrialized countries according to quality and obsolescence and to record them as a dot on the graph, presumably they would cluster in the northeast quadrant, although there would be products in all quadrants. Examples of advanced, but low-quality, products (the northwest quad-

60. See, for example, S. E. Goodman and W. K. McHenry, "Computing in the USSR: Recent Progress and Policies," *Soviet Economy*, vol. 2 (October–December 1986), pp. 327–54; and Richard W. Judy, "Computing in the USSR: A Comment," ibid., pp. 355–67.

61. Robert W. Campbell, "Satellite Communications in the USSR," *Soviet Economy*, vol. 1 (October–December 1985), pp. 313–39.

rant) can be found in all industrialized societies; indeed, products embodying frontier technologies frequently suffer from quality problems. Examples of obsolete, but high-quality products are also easy to find, either because of lags in various firms' reactions to recent developments, or because the obsolete products still can find a productive use in society.[62]

If a similar grading exercise was applied to Soviet products, the preponderance would fall in the southwest and southeast quadrants. Where the two quadrants divide is what anecdotes cannot tell. My admittedly subjective guess is that Soviet products probably cluster around the vertical axis, being of average quality by world standards. To be sure, many are well into the southwest quadrant, and some well into the southeast quadrant. In addition, there is apparently a separate cluster of primarily military hardware of higher quality than the bulk of goods produced, but still of varying degrees of obsolescence (thus it straddles the horizontal line between the northeast and southeast quadrants).

It will probably never be possible to improve on this admittedly fuzzy understanding of the situation. The measurement problems are too difficult, and in any event the Soviet Central Statistical Administration seems uninclined to take them on. It is important, nevertheless, to constantly keep in mind that these two dimensions of the quality problem are separable and have different implications for the potential solutions.

THE QUALITY OF SERVICES. The third dimension of the quality problem is the quality of services, which can be divided into two parts: the quality of services available to consumers and the quality of services available to enterprises. Both show gross deficiencies with implications for the operation of the economy.

In Marxist ideology, and in its current interpretation in the Soviet Union, services are not "productive" unless they directly contribute to the production of material goods. If a train in the USSR is carrying freight from one enterprise to another, the service is considered productive and is counted in the national income accounts; if it is carrying passengers, the service is nonproductive and is not counted as part of national income. This attitude also accounts for the general neglect of services, which has been responsible for the low quantity of services available to the population as a whole.

62. The microwave oven is an advance over the traditional stove, but has not replaced it for the perfectly good reason that the stove does some things better.

However, quantity and quality are more difficult to separate for services than they are for manufactured goods. The USSR averages 170 square meters of floor space for retail trade per 1,000 members of the population, whereas the other socialist countries average approximately two times that amount of space, and Western countries average more than four times as much.[63] Employees in the retail trade sector in the USSR are well under half the number serving the smaller U.S. population.[64] Repair services are extremely scarce throughout the Soviet Union, both for consumers and for enterprises, a problem compounded by the general shortage of spare parts. Taxicabs are frequently difficult to locate, and buses are frequently jammed beyond the rated capacities. These and other examples indicate that a significant component of the service aspect of the quality problem in the Soviet Union is simply a shortage of services in demand. Again, the only evidence is anecdotal, but it is also quite convincing in its magnitude.

In addition, there are obvious quality problems in those services. In most Soviet shops it still takes three stops to make a purchase: one to make the selection and get the price; a second to pay for the product; and a third to pick up the wrapped package in return for the proof of payment. Medical services are generally regarded as being of low, or at least variable, quality. Housing services are scarce throughout the Soviet Union, and the quality of Soviet housing construction is poor. Both have been the case for most of Soviet economic history, and this has led Soviet leaders in recent years to talk of a housing "problem" that must be resolved.[65]

The overall quality of services is probably worse in the countryside than in large cities, and probably worse in Siberia than in the European

63. Interview with Deputy Minister of Trade S. E. Sarukhanov, "Chto poluchit pokupatel'?" (What does the buyer receive?), *Izvestiia*, January 1, 1987.

64. In 1984 employees in all aspects of trade in the USSR numbered 7.7 million. *Narkhoz 1984*, p. 411. In 1983 the United States employed almost three times as many people—22.5 million—in retail trade alone to provide goods and services to a population 85 percent the size of the Soviet population. U.S. Department of Commerce, Bureau of the Census, *Statistical Abstract of the United States, 1985*, p. 405.

65. See, for example, "Politicheskii doklad tsentral'nogo komiteta KPSS XXVII S"ezdu Kommunisticheskoi partii Sovetskogo Soiuza. Doklad General'nogo sekretaria TsK KPSS tovarishcha M. S. Gorbacheva 25 Febralia 1986 goda" (The political report to the Central Committee of the CPSU at the 27th Congress of the Communist Party of the Soviet Union. The report of General Secretary M. S. Gorbachev, 25 February 1986), *Materialy XXVII S"zeda kommunisticheskoi partii Sovetskogo Soiuza* (Moscow: Politizdat, 1986), pp. 3–97.

USSR. There is very little information to confirm that generalization, but it is probably one that most Soviet citizens would not consider to be amiss. There is a good deal of information about Siberia, where the construction of social infrastructure, and the supply of services resulting from that, lag far behind the development of the productive sector itself. The problem there is so serious that it has apparently dampened the enthusiasm of new workers for living in the area and has therefore led to an explicit effort by Gorbachev to improve services.

The impact of low-quality services on consumer welfare is of course, difficult to measure, but nevertheless is surely there. It also must affect industrial performance. Difficulty in purchasing repair services and spare parts causes many enterprises to expend their own resources on those activities, or, in some cases, the services are not performed. One visible example of such a problem is the evidence that a failure to repair oil wells in due time contributed significantly to the 1984–85 decline in oil output. This is but the most visible of a large number of instances in which the shortage of repair services and spare parts has materially affected economic performance in the Soviet Union.

ECONOMIC AND POLITICAL CONSEQUENCES OF THE QUALITY PROBLEM. Soviet leaders are increasingly concerned with both the political and economic implications of the quality problem. Less clear is just how serious the implications are, or how improvements in the qualitative side of economic performance would affect political sentiments about the economy, or the performance of the system.

It would appear that the population's considerable patience with the chronic low quality of Soviet goods and services is eroding. In large measure, this is simply an indicator of the success of the system in raising living standards. In 1960 almost one out of every two Soviet families owned a radio, about one out of ten a TV, one out of three a sewing machine, and one out of twenty-five a refrigerator. In 1984 there was one radio and one TV for every Soviet family, two sewing machines for every three, and one refrigerator for every family.[66] These few figures illustrate the important general point that Soviet consumers are now much closer than they were a quarter century ago to having their basic needs satisfied with regard to food, clothing, shelter, and some basic comforts. Of increasing importance to them is not the fact that a refrigerator, or stereo phonograph, or TV, or shoes are for sale, but

66. Figures are from TsSU SSSR, *Narodnoe khoziaistvo SSSR, 1922–1972 gg.* (Moscow: Statistika, 1972), p. 373; and *Narkhoz 1984*, p. 461.

whether the quality of those products is higher than what they have. It is precisely here that Soviet industry's weakness grows increasingly apparent and important to popular perceptions of the contribution of the economy to consumer welfare. The Soviet leadership must, if only for political reasons, show a concern about the problem and have an approach for dealing with it—hence, the statements of concern at the Twenty-seventh Party Congress, and hence, also, the consumer goods program.

However, the concern about the consequences of chronic problems in the quality of consumer goods is not limited to the political side of the equation. Of equal, if not greater, significance is the leadership's conviction that the low quality of Soviet goods and services now constitutes a significant brake on the growth of labor productivity. The elaborate incentive schemes under constant debate in the USSR, particularly the recently proposed schemes designed to closely link wages to individual worker productivity, will mean very little if the rubles earned cannot be used to buy higher-quality goods and services. Soviet leaders understand this, and in later chapters I discuss how they propose to deal with it.

The other important economic consequence of the quality problem pertains to industry itself. The low quality of many manufactured goods affects the reliability of industries, forces enterprises to devote large resources to repair and maintenance, and reduces labor productivity. The obsolete character of many industrial products implies labor productivity considerably below what it could be if more advanced, labor-saving, technologies were used. In the Soviet case this seems to be a particularly important consideration in materials handling, loading, and unloading, where the USSR lags far behind the industrialized West. The low quality of services has similar effects.

There is no way to quantify these effects. But a measure of the importance the leadership attaches to them is the fact that Gorbachev has made a modernization program the centerpiece of his plans for the remainder of this century. Clearly Gorbachev understands that all of his goals ride on his resolution of the quality problem in industry.

Imbalances in the System

Supply-demand imbalances in the system constitute the third problem to attract high-level, and sustained, concern in the Soviet Union. The imbalances per se are not a weakness of the system; all countries at all times experience imbalances in the supply of and demand for some products. What is special about the Soviet case is the *persistence* of the imbalances. Either there are no feedback mechanisms to inform the system of the need to respond to an existing supply-demand imbalance, or the feedback is ignored. Whatever the case, the result is that the Soviet economy, unlike economies that rely more heavily on markets, may tolerate some supply-demand imbalances for decades. This may occur in a wide range of products and even sectors.

The primary concern here is an excess demand for consumer goods as a whole, meaning that in general disposable income exceeds the supply of goods available for purchase. This is related to, but separate from, the issue just discussed of a shortage of high-quality goods and a surplus of low-quality goods. A second concern relates to the high demand for investment goods, which translates into long gestation periods for investment projects as the economy's considerable construction capacity is spread among a formidable number of ongoing projects. Imbalances in specific sectors are still another concern as they provide inputs to much of the economy and therefore can contribute to a general shortfall in the utilization of the productive capacity of the system.

IMBALANCES IN CONSUMER GOODS. There is no direct way to test the proposition that consumer goods and services as a whole are in excess demand in the USSR. No data exist on the supply of consumer goods. Nor can the demand for consumer goods be easily quantified since that requires information on total wages, total savings, and consumer desires to spend the combination of their savings and income in any particular year. All that can be done with the existing data is to make a few observations on total consumption and savings in banks, which tell only part of the story.

Nevertheless, Soviet leaders, and many Soviet economists, take it for granted that there is an excess demand for consumer goods in the Soviet economy, and that an imbalance in this sector is not in the political and economic interests of the party. As Nikolai Ryzhkov observed at the Twenty-seventh Party Congress, "A more complete satisfaction of the purchasing power of the population is of principal significance in the social policy of the party." Resolving that problem is for him one of the highest priorities, for it is "inextricably intertwined with . . . the strengthening of material incentiveness to work, the rational utilization of nonworking time, the mood of the Soviet people, and the overcoming of negative phenomena engendered by shortages."[67]

The evidence on which Soviet economists and their leaders rely to support this proposition must, in part, be qualitative in the form of feedback from local authorities. In addition, on any given day one can easily find articles or letters to the editor in one of the major national newspapers complaining about shortages of consumer goods that sound so widespread they seem to add up to a more general shortage. Second, there is the general belief that wages paid in industry are now so loosely tied to productivity that the entire wage system has become a source of inflationary pressures.[68] Other evidence is somewhat "harder," albeit not without its own problems. Savings deposits, for example, grew at an average rate of 9.3 percent during 1975–85, whereas consumption over the same period grew at only 4.6 percent.[69] Wage growth has exceeded the growth of retail sales.[70] This, combined with the qualitative evidence, has led Soviet leaders to conclude that there is a pent-up demand for consumer goods.

Some economists in the West have been skeptical about the interpretation of the supporting data, arguing, for example, that the savings rate is not dramatically out of line with that observed in other countries at the Soviet level of development.[71] Another possibility, if the disequilibrium econometrics Portes and others have used to analyze similar issues for Eastern Europe is applied to the Soviet case, is that the results would show—as they have for Eastern Europe—no persistent pattern of disequilibriums in the markets for consumer goods.[72] Indeed it must be

---

67. Ryzhkov, "Ob osnovnykh napravleniiakh."

68. Rusanov, "Proizvoditel'nost' truda i zarplata," provides an example of this form of argumentation. He argues that whereas in the early 1950s wages in material production grew only 23 percent as rapidly as productivity, by 1976–83 the ratio was 90 percent, and in 1982 wage growth exceeded that for productivity.

69. Consumer incomes are a more meaningful measure for the latter figure, but are not available. The data are from Narkhoz 1985, pp. 411, 448.

70. Rusanov, "Proizvoditel'nost', truda i zarplata" notes that during 1970–83 retail sales grew 81 percent while wages grew 90 percent.

71. Joyce Pickersgill, "Soviet Household Saving Behavior," Review of Economics and Statistics, vol. 58 (February 1976), pp. 139–47; and Pickersgill, "Recent Evidence on Soviet Households' Saving Behavior," Review of Economics and Statistics, vol. 62 (November 1980), pp. 628–33.

72. For a review of Portes's work, see Richard Portes, "The Theory and Measurement of Macroeconomic Disequilibrium in Centrally Planned Economies," paper prepared

true that some of whatever excess demand exists for Soviet consumer goods and services as a whole is there because of the mix problem alluded to earlier. If the right mix of goods was produced, presumably retail inventories would be lower and consumers would have, to use Ryzhkov's phrase, their "purchasing power" more completely fulfilled.

In any event, the most important political point is that the leadership, Soviet economists, and the population are convinced there is a problem here, which they intend to do something about. Furthermore, they clearly intend to try to make progress on both the mix and the total demand for consumer goods.

IMBALANCES IN INVESTMENT GOODS. Several indicators point to the existence of persistent excess demand for investment goods in the Soviet Union, which may have grown much more pronounced in the past ten years as planners have sought unsuccessfully to dampen demand to make room for higher consumption growth rates. The anecdotal evidence certainly supports the notion that enterprises, and ministries, have an almost unquenchable thirst for large new projects, a natural outcome of a system that chooses bureaucratically among investment proposals and issues nonrepayable investment grants to the winners. To cite just one case in which information is available, two Gosplan officials responsible for investment planning report that, in the negotiations for the 1982 plan, ministries and their departments proposed to Gosplan 2,000 investment projects, each with a budgeted value of at least 3 million rubles, and most were presumably for much more. Gosplan's departments had to cut those down to 600 projects in the first pass, and then finally to 385 projects in a second pass.[73]

This excess demand shows up in part in the growth rates for investment that exceed five-year plans, but it also can be seen in several other ways. Most notable are the long, and apparently growing, time periods required to complete investment projects in the Soviet Union. In the 1960s the average length of time from initial design to full-capacity operation for a Soviet investment project was seven to eight years, which was two to

for conference on the Soviet Union and Eastern Europe in the World Economy, Kennan Institute, Washington, D C , October 1984.

73. N. Baryshnikov and G. Galakhov, "Kapital'noe stroitel'stvo—reshaiushchii uchastok sotsialisticheskogo vosproizvodstva" (Capital construction: a decisive part of socialist reproduction), Planovoe khoziaistvo, no. 3 (March 1982), p. 26. (Hereafter cited as Plan. khoz.)

two and a half times the normal time for investment projects in industrialized countries of the West. In the 1970s that may have stretched out to eight to ten years.[74] In his speech to the Twenty-seventh Party Congress, Nikolai Ryzhkov cited figures concerning projects approved by several ministries (nonferrous metallurgy and autos) for inclusion in the Eleventh FYP in which the *average* length of time between initial design work and final completion exceeded twenty years.[75]

The excess demands also show up in cost overruns, as enterprises purposely underestimate project costs to enhance the chances that their project will be accepted and then later on reveal the full costs. A survey of 1,600 enterprises regarding investment projects during 1971–78, which covered 20 percent of the value of all investment projects undertaken in those enterprises during that time period, showed that the actual productive capacity of the finished projects was within 3 percent of the capacity projected in original plans, but the project costs averaged one-third higher than originally planned.[76]

The evidence available hardly constitutes an unambiguous case in favor of the hypothesis that there is a growing gap between the demand for investment goods and the supply. It would be useful to have time-series data for the last several decades documenting the number and value of investment requests from the ministries to Gosplan, the number and value of investment projects approved, and the time schedule and final value of the completed projects. Presumably such data exist, but, aside from bits and pieces, they are not made public.

OTHER IMBALANCES. There are many individual imbalances in factor and intermediate product markets that can be documented only through anecdotes. The conventional wisdom, probably fully justified, is that they exert downward pressure on the general level of industrial output and at times disrupt it.

The most important and all-pervasive shortage is in labor itself. The consequent excess demand for labor, at least in the European USSR, is one of the sources of the economic security enjoyed by the labor force; at the same time, it can be a source of underutilization of capacity in the

74. David Dyker. *The Process of Investment in the Soviet Union* (New York: Cambridge University Press, 1983), p. 36.

75. Ryzhkov, "Ob osnovnykh napravleniiakh."

76. V. Kirichenko, "O nekotorykh voprosakh dal'neishego sovershenstvovaniia planirovaniia i upravleniia khoziaistvom" (Several issues concerning the improvement of the planning and management of the economy), *Plan. khoz.*, no. 9 (September 1982), pp. 63–64.

remainder of the system. The major unemployment problem in the USSR is not with people, but with machines.

Also significant, and apparently pervasive, are shortages of intermediate products, which in turn can suppress, or at least disrupt, production. From a survey of 5,000 enterprises in 52 ministries a Gosplan economist estimated that capacity utilization averaged 80.8 percent. But the variance in that figure among branches was enormous, from 104.4 percent in ferrous metallurgy to 61.9 percent in food; these differences have been attributed to access to material resources.[77] A myriad of anecdotes could be cited in support of the proposition that imbalances affect the level of economic performance, but they would do little to determine the actual significance of the phenomenon for performance. The most important fact is that the leadership considers this to be a serious economic problem.

The imbalances in supply and demand for labor and other inputs are linked to the general concern over the efficiency of the system. Thus the fact that the USSR experiences shortages in steel, but produces more steel than any other country in the world, suggests that at least part of the problem is the excess demand for steel. Likewise, the debates now developing over Gorbachev's reforms suggest a growing consensus that the shortage of labor is the artificial consequence of an excess demand for labor.

In addition to these pure supply-demand imbalances, the system is prone to generate disproportions within industry and between industry and other sectors, both of which have an impact on performance and consumer welfare.

In large investment projects there is a chronic tendency for the expenditures on the productive investment itself to outpace the investment on social infrastructure—schools, medical facilities, retail establishments, apartments, and so on. This is a major problem in the new areas of settlement, most notably Siberia, which is regarded as an important contributing factor to labor supply difficulties in those areas.

Within industry, investments tend to focus on the production line itself, while materials handling for inputs and the handling of final output are still done primarily through hand labor. In the early 1980s, hand labor accounted for 40 percent of all industrial labor, 70 percent of agricultural labor, and 60 percent of labor in construction.[78] The trans-

77. S. Zhuravlev, "Novoe kachestvo ekonomichskogo rosta" (A new quality of economic growth), *Ekon. gaz.*, no. 24 (June 1986).

78. K. K. Val'tukh, "Investitsionnyi kompleks i intensifikatsiia proizvodstva" (The

portation sector, a key link in the Soviet economy, has historically been accorded a relatively low investment priority. This has led to transport bottlenecks, which, at times, may have depressed national output.[79] Finally, there is the major imbalance Gorbachev has singled out for the Twelfth FYP: the historically low priority for the producers of machinery, which has contributed to the sluggishness of technical change in the core of the investment system.

CAUSAL FACTORS. The causal factors underlying these various imbalances are multiple and complex. Obviously the system plays a large role. The excess demand for labor and capital, and the low quality of consumer goods, are both primarily a direct result of the incentives built into the system itself.

However, it is important to note that the system is not solely to blame; planners' priorities play a role. The shortage of housing in the USSR is a result of conscious decisions by Soviet leaders to shortchange that sector. The inadequacies in the transport and social infrastructures similarly reflect conscious, if unannounced, decisions. Even the persistent quality problems in consumer goods and services may, in part, reflect the indirect consequences of the defense sector's high priority for the acquisition of labor, capital, and intermediate inputs.

As Soviet leaders move ahead with their reform agenda, these imbalances will be important indicators of the success or failure of the reform. But to address the imbalances adequately will require not only economic reforms, but also new investment priorities favoring hitherto neglected sectors in the system.

The Economic Reform Problem

The weaknesses of the Soviet economy are the driving force in the debates about economic reform. The Soviet leader, whoever he may be, must somehow be seen to be dealing with these weaknesses through changes in policy or in the system itself. If the decline in growth continues—which is the direction the exogenous forces are pushing—

---

investment complex and the intensification of production), *EKO*, no. 3 (March 1982), p. 8.

79. See Holland Hunter, Peggy Dunn, Vladimir Kontorovich, and Janusz Szyrmer, "Soviet Transport Trends, 1950–1990," *Soviet Economy*, vol. 1 (July–September 1985), pp. 195–227.

and if the quality and imbalance problems persist, then the pressure for ameliorative action from the party and the population grows.

In responding to that pressure it is also natural for any Soviet leader to try to preserve the strengths of the system. The economic security of the system is surely one of the most visible characteristics of a socialist society, distinguishing it from Western industrial countries and in effect justifying the rule of the party. Therefore the search for economic reforms can be expected to begin under the constraint of preserving economic security and the egalitarian bias, while holding on to the bias in favor of high growth rates.

The likelihood that the search will be successful hinges on the nature of the links between the strengths of the system and its weaknesses. To what extent does the considerable economic security afforded workers account for the low-quality output, falling productivity, and the excess demand for investment goods? Is it possible to sustain full employment, yet deal effectively with those problems? Is it possible to sustain price stability, yet enjoy the benefits of a flexible price system that facilitates rapid adjustment to changing supply-demand conditions?

Any reform program introduced by Soviet leaders must somehow identify and address these links between the strengths and the weaknesses. Effective reform programs will probably involve compromises. In order to understand the links and to evaluate the possible compromises, one must know how the system as it is now constituted works to allocate resources.

CHAPTER THREE

The Soviet Economic System As It Is Designed to Operate

THE ECONOMY pictured in the preceding chapter provides its citizens with a high degree of economic security, a fairly equitable distribution of income, and respectable growth rates for national income and consumption. Yet it has always been plagued by imbalances and gross inefficiencies, and innovative activity has been little more than modest. Moreover, the possibility for rapid growth is now declining as the growth of inputs has fallen off and efficiencies are not rising to compensate.

Any effort to explain this performance must take into account Soviet economic policy, exogenous elements, and the economic system itself. Although the economic system is the most important factor, the other two sets of factors cannot be dismissed, nor should they be confused with the economic system. Consider, for example, the fact that successive Soviet governments have accorded low priority to investment in housing and light industry and that goods and services from both of those industries have therefore been in short supply. Note, too, that the bias in the incentive system favors high output growth rates and thus explains in part the relative lack of concern among Soviet enterprises for the quality of their output. Furthermore, the high priority accorded the military draws resources away from research and development and contributes to the poor innovative performance of Soviet civilian industry. These are but a few examples to illustrate the simple, but quite important, point that government policies significantly affect the performance of an economic system. The system itself may reinforce these tendencies, but it is not the sole cause of them.

Exogenous factors such as the weather, raw material and energy reserves, and accumulated capital stock (both human and physical) also influence the performance of the system, whatever its configuration. Variations in Soviet climatic conditions, which can be large, not only cause agricultural output to fluctuate, but also create disruptions in transport, which in turn add to bottlenecks in the economy. The USSR's relatively strong balance of payments record since the end of World War II is explained not so much by the nature of its economic system as by the abundance of its energy resources and raw materials, which are highly valued on world markets. Economic growth has deteriorated in recent years in part because the population, and therefore the labor force, has experienced falling growth rates.

Nevertheless, it is the system that lies at the core of any explanation of economic performance. The economic system is the mechanism by which society makes the best of the environment, whatever it may be, and implements policies, whatever they may be. Soviet agriculture works under weather conditions far less favorable than those in many other parts of the globe. However, that is a well-known fact of life, and the system must compensate for this as best it can.[1] Similarly, the system must be able to minimize bottlenecks arising from decisions that favor some sectors over others.

That the economic system is of central importance is also clear from the fact that many of the policy and exogenous variables themselves emanate from the system. For example, although the existing capital stock is a "given," an exogenous variable, for the economic system functioning today, it is also a legacy of the system in the past. Inefficient factories contributing to poor performance are the products of a similar system that existed in the past. Another given is the decline in population growth, which is contributing to the slowdown in Soviet growth. However, the decline in birth rates can in part be traced to leadership policies that accorded low priority to housing in the postwar period. Moreover, although it is true that the Soviet policy has favored high growth rates over quality, it is also true that the system is better suited to focus on quantitative indicators than to implement a more sophisticated policy encouraging the production of fewer high-quality products.

1. General Secretary Gorbachev has made the point himself in a critical discussion of the inadequate response of local authorities to the severe winter of 1984–85, in which he exclaimed, "After all, a severe winter is hardly unexpected in our country." See "Kursom edinstva i splochennosti" (The course of unity and firmness), *Pravda*, February 21, 1985.

Thus it is not surprising that Soviet leaders have concentrated on the economic system in their efforts to improve, or at least retard, the deterioration in economic performance. Nor is it surprising that Western analysts of the Soviet economy have focused on the system in their efforts to explain the current pattern of economic performance. As a result, the primary concern of this volume is the economic system itself, and its reform.

This chapter and the next explain how the economic system in the USSR operates in order to set the stage for a discussion of efforts to reform it. The brush strokes are, of necessity, rather broad; much more detail is provided about some matters than about others. The goal is twofold: (1) to provide a sense of the logic of the system by identifying its major parts and their interrelations, and (2) to identify the most fundamental characteristics of the system that contribute to the particular weaknesses in economic performance discussed in chapter 2.

Both this chapter and the next analyze the system as it existed on the eve of Gorbachev's accession to the office of general secretary. These chapters provide the benchmark against which to compare the reforms emerging under Gorbachev since 1986, which is the subject of later chapters. In fact, because most of the changes actually implemented to date under Gorbachev affect the details, but not the fundamentals, this benchmark is also still an expression of the reality of the economic system that Gorbachev is trying to change.

Formal versus De Facto Systems, and the Logic of Both

I use the term "logic" here in the spirit of Marx's analysis of the capitalist system through the prism of the dialectic; that is to say, an economic system may have many parts that serve different functions, but these parts must also work more or less harmoniously with—not against—each other.[2] Any viable system has this sort of internal logic, and the Soviet system is no exception. The existence of this logic has nothing to do with whether the performance of the system as a whole is efficient or equitable. On the contrary it is quite possible to have a system

2. For an excellent interpretation of Marx along these lines, see Bertell Ollman, *Alienation: Marx's Conception of Man in Capitalist Society* (Cambridge University Press, 1971), pt. 1.

in which the parts work together superbly, but the total result is poor performance.

That logic must be kept in mind whether one is a critic or a designer of systemic reforms. The rigid Soviet price system, which leaves many important prices fixed for over a decade, and the financial system, which acts passively to distribute funds to enterprises that need them, both fit extremely well with the hierarchically organized planning system, which seeks to exert total control over resource flows. In fact, all of the major components of the system fit together rather well, and have for years. That point must be fully understood before one can simultaneously explain why the system works as well as it does and why it is so difficult to change.

Inattention to the logic of the system is apparently what has contributed to the failure of so many past efforts at reform in the Soviet Union, as well as in Eastern Europe. Soviet leaders are no different from political leaders elsewhere; they can be easily drawn to solutions that address symptoms, not the root causes. Their memories are conveniently short; their capacity for wishful thinking, seemingly boundless. Gorbachev's effort in 1985–86 to curb the ministries' power over enterprises is a good illustration. Ministries do intervene continuously, and excessively, in the affairs of "their" enterprises, but to some extent that simply reflects the pressure they are under from the center to ensure improved results for a number of indicators in all of their enterprises. According to the logic of the system, to reduce ministerial interference in enterprise affairs it is necessary not only to dilute the ministerial powers over enterprises, but also to reduce ministerial responsibilities for enterprise performance. The fate of the Kosygin reforms is ample testimony to the costs of ignoring such considerations.

It is equally important to be as clear as possible about the ultimate causes of poor performance in the system. Take, for example, the lackluster innovative performance of enterprises in the civilian economy. Enterprises do not innovate because there are other, easier alternatives open to them as a result of a lack of domestic or foreign competition and the understanding stance taken by their ministries when they fail. There is an infinite supply of reforms that will deal with the many symptoms of this basic problem without addressing the problem itself, and Soviet leaders are constantly trying them: new incentive systems, new plan indicators controlling innovation, price bonuses for new products, and so on. If an outsider is to analyze a priori the likelihood that a particular reform will have an effect on the performance problem it is addressing, he can only do so if he understands the basic causes of the problem. Only then will it be possible to ascertain which reforms, if any, are appropriate.

Such considerations suggest that the Soviet leaders' analysis of the country's economic problems should be treated with considerable skepticism. Their record in this regard is hardly one that inspires confidence. Their diagnosis of a problem should be regarded as no more than one of possibly many plausible hypotheses, the significant point being not that their version of the situation is right, but that they think it is.

The Logic of the System

Economic systems can be defined and distinguished from each other by the form of their three basic components: (1) the decisionmaking hierarchy that allocates responsibility for and power over resource allocation; (2) the information system that provides decisionmakers with the information needed to support their decisions; and (3) the incentive system with which decisionmakers use the information at hand to decide on resource allocation.

The decisionmaking hierarchy consists of the actors in the system and their interconnections defined by a distribution of responsibilities, authority, and power. Government bodies, business enterprises, individuals or workers and consumers, banks, and the many other economic institutions are all part of the mosaic that makes up the decisionmaking hierarchy. The rights and responsibilities of the various actors—for example, the limits on private activity or the rights and duties of ministries—are the other distinguishing features of this dimension of an economic system.

The information system links the actors in the decisionmaking hierarchy. It is composed of the price and various nonprice signals that move around the system providing the various actors with feedback on their actions and affording them the opportunity to adjust their decisions in the light of their goals, whether self-determined or dictated from a point higher up in the hierarchy. The quality of the information determines whether the system will function smoothly, since those who receive false or inadequate information must depend on luck to make the right decisions.

The incentive system is the sum of the incentives that induce decisionmakers to use the information at their disposal to make the millions of decisions that underlie the economic activity of any system. These may include moral incentives ("Work for the good of the party"), material incentives ("Work to improve your own living standard"), and coercion ("Work or else") and probably consist of some combination of the three.[3]

This framework is a useful device for organizing a discussion of the nature of the economic system because it enables the analyst to draw out of a highly complex reality the answers to three important questions: Who has the power to decide over resource allocation? What information do they have at their disposal? And what incentives motivate them to act on that information? This device also makes it possible to illuminate on a highly aggregated level the basic logic of the system. A multilevel hierarchy in which power is focused at the top will need an information system that can accommodate large amounts of nonprice information (plan targets, plan fulfillment, and data on inventories, to cite just three examples) and an incentive system that encourages units at the bottom of the hierarchy to send up accurate information and to respond to plans sent down the system as the center wishes. A program of reforms seeking to decentralize decisionmaking power must also alter the design of the information and incentive systems if the reformed system is to have a logic that will make it viable.

Formal versus De Facto Systems

In the Soviet Union, as in most countries, there are in fact two economic systems: the system described in laws and decrees, which represents the way that Soviet leaders would have the economic system operate (the formal system), and the system as it actually operates, sometimes at complete variance with the existing laws and decrees (the de facto system). It is far easier to obtain information about the formal system than about the de facto system; and the formal system is generally much neater, and less contradictory, than the actual system. Because of those attributes, an uncritical observer may be inclined to accept the

3. For an elaboration of these concepts, see John Michael Montias, *The Structure of Economic Systems* (Yale University Press, 1976). See also the discussion of Montias's framework and how it may be applied to the study of economic systems in Egon Neuberger and William J. Duffy, *Comparative Economic Systems: A Decision-Making Approach* (Boston: Allyn and Bacon, 1976), pts. 1,2.

formal system as an accurate description of reality, whereas a more skeptical analyst might automatically dismiss it as a facade. The actual situation in the Soviet Union, not surprisingly, lies somewhere between those two extremes. The formal system represents things as they are in some cases, but not in others. The system was designed, in part, to give Soviet leaders virtually unchallenged control over the level and structure of investment, and reality is reasonably close to that. At the same time, the formal system stipulates that prices should be determined at the center, whereas in fact the center seems to have great and increasing difficulty in controlling prices.

In general, the reason that formal and de facto systems diverge is that the formal system, although feasible in the abstract, is infeasible in reality. Typically, the problem is that the formal system cannot operate as designed unless an enormous amount of information flows to the decisionmakers. In the real world, however, the information system fails to supply the requisite information and therefore central decisionmakers are too ill-informed to fulfill their responsibilities. In some cases that leads to poor decisions; in others, to a de facto shift of power from those who are responsible, but ill-informed, to those who are not responsible, but who have the requisite information. This is certainly true in the Soviet Union, where many decisionmakers with formal responsibility in a given area find it impossible to obtain sufficient information to make the decisions they are charged to make. Thus, a significant number of the decisions are made at lower levels, where the information lies.

Because the formal system so often fails in the real world, it cannot be used to represent the system as it actually works. More important, reforms to this system will have little effect unless they interact with the de facto system.

However, the formal system does function effectively where this is feasible, and there are such places in the Soviet economy. Also, it does constrain the de facto system in many respects. Enterprises may, and do, search for ways to obtain an easy plan and then minimize the pain of appearing to fulfill the main indicators, but they cannot ignore the plan. The plan sets the agenda for them more than they set the agenda for the plan. Thus, an analysis of how the Soviet economic system actually operates cannot ignore the formal system; on the contrary, it should start with the formal system and use it as a touchstone to understanding the de facto system.

The Formal System

The guiding principle behind the design of the Soviet economic system is that the Communist party should have institutionalized control over all major aspects of economic activity in the USSR. This goal clearly dominates other possible considerations, most notably economic efficiency, although the formal system is said to be the most efficient way to meet the full range of social, economic, and political requirements of the Soviet people.

All subsystems in the formal system are designed to do their part in helping the party exercise control over the economy. Every proposal for economic reform in the Soviet Union has been, and will be, couched in terms that refer to enhancing the party's control over the economy. That basic interest is always visible, whatever part of the economy is being considered—whether it is the legal system, the price system, or the financial system. Thus, in seeking to understand why a particular reform proposal or possibility is or is not viewed with favor by the leaders, the critical factor to note is how they think that reform proposal will affect the party's control over the system.

However, "party control over the economy" is a complex concept that is open to many interpretations and that can be worked out in many ways in the formal system. Furthermore, the fact that "the party" has over 19 million members leads one to ask how control over the economy will be distributed among them. Clearly the party leadership will want to maintain control over the most important variables, but which ones will fall into this category? Some members of the leadership might only want the party to control major macro indicators, whereas others would include the output of key products, as well as many indicators of economic activity at the enterprise level (such as investment, the introduction of new products, and wage funds).

Complicating matters further is the question of how to define control. Many party members may take control to mean directly dictating, and possibly even participating in, decisions that are made at all levels of the hierarchy and that pertain to economic activity involving all of the important variables. Others will be content to manipulate incentives in an effort to induce the "right" decisions regarding key variables—that is, the decisions the party would like to see—without resorting to direct intervention.

The formal system as it exists today, with its clear Stalinist foundations, leans heavily in the direction of defining precisely all the important variables that should be controlled by central party leaders, utilizing techniques that emphasize direct intervention, and using incentives only where direct intervention is clearly unable to provide satisfactory results. I turn now to an overview of the formal system. It is organized around the three central components identified earlier: the decisionmaking hierarchy, the information system, and the incentive system.

The Decisionmaking Hierarchy

Two hierarchies work together to control resource allocation in the USSR: the party and the government. They constitute what Thane Gustafson has characterized as a "dual government by party and state," each of which counterbalances, or supplements, the operation of the other.[4] The party has clear authority over and responsibility for the most fundamental decisions affecting the economy—those that pertain to the division of national product among consumers, investors, and defense; the general thrust of investment policy; key foreign economic variables (foreign debt, for example); and policies on large projects (such as Baikal-Amur mainline). The primary responsibility of the government hierarchy is to run the economy in a way that optimally contributes to meeting the goals set by the party. One of its important functions is to provide party leaders with information on the economic system to help them reach decisions on strategic issues. Both hierarchies have a hand in operating the formal (and, for that matter, the de facto) system, but depending on the type of economic decision, one hierarchy or the other will bear primary responsibility. For example, the party decides on the general policy regarding the development of nuclear power in the USSR; whereas the government, having provided much of the supporting technical and economic information, must implement the decision and deal with the practical task of mixing nuclear with other sources of energy in order to meet the economy's energy needs.

THE PARTY HIERARCHY. The ultimate source of all authority within the party is the congress, which in recent years has been convened at five-

---

4. Thane Gustafson, *Reform in Soviet Politics; Lessons of Recent Policies on Land and Water* (Cambridge University Press, 1981), p. 2.

year intervals.[5] The Party Congress elects a Central Committee (CC) to handle all party affairs between Party Congresses. The Central Committee must, according to party rules, meet at least twice a year. The most recent Party Congress, the twenty-seventh, held between February 25 and March 6, 1986, elected a Central Committee of 307 voting members and 170 nonvoting members.[6] The Central Committee includes in its membership nationally or regionally prominent political and economic leaders, as well as a sprinkling of prominent scientists, writers, trade union officials, workers, and peasants.[7]

The Central Committee elects from its membership a Politburo, which is empowered to handle the affairs of the party between meetings of the Central Committee. As of June 1987, the Politburo consists of fourteen voting members and six candidate (nonvoting) members (table 3-1). In addition, the Central Committee elects secretaries to manage the administrative apparatus of the party. First among the secretaries is the general secretary (currently Mikhail Gorbachev), who is head of both the party and its bureaucracy.

At present eleven additional secretaries serve with Gorbachev. The Politburo is what Jerry Hough aptly characterizes as "the real cabinet of the Soviet system,"[8] the Secretariat providing the administrative support that drafts resolutions under guidance of the secretaries—some, but not all of whom, are Politburo members—and sees that they are carried out after approval.

The general secretary and the eleven secretaries who work with him supervise the work of the Central Committee staff, which is divided into twenty-one departments that together monitor and supervise the approximately eighty national-level ministries and state committees overseeing the economy, as well as all other national-level political-economic organizations. Of those twenty-one departments, ten share the bulk of responsibility for the economy.[9] These ten departments are the means

5. Unless otherwise indicated, this section relies on Jerry F. Hough and Merle Fainsod, *How the Soviet Union Is Governed* (Harvard University Press, 1979), chaps. 11–12; and Jerry F. Hough, *The Soviet Prefects: The Local Party Organs in Industrial Decision-making* (Harvard University Press, 1969).

6. *Pravda*, March 7, 1986, provides a full list.

7. Hough and Fainsod, *How the Soviet Union Is Governed*, p. 457, analyze the composition of the Central Committee in the 1960s and 1970s.

8. Ibid., p. 466.

9. The ten departments directly responsible for the economy—or, more accurately, for supervising the organs that administer the economy—are (department chief in

Table 3-1. *Politburo of the Central Committee (CC) of the Soviet Communist Party (CPSU) and Party Secretaries, June 1987*

Politburo membership[a]

Voting members
Mikhail S. Gorbachev (general secretary, CC, CPSU)
Geidar A. Aliev (first deputy chairman, USSR Council of Ministers)
Viktor M. Chebrikov (chairman, USSR Committee for State Security [KGB])
Andrei A. Gromyko (chairman, Presidium of the USSR Supreme Soviet)
Egor K. Ligachev (secretary, CC, CPSU)
Viktor P. Nikonov (secretary, CC, CPSU)
Nikolai I. Ryzhkov (chairman, USSR Council of Ministers)
Vladimir V. Shcherbitsky (first secretary, CP of the Ukraine)
Eduard A. Shevardnadze (USSR minister of foreign affairs)
Nikolai N. Slyun'kov (first secretary, CP of Belorussia)
Mikhail S. Solomentsev (chairman, Party Control Commission)
Vitalii I. Vorotnikov (chairman, RSFSR Council of Ministers)
Aleksandr N. Yakovlev (secretary, CC, CPSU)
Lev N. Zaikov (secretary, CC, CPSU)

Candidate (nonvoting) members
Petr N. Demichev (first deputy chairman, USSR Supreme Soviet)
Vladimir I. Dolgikh (secretary, CC, CPSU)
Boris N. Yeltsin (first secretary, Moscow *gorkom*)
Iurii F. Solov'ev (first secretary, Leningrad *obkom*)
Nikolai V. Talyzin (first deputy chairman, USSR Council of Ministers; chairman, Gosplan)
Dimitrii T. Yazov (USSR Minister of Defense)

Party secretaries[b]
Mikhail S. Gorbachev (general supervision)
Aleksandra P. Biryukova (consumer goods, food and light industry)
Anatolii F. Dobrynin (foreign policy, relations with nonruling communist parties and socialist parties)
Vladimir I. Dolgikh (heavy industry, energy, power, transport)
Egor K. Ligachev (cadres and ideology)
Anatolii I. Luk'ianov (administration and Politburo staff work)
Vadim A. Medvedev (relations among socialist countries and CMEA)
Viktor P. Nikonov (agriculture and forestry)
Georgii P. Razumovsky (cadres affairs)
Nikolai N. Slyun'kov (economic administration)
Aleksandr N. Yakovlev (domestic ideological affairs and culture)
Lev N. Zaikov (economic administration and military-industrial complex)

Source: Alexander Rahr, "The Composition of the Politburo and the Secretariat of the Central Committee of the CPSU," *Radio Liberty Research Bulletin*, RL 236/87, June 26, 1987.
a. Other duties in parentheses.
b. Duties in parentheses.

by which the party controls the system in that the Politburo draws from them the staff support it needs to prepare all decrees, monitor their implementation, and supervise the overall work of the ministries as well as party organizations throughout the system.

Republican and local levels replicate in all important ways the party organization at the national level. Each of the fifteen republics has a party organization that holds quinquennial congresses, which elect a Central Committee, which in turn elects a Politburo and a set of secretaries to supervise the work of the republican secretariat. In addition, the party organization in each republic has other components whose authority conforms to governmental boundaries, the most important being the *oblast* party committee, or *obkom,* which may cover areas as large as a typical state in the United States; the *raion* party committee, or *raikom,* which falls under the *oblast'* party committee; and the city committee, or *gorkom,* which is formed for all large cities.[10] The first secretary of an *obkom* or *gorkom* is generally as powerful in his region as the general secretary is on the national level, and his formal powers far exceed those of a mayor or governor in the United States.

The party hierarchy influences the operation of the economic system in many ways. Probably the most important and all-pervasive avenue of influence is the choice of personnel. The USSR Central Committee Secretariat has the exclusive right to appoint individuals to leadership positions in important social, political, economic, and cultural institutions in the entire nation. This *nomenklatura* list includes, for example, all ministerial-level positions at the national level, important department heads within those institutions, managerial positions in important factories (the director and his first deputies), and the leading posts in important institutions (research institutes, editorial positions at all national newspapers and journals, and other important positions). Other

---

parentheses) Agriculture and Food Industry (Ivan I. Skiba), Chemical Industry (Veniamin G. Afonin), Construction (Aleksandr G. Mel'nikov), Defense Industry (Oleg S. Beliakov), Economic (Nikolai N. Slyun'kov), Heavy Industry and Power Engineering (Ivan P. Yastrebov), Light Industry and Consumer Goods (Leonid F. Bobykin), Machinebuilding (Arkadii I. Vol'sky), Trade and Consumer Services (Nikolai A. Stashenkov), and Transport and Communications (Viktor S. Pasternak). The source for this listing is Alexander Rahr, "The Apparatus of the Central Committee of the CPSU," *Radio Liberty Research Bulletin,* RL #136/87, April 10, 1987. For more details on the operation of the CC apparatus, see Hough and Fainsod, *How the Soviet Union Is Governed,* pp. 411–22.

10. The hierarchy of committees is much more complicated than indicated here. See Hough, *Soviet Prefects,* pp. 8–34, for a discussion.

levels of the hierarchy have their own, even more numerous, *nomen-klatura* lists that cover leading positions for all important institutions within the region over which they have authority.

This right of appointment provides the party with substantial and sustained influence over decisionmaking throughout the economic system. The fact that each individual serves at the pleasure of the party provides a strong incentive, although far from a requirement, to set policies in conformance with the party's preferences. This works at every level of the economy, from the national-level ministries monitored by the departments of the Central Committee to the entire range of enterprises monitored by local party officials.

The second major source of party influence lies in the control it exercises over the agenda at the national level through the Politburo, with the support of the CC staff. The Politburo sets the main goals for the economy—growth rate targets, the distribution of national income among final uses (defense, consumption, investment), targets for foreign economic relations, and targets for critical products, to name just four important areas—and it decides on the most important policy directions. Put more generally, the Politburo makes all the strategic decisions that drive the entire planning process—the long-term, five-year, and annual plans. The government acts as a source of information and an executor of policy. Ideally (that is, in the formal system), the Politburo and the CC staff will not involve themselves in the detailed operation of the system; that is the government's job. The Politburo has decided, for example, to permit joint ventures with Western firms on Soviet soil and has approved a general resolution to that effect, but the government carries primary responsibility for issuing detailed regulations, approving joint venture applications, and supervising the operation of joint ventures in the USSR.

The third channel through which the party influences the economy is the party officials, whose duty at all levels is to see that party policies are carried out. At the national level, party officials in the CC secretariat and in the party committees in each ministry constantly monitor the actions of the government, making sure that they are consistent with official policy. When they are not, it is the duty of party officials to try to change the situation without interfering in operational decisions of the agency involved. An example that illustrates this point is Gorbachev's current modernization campaign in which the party committees in each of the eleven civilian machinebuilding ministries are charged with doing their utmost to ensure that ministry officials do all in their power to contribute to modernization goals.

Local party organs have identical duties in their areas of competence. It is the duty of the first party secretary of the *obkom* (or *raikom* or *gorkom*) to see that all organizations in his area perform in ways consistent with central policy, in particular that they fulfill key indicators in the plan. The expectations here are quite detailed and demanding and add up to general responsibility for the economic performance of the area covered by the first secretary's committee. Again, he must not interfere in the operational decisions of enterprise directors in his area, but must keep the pressure on so that the operational decisions they do make add up to a performance record as close as possible to targets set from above.

These rather extensive, and generally visible, links between the party and government hierarchies are supplemented throughout the society by what in a Western country would be called "interlocking directorates." At the apex of the system is the Politburo, which includes in its membership the most important leaders in the government hierarchy (indeed, it specifies who the most important members are). Currently, the Politburo membership includes the chairman of the Council of Ministers (Ryzhkov), two of his deputies (Aliev and Talyzin), the chairman of the Presidium of the Supreme Soviet (Gromyko), the chairmen of the councils of ministers of two republics (Vorotnikov of the RSFSR and Shcherbitsky of the Ukraine), two USSR ministers (Chebrikov, KGB; Shevardnadze, Foreign Affairs), and the first secretary of the Moscow *gorkom* (Yeltsin). Consequently the majority of those who participate in the deliberations of the Politburo are members of the government and thus are able to facilitate the transmission of Politburo policy directions into the government hierarchy.

This pattern of interlocking directorates is repeated throughout the system at all levels. The party Central Committee includes in its membership virtually all national ministers, the chairmen of all republican councils of ministers, and a few important enterprise directors. Republican and local-level party organizations show similar interlocking patterns.

THE GOVERNMENT HIERARCHY. In many ways the government hierarchy of the USSR replicates the party hierarchy, although not in all ways; it is an administrative organization, and as such has a much more detailed bureaucracy with which to operate the system.[11] The bicameral Supreme Soviet convenes twice a year for brief meetings devoted to major pieces of legislation. From the point of view of the economy, the most important issues considered are the annual plan drafts and the five-year plan drafts, all of which are debated and then passed as a law.

The Supreme Soviet elects a Presidium of approximately forty members, which meets every two months and is empowered to issue decrees or take other actions consistent with the constitution, subject to subsequent approval at the next session of the Soviet. The chairman of the Supreme Soviet, currently Andrei Gromyko, is the formal head of state. To judge from the infrequency of the meetings of the Presidium, its role in the system would appear to be modest.

The Council of Ministers, also elected by the Supreme Soviet, represents the apex of the administrative system guiding the economy. This body is composed of over 100 members, including its chairman (currently N. Ryzhkov), four first deputies and eleven deputy chairmen, ministers, heads of state committees, and national administrators. This rather unwieldy body meets approximately four times a year and is not involved in detailed decisions regarding the economy.

Those matters are apparently handled by a presidium of the Council of Ministers that is composed of the chairman and his deputies. This much more manageable group, approximately the size of the Politburo (and with three Politburo members), oversees the operation of the government hierarchy.

Of the 100 or more ministries and committees whose heads sit on the Council of Ministers, approximately 70 play a role in the administration of the economic system (table 3–2). Enterprises, state farms, and collective farms of national importance are directly supervised by fifty ministries. Some of these are all-union (AU) ministries, which exist only at the national level, and others are union-republic (UR) ministries, which have republican counterparts that are directly responsible to the union-level ministry. Each of these ministries oversees enterprises whose primary activity is related to the branch, and they are held responsible for the performance of those enterprises.

Twenty ministries supervise the machinebuilding and metalworking industries, the core of the manufacturing system. Of those twenty, nine

11. Unless otherwise indicated, this section relies on Hough and Fainsod, *How the Soviet Union Is Governed,* chap. 10.

supervise enterprises devoted primarily to the production of defense goods. The remaining eleven ministries supervise enterprises devoted primarily to the production of machinery and equipment for civilian use. The division here is far from simple. The enterprises supervised by the nine defense ministries also produce some civilian goods (for example, computers, refrigerators, motor bikes, and passenger ships); and enterprises supervised by the civilian ministries also produce some defense goods (for example, military trucks and some electronic equipment). Nonetheless, the distinction is a real one, as is obvious from the lack of systematic published data on the nine defense ministries in contrast to a fair amount of data on the civilian ministries. For example, plan fulfillment can be tracked on a monthly basis in the civilian ministries, whereas no mention is made of the military ministries in this regard.

Enterprises that produce fuels, raw materials, and chemicals are supervised by nine ministries. Each primary fuel source has its own ministry, as does electric power (Minenergo). Construction activities are divided up among one general ministry and six ministries specializing in particular branches of construction or regions; and the production of construction materials is supervised by a separate ministry.

Overall supervision of the agricultural and food industries now resides in the State Agro-Industrial Committee created in 1986 (Gosagroprom), which absorbed the duties, but only some of the staffs, of five former ministries and one state committee (the ministries of Agriculture, Meat, Fish, Fruit and Vegetables, and Rural Construction, as well as the State Committee for the Supply of Production Equipment for Agriculture [Sel'khoztekhnika]). In addition, five other ministries supervise other aspects of the agricultural-food complex.

The basic design of this system was conceived in the late 1930s when, on the eve of World War II, Stalin began dividing the relatively few ministries (then called commissariats) supervising the economy into more specialized bodies overseeing branches. The proliferation continued after the war, was reversed temporarily by Khrushchev in the *sovnarkhoz* reforms, and then resumed under Brezhnev and Kosygin. At present almost fifty highly specialized ministries control production units in what is by far the most complex administrative hierarchy the Soviet system has ever had, and is certainly a far more complex system than has been, or is being, used in any other socialist country.

The philosophy behind the design is clear: the center controls economic activity on the supply side, on a branch-by-branch basis. This, it

Table 3-2. *All-Union and Union-Republic Ministries and State Committees, June 1987*

Branch ministries[a]

Defense machinebuilding industries
Minaviaprom (aviation)
Minoboronprom (defense)
Minelektronprom (electronics)
Minobshchemash (general machinebuilding)
Minmash (machinebuilding)
Minsredmash (medium machinebuilding)
Minradioprom (radio)
Minsudprom (shipbuilding)
Minpromsviazi (communications equipment industry)

Civilian machinebuilding industries
Minavtoprom (automobiles)
Minenergomash (power machinebuilding)
Minneftekhimmash (chemical and petroleum machinebuilding)
Minstroidormash (construction, road, and municipal machinebuilding)
Minelektrotekhprom (electrical equipment)
Mintiazhmas (heavy and transport machinebuilding)
Minpribor (precision instrument-making, automation equipment, and control systems)
Minzhivmash (machinebuilding for animal husbandry and fodder production)
Minlegpishchemash (light and food industry and household appliances machinebuilding)
Minstankoprom (machine tool and tool building industry)
Minsel'khozmash (tractor and agricultural machinebuilding)

Fuels, raw materials, and chemicals
Minugleprom (coal)
Minnefteprom (petroleum)
Mingazprom (gas)
Minneftekhimprom (petroleum refining and petrochemical industry)

Minenergo (electric power)
Minatomenergo (atomic power)
Mingeo (geology)
Minchermet (ferrous metallurgy)
Mintsvetmet (nonferrous metallurgy)
Minkhimprom (chemicals)

Construction and construction materials
Gosstroi (construction)
Minsevzapstroi (north and west construction)
Miniugstroi (southern construction)
Minuralsibstroi (Urals and west Siberia construction)
Minvostokstroi (Far East and Transbaikal construction)
Minstroimaterialov (construction materials)
Mintransstroi (transport construction)
Minmontazhspetsstroi (installation and special construction)
Minneftegazstroi (petroleum and gas industry construction)

Agriculture and food
Gosagroprom (agro-industrial committee)
Minkhleboproduktov (grain products)
Minrybkhoz (fishing)
Minudobrenii (fertilizer)
Minvodkhoz (land reclamation and water)
Minlesbumprom (timber, pulp, paper, and wood processing)

Transport and communication
Minsviazi (communications)
Minmorflot (maritime fleet)
MPS (railroads)

Other industry
Minlegprom (light industry)
Minmedprom (medical and microbiological)

Functional ministries related to the economy

Minfin (finance)
MO (defense)
Minpros (education)
MVD (internal affairs)

Minvneshtorg (foreign trade)
MID (foreign affairs)
Minzdrav (health)
Mintorg (trade)

Table 3-2 *(continued)*

Ministerial-level state committees related to the economy	
Gosplan (planning)	Goskomgidromet (hydrometeorology and
Goskomtsen (prices)	environmental control)
GKVTI (computer technology and	Gossnab (material-technical supply)
information science)	Goskomtrud (labor and social questions)
Gosstandart (state standards)	GKNT (science and technology)
Goskomnefteprodukt (supply of	Goskomizobretenii (inventions and
petroleum products)	discoveries)
Gosbank (state bank)	TsSU (statistics)
	Gosleskhoz (forestry)

Nonministerial-level state committees related to the economy	
Gosarbitrazh (arbitration)	Stroibank (bank for financing capital
	investment)

Sources: Herwig Kraus and Alexander Rahr, "The Government of the USSR," *Radio Liberty Research Bulletin*, RL Supplement 3/87, May 5, 1987. The classification by category was done by the author.
a. Two state committees, Gosagroprom and Gosstroi, are listed with the ministries because they perform all of the duties of a ministry. The grouping here is mine, although it resembles the "complexes" emerging in Gorbachev's reforms of economic administration.

seems, is a logical extension of the philosophy within the party, which advocates direct control of a broad range of performance indicators. Also clear is the conservative design of the system, implicit in the assumption that the definition of a "branch" will remain valid for a long period of time. Furthermore, the system is imbued with optimism, for it is also based on the assumption that enterprises in different branches, supervised by different hierarchies, will somehow coordinate their activities to meet the goals set by the Council of Ministers and ultimately by the Politburo. A system that utilizes separate hierarchies to supervise oil, gas, coal, and electric power production, for example, relies on some higher authority to choose among their competing claims for resources in order to meet the energy needs of the nation.

The state committees perform that function. Among those that relate to the economy (see table 3-2), the most important are Gosplan (State Planning Committee), Gossnab (State Committee for Material-Technical Supply), Goskomtsen (State Price Committee), and Goskomtrud (State Committee for Labor and Social Questions).

Gosplan is the Council of Minister's planning agency and is charged with coordinating the construction of plans, supervising their distribution, and monitoring their fulfillment. Gosplan sets the agenda for the planning process, drives it, and is held responsible for it. It is also formally in charge of the reform process; currently, for example, N. V. Talyzin chairs, and Gosplan staffs, a Commission on Improving Management, Planning, and the Economic Mechanism.[12] Gosplan holds considerable authority over all other ministries and committees directly involved in economic affairs through its control over all major investment decisions and the allocation of commodities critical to the operation of the economy. Under Gorbachev, that authority has been recognized formally by elevating Talyzin to the position of first deputy chairman of the Council of Ministers, as well as a candidate member of the Politburo.

Gosplan is divided internally into a series of departments that reflect its function and the organization of the economy. Branch departments closely follow—in number and title—branch ministries. So-called summary departments manage the planning process itself, key problems that cut across branches (for example, foreign trade, finance, and capital construction), and the particular problems involved in attaining balance in the system, particularly for commodities managed by Gosplan.[13]

Gosplan is a union-republic committee. That is, each republic also has a Gosplan to take up planning tasks for products of republican significance. Planning committees also exist at the local level. These are charged with planning for the production of goods of local significance. The farther down the line one goes from USSR Gosplan, the more the object of the organization is consumer goods and services, which historically have had relatively low priority in the system.

Gossnab's main job is to distribute materials according to priorities set out in the plan. For the approximately 2,000 products planned by Gosplan, Gossnab will be empowered in some cases to manage their distribution among competing claimants. For another 14,000–25,000 products, Gossnab, itself, via its various departments, decides among competing claimants and thus both plans and distributes the products in these cases.

Gossnab manages this extraordinarily complex process through three levels of organization. Twenty all-union supply administrations (*souiz-*

12. This is probably the continuation of a commission chaired by Nikolai Baibakov during the last years of the Brezhnev period and into the Andropov and Chernenko periods; however, it is only under Gorbachev that it has become quite active. For reports on the work of the commission, see, for example, "V komissii po sovershenstvovaniyu upravleniia planirovaniia i khoziaistvennogo mekhanizma" (In the commission on the improvement of administration, planning and the economic mechanism), *Ekonomicheskaia gazeta*, no. 11 (March 1986); no. 18 (April 1986); no. 32 (August 1986); and no. 36 (September 1986). (Hereafter *Ekon. gaz.*)

13. For details, see Fyodor I. Kushnirsky, *Soviet Economic Planning, 1965–1980* (Boulder: Westview, 1982), pp. 57–65.

glavsnabsbyty) control commodities distributed, or planned and distributed, nationwide by Gossnab. Fifty-six territorial supply administrations actually deal with documents and handle product distribution through 1,500 local supply offices, depots, warehouses, and stores. Finally, eleven all-union administrations manage the supply of materials and equipment to construction projects.[14]

Goskomtsen (State Price Committee) either sets or supervises the setting of prices in the system. There are three basic vehicles for setting prices. At infrequent intervals Goskomtsen undertakes an enormously complex price reform that rearranges virtually all prices in the system; the two most recent price reforms were in 1967 and 1982. Second, Goskomtsen will, from time to time, revise prices in certain sectors, as it did with agricultural procurement prices in 1981 and 1983. In the intervals between price reforms, Goskomtsen promulgates and administers an elaborate set of procedures for pricing new products.

Because the Soviet economy puts out roughly 20–30 million products, obviously Goskomtsen cannot possibly establish prices for each one. In general, Goskomtsen directly sets the prices of fairly homogenous products (such as fuels, energy, and raw materials) that serve as inputs over a wide range of sectors. In the case of intermediate and finished products, Goskomtsen sets the rules for how those will be priced (during a price reform, or when new products are introduced in the interval), and it directly considers prices proposed by enterprises and ministries—which are calculated according to those rules—for goods judged to be of the greatest importance to the system as a whole. For goods of regional significance or of relatively low priority, republican price committees, committees at a lower level, or ministries will make final decisions on the prices. The price of computers, or grain, or oil, is very much a Goskomtsen USSR concern, whereas the price of television repair services in Tashkent is a local matter.

Goskomtrud's most important role in the economy is probably to oversee wage scales for state enterprises. It administers a complicated system of wage scales, which are differentiated by the type of work, its difficulty, and by branch. In effect, it sets the average wage for the system. This arrangement has important macroeconomic consequences for total consumer demand and important microeconomic consequences

---

14. This material is based on the discussion in Joseph S. Berliner, *The Innovation Decision in Soviet Industry* (MIT Press, 1976), pp. 66–69.

for the cost of production in individual enterprises. For that reason, Goskomtrud must work very closely with Gosplan and Goskomtsen.

Gosstandardt is the state committee in charge of formulating and enforcing quality standards throughout the economy, although some of its enforcement power has naturally been shared with the ministries. It is one of the committees on which Gorbachev has focused his efforts to modernize the output of the system.

Functional ministries manage other matters that cut across the responsibilities of the branch ministries. The Ministry of Foreign Trade (Minvneshtorg) manages foreign economic relations through a network of foreign trade organizations (FTOs), each of which controls virtually all exports and imports for a select group of products.[15] Enterprises generally have no rights to export or import on their own account. They apply to their ministries for the right to import, and are ordered to export; and in both cases the FTOs manage all details of the required transactions, so that enterprises have no direct contacts with customers or suppliers. This part of the system has begun to change under Gorbachev, but I postpone discussion of these changes to chapter 7.

The Ministry of Finance manages the state budget and the banking system, the most important components of the latter being the State Bank (Gosbank), the State Construction Bank (Stroibank), and the Foreign Trade Bank (Vneshtorgbank). These banks have a monopoly in the issuance of credit, and their activities add up to total formal control over the money supply. Gosbank is the most important of these institutions, and its chairman is a member of the Council of Ministers.

The Ministry of Trade (Mintorg) is primarily engaged in managing retail trade through 704,000 retail outlets and 326,000 restaurants, canteens, and other eating establishments.[16] (Much of what in the West is classified as wholesale trade is controlled by Gossnab in the Soviet Union.) The Ministry of Trade is not directly involved in setting outputs for products or deciding on their distribution. Rather, its main function is to manage the sale of the products that eventually emerge from factories operating under the Soviet planning system. This illustrates

15. For a more detailed discussion of the role of the Ministry of Foreign Trade, see Ed A. Hewett, "Foreign Economic Relations," in Abram Bergson and Herbert S. Levine, eds., *The Soviet Economy: Toward the Year 2000* (Boston: Allen and Unwin, 1983), pp. 291–95.

16. The figures are for 1984 and come from Tsentral'noe statisticheskoe upravlenie SSSR, *Narodnoe khoziaistvo SSSR v 1984 g: Statisticheskii ezhegodnik* (Moscow, "Finansy i statistika"), p. 473. (Hereafter cited as *Narkhoz.*)

the important point to be discussed in more detail below, namely, that the consumer has a weak voice in the formal system, far weaker than does the supplier through Gosplan and Gossnab.

On the industrial side of the economy, the basic economic unit in the system is the enterprise, or, in some cases, production associations, which are groups of enterprises.[17] Far more economic power is concentrated in the industrial system than is typical of industrialized Western countries. In 1983 there were only 45,539 enterprises and associations in Soviet industry. Of those, approximately 1,400, each with receipts in excess of 100 million rubles a year, controlled half of the capital stock, employed one-third of the industrial labor force, and accounted for 47 percent of industrial output.[18] This concentration of economic power gives enormous leverage to the central planners, who, through the ministries, can control a substantial share of economic activity by communicating with a relatively small number of enterprises. Planners obviously value that power, and it appears to have increased over time, and Soviet leaders clearly hope to continue that trend.[19]

In the formal system these individual economic units in industry, agriculture, and other branches of the economy are charged with providing the center with the information it needs to monitor the

17. The production association (*proizvodstvennoe ob"edinenie*) is a form primarily arising out of the implementation of a 1973 decree ordering ministries to create associations of enterprises under one common management. In some cases the leadership of the production association is as powerful as the management of an enterprise, and the constituent enterprises are in those cases more like plants. In other cases the association is much looser and the enterprises retain a good deal of their autonomy.

18. *Narkhoz 1984*, pp. 128, 158.

19. It is difficult to trace this easily, given the data in *Narkhoz*, which do not make it possible to follow the relevant shares backward for these 1,400 enterprises. One crude indication of the increased concentration is the fact that although the value of industrial production rose by 33 percent between 1975 and 1983 (*Narkhoz 1983*, p. 407), the number of enterprises in industry fell by 1,419 (*Narkhoz 1975*, p. 189; *Narkhoz 1983*, p. 118), whereas the number of enterprises with sales of at least 100 million rubles rose by 522, and the share of enterprises with sales exceeding 100 million rubles in total industrial output rose from 37 percent to 47 percent. On the agricultural side the basic unit is either the state farm (*sovkhoz*, which is directly supervised by the Gosagroprom) or the cooperative farm (*kolkhoz*, formally a collective, but still controlled closely by the Gosagroprom). In 1985 there were 26,200 *kolkhozy* and 22,700 *sovkhozy* and 10,400 other enterprises employing a total of 24.7 million people, or 21 percent of the total labor force. Although the concentration of economic power is lower than in industry, the size of individual economic units is large by international standards. In 1985 the average *kolkhoz* employed 484 people, the average *sovkhoz*, 529. *Narkhoz 1985*, pp. 277, 286, 390–91.

operation of the economy and plan for its future operation, and with fulfilling the plans coming from above. These units are instruments of the state in that they represent the interests of the owners, namely, society at large. Local units have no rights save those granted by the state, and cannot make decisions unless authorized by the state. The state begins new enterprises and can close or reorganize existing enterprises. It appoints top management (subject to party approval), determines its bonuses, and can move management to another position. In sum, in the formal system, enterprises exist at the state's pleasure to serve its purposes.

Between the ministries and the individual economic units there are sets of intermediate authorities. In the industrial ministries, almost all of these are classified as all-union industrial associations (*vsesoiuznye promyshlennye ob"edinenie,* or VPOs), and each one controls a subset of enterprises within a ministry. Historically these intermediate authorities have been the workhorse of the administrative process, keeping close tabs on enterprises and acting as their immediate superior in all relations with the governmental hierarchy. As a result of that close relationship, they have gained a reputation for meddling in enterprise affairs, which has prompted Gorbachev to move for their elimination.

Up to now this discussion has focused on enterprises supervised by national-level ministries, but it also should be noted that a substantial number of enterprises, particularly in consumer goods and services, are supervised by other government bodies, ranging from the councils of ministers of the fifteen republics to the *gorispolkomy*, the government bodies presiding over cities.

Frequently analyses of the Soviet economy will refer to "the" planners and the decisions they make within the system. Although different people may include somewhat different bodies in the category of planners, in general the term refers to the state committees and functional ministries and excludes administrative bodies from the branch ministries on down, as well as the Politburo and the Presidium of the Council of Ministers. The latter two groups are what is generally meant by the term "the leadership"; the branch ministries and all the administrative units below them constitute the objects of the planning process.

INSTITUTIONS OUTSIDE THE GOVERNMENT AND STATE HIERARCHIES. Although this system is designed to control virtually all economic activity through state institutions, there are certain limited areas in which individuals may legally produce goods, sell them, and provide services without having any direct contact with the planning system. In general all artisan or individual activity is legal unless proscribed by law; but the proscriptive provisions of the law are quite broad, so that in effect legal private activity is limited to some services and to food production and processing linked to private plots. The use of hired labor is strictly prohibited.[20]

Among the legal private activities, most are connected with the production and sale of agricultural products on private plots. Families belonging to *kolkhozy* (cooperative farm) are each entitled to private plots up to 1.25 acres in size. Employees of *sovkhozy* (state farm) can work a private plot up to 0.75 acres in size. Employees in urban areas are entitled to private plots of 0.15–0.3 acres, depending on whether the plot is inside or outside the city (the smaller plots being inside the city).[21] In 1985 land held by all these individuals totaled 7.99 million hectares, or 1.4 percent of cultivatable land in the USSR.[22] Aside from being consumed by the families working the private plots, the output is important for supplies (primarily through state-sponsored *kolkhoz* markets) of some of the basic staples of the Soviet diet. Approximately one-third of the total USSR production of meat and milk and two-thirds of eggs come from private plots.[23]

The few legal private activities aside from those associated with private plots require a license, and the resulting income is subject to a highly progressive tax.[24]

The Information System

Economic systems are composed of institutions whose basic purpose is to collect, absorb, and generate information that guides a society in

20. The relevant excerpts from the law can be found in Gregory Grossman, "Notes on the Illegal Private Economy and Corruption," in U.S. Congress, Joint Economic Committee, *Soviet Economy in a Time of Change,* 96 Cong. 1 sess. (Government Printing Office, 1979), vol. 1, pp. 854–55.

21. Paul R. Gregory and Robert C. Stuart, *Soviet Economic Structure and Performance,* 3d ed. (Harper and Row, 1986), p. 272.

22. *Narkhoz 1985,* p. 202.

23. Ibid., pp. 240–41.

24. The tax law has been changed by Gorbachev, who also legalized a wide range of individual economic activities in May 1987. The rates up until then began with a marginal tax rate of 50 percent on incomes of 1,800–3,000 rubles a year, then 60 percent for 3,000–5,000 rubles and 65 percent on all incomes above 5,000 rubles. See Grossman, "Notes on the Illegal Private Economy," note 3, p. 835. The new rates and other aspects of income taxation are discussed in chapter 7.

the efficient utilization of existing resources so as to ensure maximum social welfare. Two basic types of information are of interest.

—Production possibilities, that is, the various possible combinations of goods and services that the system could produce using available capital stock, labor, and other inputs; and the trade-offs among those combinations (the opportunity cost of producing one bundle instead of another).

—Social preferences concerning the use of those production possibilities, which pertain to the trade-offs to consumers of having any particular combination of goods and services in lieu of other possible combinations. Information on preferences covers preferences for consuming today or for forgoing consumption today in order to invest in the expansion of production possibilities. For that portion of national output to be devoted to investment, the information should indicate in what directions production possibilities are to be expanded.

The economic system must somehow bring together the information on what is possible and what society desires and simultaneously decide whose preferences are to prevail, since "society" is made up of individuals whose aggregate wants far exceed society's production possibilities. In large societies with well-developed productive capacity and complex social needs, collecting, absorbing, and generating information is an enormous problem, which grows worse as the society develops.

In the formal version of a market economy, the price system is the core of the information system, automatically generating the information needed to deal with these issues. Because markets operate on the principle of competition among existing producers and the possibility of free entry for others, the ensuing prices provide producers with information on consumer preferences, while providing consumers with information on the relative cost to society of the various bundles of goods and services they might prefer (production possibilities), where those costs are minimal, resulting from the effective operation of the competitive mechanism. Incomes earned by individuals participating in the production process determine whose preferences prevail, that is, who receives the goods and services produced. How much of the nation's output is consumed now, and how much is invested, is also determined by the savings decisions of consumers, which are in turn influenced by a special price, the rate of interest.

One of the most important attributes of prices in this system is their flexibility. As imbalances between supply and demand arise—the inevitable consequence of constantly changing production possibilities and preferences—prices move, sending signals that cause both producers and consumers to alter supplies and demands in a way that begins to reduce the imbalance.

Even in "pure" market economies the state has a role to play. It identifies external costs and benefits that the price system does not reflect and alters the incentives for individual economic units so that they will take those costs and benefits into account. It also moves to alter the income distribution in order to adjust for some of the potentially extreme consequences of resource allocation via markets.

The Soviet centrally planned economy grapples with the same information problems, but in a much different fashion. The planning process, not the price system, forms the core of the information system. By means of this process, which is supervised by the government hierarchy, society elicits information on production possibilities, combines it with information on preferences, and generates plans that direct economic units to produce the mix of goods and services that, in the judgment of the party, is optimal for society. This process is designed to identify imbalances between supply and demand when they arise and to set into motion changes that will eliminate the imbalances.

The basic rationale for using the planning process, not the price system, to allocate resources is that it enables representatives of society as a whole to have direct control over all decisions relating to the economic welfare of the population. Markets, according to their supporters, automatically make it in the self-interest of private owners to meet society's needs. Soviet leaders categorically reject that proposition, pointing to the inherent tendency of markets to produce high rates of unemployment, inflation, and a skewed income distribution, all of which rather conveniently serve the interests of those who own capital. Instead they propose to avoid those antisocial phenomena through direct and conscious control of the economic process via state ownership of capital and central planning. Among other things this means that the party directly decides whose preferences will prevail, both with regard to the choice of consumption now and investment and consumption later; and also with regard to the mix of goods produced using current capacity not devoted to investment goods (defense versus consumption goods, the type of consumption goods produced, and so on).

Many of the steps that must be taken in order to coordinate resource allocation decisions occur automatically in a market system, in a fashion that might be regarded as subconscious from the point of view of society as a whole. Under Soviet central planning those steps are deliberate, not automatic. In market economies the engine that drives events is the market, which lies outside the government hierarchy, and governments intervene to shape events that would otherwise occur automatically. In centrally planned economies the government is the machine that makes things happen. In many ways the situation is analogous to deciding to run a system manually instead of on "autopilot." The amount of information required to do that—which involves not only replicating, but improving upon, decisions made by markets—is enormous. As a result, quite naturally, the planning process is extraordinarily complex.

Plans are the primary, but not the exclusive, mechanism that the formal system utilizes to acquire information and act on it. Prices also play a role in guiding resource allocation, albeit a far more modest role than in market economies. Prices exist in the Soviet Union because they are a useful supplement to the planning process, as is reflected in the way they are determined and the way they are put to use. In addition there are a number of other ways in which planners seek to gather information about the system in their effort to run it.

THE PLANNING PROCESS. The planning process is virtually a constant bureaucratic dialogue that goes on within the government hierarchy, on the one hand, and between it and the party hierarchy, on the other. The dialogue is supervised by Gosplan and is organized around negotiations over five-year and annual plans.[25] In both cases the bureaucratic process leading up to final agreements and documents goes through four inter-mediate, and overlapping, stages.[26]

—Targets for the macro aggregates and basic branch targets—"control figures"—are set. The branch ministries participate in the negotiations by providing information on production possibilities and needs of the system.

25. I do not discuss here long-term, twenty-year, plans, which are supposed to be a part of the system but in fact have rarely been formulated. For a discussion of the hierarchy of plans, see V. F. Filippov, *Besedy o khoziaistvennom mekhanizme* (Conversations on the economic mechanism) (Moscow: Politizdat, 1984), pp. 14–20.

26. For a discussion of the planning process, see Kushnirsky, *Soviet Economic Planning*, pp. 54–86; Herbert S. Levine, "The Centralized Planning of Supply in Soviet Industry," in Morris Bornstein, ed., *Comparative Economic Systems: Models and Cases* (Homewood, Ill.: Irwin, 1965), pp. 251–77; and R. W. Davies, "Economic Planning in the USSR," in Morris Bornstein, ed., *Comparative Economic Systems: Models and Cases*, 3d ed. (Irwin, 1974), pp. 266–90.

—The control figures are approved by the Politburo, then are sent through the ministries and intermediate authorities to individual economic units as guidelines to be applied in the construction of their annual plans.

—Individual economic units negotiate with their ministries, which in turn negotiate with Gosplan, over alterations in the control figures.

—The draft plan is approved by the Politburo, the Council of Ministers, and the Supreme Soviet and subsequently becomes a law, which passes again through the ministries and intermediate authorities to individual economic units as a legal document to which each economic unit is obliged to adhere.

The similarities between the five-year and annual planning processes should not obscure some significant differences, the most fundamental being that the annual plans guide the operation of the system, whereas the five-year plans are simply guides to the formulation of the annual plans. Thus the negotiations over the annual plans are expected to be the most heated. However, the battle over the five-year plan is far from irrelevant, particularly when it comes to large projects that involve multiyear commitments of substantial investment resources.

Throughout the entire process the basic goals are to collect, absorb, and disseminate whatever information is needed to arrive at a balanced plan that conforms to targets set by the Politburo. Because the economy is divided into many subsectors supervised by ministries, the ministries are virtually guaranteed to fight doggedly for their narrow interests, and to have little concern for the national economic consequences of the plans they propose. Gosplan must search for a bureaucratic consensus, choosing among those competing claims on the basis of the national economic interest, in somewhat the same way that the U.S. Bureau of the Budget mediates the competing claims of various components of the federal bureaucracy. When the conflicts prove difficult to resolve or involve issues of fundamental importance, the final resolution can be shifted up to the Presidium of the Council of Ministers. In the most important and difficult cases, the Politburo serves as the economic equivalent of a supreme court.

Five-Year Plans

Five-year plans have been a hallmark of Soviet central planning since the current system began to take shape under Stalin in the late 1920s.

Every five years the planning system is charged with producing a plan for the upcoming first or second half of the decade. The procedure begins approximately three years before the plan is to take effect as Gosplan begins to gather information on evolving performance under the current plan and the Politburo begins to formulate general targets for the next five-year period.[27] The basic purpose of negotiations during what might be called years $t-3$, $t-2$, and the first part of $t-1$ is to establish control figures, or basic guidelines *(osnovnye napravleniia)*, which will be used to guide the negotiating and drafting of the five-year plan. The basic guidelines specify the targets for growth rates for national income, investment, defense, consumption, and—in support of those—growth for the various branches and the foreign sector. The key variables here, aside from implied output growth rates, are the level and structure of investment, and this is where the major battles occur. If a large project is to be undertaken, then it must be included in the guidelines; otherwise the investment funds will simply not be available.

After extensive negotiations, the draft of the guidelines is approved by the Politburo and the Council of Ministers, at which point the guidelines also come to embody what will be the main targets for the five-year plan itself. These are published, at least in abbreviated form, and are what Western observers typically refer to as "the" five-year plan. Although they are not the plan, either in theory or in fact, they do represent a good estimate of what planners believe the actual five-year plans of all levels of the hierarchy will add up to for the main economic indicators.

In recent years the basic guidelines have been approved and published *as a draft* quite late in the planning process. For example, the guidelines for the Eleventh FYP (1981–85) appeared in December 1980; those for the Twelfth FYP in November 1985. Even if, as is likely, the guidelines are made known to the hierarchy before they are published, they are probably finalized too late in the year for the ministries to disaggregate the figures and pass them down the line in time to finish negotiations with economic units before the beginning of the five-year plan period. Therefore, the second stage of the planning process probably overlaps

27. It is clear from reports of Politburo meetings, for example, that the Politburo and the government hierarchy were working on the Twelfth Five-Year Plan during much of 1983 and that by 1984 the entire process was in full swing. For some of the key dates, see Ed A. Hewett, "Gorbachev's Economic Strategy: A Preliminary Assessment," *Soviet Economy*, vol. 1 (October–December 1985), p. 287.

with the first to a considerable extent. Gosplan is already drafting the five-year plan itself, and the ministries are already negotiating with Individual economic units on their five-year plan drafts, at the time that the basic guidelines are being finalized.

The planning process is in one sense a massive aggregation and disaggregation operation. In the early stages Gosplan uses the ministries to draw information out of individual economic units, aggregating the details as it moves up the hierarchy toward the center. For example, the Ministry of Ferrous Metallurgy is charged with gathering information on the possibility of producing key types of steel in its factories; it obtains this information through intermediate authorities who have intimate knowledge of, and are in constant contact with, the individual enterprises.

During later stages of the process, Gosplan uses the ministries to pass down the hierarchy obligatory tasks that constitute in sum the effort to fulfill aggregate plan targets. In the Ministry of Ferrous Metallurgy, for example, the five-year plan will include targets for the output of key steel products, which Gosplan sends to the ministry, and the ministry then disaggregates through intermediate authorities into obligatory targets for individual enterprises.

However, planning consists of another important function in addition to the aggregation and disaggregation of information: during the planning process the hierarchy engages in the critical search for a balanced plan. The branch departments in Gosplan work through the ministries they oversee to find ways to increase output and decrease input use. The most important input figures pass back and forth among branch departments, while other departments charged with achieving overall balance gather information from all the branch departments in order to identify impending imbalances and act to eliminate them by ordering more output, reducing planned input use, or authorizing an increase in net imports. During the negotiations over the five-year plan this process is probably at a relatively aggregated level, and apparent gaps in the balances are probably not a matter of great concern. During the annual plan negotiations, imbalances are a much more serious matter, since all parties are negotiating over actual claims to resources in the coming year.

This process culminates in a set of five-year plans for the hierarchy as a whole, which is aggregated into the five-year plan for the nation. This five-year plan, in the form of a final draft of the basic guidelines, is one of the major items considered by the Party Congress and must also be subsequently approved by the Supreme Soviet. After that it has the force of law for the entire hierarchy and should guide the formation of annual plans.

To serve that function, the five-year plans should be prepared well in advance of the period to which they apply. According to regulations, the control figures are to be sent to the ministries and intermediate authorities, as well as the union-republic councils of ministers, eleven months before the start of the new five-year period. The draft five-year plan is to be sent to the Council of Ministers for approval five months before the start of the new five-year period.[28]

In fact the law has never been complied with. In recent years the five-year plan has been considered and passed well into the first year of the five-year period to which it applies, so that whatever guidance it provided, at least in the preparation of the first annual plan of the new period, had to be based on the evolving draft.[29]

Outsiders know only a fraction of what is included in the five-year plans. The basic guidelines have been published, in truncated form, both as a draft, and in their approved form after being reviewed by the Party Congress. However, recent five-year plans themselves have not been published, even in truncated form, with the exception of the Ninth FYP (1971–75).[30]

ANNUAL PLANS. The annual plans constitute the operational plans by which the state seeks to control the bulk of activity in the entire economic system. The process by which these plans are developed is basically similar to that for the five-year plans, but it is compressed in time and expanded in coverage. Although planners are to be guided by the five-year plan in preparing the annual plan, they must also react to changing situations, to assumptions that turned out to be unrealistic, and possibly to changing central priorities. These plans embody the decisions of the central authorities that determine how resources will be allocated in the economy. The five-year plan may call for a 3 percent growth in invest-

28. Filippov, *Besedy,* p. 33.
29. The draft of the Tenth FYP (1976–80) was accepted (as basic guidelines) by the Twenty-fifth Party Congress in March 1976 and by the Supreme Soviet in October of that year. The Eleventh FYP was accepted by the Twenty-sixth Party Congress in March 1981 and approved by the Supreme Soviet in November of that year. The Twelfth FYP was accepted by the Twenty-seventh Party Congress in March 1986 and approved by the Supreme Soviet in June of that year.
30. *Gosudarstvennyi piatiletnii plan razvitiia narodnogo khoziaistva SSSR na 1971–1975 gody* (State five-year plan of the development of the economy of the USSR during 1971–1975) (Moscow: Politizdat, 1972).

ment, but the annual plans specify precisely what resources will be devoted to investment in each particular year. The five-year plan may call for rapid expansion of nuclear power and coal, but the annual plan represents the outcome of the battle between the ministries of electric power and coal over investment resources, and it is the annual plan that determines the actual course of investment in those two industries.

It is probably useful to regard the five-year plans as a serious effort by the party and the government to come up with an internally consistent statement of possibilities, priorities, and therefore targets that they will attempt—during the annual planning process—to translate into reality. It is the plan of battle before the battle. What in fact happens will depend on many variables that cannot be, or were not, predicted at the time.

Because the annual plans are operational, they inevitably focus on a search for balance, both in aggregate categories (consumption, investment, foreign trade), and among critical commodities. The approximately 2,000 commodities judged to be of the greatest importance are the direct responsibility of Gosplan, particularly its summary departments, which negotiate with producing ministries on supplies, and with all ministries on use. For each of those commodities the summary department draws up a balance indicating sources (production, imports, stock drawdowns) and uses (industry, final users, export, stock additions). When the balance shows a deficit, the Gosplan department in question must somehow enhance sources or decrease uses in order to bring the account closer to balance. Approximately 400 of these products are designated funded commodities, the distribution of which must be approved by the Council of Ministers. Subsequently they are assigned, generally to ministries or organs of Gossnab, which then distribute them. Funded commodities include key primary and energy products (such as electric power and oil products), important intermediates (such as chemical and rubber goods), and a small list of machinery and equipment.[31] The remaining commodities are assigned by Gosplan, but without the direct approval of the Council of Ministers, and are also distributed by Gossnab departments.[32]

Gossnab, either directly or through its territorial supply administra-

31. For details from the late 1960s, see Gertrude E. Schroeder, "The 'Reform' of the Supply System in Soviet Industry," *Soviet Studies,* vol. 24 (July 1972), p. 99.

32. For details, see Berliner, *Innovation Decision.* His data on the number of commodities planned from Gosplan are for 1969. However, Morris Bornstein has found a 1981 source with similar figures; see "Improving the Soviet Economic Mechanism," *Soviet Studies,* vol. 37 (January 1985), p. 7.

tions, is responsible for the balances of a much larger group of commodities, which probably number somewhere in the range of 15,000.[33] The branch ministries are responsible for another 50,000 or so product groups.[34] During the first quarter the control figures for the coming year are developed. The control figures are based on goals approved by the Politburo, information on recent performance, and norms for improved efficiency in the use of major inputs (labor, capital, and selected materials). In the main, these figures pertain to the planned growth of national income and its distribution among final uses, which in turn will imply outputs for various branches, given plans for net exports. These data, as they apply to various branches, are sent to ministries for disaggregation and are then sent on through intermediate authorities to individual economic units. Individual economic units and ministries are charged with sending draft plans back to the center in response to these control figures. Negotiations ensue during the second and third quarters along the entire chain of authority in the hierarchy as enterprises negotiate with intermediate authorities for adjustments to the targets for outputs and inputs they received. Intermediate authorities in turn must negotiate with the ministries, and the ministries with Gosplan. Except for the most difficult cases, Gosplan is the center of these negotiations, the court to which all participants take their case for more resources.

In theory this process should conclude with a draft plan that is to be reviewed by the Council of Ministers in September, although in fact it typically goes to the council much later. It is then considered at the December meeting of the Supreme Soviet, passed into law, and sent down the hierarchy as an obligatory set of targets.

The annual plan specifies in aggregate, but considerable, detail all major aspects of economic activity in the system. Each ministry, each

33. Different sources give different numbers, and the numbers vary over time. Bornstein, "Improving the Soviet Economic Mechanism," p. 7, quotes a source for 1981 saying that Gossnab is responsible for "up to" 15,000 products. N. P. Fedorenko puts the figure at 18,000 for what must be about the same time. "Planirovanie i upravlenie: kakimi im byt'?" (Planning and management: Which will it be?) EKO, no. 12 (December 1984), p. 8. Berliner, Innovation Decision, p. 64, has sources for the late 1960s putting the figure at about 16,000.

34. Both Fedorenko, "Planirovanie i upravlenie," p. 7, and Bornstein, "Improving the Soviet Economic Mechanism," p. 7, agree on that general figure. Most of each year the government hierarchy is involved in some phase of the annual planning process, much of it focused on constructing the balances and dealing with deficits. For an account of the annual planning process see, for example, Kushnirsky, Soviet Economic Planning, pp. 57–67, 88–90.

republican council of ministers, has a set of specific output targets that add up to a target for total output of key commodities; further down the hierarchy other plans drawn up by Gossnab, the republic ministers and councils of ministers, the ministries, and local authorities specify outputs of many more commodities. The hierarchical system guarantees that the targets for those products planned centrally are disaggregated directly down to individual economic units. For the most important commodities, there are not only output targets, but also allocation certificates *(nariady)* allocating supplies among users; similar certificates are issued by Gossnab and the ministries for commodities under their control.

Those allocations imply a set of final users and uses for the key commodities in the system, both in terms of consumption versus investment and in terms of the types of consumption goods to be produced. Automobile production, for example, is divided among export, Soviet enterprises (including taxi enterprises), the government, and organizations retailing autos; under this allocation system, consumption, investment, government expenditures, and export for that commodity are directly specified. By deciding which enterprises receive how many autos the system even decides the structure of investment expenditures on automobiles, and so on. A similar story could be told for other centrally planned commodities.

In theory Gosplan has also drawn up balances from the side of users: total investment versus the supply of investment goods, total consumption versus consumer income, and so on. In some sense that information is redundant if the commodity allocation system is working well and covers all key commodities, but still it is helpful in order to keep track of aggregate uses of national income, and to detect potential balance problems, such as excess demand for consumer goods.

At the other end of the hierarchy, at the enterprise end, the plan that finally comes down the hierarchy as law is a formidable document—the *techpromfinplan*—which specifies all major aspects of enterprise activity in six categories: production, material inputs, introduction of new technology, capital construction, labor and social development, and finance.[35] For a large enterprise, the number of obligatory targets in these six categories can easily fall in the range of 200–300.[36]

---

35. Filippov, *Besedy,* p. 65.

36. For example, the head of the Nevsky Factory in Leningrad (famous for its production of 25-megawatt turbines for the large natural gas pipelines) complained recently that his enterprise must seek to fulfill 300 separate plan targets on an annual

The enterprise is given a set of obligatory targets in each category that set out in detail planners' requirements for that enterprise, filtered through the ministry and intermediate authority. The production plan has a target for overall economic activity of the enterprise (in recent years, the volume of sales), targets for the output of key products in physical units, and targets for the share of enterprise output to be accounted for by products certified as being of the highest quality in the USSR's three-tier quality standards system (highest, high, and all others). If the enterprise produces funded commodities, then it will also receive from Gossnab shipping orders *(zakaz-nariady)* specifying how planned volumes of output will be distributed among potential customers.

The input plan will specify authorized levels of input for funded commodities and the sources of input, along with *nariady* allowing the enterprise to conclude contracts with the designated suppliers (who have received the *zakaz-nariady*). Depending on the plan and *nariady,* the enterprise can proceed to negotiate contracts for inputs.

The plan for the introduction of new technology specifies innovations in products and processes that the enterprise will introduce during the year. The closely related capital construction plan specifies authorized capital construction projects and will include authorizations to acquire the required machinery, equipment, construction services, and so on.

The labor and social development plan includes a specification of the ceilings on the size of the enterprise labor force, with subtargets for the number of white- and blue-collar workers, and for the share of manual laborers in the labor force; a limit on the total wage bill; and norms that specify what share of profits can be placed in accounts the enterprise can use for premiums (Material Stimulation Account), for social-cultural projects and housing (Social-Cultural Measures and Housing Account), and for small capital construction projects (Development Account).

The financial section of the plan specifies the major financial flows for the enterprise, most notably, profits, loans incurred and repaid, and reserve funds.

The planning process also generates fairly detailed plans for *sovkhozy* and *kolkhozy,* although of a somewhat different nature. Since the mid-1950s Soviet planners have pulled back from efforts to plan the entire production process of each agricultural unit, from inputs through out-puts. Instead the plans have concentrated on obligatory deliveries of a

basis. "Korennye zadachi mashinostroitelei" (Fundamental tasks of the machinebuild-ers), *Sotsialisticheskaia industriia,* November 12, 1986. (Hereafter *Sots. ind.*)

list of products for each farm unit, along with a price schedule for deliveries up to the quota, and a second (higher price schedule) for above-quota deliveries. These obligatory deliveries are sufficiently large and detailed to make them almost as constraining as the output plans sent to industry.[37]

THE PLANNING PROCESS AS AN INFORMATION SYSTEM. The most striking characteristic of central planning institutions as elements of an economic information system is their bias toward the supply side of the information problem. The entire hierarchy is built around suppliers, not purchasers. Much of the planning process is devoted to eliciting information on the production possibilities of the suppliers and to searching for balanced plans that will meet the mutual needs of the production system and fulfill demand targets for various products.

The main link to final customers is the Politburo and Council of Ministers, who together set the basic targets for the system and allocate national product among competing claims on final output from consumers, investors, the military, other government purchases, and foreign trade. Thus in the centrally planned economy, the allocation among claimants is a political decision handled outside the system. It is the Politburo, for example, not the population acting through a market, that sets the savings and investment rate.

Given that basic allocation of national product, there is still the question of what goods each set of final demand claimants will receive. Here the power of the competing groups varies enormously. There is no obvious mechanism that allows consumers to register their preferences for goods and services. Investors have a better chance than consumers of having their preferences taken into account because they are part of the supply problem of direct concern in the planning process. The military has the best chance of all because of its long-standing high priority.

Clearly the task of replicating markets is a formidable one requiring designs that minimize the information required by the bureaucracy to do the job. That is why, in fact, much of the planning actually occurs in ministries or in governmental bodies below the national level (republican, *oblast*, or city). The center tries to focus only on the most important commodities and leaves the lower levels other parts of the planning problem. Also, planners work with commodities aggregated into cate-

37. Jerzy F. Karcz, "An Organizational Model of Command Farming," in Bornstein, ed., *Comparative Economic Systems*, pp. 291–312.

gories, not the individual commodities, leaving to lower levels the disaggregation to actual products. There aggregations are one important reason why commodity values, and therefore prices, are indispensable to planners. But even if planners rely on these devices to cut down on the information load, they are left with an enormous information problem. In the next chapter I discuss the other practices that have evolved as a de facto response to the problem.

THE PRICE SYSTEM. The Soviet price system is designed to support the planning system, not the other way around. Like the planning system, the price system is biased toward the supply side. Whereas prices in market economies are rich with information on both the demand for products and the costs of producing them, Soviet prices in general provide information only on the relative costs of goods and services, which serve as an input into planning decisions. These cost-based prices are also useful to planners as a means of evaluating enterprise performance and controlling it, by inducing enterprises to use their relatively small room for maneuver within the plan in ways that reduce costs. In brief, the Soviet price system is an appendage to the planning system, purposely designed to facilitate planners' efforts to collect information on production possibilities and to control individual economic units.

Because planners must constantly be on the alert for ways to cut down their enormous information load, prices are set for long time periods to facilitate the construction of plans to cover those periods, and to avoid the daunting task of recalculating the myriad of interrelated prices in the entire economic system. For example, following a price reform in 1966–67, prices in industry were not changed again in a large-scale fashion until the price revisions of 1982. In the intervening fifteen years industrial prices in the USSR remained essentially unchanged.

This is what is frequently called a passive price system: that is to say, it is affected by plans, but does little to affect them. One of the most striking testimonies to the passive nature of the system is the fact that in reality there are a multitude of price systems in the Soviet economy, which are only weakly interconnected, if at all. Several categories of prices are important.[38]

—Industrial or "wholesale" prices that prevail in transactions be-

38. The first six categories in this listing are taken from Morris Bornstein, "The Soviet Industrial Price Revision," in G. Fink, ed., *Socialist Economy and Economic Policy: Essays in Honour of Friedrich Levcik* (New York: Springer-Verlag, 1985), pp. 157–58. The last category is my addition.

tween producers which can be divided into three subcategories: (1) enterprise wholesale prices, which are those received by suppliers; (2) industrial wholesale prices—those paid by enterprises for the purchase of goods of other enterprises—which equal the enterprise wholesale price plus, possibly, a tax on the product, a wholesale markup, and transportation costs; and (3) "settlement prices," which differ for each producer, used in branches such as mining, where costs very widely among producers.

—State retail prices, which are charged by state retail outlets. These equal industrial wholesale prices plus any other taxes and charges that may be added or subsidies. The taxes are used to dampen demand for products in short supply; the subsidies (for example, on housing or food) are a matter of social policy.

—Agricultural procurement prices paid to farms for products procured by state agencies.

—Collective farm market prices, which are prices charged by individuals and collective farms for produce marketed through the collective market system (produce not subject to state procurement, and produce grown on private plots).

—Foreign trade prices, which are the prices the USSR charges foreign customers for its products. There are four price systems here: one each for exports to and imports from the Council for Mutual Economic Assistance (Communist-bloc nations), denominated in transferable rubles; and one each for exports to and imports from developed countries and most developing countries, denominated in dollars. None of these four sets of prices is linked in any systematic way to Soviet domestic prices because Soviet planners are unwilling to allow foreign markets to directly influence the economy.

—Wages and various bonus schedules. Wages in state industry and *sovkhozy* are generally governed by a centrally determined, six-tiered wage scale (linked to skills), with numerous additional gradations for the difficulty, conditions, and location of the work. Soviet planners use the gradations to influence the movement of labor among industries, skills, and regions.[39]

—What I call planning prices, which are set to guide internal decisionmaking within the system, but which do not actually apply in specific transactions. There are many of these, the most important being (1)

39. For a brief summary, see Leonard Joel Kirsch, *Soviet Wages: Changes in Structure and Administration since 1956* (MIT Press, 1972), chap. 1.

"closing prices" *(zamykaiushchie zatraty)*, which are rough approximations of shadow prices from large linear programs and are used to plan investments (for example, in choosing among power plants using different fuel inputs, Soviet planners used the ZZ to price the inputs);[40] (2) "normative net output" for each product produced by an enterprise, calculated as the value that would be added in the production of a particular item by an enterprise if the enterprise used labor in quantities and quality mixes specified in centrally determined norms for that branch (essentially this works out to planned labor costs, social insurance cost, and planned profit on the product); these are "prices" for the enterprise because the normed value added coefficients are used to calculate normative net output *(normativnaia chistaia produktsiia)* for each enterprise, which determines some of the bonuses that an enterprise will receive;[41] and (3) various bonuses established in annual plans, which inform enterprises of the relative rewards for fulfilling individual targets in the plan.

Various national entities determine, or supervise the determination of, these prices. Wholesale, retail, and procurement prices are set by Goskomtsen. Collective farm market prices are basically market prices, although the state monitors them. Foreign trade prices are negotiated by the Ministry of Foreign Trade under the general guidance of the Council of Ministers and the specific guidance for politically determined prices relating to important commodities traded with Eastern Europe. Goskomtrud sets wage rates. The planners' prices are generally set by Gosplan and the branch ministries.

This potpourri of prices and price authorities, although formidable, is not what distinguishes the Soviet Union from other developed economies. Markets may "determine" prices in Western countries, but in reality an equally long list of types of prices and price authorities could be compiled for any Western country. Rather, the Soviet pricing arrangements differ markedly from those typical of a Western industrial country in other ways, and they differ so much that it is stretching the point to talk of a Soviet price "system."

---

40. For a discussion of ZZ for the energy sector, see Robert W. Campbell, "Energy Prices and Decisions on Energy Use in the USSR," in Padma Desai, ed., *Marxism, Central Planning and the Soviet Economy: Economic Essays in Honor of Alexander Erlich* (MIT Press, 1983), pp. 249–74.

41. The normative net output procedure is discussed in Bornstein, "Improving the Soviet Economic Mechanism," pp. 9–10.

First, the various types of prices are weakly connected. Foreign trade prices have little influence on domestic prices, with the possible exception of imported machinery and equipment.[42] If, for example, the price of oil falls from $25 a barrel to $10, Soviet export prices will follow that, but the domestic wholesale and retail prices of oil and oil products will remain unchanged, unless Goskomtsen moves to change the price. During the 1970s when the world price, and Soviet export price, of oil exploded, Soviet domestic prices of oil and oil products did not change.[43] Fluctuations in the world price (and Soviet import price) of grain have no direct influence on Soviet feedgrain prices or the price of grain products. Similarly, although wages are a component of costs used to calculate prices during infrequent price revisions, when they move subsequently, the price of the product does not follow.

The lack of connection among the various price systems can, at the very least, lead to disproportions in the economy that can only be addressed through complex price revisions at irregular intervals. But, in addition, the poor connection between wholesale and retail prices can postpone necessary changes with potentially serious political consequences. For example, the rapidly rising costs in Soviet agriculture in the 1980s, which have not been passed on to consumers, have made it necessary to introduce subsidies to cover the difference between procurement and retail prices, which amounted to 29.9 billion rubles in 1982 and 54.7 billion rubles in 1984.[44] The 1984 figure amounted to 14.2 percent of the state budget for that year.[45]

There are areas in which prices are interconnected closely; this is particularly the case for industrial wholesale prices. Price reforms take years to prepare because Goskomtsen is seeking to set prices for all of industry, where the inputs of one enterprise are the outputs of another,

42. Price regulations specify that imported machinery and equipment will be priced according to comparable Soviet domestic machinery, or a best guess at that. In fact, Vladimir Treml's research suggests that such a cumbersome procedure has not worked and that imported machinery tends to receive a price equal to the import price, converted at the official ruble-dollar (or yen, and so on) exchange rate. See Vladimir G. Treml and Barry L. Kostinsky, *Domestic Value of Soviet Foreign Trade: Exports and Imports in the 1972 Input-Output Table*, Foreign Economic Report 20 (U.S. Department of Commerce, 1982), pp. 20–21.

43. Ed A. Hewett, *Energy, Economics, and Foreign Policy in the Soviet Union* (Brookings, 1984), p. 135.

44. V. V. Dementsev, "Finansovye richagi intensivnogo razvitiia" (The financial means for intensive development), *Ekon. gaz.*, no. 13 (March 1985).

45. *Narkhoz 1985*, p. 559.

in a way that preserves profitability throughout the system at a relatively constant level across branches.[46]

Enterprise wholesale prices are set to reflect branch costs of production, so that individual enterprises operating at lower than branch costs will be rewarded, and those above penalized, while overall the branch is profitable. If products are not selling but are piling up in warehouses— as happens all too frequently in this system—the result is not a drop in the price. At most, if planners are on to the problem, the enterprises responsible will be pressured to develop a better product or there may be a "sale" in which the retail price of the product (if it is a consumer good) is reduced; but the enterprise wholesale price does not change. Likewise, if an enterprise is producing an item that is highly valued by society or foreign buyers (for example, oil in the 1970s), the enterprise wholesale price does not deviate from the centrally determined, cost-based, price. The only way enterprises will know their product is highly valued is through nonprice signals (direct communication from the customer or possibly a thriving black market for the item).

Another distinguishing feature of Soviet price arrangements is the long time periods for which prices are fixed, particularly industrial wholesale prices, which are at the core of the system. Because the costs of production, even at fixed prices, will change, over time the fixed set of cost-based prices will become obsolete even as a reflection of supply conditions for products. This can easily be seen in the drop over time in profit rates for some branches, particularly those involved in resource extraction, for which input costs can grow rapidly even at fixed prices as diminishing returns force physical inputs to increase.

The experience of the coal industry is typical. In 1970, three years after the price reform, coal industry profits were 7.3 percent of capital (fixed and working). By 1981 the industry as a whole was running losses equal to 9.4 percent of capital. The 1982 price revisions reduced the loss to 3.2 percent in that year, but then losses rose to 5.4 percent on capital in 1984.[47]

Between price revisions, when prices are "fixed," the price system is nevertheless in constant motion as some items leave production and new ones are introduced. Indeed much of Goskomtsen's time between

46. For example, preparation for the 1982 price revisions began in 1979 and occupied the bureaucracy for three years. See Bornstein, "Soviet Industrial Price Revision," pp. 157–70.

47. *Narkhoz 1984*, p. 565.

price revisions is probably taken up with monitoring the process by which new product prices are determined. New products developed by enterprises, typically in fulfillment of plan obligations, are initially sold at provisional prices determined by the ministry (from information supplied by the enterprise), which cover the initial serial production costs plus a profit. Then within several years the ministry is required to apply for a permanent price, which is determined by a complicated set of procedures set out by Goskomtsen.[48] A number of authorities must approve the proposal, but final approval, which can involve an enormous amount of work, is left to Goskomtsen.[49]

OTHER INFORMATION MECHANISMS. Planners also rely on many other sources of information about the system, but I can only touch on them here. One of the most important is the Central Statistical Administration (TsSU), formerly part of Gosplan until it attained independent status in the late 1940s. Now a ministerial-level entity, this is Gosplan's most important source of information on the performance of the system and its capabilities. Some of the data collected by the TsSU are published and are an important resource for any research on the Soviet economy. However, much of the data are fairly detailed and of direct use to planners, and are not available to outsiders.

In addition various levels in the hierarchy collect their own information, in part in an effort to carry out the orders from the center. Much of this information does not go all the way up the hierarchy, nor is that necessary. What is important is that as the ministries and local authorities negotiate with individual economic units and the center over resources,

48. For an excellent discussion of new product pricing, as well as other aspects of the administration of price formation in the Soviet Union, see Morris Bornstein, "The Administration of the Soviet Price System," *Soviet Studies*, vol. 30 (October 1978), pp. 466–90; on new product pricing in particular, see pp. 474–75.

49. A recent account of the work of the Ukrainian Goskomtsen regarding a proposed price for a single product provides some flavor of the enormous effort required to do this job properly. The Prikarpatpromaratura Association in Minkhimmash sent Goskomtsen Ukraine a proposal for a price for a detergent. They estimated their production cost at 18.30 rubles for some unspecified unit. They proposed a wholesale price of 20 rubles, and a retail price of 23 rubles. However, Goskomtsen knew that other associations were producing a similar product at much lower cost; therefore specialists on the price committee delved deeply into the documentation accompanying this application. The price was the outcome of costing out 124 operations; Goskomtsen specialists checked the norms for each, and found 107 were artificially inflated. They redid the calculations with proper norms, and concluded that the cost would be approximately 15.5 rubles, and that the retail price should be 18 rubles. See L. Ogienko, "Obosnovannost' tseny" (The soundness of a price), *Sots. ind.*, February 18, 1986.

they use their own capabilities to gather data in order to conduct a negotiation with maximum information.

One example of the type of information the center and ministries attempt to collect and use concerns the enterprise *pasport*, which each enterprise has had to prepare annually since about 1980. The *pasport* consists of thirty-nine forms that the enterprise must fill out in order to ascertain the productive capacity of the enterprise, its full inventory of capital stock and working capital, its labor force, and its recent performance record. This is clearly an attempt to develop a data bank for the economy as a whole showing the productive capacities of each enterprise. Such a data bank, if complete and accurate, could prove an invaluable aid in the planning process.[50]

The Incentive System

In the best of all possible worlds the *pasport* would provide the central planner with precise information on production possibilities in his system, and he would have the computing capacity to use that information to devise a consistent plan that maximized the goals of the political leadership. Then it would be possible to order each economic unit to produce a specific mix of goods and services by using a specific mix of inputs and by assuming a certain set of efficiencies for the use of inputs to produce outputs. Enterprise managers in this situation would have no room to maneuver, their sole job being to see that in fact the enterprise was operating as efficiently as the center knew it could. Violations of any part of the plan could be dealt with by the center swiftly and with confidence; they know what each economic unit is capable of, and if they fall short of those capabilities, the management will be replaced.

In this world planners resemble the captain of a ship whose passengers are also the crew. Planners know precisely the performance characteristics of the ship, and can—from the bridge—utilize a wide array of controls to bring the ship up to the edge of any or all of its engineered capabilities. The problem for them is to decide where to go, how to get there, what to do on arrival, and how much of the scarce time of the passengers should be devoted to repairing and improving the ship, as opposed to enjoying the cruise. They know the capabilities of their

50. The *pasport* requirement was part of the 1979 decree. For a brief discussion, see Filippov, *Besedy*, pp. 37–45.

system perfectly; what they must focus on is their preferences and how this well-known system can best serve those preferences.

Even the most visionary and optimistic advocates of central planning will readily admit that such a utopian (or nightmarish) vision of an omniscient, and omnipotent, planning authority is currently not even remotely attainable. Soviet planners have learned through long, and sometimes bitter, experience that information is a commodity that can be extremely difficult and costly to purchase and difficult to manage. As a result, they know that to some extent they are flying blind.

To return to the analogy of a ship, in a real-world economy that is centrally planned the planners are on the bridge, facing an array of gauges and controls that report on the status of the ship and control its movements. However, none of the gauges or controls are directly linked to the systems that run the ship. Rather, they are linked to a hierarchy of control panels on various of the lower decks, each of which is manned by other members of the crew who enter data from above that are to be sent down and aggregate data from below that are to be sent up. Speed, direction, fuel consumption, the state of the machinery—all these details come indirectly to planners through a hierarchy of individuals, all of whom have good reasons in some cases to distort the information traveling to the top. By turning the wheel or shouting instructions to other levels, planners issue commands to stop, start, turn, speed up, or slow down the ship. However, individuals at those other levels actually determine what happens. Sometimes what happens is what planners expect, sometimes not. Sometimes they think they know why something happened; at other times, they are baffled. They can run down to this or that station in the ship to check up on some part of the system, but if they do much of that, they won't have time to run the ship. Basically they have to stay on the bridge and cajole the crew into sending up accurate readings and responding to commands.

The formal system in the Soviet Union reflects the scarcity of information and the limits of planners' powers. Implicit in the system is the recognition that the center can never know enough to eliminate the enterprise director's room for maneuver—plan targets will inevitably be internally inconsistent, situations will change, and so on; therefore the incentive system is designed to induce individual economic units to make choices that central planners would make if they knew everything that the management of the individual economic unit knows.

This has obvious potential for becoming an elaborate game in which the center needs information—and can offer rewards to enterprise management and workers—as well as access to scarce resources in exchange for the information. The individual economic units want those rewards and need the access to scarce resources, and can manipulate the information in an effort to acquire them.

The passage of time makes the game infinitely more complex and interesting than it otherwise would be. Year after year the two sides engage in the game, using the information they have accumulated in an effort to gain an advantage for the future. The past is the major source of information available to the center in its effort to verify independently the current flow of information coming from individual economic units. For example, the norms so critical to the construction of control figures and to the setting of prices are heavily influenced by information on input use in the past. Enterprise managers know this and therefore try as best they can not to take actions which will reveal too much and cause them difficulties in future years. The center knows they know that and is doing its best to draw them out. In the midst of all this stand the ministries, which are also seeking to draw information out of enterprises and control them while dealing with the center on behalf of those units.

The center relies on two types of incentives to make the system operate. The primary mechanism is material incentives: bonuses and penalties, but primarily bonuses, designed to elicit cooperation from individual economic units. The secondary mechanism is moral incentives introduced through general propaganda, but also directly through the local party organizations, which are used to supplement material incentives.

The two basic problems the center faces—obtaining information on production possibilities and inducing individual economic units to work up to their full capabilities—are clearly interrelated. Inducing enterprises to do what you want them to do is much easier if you have a good notion of their capabilities. If you are uncertain about those capabilities, the problem of controlling enterprises is much more difficult. When you send a plan down to enterprises and they complain it is outside their capabilities, you cannot be sure that they are telling the truth. In reality the two problems become one, and what the planner must do is keep constant pressure on enterprises to improve their performance, using the information on plan fulfillment to sustain the pressure in subsequent periods.

MATERIAL INCENTIVES. The material incentive mechanism within Soviet central planning rests on the ability of the center to tightly control the size of earnings retained by the enterprise and their distribution among accounts, which can be used to significantly affect worker welfare and investments in the enterprise. A detailed set of national-level regulations, supplemented by regulations promulgated by each branch ministry, specifies the accounts (*fondy*) that an enterprise can establish, the amount of net earnings that can go into each account, and the uses to which the funds in each account (bonuses, small investments in the factory, and expenditures for housing and other facilities for workers) may be put. Annual plans specify in considerable detail the flow of earnings into those accounts as a function of fulfillment of key targets. The implicit assumption is that enterprise managers will be sufficiently motivated to bring funds into those accounts—in order to pay bonuses, provide amenities for workers (including housing), and make small investments—and that they will make every effort to fulfill the key targets in the plan and thus earn the right to retain and use the funds.

The rules for the distribution of earnings among these accounts constitute one of the policy instruments most frequently resorted to by planners in their effort to improve the operation of the system without dramatically changing it. Every reform introduced since 1965 has included, but has not been limited to, numerous changes in the bonus rules. They are discussed in somewhat more detail in subsequent chapters. For present purposes it is sufficient to outline the basic approach.

The nature of the centrally imposed accounting system under which managers work can best be explained by examining a simplified version of 1985 accounts for all industrial enterprises in the Soviet Union. Table 3-3 shows the distribution of profits in 1985 between contributions to the central budget and retained earnings, and the general distribution of retained earnings. Table 3-4 shows the breakdown of actual disbursements from all the accounts under the heading "economic stimulation" (*fondy ekonomicheskogo stimulirovaniia*), which are the basic accounts that enterprise management can draw on to pay bonuses, finance other expenditures affecting worker welfare, and undertake small capital projects in the enterprise.

Table 3-3 shows that during 1985 enterprises were authorized to retain a total of 45 percent of their profits in various accounts, the two most important being the economic stimulation accounts, discussed below, and those accounts reserved for interest and debt repayments; together

Table 3-3. *Distribution of Profits in Soviet Industrial Enterprises,*
1985

Profits	Percent	Amount (millions of rubles)
Total	**100**	**100,619**
Paid to state budget	55	55,340
Capital charges	26	26,161
Rent (resource), miscellaneous	6	6,037
Residual to state	23	23,142
Retained by enterprises	45	45,279
Economic stimulation accounts	17	17,105
Inventory and planned losses	4	4,025
Capital expenditures	4	4,025
Other (interest, debt repayment)	20	20,124

Source: Tsentral'noe statisticheskoe upravlenie SSSR, *Narodnoe khoziaistvo SSSR v 1985 g.: Statisticheskii ezhegodnik [Narkhoz]* (Moscow: "Finansy i statistika," 1986), pp. 548–49.

Table 3-4. *Funds Paid out of Economic Stimulation Accounts in*
Industrial Enterprises, 1985

Account	Percent	Amount (millions of rubles)
All	**100**	**21,881**
Economic stimulation	93	20,268
Material stimulation	39	8,473
Social-cultural and housing	15	3,203
Development of production	39	8,592
Other	7	1,613

Source: *Narkhoz 1985*, p. 557.

these accounts hold 79 percent of retained earnings. The remaining 55
percent of total profits reverted to the state via two mechanisms. Some
of the profits were paid to the state for specific charges, the largest being
the charges for fixed and working capital, which amounted to 45 percent
of the payments to the state budget out of gross profits of industrial
enterprises. These charges on capital, instituted during the 1965 reforms,
represent an effort to induce enterprises to economize on capital that
they received free of charge from investments financed out of the state
budget.

When all direct payments to the state budget are calculated, along
with authorized payments into enterprise accounts, the remainder of

profits reverts to the state budget. In 1985 that amount was 23.14 billion rubles, which was 23 percent of gross profits in that year.

Table 3-4 shows the breakdown of payouts from the economic stimulation accounts, the three important accounts being (1) Material Stimulation, (2) Social-Cultural Measures; and (3) Development of Production.

The Material Stimulation Account is a critical one for enterprise management. It is the sole source for their bonuses (top management's bonuses are determined by the ministry; the remainder of management's bonuses by top management). This account, along with a portion of the Wage Account, is the source of all bonuses to workers. Because wage scales are fixed centrally, these bonuses are the primary device available to management for rewarding those workers who contribute most to plan fulfillment.

Data on the share of worker's income from bonuses are difficult to find. According to the latest data, in the early 1970s bonuses for manual workers constituted 15 percent of their base pay, and that share was rising. Technical staff and management were receiving bonuses averaging about 20 percent of their pay. The top managers, who have the most influence over the performance of an enterprise, also have the largest share of bonuses in their income. A Gosbank inquiry in 1974 reported that almost one-quarter of top managers received bonuses in the range of 38–50 percent of their salary. About half were in the 51–60 percent range; 16 percent received bonuses equal to 65 percent of their salaries; and the remaining 11 percent were above that.[51]

Although more recent data, should they become available, may show somewhat different numbers, the basic fact will remain that bonuses

51. Cited in Jan Adam, "The Present Soviet Incentive System," *Soviet Studies*, vol. 32 (July 1980), p. 360. The data here are spotty and should only be taken as a general order of magnitude. For example, Adam quotes a source that estimates bonuses to be 22.1 percent of the salaries of engineering and technical staff in 1973. David Granick has found a source estimating that bonuses represent 27.5 percent of the total earnings of the same group, which would imply that bonuses were 38 percent of their base earnings (0.275/0.725). Granick also quotes a Gosbank study for the Russian Republic showing that one-third of all "upper" managers in enterprises in that republic had total earnings at least double their base salary, so that bonuses must have been at least 100 percent of base salary, a figure considerably higher than appears in Adam's sources. David Granick, "Institutional Innovation and Economic Management: The Soviet Incentive System, 1921 to the Present," in Gregory Guroff and Fred V. Carstensen, eds., *Entrepreneurship in Imperial Russia and the Soviet Union* (Princeton University Press, 1983), note 34 on p. 246.

make up a significant portion of the income of all enterprise staff, even manual workers. For that reason the Material Stimulation Account is important to top management. Historically, planners have relied on that interest to stimulate enterprise management to fulfill plans by linking authorized payments out of profits in the accounts to the fulfillment of key plan indicators. That was a fundamental feature of the 1965 reforms and has continued to be one of the main measures included in all efforts at reform since then.

The Social-Cultural Measures and Housing Account can be used by enterprise management to contribute to the construction of housing for workers (the remainder of the cost is covered by local government), for housing repair, and for the construction of children's institutions (for example, day care facilities), clubs, or sports facilities. Because labor is scarce in the USSR, the workers' amenities financed out of this fund are important to management as they seek to lure workers from other enterprises; hence their interest in this fund is also quite high. Payments into this account have generally been keyed to payments into the Material Stimulation Account (that is, simply some share of those payments).

The Production Development Account is used by the enterprise to make small investments involving, for example, technical refurbishing of a plant. Payments into the fund come from gross profits according to norms, a share of amortization allowances (the remainder reverting to the state), and proceeds from sales of used equipment.

In brief, this is a system in which planners use state ownership of the means of production to link enterprise-retained earnings and the uses to which they are put to enterprise performance indicators of importance to planners. The critical assumptions behind the system are (1) that planners can specify enterprise performance indicators that accurately convey to enterprises information on how the actions they take are valued in terms of society's preferences, and (2) that enterprise directors can only earn rewards via those indicators by in fact doing what planners would have them do if they (the planners) were in the place of each individual enterprise director. As will become clear in the following paragraphs, both critical assumptions are problematical.

Moral Incentives

In the Soviet economy, as in all other systems, people are motivated to participate in economic activity for a rich variety of reasons, of which material rewards are only one. Productive activity can be a source of personal gratification, which can come from pride of accomplishment, status, satisfaction in taking responsibility, and so on. In addition some people may be motivated by patriotism or feelings of nationalism as is often the case during a war. Historically Soviet leaders have tried to tap all of these motives to reinforce material incentives that may help to elicit information and induce compliance with central plans.

At a general level this is one of the main functions of the mass media. The press is replete with stories praising the work of exemplary workers and criticizing those who fail to show sufficient zeal or initiative in their work. However, the duties of the press in this regard go beyond general propaganda. Each major newspaper has a large staff divided up into departments similar to those in the hierarchy of the economy. The duty of staff in these departments is to follow affairs in their sectors and to publish investigative reports on the activities of ministries or enterprises in their area of responsibility. These reports can be devastating at times and may lead to disciplinary measures against enterprise management, and possibly even dismissal. The pressure of such reports is part of the environment designed to encourage enterprise managers to do their best to fulfill the plan.

Aside from the general propaganda and investigative reporting, there are constant government campaigns to stimulate higher productivity in enterprises. One example is the recurring effort to rekindle the Stakhanovite movement of the 1930s in which a group of workers or individual workers set an example for others by their extraordinary efforts to increase productivity. A myriad of similar devices—awards to factories that fulfill or overfulfill the plan, or honorary awards to individual workers who are exemplary in their work—serve similar purposes. Such approaches are not uncommon in businesses and governments in Western countries, and for the same reasons. Enthusiastic workers are generally better workers, and well-run organizations try to tap all the determinants of that enthusiasm—material or otherwise. "Best Worker of the Month" awards or "Best Plant of the Year" are common ammunition in that effort, both in the East and in the West.

One of the main features that distinguishes the USSR from countries in the West is the complicated and important role of the party in imbuing workers with moral incentive. Every unit in the economic hierarchy—the ministries, the production associations, the individual enterprises—has a party committee. And, because the leadership of each unit is composed of party members, the party committee has formal authority over those members and the responsibility to see that their activities within the unit serve the best interests of the party, and therefore the state. In addition party organizations all the way up to the Politburo have a potential interest in and are indirectly responsible for the performance of individual economic units. Normally the direct surveillance of and work with enterprises is carried out by the local party committees (*gorkomy, obkomy,* and *raikomy*), which are expected to be informed about the performance of enterprises in their jurisdiction and are held responsible for shortcomings in the enterprises.

This means that party pressure for improved performance is normally exerted on enterprises from two sources: the party committee within the enterprise and the local party organization. The party committee within the enterprise—which is composed of the enterprise director, the party secretary for the enterprise, and the leader of the trade union—acts like a board of directors and discusses major aspects of enterprise activity. An ideal enterprise party secretary is well informed about the operation of the enterprise, able to engage the director in an intelligent discussion about all aspects of the plan, and also able to provide the director with valuable information on problems from the shop floor. The enterprise party committee cannot make binding decisions governing the operation of the enterprise, but the enterprise secretary is one of those held responsible for enterprise performance (within the party hierarchy). If there is something terribly amiss with enterprise performance, he had better be able to show that he did his best to rectify the problem, working with top management.[52]

The local first party secretary, outranking the enterprise director and his party committee, has a direct interest in, and is responsible for, the performance of all enterprises in his area. His role is to keep track of enterprises and also to guide them in setting policy to ensure that it is consistent with central preferences. His staff will undertake investigative work to analyze problems in individual enterprises, will help management to solve them, and in some cases will use the power of the *nomenklatura* to replace some of the top management.[53]

52. Hough, *Soviet Prefects*, pp. 87–100.
53. For a discussion on this subject, see ibid., pp. 101–25, 178–96. To give an example, consider the case of a factory under the Ministry of Light Industry for the RSFSR that was performing poorly in that it was failing to fulfill the plan and producing low-quality goods in a mix not consistent with what consumers wanted. The Vologodskii

In addition, party pressure may be exerted on enterprises by the CC itself, which may single out enterprises for attention when a particularly important matter is involved, about which the CC wishes to make a point and set an example. A recent example that illustrates the role of the central apparatus here is the June 1986 decree concerning the quality of television receivers produced by the Ekran Production Association in Kuibyshev *oblast'*.[54] The decree charges that television receivers produced by the Ekran association are of poor quality and frequently in need of repair. The factory, the decree goes on, is poorly managed, allows equipment to go unrepaired, tolerates poor work habits, pays little attention to worker amenities, and so on. The party committee of the association was accorded part of the blame, and the leader of the committee was reprimanded. The enterprise director was fired; the minister heading the Ministry of the Radio Industry (P. S. Pleshakov) was reprimanded for not paying more attention to increasing the quality of consumer goods produced in his enterprises. The Kuibyshev *obkom* first secretary, who escaped censure, was ordered to assist the association's party committee and new manager in setting things right.

As this case illustrates, even the central apparatus of the party takes direct interest in individual economic units and will use them to set an example where an important policy goal (in this case the production of consumer electronics) is involved. Conversely, individual enterprises may be praised for a particular approach to a matter, also to set an example.

Moral incentives probably play an even greater role in the effort to induce ministries to lead the way in the fulfillment of plans. Ministries, like enterprises, have obligatory plans, but there are no well-defined criteria linking the fulfillment of those targets to the incomes of ministers or their staff. Although the performance of a ministry's enterprises may, over the long run, affect the income and job prospects of a minister, the link is probably poorly defined.

Here the party committees are expected to play an important role, although it is not noticeably different from that played by the party

---

gorkom responsible for the enterprise investigated the situation and concluded that the enterprise leadership was at fault. The director was fired, and the chief engineer replaced him because "he had the ability to unite and mobilize people." See V. Kuptsov (first secretary of the Vologodskii *gorkom*), "Effekt khoziaistvennoi initsiativy" (The effect of economic initiative), *Ekon. gaz.*, no. 33 (August 1984).

54. See the resolution by the Central Committee under the heading "V Tsentral'nom Komitete KPSS" (In the Central Committee of the CPSU), *Pravda*, June 3, 1986.

committee within the factory. The basic expectation is that the ministerial party committees will reinforce signals from the Council of Ministers and the party apparatus regarding the importance of working to fulfill the plan and that they will take initiatives consistent with party preferences. Like the committees within enterprises, party committees are expected to be familiar with the operation of their ministries, alert to problems, and diligent in their search for solutions. This may involve, for example, pushing a reluctant bureaucracy into accelerating the development of precision machine tools and numerically controlled machines, as the party committee of the Ministry of Precision Instruments, Automation, and Control Systems (Minpribor) apparently did with success in the 1960s.[55] On the other hand ministerial party committees can come in for heavy criticism if they fail to address chronic problems in the ministry, as the head of the party committee for the USSR Ministry of Light Industry recently discovered.[56]

Ministries also come under party surveillance and pressure via the departments of the Central Committee apparatus. Each of the economic ministries and state committees is supervised by one of ten departments in the Central Committee. Those departments are expected to maintain close ties with the units of the administrative apparatus that are their responsibility, monitoring performance and urging actions where there are shortcomings. Aside from virtually constant contact with each organization, this can also take the form of meetings in CC headquarters relating to the affairs of a ministry or a group of ministries. The party secretary responsible for that CC department (and therefore the ministry or ministries involved) will attend and speak; if the topics are important, a number of other secretaries may be involved, including—for high-priority issues—the general secretary.

Together the material incentives associated with the enterprise's plan

55. Ronald Amann and Julian Cooper, eds., *Industrial Innovation in the Soviet Union* (Yale University Press, 1982), p. 29.

56. An investigative article in *Sotsialisticheskaia industriia* castigates the head of the ministry's party committee for being subservient to ministerial leadership and for not making a genuine effort to deal with long-standing tendencies for enterprises in the ministry to produce low-quality goods not responsive to consumer demand. The article cites specific cases in which the party committee did actually investigate the problems, but then concluded they were not serious or that they were fixed, when in fact they were serious and nothing had been done to rectify matters. Because this situation is from the Gorbachev era, it may well include an element of new-found enthusiasm for the role of party committees in ministries, but the expectations have always been there. "S ogliadkoi na rangi" (Being very careful of rank), *Sots. ind.,* June 1, 1986.

and the moral incentives throughout the system (which are conveyed primarily through complex and multiple links between the party and government hierarchies) add up to formidable pressure at all levels of the hierarchy to take the plan seriously and to attempt to fulfill the most important indicators. No enterprise director ignores the plan or the many supplemental signals he receives from his ministry or the various party organizations with which he is linked and deals. No minister will lightly ignore the main indicators he receives from Gosplan.

In this sense the formal system and the plans that result from the operation of that system are the driving force behind the de facto system. However, they function with inadequate information. As a result, local units have ample room in which to maneuver and thus still seem to (and even actually do) meet plan indicators, although they fall short of the basic goals planners sought to achieve through those inadequate indicators. That room for maneuver and the quite natural inclination of enterprises to exploit it in search of the easiest way to obtain bonuses constitute the foundation of the de facto economic system, which differs in important ways from the formal system portrayed here.

The Formal System in Action

The logic of the formal system cannot be fully understood without some idea of the procedure used to identify and respond to changes in underlying economic forces. The design of that procedure strongly influences the performance of the system. The elements of critical importance are the devices used to (1) identify and respond to changes in supply conditions (for example rising costs of extracting raw materials); (2) identify and respond to changes in demand; (3) decide how to expand productive capacity; and (4) stimulate technical progress (innovation in production processes or products), which in turn leads to changes in supply conditions or demand (for example, for inputs). I discuss each of these briefly, using hypothetical examples to illustrate the operation of the formal system.

Changes in Supply

There are three questions of interest concerning supply. First, what are the actual changes in supply conditions, and how rapidly are they occurring (gradually over years, or quickly over days or weeks)? Second, how is the system designed to identify changes in supply? And third, how does it move to adjust?

Consider an example with relevance to the Soviet economy: the sustained rise in the costs of extracting oil. This is an unavoidable consequence of declining returns in an extractive industry; it comes gradually, over a series of years. Because the Soviet economy is a fixed-price system, prices will not automatically rise to reflect changing real production costs, except during infrequent price reform cycles. The only signals planners receive between those cycles are declining profits in oil extraction. Their main source of information is the negotiations with the Minnefteprom (oil industry), during the annual planning process, when it becomes clear that either input allocations to that industry must rise or output plans will have to be adjusted downward. That information, confirmed probably over several planning periods in which planners see underfulfilled output targets despite heavy pressure on the oil industry, is what eventually convinces planners that they are faced with different (and continuously changing) supply conditions for that product.

In the formal system, the reaction to recognized changes in supply conditions will be some combination of centrally directed increases in input allocations (including capital expenditures to expand productive capacity) to the oil industry and efforts to curb demand (direct cuts in petroleum product allocations to some users; new incentives to conserve on oil or to switch to natural gas). The reaction may also include cutbacks in exports (or increases in imports, depending on the product). All of this is managed within Gosplan and Gossnab through the material balance system and the bureaucratic bargaining process that it both reflects and drives. The important point here is that, if planners do nothing, then the supply begins to shrink (as fixed inputs produce progressively less oil), and a widening gap forms between demand (since customers know nothing of scarcity other than what the center communicates to them through the planning process) and shrinking supply—or so the design of the formal system suggests. Planners in this system are the main adjustment mechanism; if they refuse to see a problem or react to it, then it persists or grows worse until they change course.

Suppose, however, that the change in supply is sudden, say, in the first months of the year after the plan for that year has been approved; it could, in addition, be temporary. A particularly cold winter that creates a shortage of transport capacity is a case in point. The difference between this and a longer-term change in supply is that it occurs between planning cycles and therefore bypasses the major mechanism that the formal system uses to identify problems in supply. There is no explicit provision for such a development in the system. Of course, in fact, the planners are constantly monitoring the performance of the system and will be aware of such problems as they arise. The result, quite naturally, will be within-plan modifications of targets.

Changes in Demand

Typically the goods and services in a system are divided between intermediate commodities traded between enterprises (raw materials, semifabricates) and goods to final users (consumers, defense, enterprises undertaking new investments). However, in the Soviet economic system the more relevant distinction is between goods purchased by enterprises or the government and those purchased by consumers, since information on demand by those two groups is treated differently. Time is also a factor here, as it is on the supply side.

Long-term shifts in enterprise demand for intermediate or final goods (investment goods) will show up in the formal system through the planning process as enterprises and their ministries request more of some inputs and less of others. Heavy and light trucks might be an example. As enterprises come to emphasize increased reliance on trucking for short hauls, they may have an increased demand for small trucks and therefore will put in requests for increased shipments of that item. Suppliers of trucks will have no direct way of perceiving and responding to that increased demand except through the planning process. As the material balance system identifies the developing imbalance, it should react by some combination of cutting demand (refusing requests for more light trucks), ordering increased output of light trucks (increasing direct targets for light truck production, with bonuses attached to them), and directing investments to the expansion of productive capacity for light trucks. Typically planners will use norms to indicate whether the increased demand for light trucks is legitimate (say, because enterprises are moving into activities that require greater use of light trucks). If nothing is done, the imbalance will persist, and may grow worse if other aspects of the plan sent to enterprises tend to raise the derived demand for light trucks.

Consumers, on the other hand, do not participate in the planning process, and shifts in their demand for products must be communicated to planners through intermediaries. They are represented by the Ministry of Trade and by the enterprises producing consumer goods, which—through negotiations with retailers—learn of shifts in demand. An increased demand for, say, automatic washing machines can only make its way up to the center through those avenues. If the information somehow does not get into the system, or if it is ignored, then the resulting imbalance persists. If planners decide to close the deficit in some consumer goods market, they will build that into plan targets. However, for many consumer goods the all-union authorities are dealing in targets for ruble sales, and it is up to the republican planning authorities and the responsible ministries to identify and respond to specific imbalances. Note the difference between imbalances in the supply and demand for consumer goods, and for intermediates or final products to enterprises. The latter can cause imbalances that directly affect the production process. Imbalances in consumer goods markets will not have such a direct effect, although persistent imbalances may affect the supply of labor.

Investment Decisions

One of the most important aspects of the system's procedure for responding to changes in supply or demand is the method of allocating investment funds among sectors. In developed market economies enterprise-retained earnings and funds obtained through financial intermediaries jointly determine how investments are allocated to various sectors. The bidding process involved strongly favors investments with high rates of return, those being directly linked to the price system in its capacity as a source of accurate information on supply and demand conditions. In a market, increases in demand for a product will not only cause short-term increases in production (if productive capacity will allow that), but will also draw in new investment funds on the strength of an increase in anticipated returns.

In the Soviet system, Gosplan plays the role that financial intermediaries play in market economies: it decides who will receive available investment funds, or—what is more important—who will receive authorization to purchase specific equipment needed to undertake specific investments. In fact, Gosplan is a pseudo-financial intermediary, and more, because enterprises are allowed to retain so little of their earnings for investment purposes (in the Development Account).

The allocation of investment funds within Gosplan is an important part of the planning process and is accomplished through bureaucratic bargaining in which the various ministries supervising productive enterprises fight for a share of total investment resources. No explicitly defined criterion governs this process, but clearly decisions on investment are closely linked to the information that is generated through planning, particularly through material balancing. Ministries producing goods in short supply (for example, coal or oil) have an obvious case for more investment funds. That does not mean they will win their case; there are more shortages than there are investment funds to eliminate them. However, a proven shortage is the required foundation for a ministry's argument for investment funds.[57]

This procedure for allocating investment funds among sectors, although it differs significantly from that used in market economies, does not necessarily lead to a dramatically different result. After all, the mechanisms allocating investments in market economies are ultimately reacting to changes in supply and demand, which cause imbalances, which in turn change relative prices. The result is to draw funds away from areas in which surpluses are rising (and prices falling) to areas in which shortages are rising (and prices are rising). When the Soviet material balance system is working well, it does the same thing. The differences may be in the choices that the two systems make in an environment of scarce investment funds. Soviet central planners may be quicker to invest in expanding capacity in some sectors that in market economies would instead see rapidly increasing prices leading to significant reductions in demand.

Stimulating Technical Progress

In the Soviet system the stimulus to develop new products, or to develop and introduce new production processes, comes primarily from the center. The performance indicators for the manager include targets for increases in product quality, new investments designed to modernize

---

57. Planners are supposed to use an elaborate set of criteria in choosing among closely related alternative investment projects relating to an expanding capacity to produce a product in a particular sector. I do not discuss those here since my main concern is intersectorial investment allocations.

the enterprise, and increases in efficiency (which may imply process innovation). This system leaves room for innovation from below, that is, for the development of innovative ideas in individual factories in response to real customer needs, or in response to a need to reduce production costs. Indeed, the principal purpose of most moral incentives, and one of the main functions of the party, is to attempt to draw innovations out of enterprises.

Notice, however, that this system is designed around well-defined sectors that are supervised by individual ministries; it is therefore best able to generate those innovations that can be developed within the enterprise, or at least within the given ministry. Innovations that require the cooperation of enterprises in different ministries will have to be negotiated through the planning process. Furthermore, innovations that require close cooperation with the eventual user will similarly require negotiations through the planning process. All of this suggests that, although the formal system does not openly discourage innovation, neither does it make innovation terribly easy. Here, as elsewhere, planners play a pivotal role.

CHAPTER FOUR

The Soviet Economic System
As It Actually Operates

THE SOVIET economic system, like any economic system, works differently in fact than in theory. It is more complex and much less clear-cut than Soviet leaders wish it were. An understanding of the de facto economic system is indispensable for understanding the roots of Soviet economic weaknesses, and of Soviet economic strengths. An analysis of the potential effect of reforms on the system must rest on an understanding of how those reforms will interact with the system as it actually functions, rather than as it is supposed to function.

But there is also much to be learned from analyzing the reasons for a divergence between the formal and de facto systems. In some parts of the system the divergence is small; in others it is enormous. An understanding of the roots of this variance provides insights not only into the determinants of Soviet economic performance, but also into the types of economic reforms which are most likely to improve that performance.

Comparison between the Formal and De Facto Systems

The de facto system is not entirely different from or counter to the formal system. It is a product of the formal system and in many ways complements it. The hierarchy of actors in the formal system, with its complex set of rights, responsibilities, and procedures, finds an imperfect, but nevertheless recognizable, counterpart in the hierarchy of actors in the de facto system, where the rights, responsibilities, and procedures have evolved over time.

In the formal system, Goskomtsen either determines or tightly controls the determination of prices in the economy. In fact, although it exercises considerable control over price levels and structures, it "shares" its price-setting rights with enterprises and ministries. In the formal system, Gosplan and Gossnab enjoy formal monopoly rights over the materials distribution system, allocating rights of purchase for scarce products of national economic importance. In the actual system the official allocation mechanism is supplemented by an active black market in which enterprises unable to obtain the product they need through formal channels can barter for, or buy, those products from others with surplus stocks. In the formal system consumers have their autos serviced at state-run service centers. In fact some go there, but some also go to private individuals or to state employees working outside regular hours, who repair autos much more quickly and more reliably than state service centers can manage, although at considerably greater expense.

Areas of Convergence and Divergence

The differences between the formal and de facto systems stem from two basic factors: (1) the mismatch between the responsibilities assigned to particular central authorities and their capability to collect and process information; and (2) differences between preferences of central authorities and those of consumers and enterprises.

CONSEQUENCES OF LIMITED CENTRAL CAPACITY TO COLLECT AND PROCESS INFORMATION. By far the most important source of problems in the Soviet economy today is the fact that in the formal system particular central bodies have been assigned responsibilities they cannot fulfill because of the amount of information that must be collected and processed to do the job. This is also the greatest concern, although not always articulated, behind efforts to reform the system. Right now many of the most prominent central institutions have formal powers they cannot hope to use intelligently because much of the information they require is locked in lower levels of the hierarchy. Such are the limits to commanding this very large ship from the bridge.

This mismatch between formal power and the capability to collect and process information has different consequences in different situations. In some cases, lower bodies that have the information gain power and use it to their own ends, which are not always congruent with state goals. In others, incentives in the system are so structured that actors devise ways to compensate for problems arising from this mismatch.

Goskomtsen provides a good illustration of the first phenomenon. Given the reasonable limits on its staff and computing capability, that body can never hope to control fully the level and structure of the prices of manufactured goods in the USSR without the help of market pressures. It must primarily resort to rules to control the formation of prices by enterprises and ministries. The mere fact that it issues rules indicates that it has neither the time nor requisite information to set prices directly and also creates opportunities for producers and ministries to use their de facto power to inflate prices and profits. Goskomtsen can, and does, use spot checks to catch individual producers in the act. But the "spots" it can check are minuscule compared with those it must simply assume are satisfactory.

The operation of the materials distribution system illustrates the self-healing devices—sometimes but not always illegal—that actors in the de facto system use to replace or supplement the unworkable or poorly working parts of the formal system. Here, too, the duties and information-gathering and processing capabilities of central authorities are mismatched. Gosplan and Gossnab find that, even for the 16,000 or so products they directly distribute, they cannot consistently obtain information on supply and demand of sufficient accuracy to avoid serious bottlenecks during the year. Thus enterprises may find that they have certificates authorizing them to purchase products (and they have the rubles), but the products are not available. Yet the enterprises must try to fulfill the main plan targets, and so they go to black markets to obtain their products. As a result a system has evolved in which expediters (*tolkachi*) working on behalf of enterprises sell surplus commodities and purchase products the enterprises need. This secondary supply system is illegal yet openly discussed in the Soviet press; it has no place in the formal system, although it is an important component of the actual system that allocates resources. More important, without this secondary system, economic performance would clearly be worse than it now is.

Here the de facto system complements the formal system, compensating for flaws in its design. Notice also that the compensatory mechanism is a market in which the price (barter or monetary) of goods traded fluctuates according to supply and demand.

In other cases the efforts of individual economic units to protect themselves from the consequences of the center's problems with collecting and processing information may have harmful effects on the economy. Enterprises and ministries therefore tend to strive for self-sufficiency in inputs (as discussed below), but this merely leads to a substantial amount of small-scale, low-technology, high-cost production that reduces the efficiency of the system.

DIFFERENCES BETWEEN CENTRAL PREFERENCES AND THOSE OF THE POPULATION. Historically Soviet leaders have used various strategies to impose their preferences on the country's population and enterprises. An important point to note at the outset is that the phrase "their preferences" refers not to the personal preferences of Soviet leaders, which do not differ substantially from those of the population as a whole, but to state preferences, which favor investment over consumption and heavy industry over light. In fact, Soviet leaders seem to have typical preferences, but their special privileges make it possible to realize them in a way not open to the population at large. It is this special access that allows them, without great personal sacrifice, to impose state preferences on the system as a whole.

Although one can only speculate, it seems likely that the state and the population differ most significantly in their time preferences. The Soviet Union has consistently invested one-third of its GNP, but most of that goes toward expanding productive capacity. One suspects that, if the population as a whole could effectively express its preferences, the investment share of GNP would be lower, probably approaching one-fifth of that characteristic of Europe. In addition the distribution of investment imposed by the leadership favors heavy industry over light industry and housing. Here, too, the population would surely opt for a different set of choices.

These differences relate to the level and distribution of additions to Soviet productive capacity. Clearly, the population and the leadership also differ with respect to how that productive capacity should be used, as is evident from the chronic shortage of a broad range of consumer durables and services. A population able to express its preferences over government expenditures might also opt for more social services and significant new investments in infrastructure, financed by a reduction in the 15–17 percent of GNP devoted to defense expenditures.

In the formal system, the possibility that preferences may differ is ignored, and the party is purported to represent the interests of society as a whole. Furthermore, the formal system provides the party with the necessary tools to impose its preferences on the system. Yet evidence that popular and leadership preferences differ is constantly present in the population's complaints about inadequate supplies of consumer goods, the long lines for many of those goods, and the persistent upward pressures on their prices. It is the existence of those diverging preferences that has given rise to the USSR's "second economy."

The state withholds resources allocated to the production of consumer goods and services, but puts a lid on their prices to obscure the extent of the shortage. The result is long lines for the consumers and substantial profits for those willing to break the law and supply goods and services on the black market. Automobile repair is just one of many examples in which private entrepreneurs operate illegally, using time, materials, and even productive capacity sometimes stolen from the state to supply goods and services in amounts, qualities, and quantities greater than the state intended. Again a market springs up, but here it undermines, rather than supports, official state goals. Black markets for housing construction and rental, various manufactured goods, and other services yield additional examples.

Enterprises, too, have their own preferences, which differ from those of the state, and they have developed mechanisms—with sympathetic assistance from ministries—to undermine, or at least dilute, state preferences. The virtual conspiracy among design bureaus, ministries, and enterprises to build new plants rather than to renovate and modernize existing plants, as the state would prefer, is but one of the numerous ways that the de facto system operates to produce investment decisions different from those the center would prefer.

The Significance of Comparing the Two Systems

It would be impossible to present a definitive account of how the de facto system operates in a single chapter. The purpose of this chapter is narrower and therefore more feasible: to provide a context in which to analyze current debates on Soviet economic reform, and actual reform measures as they are introduced. The goal is to understand the principles by which the system operates, without being overwhelmed by details.

To construct a context useful for analyzing economic reforms, one must first understand the logic of the existing system. That is, one must identify the various parts and determine how they relate to each other. Second, one must examine the links between the de facto system and economic performance to determine why its performance record has been strong in some cases and weak in others.

THE LOGIC OF THE DE FACTO SYSTEM. If there were such a thing as an economic systems engineer and he were given the blueprints of the USSR's formal economic system, he could quickly explain why this system cannot work, or, at least, cannot work very smoothly. Certainly the institutions that make up the formal system are mutually consistent. However, they alone cannot conceivably handle the information needed to complete the tasks formally assigned to them.

Nevertheless the Soviet economic system "works" reasonably well by world standards and has done so for over a half-century. Growth rates have been respectable; industrialization has occurred at a rapid pace; Soviet military power, constructed on the base of the economy, is rivaled only by that of the United States. This "implausible" system somehow works. All of this suggests that the de facto system contains mechanisms that are not part of the formal system, that have a logic of their own, and that make the economy operate more smoothly than it otherwise could be expected to operate.

The analyst must identify those mechanisms in order to explain the present system and to evaluate economic reforms and their potential for affecting those mechanisms. Reforms are debated within the context of the formal system, yet by definition they are effective only if they have an impact on the de facto system. To have an impact, the reforms must incorporate elements of the de facto system into the formal framework—for example, previously illegal private activity might be legalized—or they must introduce changes in powers and responsibilities that will alter the way the system actually operates. In either case, only in the context of the de facto system is it possible to analyze what the consequences of such reforms might be.

Consider, for example, that Gorbachev's reforms include stricter laws on unearned incomes from sources such as speculation and price gouging. Note, however, that the *tolkachi*, whose actions add up to a de facto mechanism that makes it possible to trade surpluses for deficits throughout the system, could easily be labeled speculators, not without justification in some cases. The effects of such a reform on economic performance would depend on the mechanisms simultaneously put in place to compensate for the loss of the services of *tolkachi*, or to protect them.

To take another, less obvious example, one of the goals of Gorbachev's reforms is to reduce ministerial interference in the daily affairs of enterprises, and thereby to reduce their authority, vis-à-vis enterprises, within the formal system. Yet ministries are not only pests for enterprises, but also an important intermediary with the center, aiding enterprises and interceding on their behalf in cases where other avenues have been unproductive. Therefore an important question to ask is whether the reforms, should they prove successful, would destroy this valuable channel for enterprises, and, if so, what would replace it.

THE DE FACTO SYSTEM AND ECONOMIC PERFORMANCE. To explain the performance record of the de facto system, the analyst must turn to the interlocking institutions that together provide an extraordinarily high degree of economic security. That economic security is both the greatest strength of the system and the source of its weakness: the general inertia of the R&D process, the apparent lack of feedback (which helps to perpetuate imbalances in the supply of and demand for many products), and the tendency toward extreme inefficiency in the use of human and material inputs. The leadership has used each of these to justify economic reforms; and each is the subject of specific reform decrees. To understand the likely effects of the reforms, one must understand how they are linked to the actual system.

In analyzing the links between the system and performance, one must also be constantly alert to the danger of painting black and white pictures that add up to caricatures of the true state of affairs. This is a system full of paradoxes or contradictions, the causes of which it is too easy to assume are exceptions in the system. Is it just happenstance or some complex order that is responsible for the fact that the Soviet system produces some of the world's most reliable turbines for electric power stations, whereas its television sets are by and large obsolete and unreliable? Was it just a quirk that the USSR, when faced with the Reagan embargo, managed to finish its natural gas export line ahead of time by using Soviet technology almost exclusively, although it clearly had planned to rely heavily on imported turbines for the line? If this is a system constantly fighting incipient balance of payments problems, then why have dollar trade balances been consistently positive, and why has net debt remained so low for most of the postwar period?

These are but a sampling of questions that together suggest the system not only is more complicated than it might seem at first glance, but may have within itself the power to improve its performance.

Issues Concerning Evidence

The difficult problem in studying the de facto system is the lack of reliable data. No one in the Soviet Union has yet published, or at least written, a much needed book on the Soviet system at work—myth versus reality—but the newspapers and the scholarly literature contain countless anecdotes that could go into such a book. Although some of these are quite frank in their portrayal of systemic failures, they must be viewed with healthy skepticism. Recall that the press is part of the system that monitors and critiques the activities of economic organizations at all levels in the hierarchy below the Politburo and Council of Ministers. Some of that involves praising various economic activities that Western readers tend to ignore; they focus instead on the critiques that also reflect part of the media's duties, and part of the reality of the Soviet economy. The implicit assumption (in the West and the USSR) is that the ratio of praise to condemnation in officially sanctioned publications far exceeds the ratio of what is praiseworthy to what is condemnable in the system. Although that may be true, it is also likely that the stories of praise reflect some aspect of the reality that makes up the Soviet economy.

The problem is one of weighting the various anecdotes, and there is no easy solution. Drawing inferences from a mass of anecdotes is a highly subjective exercise and is not amenable to replication by others. The best one can do is to make prior assumptions (or biases) clear. My bias is to find anecdotes that help to explain how this system works as well as it does. Clearly the system has many weaknesses; the anecdotal evidence documents those; and they should not be ignored. However, the challenge is to explain how a system with all those failings has nevertheless made it possible for the Soviet Union to emerge as one of the world's two military superpowers, while sustaining respectable GNP growth rates. Explaining why this system cannot work, and should be changed, is elementary. Explaining why it nevertheless has worked for so long is a daunting task indeed.

The approach in this chapter, as in chapter 3, is to focus on the decisionmaking hierarchy and the information and incentive systems.

The time frame is again the mid-1980s, although that is a less important caveat here than it was in the discussion of the formal system, since in its basic principles the de facto system has existed in its present form for at least the last quarter century; and some would go back to the 1930s in their dating.

The Decisionmaking Hierarchy

The decisionmaking hierarchy in the de facto system differs from that in the formal system in several ways. To mention the obvious ones first, the popular elections for the Party Congress, the Central Committee, the Politburo, and so on, are facades behind which the power brokers who constitute the Politburo hold and exercise power. That does not mean the system is devoid of politics in the traditional sense; nor does it signify that the issues are unrelated to genuine concerns of the population, or to its welfare. On the contrary, it appears that in the struggles over the choice of a general secretary, or the Politburo, many of the large social and economic issues that play a role in Western elections also loom large here. At least one factor that contributed to Khrushchev's demise was the modest results of his expensive Virgin Lands scheme for producing wheat in semiarid Kazakhstan; and Gorbachev's plans to revitalize the economy probably helped him become general secretary.

Nevertheless, the elections and "campaigns" surrounding them, both in the government and in the party, have an essentially formal character and as a result reflect, rather than constitute, the debates among those who actually make the choices. Elections below the level of the Politburo are occasions to signal shifts in power within the leadership, as in the election of a new Central Committee at every party congress, or the choice of a republican party leader. Elections to the Politburo itself signal how the general secretary has managed to construct the coalition with which he will govern the system. Retirements "for reasons of health" may accurately describe the situation in some cases, but can also provide a cover for a dismissal.

Aside from that obvious difference, there are several important ways in which the hierarchy in the Soviet Union differs from the formal description, or at least is a good deal richer than the formal description implies. The most notable of these differences have to do with the role of the party in the economy, the distribution of power among government institutions, and the role of nongovernmental institutions in resource allocation.

The Role of the Party in the Economy

In the design of the formal system the party is given awesome powers over the economy in large and small decisions. In fact it realizes all of those powers, and then some. The distinction here between the formal and de facto systems is primarily one of degree. Whereas the formal system specifically excludes party organizations at all levels from involvement in the operational side of the economy, the party in fact plays an important, if not constant or consistent, role even there. That role is most evident in the activities of the Politburo and of local party organizations.

THE POLITBURO. On December 11, 1982, Iurii Andropov, then general secretary, began a tradition, still honored, of publishing a selective summary of topics discussed at each week's Politburo meeting.[1] As is clear from the summaries themselves, some topics discussed in the meetings are not enumerated in the summaries; and presumably some of the topics omitted are of major importance. Further, it is not guaranteed that a summary will be published after every meeting of the Politburo, although there have been no hints to the contrary. Those limits on what is known do not change the fact that we know much more than we have in the past about how the Politburo and the powerful CC staff operate, what topics interest them, and how they seek to control the system.

In general the Politburo does everything one would expect from its position in the formal system. Consider, for example, the role of the Politburo and CC staff in the formulation of the Twelfth FYP (1986–90). In 1983 the Politburo was already discussing plans for particular sectors to be built into that five-year plan.[2] The May 31, 1984, Politburo meeting included a general discussion of the party's economic strategy in the context of general guidelines for the plan.[3] On July 20, 1984, a major

1. "V Politbiuro TsK KPSS" (In the Politburo of the CC of the CPSU), *Pravda*, December 11, 1982.

2. See, for example, "V Politbiuro TsK KPSS," *Pravda*, September 24 and December 24, 1983, in which a program for consumer goods and services to be built into the Twelfth FYP is discussed.

3. "V Politbiuro TsK KPSS," *Pravda*, June 1, 1984.

meeting on the Twelfth FYP was arranged by CC staff at CC headquarters and was attended by heads of ministries at which (then second secretary) Gorbachev spoke.[4] Increasingly detailed and numerous meetings (including full-scale reviews of the Twelfth FYP drafts in the May 24, 1985, Politburo meeting) followed in government and party institutions under the leadership of the Politburo and Gorbachev in particular.[5] Another general meeting was held at CC headquarters on August 23, 1985.[6] The full (probably by now at least the fourth) draft of the plan was considered at the November 14, 1985, meeting, after which it was published for general consideration.[7] That draft was considered at the Twenty-seventh Party Congress in February–March 1986, then modified, and, after yet another discussion in the June 13, 1986, Politburo meeting,[8] was passed by the Supreme Soviet on June 19, 1986.[9]

This presumably partial list of high leadership meetings devoted to the Twelfth FYP illustrates the considerable and sustained attention the Politburo gives to the general direction of the planning process. It also does this for other aspects of the planning process and economic reforms. At various times during the year it reviews economic performance; every December it devotes a major meeting to assessing the year's performance and plans for the following year. Throughout the year Politburo staff discuss particular topics relating to major issues in the economy, make decisions, issue orders to CC staff, and so on. In this sense the Politburo and CC staff are just as active and powerful as one would expect, to judge by the formal system.

What is most interesting about the Politburo, and at variance with the formal system, is that it does not limit its concerns or its activities to the general and most critical goals and decisions of the system. Nor can it do so. Its immense power also draws it into decisions on countless matters that in Western countries are frequently decided by the boards, or even the management, of large corporations; the number is so great,

4. "Soveshchanie v TsK KPSS" (Meeting in the CC of the CPSU), *Ekonomicheskaia gazeta*, no. 31 (July 1984). (Hereafter cited as *Ekon. gaz.*)

5. "V Politbiuro TsK KPSS," *Pravda*, May 25, 1985.

6. "V Tsentral'nom Komitete KPSS" (In the Central Committee of the CPSU), *Sotsialisticheskaia industriia*, August 23, 1985. (Hereafter cited as *Sots. ind.*)

7. "V Politbiuro TsK KPSS," *Pravda*, November 15, 1985.

8. "V Politbiuro TsK KPSS," *Pravda*, June 14, 1986.

9. "Zakon Soiuza Sovietskikh Sotsialisticheskikh Respublik. O gosudarstvennom plane ekonomicheskogo i sotsial'nogo razvitiia SSSR na 1986–90 gody" (Law of the Union of Soviet Socialist Republics. On the state plan for the economic and social development of the USSR during 1986–90), *Ekon gaz.*, no. 26 (June 1986).

in fact, that the threat of information overload is ever present. In the four meetings that normally occur every month, the Politburo can hear reports and issue decrees relating to the Yamburg natural gas pipeline, the preparation of livestock for winter, the development of the television industry, changes in selected retail prices, and the rational use of the various bus fleets in the USSR.[10] The development of a particular town, the state of shoe production, the use of a Soviet-developed technology in assembly lines, techniques for stock-breeding, the management of the Chernobyl' disaster, and the fall harvest are additional, fairly random samples of what Politburo members discuss and make the subject of decrees. Although many of these discussions and decisions represent no more than a ratification of proposals and detailed work by the CC staff and government bureaucracies, the number of detailed decisions ultimately discussed and approved by this very small group of leaders is striking and leaves no doubt that they have an abiding interest in everything that happens throughout the system.

In addition to overseeing economic affairs, the Politburo directs foreign policy and domestic policy in other areas. Those duties, combined with the various ways it seeks to control the economy, add up to a set of powers and responsibilities that have no counterpart in a developed Western country. If it is viewed in the U.S. context, the Politburo has all of the powers and duties of the president's cabinet, a good portion of congressional power, some judicial powers, and a portion of the power and responsibilities that in the United States are held by boards of directors of major corporations.

The authority over the economy left to government institutions is a residual composed of all of the mundane details of economic administration (save those few in which the Politburo happens to take a particular interest) and some of the middle-level economic decisions that the Politburo cannot or does not involve itself in (concerning the types of conventional plants used to generate power, allocation of investments within sectors, and so on). Because the Politburo is the court of last resort in both the party and the government, the residual authorities of the government can change dramatically, and quickly, over time. When, for example, the Politburo decides that conveyor-rotor technology should be pushed in Soviet manufacturing, then the government has just lost control over what should have been a middle-level decision.

10. This is a sampling of the topics included in the published reports for the Politburo meetings in August 1984, under the leadership of Konstantin Chernenko.

LOCAL PARTY ORGANIZATIONS. Local party authorities (*obkom*, *gor-kom*, and *raikom* secretaries) are held responsible for the economic performance of "their" regions, and their formal powers (control over appointments through the *nomenklatura*, influence through party members holding important posts in the enterprises, general influence with higher party officials) give them tools to influence enterprises in their geographic areas. Formally, however, they are enjoined to stay out of operational decisions in enterprises. Party authorities are to achieve their goals through general propaganda and education, which will motivate party workers and the enterprises in which they work to fulfill plan targets and to meet the more general expectations of party authorities.

That is one of the concerns motivating local party leaders, but not the only one. Local first party secretaries are responsible for the general economic performance of their region, and for many of the details: "The first secretary of the party committee is concerned with a broad set of problems. Those include technical progress, science and culture, ideological work, the education of people, questions concerning the development of trade, services, health. . . . He must thoroughly scrutinize everything; he is held responsible for everything."[11]

These expectations create a strong incentive for local party officials to intervene directly in enterprise activities, to become advocates for their enterprises, and at times to become apologists. Furthermore, because party organizations are in general responsible for all aspects of local welfare, they find that they must use enterprises to serve local interests, even though at times that interferes with enterprises' efforts to fulfill plan targets from above. The formal system implies that these party organizations will be one-way transmission belts representing the interests of the party at a local level. In other words, they are meant to act as party "prefects," to use Jerry Hough's term, without interfering in economic decisions best left to trained industrial managers. In fact they have to some extent become, quite naturally, miniature images of the national Politburo, mixing work on "pure" party issues with considerable involvement in detailed decisionmaking in individual enterprises.

One of the responsibilities of local party organizations, for example, is to do everything possible to ensure that supplies of food are regular and adequate and that local *kolkhozy* and *sovkhozy* fulfill procurement targets from the plan. One of the major devices local party organs use in

11. "Pervyi sekretar' " (The first secretary), *Pravda*, July 22, 1986.

an effort to fulfill these expectations is a "patronage" (*shefstvo*) system in which workers in a particular factory are encouraged by the local party organization to adopt a local farm and to provide "voluntary" work and materials. This may involve assistance during the harvest or in the construction of buildings. Such assistance can be provided during the regular working hours of the enterprise, in which case it still must pay the workers wages, or it can be on the weekends, during harvesting, for example, or when the crop is being unloaded. In the latter case the workers "volunteer."[12] In some cases the activity may be fairly loosely organized and sporadic, whereas in others the local party organs may systematically use "volunteers" to assist agriculture. The head of the ZIL Production Association based in Moscow, one of the USSR's major producers of trucks, complains that up to a thousand or more workers from each of his factories are requisitioned annually for agricultural work, and as a result the association must incur the additional expense of overtime and extra shifts to fulfill its own plan.[13]

The Karaganda *obkom* studied the *shefstvo* system and concluded that firms were providing slow and inefficient support to agricultural enterprises, the main sign being a great deal of unfinished construction. The *obkom* then reorganized the system so that local enterprises used standard blueprints in producing parts for prefabricated buildings and plants for use in villages. Now construction projects that before required ten to twelve months of work are completed in three.[14]

The more general responsibilities of local party secretaries make it necessary to requisition the labor force and materials of local factories for various other tasks. During the 1970s provincial cities and towns received virtually no funds earmarked for local public projects. These were nevertheless their responsibility, and they turned to local enterprises for work on roads, sewage systems, municipal services, and so on.[15] The result is a tax in kind on the enterprise which, according to one

12. Jerry F. Hough, *The Soviet Prefects: The Local Party Organs in Industrial Decision-making* (Harvard University Press, 1969) pp. 157, 236.

13. "ZIL: Vozmozhnosti, zaboty, sversheniia. Beseda korrespondenta EKO s general'nym direktorom proizvodstvennogo ob"edineniia ZIL E. A. Brakovym," (ZIL: Possibilities, concerns, accomplishments. A conversation by EKO's correspondent with E. A. Brakov, general director of the ZIL Production Association), *EKO*, no. 10 (October 1986), p. 7.

14. A. Korkin, "Predpriimchivost' rukovoditelia" (The enterprising nature of an enterprise director), *Sots. ind.*, September 27, 1984. Korkin was at the time the *obkom* first secretary in Karaganda, so there may be some hyperbole in this account.

15. Fyodor I. Kushnirsky, *Soviet Economic Planning, 1965–1980* (Boulder, Colo.: Westview Press, 1982), pp. 73–74.

of the deputy directors of Gosplan's Economic Research Institute, has grown with extraordinary rapidity in the past fifteen years. "Besides the economic losses," he goes on to say, "this has brought enormous social damage, worsening the relationship of people to their main duties."[16] How large that tax in kind may be, and whether in fact it has grown in recent years, is something anecdotal evidence cannot shed light on.

Local party officials play as great a role in the agricultural affairs in their district, if not greater, than they do in industry. The main purpose of the *shevstvo* system—to requisition urban labor for agriculture—emphasizes the organic relationship between local party organizations and the *sovkhozy* and *kolkhozy* in their area. The local party official is the guarantor of the welfare of the population in his area, which means he must be concerned with food supplies and must do all he can to keep those supplies coming to his area as well as to the national economy.

Alec Nove argues that the local party may be even more intrusive in agriculture than in industry, in part because the agricultural laborer can violate the plan in many more ways than his urban counterpart (for example, by working his private plot instead of state or collective land), but possibly also because of a lingering fear of the political challenge that could come from the countryside.[17] The party's role in agriculture could also be the natural consequence of the persistent attempt by planners to treat agriculture as they do industry—by managing it through detailed annual plans—even though the costs of overcentralization are somewhat greater in agriculture than in industry. The continuing poor performance inevitably draws the party more and more deeply into the operations of the sector.

Because local party organizations are expected to participate in economic affairs in their regions, and in fact do help local economic organizations make operational decisions, they have taken on an advocacy role. Quite often they plead their enterprises' cases for more investment funds before higher authorities in the party and government. Successful pleas may not only improve the performance of their enterprises, but may also mean more staff, not to mention more influence and prominence for the party secretary.[18] In some cases the local party organs may even act as *tolkachi* and attempt to secure scarce inputs that

16. V. Kostakov, "Zaniatost': Defitsit ili izbytok?" (Employment: deficit or surplus?), *Kommunist*, no. 2 (January 1987), p. 81.

17. Alec Nove, *The Soviet Economic System* (London: George Allen and Unwin, 1977), pp. 127–28.

18. Hough, *Soviet Prefects*, pp. 256–57.

enterprises need and have been unable to obtain through regular channels.[19] Party secretaries may even be sorely tempted on occasion to look the other way when an enterprise director breaks the law in an effort to fulfill a plan target of importance to the center.[20]

The fact that local party organizations have been drawn into operational decisionmaking throughout the system, far beyond what is considered wise or justified by the principles of the formal system, is generally recognized. Party officials have on numerous occasions indicated a desire to reduce the burden of operational decisions by shifting it back to local governmental bodies and enterprises.[21] However, the party's strong signals to local party organs that they will be judged by the economic performance of their areas do not jibe with the party's admonitions to stay out of operational decisions. It is not surprising that local party officials respond by doing all in their power to see that their region performs well, even to the point of becoming directly involved in detailed decisions.

THE PARTY AS A STRENGTH AND WEAKNESS OF THE CURRENT SYSTEM. The de facto powers here do not add up to an omnipotent party, simply because omnipotence is beyond the capabilities of the organization. Rather, the party is more like a "spotlight," which, when it focuses on one part of the system, must perforce ignore others. What these powers do is to make particular parts of the system work extremely well, relative to, and maybe even at the cost of, the rest of the system. When the party has a particular goal and that goal is an important one, it can utilize the innumerable links between the party and the economy, each with its particular history of debts and commitments, to mobilize the economy in service of that goal.

The Soviet reaction to President Ronald Reagan's pipeline sanctions is a good case in point.[22] By 1980 the Soviet Union had already outlined a very ambitious program to rapidly expand the capacity of its gas transportation system during 1981–85 by 40,000 kilometers (from a total of 130,000 kilometers in 1980). Half of that increment was to be accounted for by six 56-inch-diameter lines stretching from West Siberia to the

---

19. Ibid., p. 227.

20. Ibid., p. 200.

21. See, for example, Konstantin Chernenko's speech accepting the post of general secretary (*Pravda*, February 14, 1984); or L. N. Zaikov's complaints at the time he was Leningrad *obkom* first secretary about the excessive burden of operational decisions on his staff (*Leningradskaia Pravda*, March 20, 1985).

22. On the history of this, see Ed A. Hewett, "The Pipeline Connection: Issues for the Alliance," *Brookings Review*, vol. 1 (Fall 1982), pp. 15–20.

European USSR. One line was to be dedicated to exporting an additional 40 billion cubic meters (bcm) of Soviet natural gas to Western Europe.[23] There were strong indications that the Soviet Union intended to rely heavily on imported compressors and turbines, which were far superior to its own, to implement this ambitious program. The equipment was either of U.S. or European origin, but embodied U.S. technology for critical parts.

President Reagan, in response to developments in Poland, placed an embargo on exports of that equipment that lasted less than a year and had the effect of delaying some shipments of turbines and blades. The Soviet response to this action was to mobilize local party and government organizations in an all-out effort to meet the goals of the pipeline expansion program by relying almost exclusively—contrary to the original strategy of the ambitious plans—on Soviet turbines and compressors. That is precisely what happened, and more. The entire pipeline expansion program was completed ahead of schedule, and without further imports of western turbines and compressors beyond those few purchased before the Reagan embargo.

This was no mean feat, and how the Soviets managed it is still somewhat of a mystery.[24] What is clear is that the Soviet leadership responded to the Reagan threat by mobilizing the entire system through the party, signaling to all levels that the gas pipeline program was a first priority. There can be little doubt of the importance placed on this when, as one official in Minneftegazstroi (the ministry charged with overseeing the pipeline construction program) noted, his ministry was required to produce a full report daily on the previous day's work throughout the entire system, a report that went to Gosplan, the government, the relevant ministries, party organizations, and trade union offices.[25] Local party officials all along the route of the lines were mobilized to see that

23. See Thane Gustafson, *The Soviet Gas Campaign: Politics and Policy in Soviet Decisionmaking*, R-3036-AF (Santa Monica, Calif.: Rand Corp., 1983); and Ed A. Hewett, "Near-Term Prospects for the Soviet Natural Gas Industry, and the Implications for East-West Trade," in U.S. Joint Economic Committee, *Soviet Economy in the 1980s: Problems and Prospects*, Joint Committee Print, 97 Cong. 2 sess. (GPO, 1982), vol. 1, pp. 391–413.

24. I had concluded from an analysis of Soviet capabilities in turbine and compressor technology that the Soviet Union would not be able to bring the new lines up to full pressure as quickly as it did. See Ed A. Hewett, *Energy, Economics, and Foreign Policy in the Soviet Union* (Brookings, 1984), pp. 77–78. They clearly have done it, but there are many unknowns on how and at what cost.

25. "Velikaia stroika piatiletki" (The great construction project of the five-year plan), *Izvestiia*, February 18, 1982.

construction moved on schedule. Ministries were mobilized to see that they contributed their part in the supply of necessary equipment, and where possible Eastern European technology was substituted for what were to have been imports from the West.

This is but one example of an important source of strength in this system: its ability to see that a certain limited number of things are done when and how the leadership wishes them to be done. However, the limits to the party's capabilities are real, and if the party identifies too many "first" priorities, or if those matters identified as high priorities are difficult to express in terms of easily verifiable performance criteria (such as kilometers of pipeline brought up to full pressure), the results will be far less impressive than they were in the pipeline case. A general campaign to increase the quality of goods and services might be a case in point. No matter how intense the party's desire is in this area, there are too many escape routes available to an enterprise for the party pressure to produce results commensurate with the effort.

The Distribution of Power among Government Institutions

The de facto distribution of power among the ministries and state committees and between them and the lower-level economic units differs in important ways from what the formal system would suggest. Most important is the constant effort of the ministries to avoid cooperating with other ministries. As a result, many of them try to minimize contacts with the remainder of the system, sometimes on an enterprise-by-enterprise basis.

Outsiders tend to view the Soviet Union as an autarkic economic system that avoids contacts with the outside world so that the leadership can keep a strong hold on the system. There is much to be said for this hypothesis, but for the purposes of this discussion the more interesting proposition is that this desire to keep contacts with the outside to a minimum pervades the entire system, from the ministries to the enterprises themselves. Individual enterprises, and their ministries, will strive for vertical integration, by producing most of the inputs and services required to produce the outputs for which they are held responsible in the plan. This is a natural consequence of an uncertain material-technical supply system in which even enterprises with the authorization and rubles necessary to purchase an important input may find they cannot acquire it. Yet they are still held responsible for meeting the plan objectives. Difficulties in acquiring inputs, although formally a valid excuse for not meeting a plan target, are so common that planners expect managers to somehow deal with them.

In some cases *tolkachi* can be used to solve the problem, particularly if the input involved is already being produced somewhere in the system. The more difficult, and probably more common, situation is the one in which the enterprise is developing new products and requires new inputs from suppliers in other ministries. The typical experience is probably that of A. I. Shokin, who in 1965 founded the Ministry of the Electronics Industry (Minelektronprom, one of the nine defense machine-building ministries) and was its head until 1985. In discussing the initial years of operation in the 1960s, he provides a quite frank and spirited defense for self-sufficiency:

> When starting to organize our sector, we spent 4 years searching for suppliers, and ran up against departmental barriers. The reply we constantly heard was: "We don't know anything about that, we're unable to do it." We finally concluded that we would have to do it ourselves, since nobody could make this complex and very precise equipment except its immediate customers.
>
> As a result, a scientific and production base was set up for specialized technological equipment without which the development of electronic equipment would have been inconceivable. That, as time has shown, was justified. Other ministries have followed such a path. The electronics industry includes the production of equipment which, according to existing specialization, would belong to [sectors producing] machine tools, electrotechnical, chemical, radiotechnical, non-ferrous metals, instrumentmaking, construction materials.[26]

This is a system in which customers are far less important than ministries, and the logical consequence is not only dissatisfied consumers, but also dissatisfied enterprises that cannot purchase the inputs they need. As a consequence, the successful enterprise is the vertically integrated enterprise, and the successful ministry, the vertically integrated ministry.

DATA ON AUTARKY. The result is what the Soviets call a "natural economy" (*naturnalnoe khoziaistvo*) in which enterprises are designed to come as close to self-sufficiency as possible and ministries encourage that. No general statistics are available to give a clear idea of ministerial self-sufficiency and changes in it over time, but bits and pieces of

26. "Podkhod—gosudarstvennyi" (State approach), *Pravda*, May 27, 1984.

information suggest it is an important phenomenon. For example, Minpribor (Instrument-making, Automation Equipment, and Control Systems) produces only 57 percent of such equipment; only 59 percent of the wood products are produced by Minlesbumprom (Timber, Pulp, Paper, and Wood), and Minlesbumprom shares with almost seventy ministries the production of sawn timber; sixty ministries and other institutions produce construction materials.[27]

More aggregated data are available on machinebuilding, the core of the industrial economy. Twenty of the approximately fifty ministries supervising economic activity share responsibility for machinebuilding. Together they account for 11.8 million employees and 3.7 million units of metalworking, stamping, and other equipment valued in excess of 100 billion rubles.[28]

Entire enterprises are devoted to producing machines in other sectors and employ a total of approximately 3 million workers. Most of the equipment in these enterprises is quite old, so that operating costs must be quite high.[29]

Some departments in nonmachinebuilding enterprises also produce machinery. Forty-five percent of all metalworking equipment in the Soviet Union can be found there, a stock that by itself exceeds in value the entire capital stock of the U.S. machinebuilding sector. Those departments account for 5 to 6 million workers, approximately one-third of all those employed in machinebuilding in the USSR.[30] These, also, must entail very high unit production costs. The one piece of corroborating information that is available comes from a survey of small metalworking shops in Belorussia, which found that castings produced in those shops were one and a half to two times as expensive as the average for Belorussia as a whole.[31]

27. R. G. Karagedov, "Ob organizationnoi strukture upravleniia promyshlennost'iu" (On the organizational structure of the management of industry), *EKO*, no. 8 (August 1983), p. 57.

28. G. A. Dzhavadov, *Mezhotraslevoe upravlenie proizvodstvom* (Intrasectoral management of production) (Moscow: Ekonomika, 1983), p. 47.

29. Ibid., p. 48.

30. S. A. Kheinman, "Razvitie mashinostroeniia: organizationnye i strukturnye faktory" (The development of machinebuilding: organizational and structural factors), *EKO*, no. 6 (June 1984), pp. 91, 109.

31. David A. Dyker, *The Process of Investment in the Soviet Union* (Cambridge University Press, 1983), pp. 38–39.

Most new enterprises are specifically designed to be as self-sufficient as possible. A Central Statistical Administration survey (for probably a recent, but unspecified, year) showed that for every 100 machinebuilding enterprises, 84 produce their own forgings (*pokovki*); 76 their own stock (*shtampovannye zagotovki*); and 65 their own metal hardware (*krepezh* and *metizy*).[32]

Vertical integration per se is not necessarily bad. However, to be rational it must come primarily as a consequence of cost calculations that show that outsiders cannot produce the goods as cheaply or as well as insiders. It appears that in the Soviet economy extraordinary uncertainty and unwillingness to accommodate customers lead to vertical integration at almost any price. This, also, is the result of a rational calculation by enterprises, and one they are probably reluctant to make since it takes them into a wide range of activities outside their assigned product mix and their expertise. The result is costly for society: large quantities of goods and services produced in small batches at very high cost and probably of variable quality.

A related symptom of the problem can be found in the quantity of cross-shipments in Soviet transport, particularly railroads, as ministries ship "their" products back and forth among their enterprises, while other ministries ship identical products, possibly in opposite directions. Timber products provide a good example. Sixty ministries and twelve Gosplans (the all-union and eleven republican Gosplans) distribute timber products. They tend to look out for their own enterprises, irrespective of the cost to the economy. Minenergo (Energy and Electrification), for example, ships sawn timber produced by construction firms at the Bratsk and Krasnoiarsk hydroelectric stations in Siberia 3,000–5,000 kilometers away to its enterprises in the European USSR. Simultaneously Minlesbumprom ships sawn timber to Siberia from its enterprises in the European USSR.[33] Nearly one-half of the reinforced concrete produced in major industrial centers is transported by ministries to "their" projects in other *oblasti* or *krai,* irrespective of distance.[34]

32. Iu. Lavrikov and V. Andreev, "Put' k mezhotraslevym proizvodstvam" (The road to intersectoral production), *Sots. ind.,* July 12, 1985.

33. V. Medvedev, "V poriadke iskliucheniia. Pochemu prodolzhaiutsiia neratsional'nye perevozki?" (In the nature of an exception. Why are irrational shipments continuing?), *Sots. ind.,* October 2, 1985.

34. N. Solov'ev, "Proizvodstvennaia infrastruktura: rezervy rosta" (Industrial infrastructure: the growth of reserves), *Ekon. gaz.,* no. 5 (January 1986).

The tendency of enterprises and ministries to shun cooperation outside their bureaucratic territory and to perpetuate costly output and transport patterns just to remain independent of the rest of the system is a major target of current efforts at reform. At the same time self-sufficiency, or at least production outside the normal mix, is encouraged in selected areas of consumer goods and food, even though the efficiency of output may suffer.

MIXED SIGNALS ON AUTARKY. Soviet enterprises have for some time been encouraged to produce consumer goods regardless of what they normally put out. Thus defense industries have become important sources of consumer goods, some of which are the highest-quality goods available. Julian Cooper has done a superb detective job in identifying consumer goods supplied in significant measure by defense. To give some of the more striking examples from his data for 1980, Minmash (the Ministry of Machinery, prime supplier of ammunition to the military) produced about 30 percent of all bicycles; Minobschemash (General Machinebuilding, main supplier of strategic missiles) produced 60 percent of the tramcars; Minoboronprom (Defense Industry, supplier of conventional army material) produced about 27 percent of the railway freight wagons, 10 percent of the passenger cars, and all of the motor-scooters; and Minaviaprom (Aviation, producer of aircraft and parts) produced about one-third of all the vacuum cleaners. All of the television sets, radios, video cassette recorders, and cameras produced in the system come from the defense ministries.[35]

The defense ministries are not the only ones to be pressured for consumer goods. Each ministry and each enterprise now receives a target for the production of consumer goods. In recent years heavy industry (the twenty machinebuilding ministries and those in fuels, raw materials, chemicals, timber, and construction materials) have produced about 30 percent of the consumer goods.[36]

These blanket requirements for all enterprises, whatever their basic production profile, to produce consumer goods are probably leading to

35. The figures are from Julian Cooper, "The Civilian Production of the Soviet Defence Industry," in Ronald Amann and Julian Cooper, eds., *Technical Progress and Soviet Development* (Basil Blackwell, 1986), p. 41. The product responsibilities of the defense machinebuilding ministries are from David Holloway, *The Soviet Union and the Arms Race* (Yale University Press, 1983), p. 120.

36. "Tsentral'noe statisticheskoe upravlenie SSSR, *Narodnoe khoziaistvo SSSR v 1983 g: Statisticheskii ezhegodnik* (Moscow: "Finansy i statistika"), p. 122. (Hereafter cited as *Narkhoz.*)

some serious losses for the economy. Consider the Tochmash factory in Tula, whose story probably has far too many counterparts throughout the USSR. Tochmash produces machinery for making hosiery and socks, both scarce items in the USSR because the capacity to produce them is fully utilized. Therefore it would appear that an expansion in Tochmash's output of machinery would expand production of consumer goods in short supply. Nevertheless, Gosplan has stood firm in requiring Tochmash to produce consumer goods in which it has no experience, even at the cost of developing and introducing into serial production a new, more efficient machine (which it already has in prototype) for producing hosiery and socks. Instead, Tochmash produces motorcycle parts, flashlights, and a plastic brain-teaser game for children, each of which its own staff helped to develop and it produced at enormous cost.[37]

Planners also encourage all enterprises to produce food. A first party secretary in Volgodonskii *gorkom* reports with pride that a factory in his area whose main task is tractor repair has, with its own labor, constructed a 12,000-square-meter greenhouse. Over the last two years it has produced 29 tons of cucumbers, tomatoes, and greens. In addition it produces 15 tons of pork annually, 40 kilograms per worker.[38]

Nikolai Ryzhkov, in discussing the Twelfth FYP, noted that most industrial ministries showed a willingness to do their part in boosting agricultural output by proposing targets for live-weight production of livestock and poultry in the range of 15–20 kilograms per worker. However, he complains that the ministries of instrument making and communications (Minpribor and Minsviazi) fell far short of that, proposing live-weight production of less than 4 kilograms.[39]

Obviously the de facto distribution of power among ministries is far more complex than the formal system suggests. The ministerial system was designed to enable the center to supervise economic activity by

37. Iu. Voevodin, "Schet ne obmanet" (The count should not fool you), *Sots. ind.*, January 6, 1987. The most eloquent testimony this story offers to the irrationality of the current approach lies in the fact that when Tochmash was ordered by Gosplan to undertake the production of scarce consumer goods, the factory was given a list of such goods from which to choose, and socks and hosiery were on the list.

38. V. Kuptsov, "Effekt khoziaistvennoi initsiativy" (The effect of economic initiative), *Ekon. gaz.*, no. 33 (August 1984).

39. "O gosudarstvennom plane ekonomicheskogo i sotsial'nogo razvitiia SSSR na 1986–1990 gody. Doklad Predsedatelia Soveta Ministrov SSSR deputata Ryzhkova N. I." (On the state plan of economic and social development of the USSR during 1986–1990. Report of the chairman of the Council of Ministers of the USSR, Deputy N. I. Ryzhkov), *Pravda*, June 19, 1986.

product group: the steel industry would handle the production of steel, the timber industry the production of sawn timber, the electric power industry the production of electric power. Gosplan is divided into departments that supervise ministries; Gosplan distributes products among ministries.

In most cases it appears that the responsible ministry produces more than half of its assigned products, but in some cases it is not much more. The fifty ministries that supervise production increasingly resemble self-sufficient conglomerates focused on the production of a narrow range of final products, supplemented by a range of intermediates and final products from a wide range of product groups. Planners support those trends in their effort to deal with shortages of food and consumer goods by requiring each enterprise to contribute to supplies. What planners do not support, but have been powerless to stop, is the more general tendency toward ministerial autarky, referred to in the Soviet literature as *vedomstvennosti* ("departmentalism").

Part of what is coming to constitute economic reform under Gorbachev is an effort to strengthen interministerial ties, by increasing specialization and interministerial trade, in order to increase efficiencies and stimulate technical change. However, the logic of the de facto system suggests that if ministries are to move voluntarily in the direction of opening up to other ministries, then the material-technical supply system will have to become far more secure and responsive than it now is. Otherwise *vedomstvennosti* will continue to be a rational response to the system as it now functions.

Economic Institutions outside the Formal System

By now it should be clear that enterprises must resort to a wide range of tactics, not all of them legal, if they are to fulfill their plans. As a result a set of institutions has developed outside the formal system through which enterprises do what they otherwise could not. Consumers are in a similar situation, finding that in many cases they have rubles, but the goods and services they wish to purchase are unavailable either in state stores and cooperatives or in legal private markets. Here, too, institutions have arisen to serve those needs outside the parameters of the formal system, and the law.

THE SHADOW ECONOMY. In the search for ways to fulfill their plan and meet the other needs of their enterprise, managers find it necessary to rely on what has been called the "shadow economy" to obtain goods and services that the official, or formal, system cannot supply.[40] There are no formal organizations in the shadow economy, only individuals and transactions. Yet together they constitute institutions that supplement Gossnab and Gosplan in ways that allow the system to perform better than it otherwise would.

Tolkachi are part of this system, assisting in or carrying out barter deals between enterprises, black market transactions, and bribes. *Shabashniki* (moonlighters) who provide construction services for cash are also a part of the system, allowing enterprises to undertake construction projects that the official system will not permit. The production of goods and services well outside the product mix of the enterprise is also part of the shadow economy.[41]

The case of V. Mizin, director of Tulachermet, illustrates what all of this can involve.[42] Tulachermet is a scientific-production association (combining in one organization research, testing, prototype, and serial production facilities), which presumably produces ferrous metal products. Mizin was pushing for the firm to expand, but could not receive approval for the investment projects he desired. He decided to go ahead anyway by relying on the shadow economy. He purchased a brick factory that had been closed down and used the workers in his research institute to bring it back into operation. *Tolkachi* were used to find concrete blocks in the neighboring *oblast'* and to forge an agreement with a concrete factory that it would supply concrete if Tulachermet would send the labor to operate a third shift. Other materials were acquired in a similar fashion, for example, by requesting more of some products in the planning process than Tulachermet required and then using those to barter for the needed products not available through the material-technical supply system. Mizin apparently managed in the end to have his new projects completed but at considerable cost and considerable

40. See Gregory Grossman, "The 'Shadow Economy' in the Socialist Sector of the USSR," in *The CMEA Five-Year Plans (1981–85) in a New Perspective: Planned and Non-Planned Economies* (Brussels: NATO Economics and Information Directorates, 1982), pp. 99–115.

41. Ibid.

42. See L. Obukhov and E. Mokhorov, "Zakon vedomstvennogo tiagoteniia" (The law of departmental gravitation), *Sots. ind.*, January 16, 1985.

risk. However, as the account of this enterprising manager's handiwork suggests, he had no other choice: "It was necessary to fulfill state tasks."[43]

Much of what Director Mizin did is illegal, yet it is also a type of activity familiar to the manager of any large Soviet factory. From the manager's vantage point, he has plan targets that he knows are of first importance to the center, and more specifically to his ministry and local party first secretary. He quite naturally does all in his power to fulfill those targets, relying (probably without thinking consciously about it) on a mix of legal and illegal devices, getting what he can from the planning system and the rest through the shadow economy. The planners know their enterprise directors are doing this; implicitly they expect it of them. An enterprise director would be a fool to "work according to rule" and fail to fulfill the plan because he chose not to rely on the shadow economy. He would either have to change his ways or lose his position. It would be equally foolish to minimize contact with the formal system; the safest, fully accepted behavior is to use the shadow economy only insofar as the formal system (including not only the ministry, but also local party officials) cannot, through legal channels, meet the enterprises' legitimate needs; namely, those created by plan targets.

No data are available by which to measure the contribution of the shadow economy to economic activity in the Soviet Union, nor are they likely to be constructed. Conceptually, the shadow economy makes possible a higher national income because surpluses and deficits created by the formal system are traded off outside the system, in its shadows, heading off what would otherwise be more severe bottlenecks. This translates into a "what if" question that is impossible for an outsider to answer and is unlikely to be asked or answered within the USSR. This also demonstrates that the anecdotes, entertaining as they may be, are of no use in analyzing the significance of the institutions involved.

THE SECOND ECONOMY. Consumers, like enterprises, have many needs that the formal system cannot meet. There is a wide range of clothing, services, food, and other commodities for which excess demand is persistent in the USSR. The problem is not, as noted in chapter 2, an across-the-board shortage of goods. Many goods are available in adequate quantities; some are in surplus. The problem is the shortage of high-quality goods, or goods embodying the latest technology. More-

43. Ibid.

over, services are almost universally in short supply and of variable, generally low quality.

Because consumers have money that they are willing to spend on these goods and services in short supply, there are substantial profits to be made for any individual willing to violate the laws on private economic activity or for any enterprise willing to engage in private economic activity on the side.[44] The result is what Grossman has called the "second economy," that being the sum of production and exchange that is directly for private gain or in known contravention of existing laws.[45] Several types of activity are involved here:[46] work by single artisans operating without the legally required license; use of the "putting-out" system to produce illegal products; private production on the job (for example, an employee in a state garage repairs a car for a fee); parallel production in a plant, using extra materials to produce unreported output distributed through the system using bribes; private, organized production in a state enterprise or collective farm; private underground manufacturing; construction by private teams (*shabashniki*); and brokering and information selling.

The important distinction between the second and shadow economics is that the former is based on the search for private gain. The shadow economy evolves from the enterprise directors' search for ways to meet their plan; it is the consequence of an effort to achieve the most important targets set in the formal system, at the cost of less important targets and norms. In the second economy the motivation is to make money. Enterprises are simply making goods on the side, outside the planning system, which they sell for profit. Here individuals are knowingly operating without a license and in some cases are undermining state monopolies in search of profits.

The two economies overlap in some areas. Enterprise managers making investments outside the plan in an effort to fulfill output targets may deal with *shabashniki* who are offering construction services as a team, in contravention of the law. Unneeded inventories accumulated

44. As noted in chapter 3, the legal limits for private activity are narrow, and even within those limits most activities require a license, which means a hefty income tax. The law clearly forbids enterprises and farms to enter into economic activity outside of that specified in the plan.

45. Gregory Grossman, "Notes on the Illegal Private Economy and Corruption," in U.S. Joint Economic Committee, *The Soviet Economy in a Time of Change*, Joint Committee Print, 96 Cong, 1 sess. (GPO, 1979), vol. 1, pp. 834–55.

46. Grossman, "Notes," pp. 837–39.

by an enterprise seeking to barter for needed goods not available in the formal system may be traded to other enterprises that need the goods for purposes of parallel production. The distinction is in the motives of buyers and sellers. As a result, the two economies are in fact intertwined.

There is no question that the second economy is important in the USSR, although its importance for economic activity is difficult to measure. Two Soviet authors estimate that second-economy services alone involve the labor inputs (not necessarily full-time) of 17–20 million persons (the higher figure being 15 percent of the 1984 labor force)[47] and account for 5–6 billion rubles in receipts a year. They also estimate that urban dwellers go to the second economy for about 45 percent (presumably in value terms) of their apartment repairs, half of clothing repairs, 30 percent of home appliance repairs, and 40 percent of auto repairs.[48]

The servicing of automobiles is an increasingly important activity in the second economy. In 1984 about 4 percent of the Soviet population owned automobiles, up from 0.5 percent in 1970.[49] State auto service centers, supervised by Minavtoprom (Automobile Industry) are widely regarded as inadequate in the quality and speed of service they offer and the stocks of spare parts. A survey by Mintorg (Trade) concluded that by 1982 only half of the automobile owners were using the state centers to service their automobiles. The remainder were relying on private services, which are faster, frequently of higher quality, and sometimes cheaper. Consumers also resort to the private market for about half of all spare parts purchases, frequently paying prices well above the official state price. Spare parts are generally in short supply, and those particularly in demand show a "remarkable ability . . . to secretly disappear from the stocks of stores and stations for technical service, and show up in the hands of speculators."[50]

Most Soviet consumers, like enterprise managers, rely on a mix of the formal economy and the range of de facto institutions to meet their needs. The second economy is important to them as it provides a way to circumvent state-determined priorities. The state has committed relatively little in the way of capital resources to the expansion of the capacity

47. *Narkhoz 1984*, p. 408.

48. G. Gukasov and V. Tolstov, " . . . i drugie zainteresovannye litsa" (. . . and other interested persons), *Izvestiia*, August 19, 1985.

49. "Lichnyy avtomobil'—ne lichnoe delo" (The personal automobile is not a personal matter), *EKO*, no. 5 (May 1985), table on p. 103.

50. G. N. Andrienko, "Legkovoi avtomobil' v sem'e" (The light automobile in the family), *EKO*, no. 5 (May 1985), p. 113.

to produce services. Thus it has created the incentive for private individuals to fill the gap, sometimes by diverting state resources from their intended uses.

If there was no second economy, possibly because law enforcement officials somehow managed to eradicate it, the supply of services would be inferior to what it now is. The supply of goods would be somewhat worse; in particular, the mix and distribution would be different. The precise decline in the supply of services and goods would presumably be less than the total value of second-economy services, if it is assumed that the theft of state time and materials ceased and therefore supplies from state outlets increased.

To imagine a world without the second economy is to engage in fiction, a fiction that Soviet leaders are too politically wise to contemplate. Instead, they have chosen to try to co-opt it through new laws on individual and cooperative activity, which are discussed in chapter 7.

AN OBSERVATION ON THE ENTREPRENEURIAL SPIRIT. This discussion on the shadow and second economies suggests an important and sometimes not sufficiently appreciated point about Soviet managers: one of the potentially formidable barriers to a successful radical economic reform in the USSR is the management cadre itself. Is it possible, one might ask, for managers who have been nurtured for a half-century by a central plan to suddenly accept the responsibility for their own actions, live with the uncertainty associated with markets, and take initiatives on their own? There is no simple answer to these questions, but at least part of the answer lies in the reality of the shadow economies.

It is true that Soviet enterprise directors do not face uncertainties concerning output markets that are the hallmark of private sectors in Western countries, nor do they face the risks associated with investment decisions in that uncertain environment. However, their uncertainty is palpable where input markets are concerned, and the reliance on the second and shadow economies suggests a willingness to take initiative and risk that might elude many businessmen educated in a different system. Similarly, the second economy suggests the existence of a private entrepreneurial spirit despite formidable barriers to private economic activity in the USSR.

The consequences of radical economic reform for Soviet managers have less to do with whether they can learn to live with uncertainty and more with what new skills they may have to develop as the uncertainty they face shifts from their dealings with the government and party hierarchies to their dealings with markets, and from input to output markets. It is also in that sense that the use of reforms to coopt portions of the de facto system seems promising for a leadership looking for inexpensive ways to improve performance.

The Information System

The divergences between formal and de facto institutions are particularly noticeable in the information system. Although the planning process represents a genuine effort to cope with horrendous amounts of information, it is simply not up to the task. This system is incapable of gathering reliable information in the necessary detail regarding production possibilities and true demands for goods. Moreover, it is poorly equipped to detect and react quickly to shortages and surpluses as they arise. Poor information leads to infeasible plans, or potentially feasible plans that individual economic units will tend to ignore because they know better than the center what the true possibilities are. That weakens central control over the system. Although the system may produce plans and there may be economic activity, the link between the two is not always clear as economic units use their room for maneuver to pursue their own goals.

The price system is consciously designed as a secondary mechanism supporting, not supplanting, the plan. For that reason it is focused on supply-side information and therefore cannot be an active institution identifying and reacting to shortages and surpluses, or changes in demand and supply that precede those conditions. Furthermore even as a source of supply-side information on changing relative costs, the system has glaring weaknesses. A fixed price system with tight rules on cost-based prices invites enterprises to introduce new products and obtain higher prices in the process. Soviet enterprises have accepted the invitation, and thus the de facto price system in the Soviet Union is a combination of some fixed prices and the prices that come out of a myriad of new prices set every year, only some of which are closely scrutinized by Goskomtsen.

Neither the planning nor price system is remotely adequate to monitor changing supply and demand conditions and to initiate reactions to them. In many cases this simply means that shortages or surpluses persist for what would be extraordinarily long time periods by the standards of a developed economy. But a set of institutions has arisen in the de facto economy that partly compensates, in a crude fashion, for the inadequacies of the planning and price systems as information systems.

The Planning System

Soviet economists frequently state, with an understandable lack of precision, that the Soviet economy produces about 24 million products.[51] That the number could be off by several million is of little consequence; it seems a reasonable approximation. In round numbers, there are about 50,000 enterprises in Soviet industry and 50,000 collective and state farms in agriculture. Therefore the average farm or enterprise produces roughly 240 products. Many of the products, probably the majority, are inputs into other products.

Nevertheless, Gosplan's task is to coordinate the production of the 24 million products in a way that at least fulfills or overfulfills targets for variables important to the leadership: output (aggregate and for important commodities), efficiency, balance of trade and payments, and quality. To attack the task on a commodity-by-commodity basis would require not only targets for each of the 24 million, but also knowledge of input requirements for producing each (the steel, plastic, rubber, and glass that goes into the production of an auto, along with the machinery and equipment required, and so on). In order to choose among investment options the center would also need to know the alternative ways each product could be produced (alternative possibilities to produce autos from steel, plastic, rubber, glass, and various types of machinery) so that it could make socially rational choices.

Impossible as this problem sounds, it probably understates the task facing Gosplan. The various interconnections implied in the wide range of choices are well beyond any conceivable set of capabilities Gosplan could hope for in this century. Indeed, even if Soviet authorities were given unrestricted access to the world's most advanced computer hardware, they would still be faced with an impossible task. Clearly Gosplan must compromise, devoting its scarce resources to address directly those decisions critical to the entire system and leaving to

51. See for example, the interview with N. P. Lebedinskii, a deputy chairman of Gosplan, "Distsiplina planirovaniia" (The discipline of planning), *Pravda*, September 21, 1983.

ministries and enterprises most of the decisions, according to rules designed to induce those bodies to decide as Gosplan officials would if they (the Gosplan officials) were faced with the detailed decisions made at lower levels and had all the information lower levels have.

How this planning system actually operates, which aspects of its operation actually affect economic activity, and which have little or no impact are all questions relating to Gosplan's compromises and their implications for the system. Michael Ellman surely goes too far when he compares Soviet planning to a "rationality ritual" that conveys "the illusion that the chaos we see around us is in fact part of a rational order . . . [and ascribes] to the priests (planners, economists and other technicians) and the rulers they serve, the function of bringing order out of chaos, of leading society to the Glittering Future."[52] But he does introduce a valuable note of caution into any study of links between the planning process and economic activity. The fact that plans are made and that economic activity then occurs need not mean that the two are closely linked in all, or even many, ways.

In fact Gosplan does have tremendous influence over the operation of the Soviet economy, but the sheer magnitude of its information problem limits that influence. In addition the compromises Gosplan has made to bring its information collection and computational capabilities into line with the task it faces may have been misguided, having the effect of reducing Gosplan's actual influence over economic activity relative to its conceivable influence if it had made all the right strategic choices in its compromises. The implication is that not all of Gosplan's obligatory plans or the elaborate procedures that produce them have an effect on the system, but some may. From the data in chapter 2 it appears that the five-year planning cycle has little influence on economic activity. Some evidence in the same vein can be compiled for the annual planning process. The crux of the matter lies in how Gosplan has chosen to make an otherwise impossible task possible and what evidence there is on how the resulting planning system affects economic activity.

GOSPLAN'S COMPROMISES. Gosplan has arrived at three important compromises in an effort to make its problem manageable: it attempts to control only a few commodities directly, leaving most of the commodity-by-commodity control to lower-level bodies; it relies heavily on planning on the margin (growth rates or absolute increments) to minimize the

52. Michael Ellman, "Changing Views on Central Economic Planning: 1958–1983," *ACES Bulletin*, vol. 25 (Spring 1983), p. 14.

information requirements; and it allows corrections to be made to plan targets that cannot be fulfilled to ensure that many specific targets are, ex post, fulfilled.

Delegation of authority. Gosplan's first and most obvious compromise was unavoidable. Gosplan directly controls output and distribution of only a few key commodities. In recent years its departments have, as indicated in chapter 3, computed balances for 2,000 commodities; Gossnab is responsible for another 15,000. Each of those numbers is quite "soft," and the total number of commodities controlled by Gosplan and Gossnab together could be 15,000 or 25,000. Furthermore, these numbers would surely be higher if they were tallied in the same way that the entire output of the economy is counted to reach an estimate of 24 million products. Nonetheless, the fact remains that Gosplan attempts to exercise direct control over only a tiny fraction of the products produced in the system.

Commodity-by-commodity control has instead been delegated to middle-level authorities. The fifty ministries, republican gosplans, and republican ministries divide among themselves all remaining products of national or regional importance. Targets for these products are determined within more general targets set by Gosplan for the output of key products in each ministry or republic, along with targets on the value of output, targets for key inputs (with explicit or implicit efficiency targets linking output to input), investment and foreign exchange limits, the quality of goods and services produced, and technical innovation in the sector.[53]

By reserving for itself full control over the intersectoral allocation of investment funds and foreign exchange (under the sometimes very tight supervision of the Politburo), Gosplan makes certain it has a say in the expansion of new capacity in the system. Ministries vie with each other for access to those scarce funds using arguments linked to their ability to meet targets for output, efficiency, and quality. Minugleprom (Coal)

---

53. Many of the products that the ministries plan are actually detailed varieties of those planned by Gosplan or Gossnab; another large group includes products intermediate to the ministry, for which the issue is not so much control as a proper estimate of detailed input-output coefficients. This bundle of detailed targets adds up to a set of constraints that reduce a ministry's room for maneuver, without removing it. For example, Minchermet (Ferrous metallurgy) receives a target for steel output and targets for the mix of steels produced. Its task is to determine detailed targets, theoretically in ways responsive to demands in the system, but the resulting outputs should at least add up to the value and quantity targets from Gosplan.

will argue for funds to build new mines and refurbish old ones; Minneft-prom (Oil) will argue instead for investments in oil production. Both will be facing machinebuilding ministries pleading for funds to enable them to modernize, one effect being energy conservation. All will make cases for imported equipment, cases that must be balanced against the use of hard currency for imports of food and intermediate goods.

The problem with the compromise on products is that it does not relieve Gosplan of the crushing information burden implicit in what it is expected to do. When Gosplan sets targets for growth in the value of outputs of each ministry, it is implicitly concerned with the output of particular products. What other reason can there be for setting growth rate targets for output in each of fifty ministries? When Gosplan sets efficiency indicators (labor inputs per unit of output, capital-output ratios, reductions in the use of key raw materials and fuels), it implies a knowledge of the possibilities available to each ministry to achieve such goals on a commodity-by-commodity basis. When Gosplan allocates investment funds among ministries, it is also allocating real machines and equipment and by implication is making choices among technologies.

In that sense it has not compromised. The question, then, is how does it nevertheless manage? Here there is the obvious potential to set plans that have little to do with reality.

Note also that ministries face the same problems Gosplan faces. They cannot possibly have sufficient information to specify in detail all outputs and inputs for their share of the 24 million products. They also must compromise, in this case giving some of their power to enterprises, but within general parameters that constrain enterprise choices.

Planning on the margin. For both Gosplan and the ministries a major component of the solution is planning on the margin, or "planning from the achieved level."[54] Anyone who has read Soviet plan documents is struck by the heavy reliance on growth rates and absolute increments, but particularly growth rates, to express targets. It is the growth rate of national income, investment, per capita real income, industrial production, and so on that receives attention. This could, of course, be simply the final outcome of a complex process that begins with recalculating all production possibilities, comparing them with current levels, and making

---

54. Igor Birman, "From the Achieved Level," *Soviet Studies*, vol. 30 (April 1978), pp. 153–72, provides an excellent discussion of this often-used phrase and the concept behind it.

choices among those that appear likely to generate the same or higher growth rates than those achieved in the previous year.

In fact, appearance and substance coincide here. Soviet authorities have quite naturally fallen into the practice of basing plans for next year's performance on increments related to this year's performance. There are adjustments, responding to clear signs of surplus or shortage (for example, investment acceleration responding to difficulties in the oil industry); and there are clear indications of relative priorities in the growth rates for particular sectors (for example, high growth rates for numerically controlled machinery). However, the general language of the plan is growth rates, from macro indicators down to indicators for individual enterprises (growth of output or sales, growth of labor productivity, growth of output of consumer goods, and so on). Gosplan communicates its expectations to ministries primarily through growth rates; ministries in turn deal with enterprises primarily via targets expressed as growth rates. Gossnab, which must actually issue rights to purchase certain quantities of products and issue orders to suppliers to sell them, still runs its balances on the basis of increments.

There is nothing surprising about this. Budgetary processes in Western governments work according to similar principles, as indicated by occasional attempts to go back to "zero-based budgeting." But it has the same inertial effects in the Soviet economy that it has in governments. The working assumption is that things will move "from the achieved level," with no automatic reconsideration of the wisdom of the achieved level. If energy efficiency in a factory improved 2 percent last year, then the plan will call for at least that improvement this year, probably more. If labor productivity in a particular ministry rose 3 percent last year, then this year should be at least that much, if not more.

The strength of this approach is its tendency, in the right hands, to produce plans that are not totally irrelevant. As long as this year's plans do not depart significantly from last year's achieved level, it should be possible to come within an acceptable range of the targets. On the other hand if there is something going on that planners do not understand, then the planning procedure runs the risk of recording hopes, rather than targets with a decent chance of fulfillment.

The best illustration of the operation of planning from the achieved level can be found in figures 2-2 through 2-6, which explore the link between planned and actual growth rates. Those figures clearly indicate how plans follow actual performance, seeming to "learn" from large deviations between actual and planned magnitudes; hence the tendency for annual plans to be reasonably close to actuals. Yet, because they are "learning" from actual performance, they lag behind it. And in the growth slowdown of the 1970s and 1980s this has meant that plans for output growth rates are frequently underfulfilled, whereas plans for investment growth rates tend to be overfulfilled.

However, given that tendency to miss changes and to have to correct during the next year, it is puzzling that ministries nevertheless manage to fulfill their output plans with almost monotonous regularity, and with surprisingly few exceptions.[55] Similarly, enterprises meet their plans frequently even though the system as a whole is falling well short of aggregate plan targets. The existence of this persistent inconsistency reflects the third compromise Gosplan (and in this case the ministries) has made: it allows plans to be corrected.

Plan corrections. Corrections are the last resort for planners faced with plans that obviously are not going to be fulfilled. They take two basic forms: a reduction in planned growth rates in order to match the plan, ex post, to the actual situation; and a change in plans within a year in an effort to change the supply or demand for a product in which imbalances are emerging.

The change in a plan target toward the end of a plan period simply to indicate the occurrence of fulfillment is apparently quite common, particularly in the plans for ministries, but also in some specific indicators for enterprises. N. P. Lebedinskii, a deputy chairman of Gosplan, describes the game well. "Many ministries, establishing lower plan indicators during the first half year, transfer the pressure to the second half, particularly to the last quarter, which artificially leads to an unrealistic series of plan tasks. And then the ministries turn to the corresponding organs with requests for corrections in the plan in the downward direction."[56]

Given the fact that planners are operating with a highly imprecise notion of what actual production possibilities are in the system, and thus are working from the achieved level, there is little they can do when faced with the reality that a plan they have devised will be substantially underfulfilled. Willingness to "learn" from last year's achievements

55. See Alice C. Gorlin and David P. Doane, "Plan Fulfillment and Growth in Soviet Ministries," *Journal of Comparative Economics*, vol. 7 (December 1983), pp. 415–31.
56. "Distsiplina planirovaniia."

translates into willingness to learn from last month's achievements, or failures; hence plan corrections.

The practice is similar for similar reasons in the relations between ministries and enterprises, and is strengthened by the symbiotic relationship between the two. Enterprises frequently find that with some effort they can convince their ministry to agree to amendments to their plan targets that will make them easier to achieve than they originally were. Indeed some regard the "battle for corrections" as a test of their strength, and the winning of corrections a badge of bureaucratic prowess.[57]

The general practice of corrections leads to many ex post inconsistencies in what was never a terribly consistent plan in the first place. One has already been mentioned: ministries can fulfill their plans while the major macro targets are underfulfilled. Similar phenomena are observed at the enterprise level. The first party secretary of Lithuania complains that nineteen of twenty-one enterprises in his republic significantly underfulfilled their delivery commitments while simultaneously overfulfilling their plans on sales as a result of corrections to the sales plans.[58]

Within-year plan corrections in response to an imbalanced plan are a constant phenomenon, and a major source of complaint within the system. If, for example, it becomes clear early in the year that targets for energy conservation are too ambitious, Gosplan may allow corrections, but at the same time will move to "correct" upward the plan for the output of various forms of energy. Or, a ministry may tell an enterprise that it can retain a certain amount of its depreciation funds for investment purposes, then change the target if it decides the money is needed elsewhere. These constant adjustments to the plan—what one Soviet author has referred to as an "epidemic" of corrections—are a major irritant within the system, especially for enterprises.[59] It provides them with a clear rationale for hiding reserves—aside from the rational flowing related to the practice of planning from the achieved level.

THE CONSEQUENCES OF GOSPLAN'S COMPROMISES. By using these compromises to reduce the informational requirements of its job, Gosplan has managed to maintain significant influence over economic activity.

57. V. F. Filippov, *Besedy o khoziaistvennom mekhanizme* (Conversations on the economic mechanism) (Moscow: Politizdat, 1984), p. 30.

58. P. P. Grishkiavichus, "Otvetstvennost' za dogovor" (Responsibility for the contract), *Ekon. gaz.*, no. 22 (May 1984).

59. Filippov, *Besedy*, p. 30.

Gosplan has real investment funds and controls the allocation of the most important products in deficit, both of which give it some influence over enterprises and the direction of economic activity. No matter how skillfully ministries and enterprises play the game of correcting plans, Gosplan, not the ministries and enterprises, sets the rules by which the game is played. It is therefore an exaggeration to suggest that the planning process is a ritual without meaning. It is probably far more appropriate to look at planning as a ritualized battle for real resources, the outcome of which has a major impact on the performance of the system.

This description of the system as it actually works helps to explain how this system manages to operate in the face of what appear to be insuperable odds. The fact is that planners resort to rules of thumb wherever possible in order to make their problem tractable. They are not in any conceivable sense optimizers. They are trying both to understand a highly complex system in constant movement and to influence it. And they are always behind the game, but never enough to say that they are out of it.

Notice also that the system is not as inflexible to intrayear perturbations as the description of the planning process would suggest. It is true that in this system the focus is on making major decisions once a year, but the plan corrections compensate for unforeseen circumstances, or for miscalculations. Although this explains how the system can react fairly quickly to a shock, it still indicates a fundamental weakness in the sense that the system does not have a regular, smoothly functioning mechanism by which to identify changes and respond to them.

It is another matter whether Gosplan is a government service that, to use the language of economists, has positive value-added. Does the presence of Gosplan, other things being equal, lead to increased national welfare, or even to increased national income? Because one of the other things remaining equal is the absence of a set of markets and flexible prices, the answer is probably yes, but to a very narrowly construed question. The broader question of whether a Gosplan making different compromises might contribute to higher economic welfare is more interesting, and, in effect, the question behind efforts to reform the system.

The operation of the de facto planning system suggests two good reasons for economic reforms. First, a rational enterprise director or minister in this system will go to considerable lengths to hide the production capabilities of his enterprise or the enterprises in his ministry. Planners have an automatic adversarial relationship with lower levels, which is a direct consequence of planning from the achieved level and of the corrections designed to adjust to imbalanced plans. This is clearly the opposite of the intended result, and much of the history of reforms is a story of attempts by leaders to find a formula that would induce lower levels to reveal hidden reserves.

Second, the constant increase in the complexity of the system is eroding the effectiveness of Gosplan's devices for compromising. The economy is not standing still; the information problem is growing worse. Already weak, Gosplan's grip on the reality of the system grows weaker; and the bargaining power of the enterprises and ministries grows stronger. That also motivates the search for a system that will reassert the strength of the center, but through a different set of compromises.

The Price System

The price system is one area in which the formal design and actual practice are relatively close, although there are still important areas of divergence. The set of weakly interconnected price subsystems, with prices fixed for long periods and driven primarily by supply-side considerations, exists in reality in the USSR. When the world price of oil drops from $30 to $10 a barrel, there is no impact on domestic wholesale or retail prices for crude oil or its products; nor will a price rise have any effect. A shift in demand for a product causes no change in its state price—indeed, there is no mechanism to accommodate that—but rather long lines, and possibly associated bribes. On those infrequent occasions when a general price revision occurs, it is production costs alone, and not demand elements, that enter into decisions on the new prices. Production in excess of current demand does not result in a price decline for the producer. Therefore, the price system is in fact, as well as in theory, not used to signal emerging disequilibriums.

Several factors have combined to create pressures that drive de facto price determination away from the system as designed. As a result the system contains even less information than the modest, narrowly defined information that planners are seeking.

GOSKOMTSEN'S COMPROMISES. Like Gosplan, Goskomtsen is forced to make compromises.[60] It is infeasible for Goskomtsen and its republican

---

60. In discussing Goskomsten here, I refer both to the all-union organization and its

departments to set prices on all new products. In fact most prices in the USSR are set not by Goskomtsen, but by enterprises and ministries, according to rules issued by Goskomtsen. Goskomtsen's role here is to enforce rules; apparently it actually sets prices for only a few products, primarily raw materials, fuels, and food.

But even as an enforcer, Goskomsten has an enormous job, and presumably many of the price proposals it considers receive only brief attention. As it is, Goskomtsen considers approximately 200,000 price proposals per year, which averages out to 770 price proposals per working day, or three to four price decisions per day for every price specialist in Goskomtsen.[61] According to one source, that is only 42 percent of the prices proposed; the remainder of what are presumably about 500,000 price proposals per year are handled by ministries or other authorities.[62] Goskomtsen reportedly responds to 90 percent of the price applications within two to three weeks, and 99 percent within three to four weeks, of receipt.[63]

It is difficult to believe that Goskomtsen gives serious consideration to any but a few of that 42 percent of proposals. It is probably forced to make decisions on which proposals to explore in depth in much the same way that the U.S. Internal Revenue Service decides on which tax returns to audit, by searching for apparent oddities (relatively high costs for a particular input, high price relative to similar products, and so on). Computers are probably relatively lightly used as of yet. It is more likely that the core of the system is the human equivalent: specialists in the prices of particular groups of products who develop a "feel" over the years for reasonable and unreasonable prices for "their" products.[64] For relatively small anomalies price authorities may do a cursory check and reduce price proposals by a small amount, and for a few they may carry out the full review.[65]

republican offices, the latter taking on much of the burden relating to the prices of products of less than national importance.

61. N. Petrakov, V. Volkonskii, and A. Vavilov, "Tsena: Nuzhny krutye izmenenia" (Price: radical changes are needed), *Sots. ind.*, April 3, 1987.

62. I. Lipsits, "Tsena izdeliia" (The price of a product), *Pravda*, September 6, 1985.

63. V. I. Shprygin, "Kak sozdat' protivozatratnyi bar'er?" (How to create an anti-cost barrier?), *Ekon. gaz.*, no. 32 (August 1986).

64. Recall, for example, the work by the Ukraine Goskomtsen (see chap. 3, n. 49) in which an initial check of prices of comparable products produced by other factories suggested the price was too high, after which an extensive audit of the price proposal revealed a number of irregularities.

65. This is, I suspect, what would happen if, as one Soviet economist reports, Goskomtsen had to correct two-thirds of the price proposals it received because they

This means that in effect most prices actually set in the USSR between price revisions are probably proposed by enterprises, but are still consistent with the general parameters for prices of similar products. This is the price equivalent of "planning from the achieved level," which has the same advantages and disadvantages it has for the planning process. For enterprises, much as for tax evaders in the United States, the goal is not to trigger an audit. For the price authorities, the goal is to convince enterprises that audits are plentiful, easy to trigger, and thorough.

Most important is the fact that the system tends to perpetuate high prices in sectors that have relatively high prices by world standards, or by standards of what is possible. As one persistent critic of the system notes, it ratifies inefficiencies and hides reserves.[66] The price specialist for each category of goods only has Soviet producers as his referent; if a particular branch is generally inefficient, then the best the price specialist can do is to "lean" toward prices that reflect below-average costs in the branch.

Given the way this system operates, the clear incentive is for enterprises to introduce new products, even if they are not new. This allows them to propose new prices, which probably mean higher profits for them, with only a small risk that Goskomtsen will spend the time to find out if the product is really new and if the proposed price is justified.

THE ECONOMIC ENVIRONMENT AND THE SELLERS' INTEREST IN HIGH PRICES. A second important factor placing a wedge between the formal and de facto price-determination mechanisms is the economic environment itself. Economic power is highly concentrated in a few enterprises in each sector, with high barriers to entry and no effective competition from imports. Enterprises are primarily concerned about plan fulfillment, not costs, since cost overruns are much more easily forgiven than violations of plan targets. The result is a sellers' market in a general climate of excess demand flowing as a natural consequence of the constant pressure for high growth rates. In this context the inability of Goskomtsen to control prices allows producers to inflate prices without opposition from buyers, who in fact even formally agree to such rises.[67]

were too high. A. Komin, "Tseny na novuiu tekhniku" (The price for new capital goods), *Sots. ind*, June 6, 1986.

66. See N. Petrakov, "Tsena—rychag upravleniia" (Price—tool of management), *Ekon. gaz.*, no. 16 (April 1986).

67. It is a common complaint in the Soviet literature that when price authorities discover inflated prices, they frequently discover that buyers readily accepted those

Goskomtsen's fragmentary control over the process combined with the effective power of the seller is particularly important because sellers have a strong interest in high and increasing prices. In part the interest stems from the importance of the value of output, net normative output, or sales (which one depends on the time period and the industry) as a bonus-forming indicator.[68] Hidden inflation swells any of these indicators, reducing the effort necessary to fulfill sales or output targets, and thereby reducing the effort necessary to fill bonus accounts in the enterprise.[69] Even a shift to higher-priced products within the year can inflate the output or sales indicator, so that Soviet enterprises will prefer the high-priced end of their output mix.[70] Notice that the corollary of this interest is a distinct lack of enthusiasm for decreasing the cost of output, hence the value of output, sales, or net normative output. Reductions of that sort increase the difficulty of fulfilling the plan and forming bonus accounts.

Enterprises also have a direct interest in high profits, although they assume only a fraction of the importance of plan fulfillment, and that, too, can lead them to seek higher prices. At a minimum, enterprises strive to be profitable in order to avoid the stigma of reporting losses and the difficulties of negotiating with authorities for subsidies. Price officials show great sympathy for that concern. One clear motivation during price revisions is to make sure that most enterprises come out profitable.[71]

---

prices. It was discovered, for example, that Mistankoprom (Machine Tools and Tool Building) had, with the agreement of its customers, inflated by an average of 30 percent the prices of over 100 types of forges and presses (Komin, "Tseny na novuiu tekhniku"). See also Shprygin ("Kak sozdat' protivozatratnyi bar'er?"), who reports on research by the Research Institute on Prices showing that on the average one-half of the price proposals reaching Goskomtsen, after they were approved by sellers, buyers, and—where required—the State Committee for Science and Technology, were inflated by 10–30 percent; one-tenth of the proposals were inflated by more than 50 percent. He also comments that even after sellers admitted to inflating their initial proposed prices, in many cases their amended proposals were still significantly inflated relative to actual production costs.

68. Net normative output, which is to be discussed in more detail in chapter 5, is the value added in producing a product, where the value-added weights are not actual but the normed labor inputs for a particular industry.

69. It is clear how hidden inflation would raise the sales or output indicators. Net normative output also provides opportunities as enterprises negotiate with the center over what norms are appropriate for a "new" product.

70. Since 1980 an increasing number of enterprises have been switched to an indicator linking net normative output directly to the wage fund, which increases the incentive to shift to costly products within the mix.

71. As Morris Bornstein notes, for example, a major signal of the need for price

This is not an absolute requirement. After the 1982 price reform, 13 out of every 100 enterprises in industry were still incurring losses, including one-half of the enterprises in Minugleprom (Coal), one fourth of those in Minudobrenii (Fertilizer), and a significant number of enterprises in construction materials, food, timber, and other sectors.[72] Nonetheless, it is an important consideration for authorities.[73]

CONSEQUENCES OF THE PRICE SYSTEM IN OPERATION. The price system is supposed to provide planners with an accurate reading of relative costs of production that will be useful in making choices and in evaluating the performance of enterprises. In fact it falls far short of that goal. Enterprises have a clear motive to inflate prices, and Soviet authorities generally acknowledge that fact. The result is a constant game between price authorities and the enterprises in which the enterprises look for ways to raise prices and the authorities, aware of that urge, seek to control it. Official Soviet price indexes are so few and so flawed that we have no official information on the rate of inflation that this system allows. As indicated in chapter 2, there is evidence of a significant rate of inflation. On the other hand, things are not by any means out of control. The combination of Goskomtsen's rules, the threat of an audit, and the relatively common price corrections seem to add up to a system that keeps the lid on the price level. As one Soviet economist has noted, Goskomtsen appears to be this system's major line of defense against high rates of inflation.[74]

From the economic point of view, probably a more serious problem is that the system tends to favor individualized deals between each enterprise and the center. The goal is to set prices that reflect branch average costs, but in fact there is considerable evidence that quite

---

revisions in the late 1970s was the falling profit rates in extractive industries. See Morris Bornstein, "The Soviet Industrial Price Revision," in G. Fink, ed., *Socialist Economy and Economic Policy: Essays in Honour of Friedrich Levcik* (Vienna: Springer Verlag, 1985), p. 160.

72. G. Chubakov, "Tsena i plan" (Price and plan), *Ekon. gaz.*, no. 17 (April 1986).

73. Aside from a desire to avoid losses, enterprises have good reasons to strive for high profits, the easiest way being to raise prices. Profitability (as a percentage of capital) is a direct success indicator for some enterprises. It is the source of payments into enterprise accounts. And, on an informal basis, high profits are probably a useful bargaining chip when the enterprise is applying to the ministry for authorizations on large investment projects. Berliner noticed this in his interviews with Soviet emigrés who had worked in Soviet enterprises before the war, and it seems likely that it is still the case today. See Joseph S. Berliner, "The Informal Organization of the Soviet Firm," *Quarterly Journal of Economics*, vol. 66 (August 1952), p. 352.

74. See Lipsits, "Tsena izdeliia."

possibly most prices for manufactured goods reflect not branch but individual enterprises' costs of production, and thus weaken the pressure on enterprises to economize.[75] As a result, it is even radical now to argue that prices should be set strictly on the basis of average costs of production in a branch—even though that is the formal requirement for the system—because the effect would be to render unprofitable half the output of that product.[76]

Demand considerations are almost as irrelevant in the de facto system as they are in the formal system. The persistent high demand for the output of most enterprises may only provide the means to raise prices; but the prime motive is to reduce the effort required to fill enterprise accounts. Of course if the economic environment was different and enterprises encountered resistance from the center or customers in attempts to inflate the value of sales, then the desire to feed enterprise accounts could translate into an effort to reduce costs. That, in turn, could introduce into the system demand-side pressure on prices. But the environment has taken its present form for virtually all of the history of Soviet central planning, and unless it is changed, the incentives to ignore demand considerations are tremendous.[77]

Other Information Mechanisms

The planning system, although somewhat more flexible than the formal description would suggest, has few mechanisms to identify shortages and distribute scarce goods among competing users. The price system is certainly little help in that regard. Other mechanisms must be allowing enterprises to sense increasing scarcities and react to them. Otherwise the system simply would not work as well as it does.

Although little systematic research has been done on these mechanisms, at least one path-breaking study has been carried out by Raymond Powell, who was fascinated by the cindynophobic (ability to avoid

75. A. Buzhinskii, "Obosnovannost' urovnia tseny" (The validity of the price level), *Ekon. gaz.*, no. 8 (April 1986); and Petrakov, "Tsena—rychag upravleniia."

76. The more traditional remedy suggested by economic theory—marginal cost pricing—can lead to disastrous results in a system dominated by sellers who are negotiating with the center, since basically they can use marginal costs to justify prices far above the average for the branch without any fear that buyers will shun them. See Chubakov, "Tsena i plan."

77. A point made, for example, by Lipsits in "Tsena izdeliia."

danger) character of the Soviet system.[78] He concluded that enterprises rely on a surprisingly large number of indicators to signal scarcities. "For a given decision, they may include money price and other money costs of acquisition; psychic costs of time and effort and risk of penalty; quantity indicators in the form of physical stocks and flows, queue lengths in their various manifestations; and verbal messages of entreaty, threat, etc. Information may come free, or it may be acquired at a cost. Its vehicle may be anything from a formal official report to a wink of the eye or a shrug of the shoulders."[79]

Powell's point is a critical one. Faced with an "inactive" price system and an imperfect planning system, enterprise management has been forced to develop other mechanisms for sensing scarcity and dealing with it. The shadow economy provides a considerable amount of information on scarce products, but the official system can do so as well.

Even here, however, the system tends to be asymmetrical. It sends far clearer signals on emerging shortages than it does on emerging surpluses; and it sends higher-quality information on physical shortages than it does on inefficiencies (although those may lie at the source of shortages). In that the de facto system cannot compensate for the failings of the formal system. It is the way this system forgives persistent surpluses, as well as persistent shortages, that forms part of the agenda for economic reform.

The Incentive System

Enterprises and individuals face a complex set of incentives in the de facto system, only some of which are intended incentives in the formal system. The constant pressures from above for improved performance, combined with the extraordinarily complex regulations and the persisting shortages, create a complicated and rich milieu in which individuals, the enterprises, ministries, and central organs find themselves in a never-ending game in which they are motivated to do things that outsiders sometimes consider strange.

The central institution in the entire system is the enterprise, the basic unit through which society brings together the labor force and capital to

78. See Raymond P. Powell, "Plan Execution and the Workability of Soviet Planning, *Journal of Comparative Economics*, vol. 1 (March 1977), pp. 51–76.
79. Ibid., p. 61.

produce goods and services. The enterprise hires labor and sets up the incentives that by and large determine how the labor force functions. Plans revolve around enterprises, which are used to control the composition of the aggregate supply of national income and the demand for that national income. By understanding the world of the enterprise as it actually exists, one can understand a great deal about the incentives that drive actors in the system and therefore the system itself.

Formally the system appears to be a conceptually neat, if extraordinarily bureaucratic, incentive system created by the state to entice enterprises to reveal their true production possibilities so that they can be used in the most efficient way possible to fulfill centrally determined plans. Enterprises operate in the context of bonus rules linking what they do to possible bonuses. They respond, and the bonuses result. Dysfunctional behavior leads to modifications in the bonus schemes. Pathological behavior can trigger a new reform.

The de facto system differs from this formal description in several fundamental ways. First, because the center wants so many things, not all of which are consistent with each other, enterprise management is forced to choose which parts of the plan to fulfill and which to violate. In essence the life of an enterprise manager in the Soviet Union is a constant flow of economic triage decisions for which the plan offers little help; thus informal communication with all levels of the party and government hierarchy is essential. Sometimes managers must rely on subtle indications of which targets are truly important to the center and which are expendable.

Second, enterprise directors have personal motives as well as the desire to meet the needs of their enterprise and the objectives of their local party and government officials. The resulting goals need not, and usually do not, coincide with those of the center. As might be expected, enterprise management attempts to fulfill the indicators judged most important to the center in ways that best serve the other complex motives of enterprise management.

These two factors give rise to another distinction: the central planners, faced with the de facto inconsistency of their assigned objectives and the efforts of managers to serve many motives, begin to make special deals with each enterprise, through the ministries. The resulting relationship between the state and enterprises is far more complex and individualized than the regulations would suggest, as both sides are forced by circumstances to reach a tacit agreement that they will ignore regulations and norms in the service of higher goals. The enterprise must therefore pay constant attention to bureaucratic politics; the assiduous enterprise manager is rewarded with considerable benefits that may not even be achievable under the regulations. However, it is an arbitrary system in which published regulations are obeyed irregularly and unpredictably. The successful "entrepreneur" in this system is not a person who develops new products and new technologies, but one who successfully develops a workable relationship with the government and party authorities supervising his enterprises.

The Enterprise Director as a Master of Triage

Regulations governing the indicators included in enterprise plans are extraordinarily complex and are changed with some frequency, although the fundamental structure of the system has remained intact since it was set in the 1965 reforms. I discuss here the system as it existed in the mid-1980s, leaving to chapter 5 an account of how procedures changed in the 1960s and 1970s.

The targets conveyed to enterprises in their five-year and annual plans are set by ministries, which are guided by general regulations outlining ministerial rights in this area. Each enterprise receives a set of targets from the annual plan, which is the operational plan from its point of view. These targets may be divided into the following categories.[80]

1. Output, including the output in physical units of the most important products, the volume of normative net output, sales (to measure contract fulfillment), and the growth of output of goods in the highest-quality category.

2. Labor productivity, the size of the labor force, and the size of the wage fund.

3. Finance, including targets on the cost of production, limits on expenditure of materials per unit of output, and profits and payments to the state budget.

4. Capital construction, including targets for additions to capacity from new machinery and modernization of existing plant.

5. Technological progress, including targets for the R&D program of the enterprise, for the introduction of new technologies embodying

80. M. G. Greshchak and others, *Sovershenstvovanie planirovaniia na promyshlennom predpriiatii* (The improvement of planning in the industrial enterprise) (Kiev: Tekhnika, 1983), pp. 19–20; and Filippov, *Besedy*, p. 65.

increased efficiencies, and for the organization of production processes and management.

6. Inputs, including deliveries of key inputs linked to plan fulfillment, and targets for reductions in the use of key inputs.

The center mandates which indicators of this group are most critical to measures of output, quality, and labor productivity for all enterprises. Beyond that, ministries have substantial latitude on particular indicators they use for their enterprises, although they must bear in mind the performance indicators by which Gosplan judges their branch total output, output for key products, productivity, and quality.

Numerous specific targets are formed in each of these categories, which can easily add up to several hundred obligatory targets, ranging from indicators of overall activity of the enterprise (profits or sales) to the smallest details of the enterprise operation. The head of a metallurgical enterprise complained that of the more than 100 indicators in his plan, 28 were for the output of specific products, and 15 of those products were intermediate products used only within the enterprise.[81] Similarly, one of the top managers in the Kama Truck Association—a premier Soviet enterprise built primarily with Western technology—complained that the organization receives a plan with 150 targets. As with the metallurgical plant, the targets include a number of detailed products that are only shipped between factories within the association.[82] G. F. Beliakov, the head of Leningrad's Nevsky Factory, complained recently of having to cope with 300 specific targets.[83]

The most striking characteristic of this system of targets is that an entity outside the enterprise attempts to control its entire operation, specifying not only final results, but also intermediate results, which are inextricably intertwined. The plan specifies total wages *and* wage rates; total output *and* the output of key products, including intermediates; labor productivity *and* the introduction of new technologies. The several hundred indicators and their myriad interconnections guarantee that the enterprise director will face an inconsistent plan. If the ministries knew enough about enterprise production capabilities to specify the structure

81. "Govoriat uchastniki vstrechi v TsK KPSS," (Participants speak in a meeting of the CC of the CPSU), *Sots. ind.*, April 12, 1985. The speaker was B. I. Kolesnikov, director of the Norilsk Mining and Metallurgical Kombinat.

82. G. Popov and V. Shcherbakov, "Podriad dlia zavoda" (Contract for a factory), *Pravda*, June 8, 1985.

83. See chapter 3.

of outputs accurately and to identify the key links between inputs and outputs, they would not have to rely on plans with bonuses for overfulfillment and penalties for underfulfillment. In fact they know much less than they need to know, and the plan tends to contradict itself.

The enterprise may find, for example, that to meet the targets for increased quality of output it will have to violate targets requiring that the use of key inputs be reduced. The plan to introduce new technologies may conflict with the plan for outputs of key products, since the introduction of new technologies can easily involve interruptions in factory operations. The plan to increase the output of certain products may violate targets for the output of intermediate products. The plan to increase labor productivity may conflict with restraints on wage levels. The list is endless.

What it goes to show is that enterprise directors must choose which targets to violate and which to try to fulfill. Their choices will be based on their assessment of which targets are truly important to the ministry; that judgment in turn is determined by the indicators to which Gosplan attaches the most importance. The bonus schedules themselves give important signals; only a few of the targets actually form inputs into bonus determination, and of those only a few determine the majority of bonuses. In addition to issuing bonus regulations, ministries make clear to enterprises in many ways what the truly important indicators are.

Historically the list of critical targets has been short and stable: the growth of total output and the output of key products. Factory managers who are contemplating violating those targets, even in order to fulfill other targets, risk the ire of their ministry in much the way that is depicted in Aleksandr Avdeenko's story of the deputy director of a large metallurgical combine who has decided to push ahead with the reconstruction of his factory. " 'You've gone in for reconstruction,' they think up there [in the ministry]. 'Fine. That's all to your greater glory. But be so kind as to fulfill your quotas of cast iron, steel and rolled metal as you did previously, before reconstruction. If you don't improve your basic work in the next few days, we'll tighten the purse strings.' And they do. They cut bonuses. Or don't give them at all. . . . That's what reconstruction means if you look into it."[84]

The existence of several hundred indicators and the rhetoric surround-

84. Aleksandr Avdeenko, "The Sweat of One's Brow," excerpt in Martin Crouch and Robert Porter, eds., *Understanding Soviet Politics through Literature: A Book of Readings* (London: Allen and Unwin, 1984), p. 114.

ing them suggest that although output indicators are vitally important to planners, many other things are significant, indeed too many things. Moreover, there have been periods in which regulations have signaled a move away from output indicators toward indicators of efficiency and quality (these are discussed in more detail in chapter 5). All the same, the factory manager must try to see through the new regulations and accurately assess what is truly important to his ministry. Even if the new regulations accurately express a shift in the underlying priorities in the system, the wise factory manager treats the new situation as no more than a working hypothesis to be tested in the course of day-to-day negotiations with the ministry.

It is not decrees and resulting regulations that ultimately determine the true priorities associated with the mass of plan indicators. Rather, it is the underlying logic of the system expressed in the way planners seek to control the system and the resulting performance criteria the center uses to judge ministries and party secretaries. The main concern today, as in the past, is to control and coordinate production on a commodity-by-commodity basis. That is how the system generates plans for the output of key products; that is what drives the interest in increases in output. As long as Gosplan judges ministries (and local first party secretaries) by those few output indicators, those will be first priority for ministries, first party secretaries, and enterprise managers.

The Problem of Fulfilling the Indicators

The reasoning implicit in the system of targets used in the formal system, although not made explicit by Soviet economists, nevertheless exerts a powerful influence on the way the system operates and the way that economists and their leaders think about the system. It begins with the assumption—which is almost universally accepted in the USSR, at least by those who make policy—that no single enterprise performance indicator can adequately convey the diverse objectives the state has for enterprises. This does not necessarily constitute a defense of several hundred targets, but it does indicate little support for the notion, say, that profits are appropriate as the sole indicator of an enterprise's success. In its most extreme form this assumption asserts that enterprises will only do what the state wishes if targets are set for them, and will do many things contrary to state wishes if they are not explicitly forbidden to do so.

The second assumption, which is really an article of faith, is that everything important to the state is measurable. Outputs, whether they are apples, drafting services, research, or computer production, are all measurable and therefore can be controlled by targets in the plan. Output quality can be measured to ensure that enterprises will not only increase output, but also quality. Efforts to introduce new technology, save energy, protect the environment, develop new products can all be measured, and controlled by targets. All outputs and the efforts that go into their production can satisfactorily be measured. It is possible therefore to specify the quantity and quality of goods and services to be produced, to ensure that they are produced efficiently, and to induce enterprises to constantly innovate in the output mix and production processes they use. Bonuses can be attached to all these indicators to signal the state's priorities, should enterprise directors find a need to choose. The idea is that this is *possible,* not that the current system of indicators actually does that perfectly; hence the constant need to "perfect" the system.

The final assumption is that, where quantitative indicators leave room for doubt, and therefore for maneuver by the enterprise, moral incentives (supplied by the local party apparatus) will induce enterprise management to fulfill the spirit, not merely the letter, of the targets. If there are two ways to increase the quality of a product, both of which would satisfy quantitative quality targets and earn bonuses but one of which would clearly benefit society more than the other, the enterprise director will choose correctly from society's point of view. This is in part an assumption that spontaneous goodwill on the part of managers will lead them to make an effort to "read" the spirit of the plan and strive to fulfill it. In addition it is presumed that party officials will, in the course of their duty, nourish that spirit of goodwill.

All three assumptions have their weaknesses. The greater the number of indicators, the more room for maneuver by enterprises. The assumption that everything is quantifiable is obviously flawed; yet Soviet leaders stubbornly adhere to it and thus keep the entire system of targets and bonuses in fairly constant flux as they search for what can never be found. The third basic assumption actually consists of two ideas: that somehow one can induce enterprise managers to adhere to the spirit of targets that are otherwise ambiguous out of good faith and that such a good faith effort will adequately compensate for ambiguities in the incentive system. Both are problematic.

Without even referring to Soviet experience, a moment's reflection suggests how difficult it is for any central authority to quantify the activities of enterprises in a way that unambiguously identifies what is "good" or "bad" from the point of view of the state. How does one measure, for example, the output of computers and thereby set targets? Using the value of computer output invites the production of expensive, but possibly not very good, computers. Simply manufacturing computers that have old transistors and tubes, which are now expensive to make, would generate high value output totally counter to social interests. Computing power, measured possibly in nanoseconds required to make a computation, is a possible indicator, but would probably result in computers that are fast, but that have few other redeeming characteristics (such as flexibility or memory). A mixture of indicators outlining the basic capabilities deemed desirable in a computer would be a potential solution, but for most products there are generally enough characteristics so that planners cannot specify all of them.

The problem is that even managers with the best of intentions are drawn quite naturally to try to maximize the indicators and therefore will tend to ignore product characteristics or aspects of their operation not specified in the plan. Furthermore, unless planners are extraordinarily lucky and skillful, managers will find ways to fulfill the indicator(s) but shortchange other variables of concern to the center.

The Soviet economic system is rich with examples of distortions caused by relying on quantitative indicators to measure enterprise activities. In research institutes attached to industry, budget utilization, not project completion, has been the main performance indicator. In many cases the result is much research and little output.[85] Design bureaus, which are judged by the number of designs they produce, are flooded with designs, most of which embody few new ideas, a great deal of obsolete technology, and a low level of standardization (because standardization would reduce the number of designs required).[86] Enter-

85. Ronald Amann and Julian Cooper, eds., *Industrial Innovation in the Soviet Union* (Yale University Press, 1982), p. 14. One recent, extreme illustration is a research institute in Minstankoprom (Machine tools) with a 600-person staff that had generated two patentable inventions over the last nine years of its existence. Nikolai Ryzhkov announced its closing in his speech on the Twelfth Five-Year Plan: "O gosudarstvennom plane" (see note 39).

86. On the bias against standardization, see Amann and Cooper, eds., *Industrial Innovation*, p. 14. Ryzhkov in the speech cited in n. 39 indicated that a survey of designs for new factories approved by machinebuilding ministries showed that half needed significant revision to bring technologies up to current levels, and 10 percent were not worth continuing, "O gosudarstvennom plane."

prises producing durables also receive targets for the production of spare parts, but the targets are in rubles. Therefore they concentrate on the spare parts easiest to produce, irrespective of consumer needs. The output of many important manufactured products is still measured in simple units (numbers of computers or numerically controlled machines), with the result that enterprises are induced to focus on quantity, not quality.

The main game between the planners, ministries, and enterprises is not over quantities per se, which are so important—both formally and de facto—that enterprises tend to fulfill those targets. Rather, the problem is that enterprises tend to compromise on quality or ignore customers' needs, or allow input usage to go out of control. Planners respond with other indicators or procedures designed to reduce enterprises' room for maneuver. The dynamic of that battle explains much of the history of efforts to reform the economy over the last quarter century and the tendency for targets to proliferate.

The game between enterprises and the state over measuring product quality illustrates the pitfalls of the Soviet approach. The key instrument used to measure output quality and to reward or penalize improving or deteriorating quality is the quality certification system. Since the late 1960s Soviet planners have developed an increasingly elaborate system for checking the quality of enterprise outputs, which they classify as highest (which receives a seal of quality, or *znak kachestva*), first, or second.[87] The highest category includes products up to the best world standards, and the first category contains products up to best Soviet standards. The second category has not been recognized since 1984, although many products that would be classified as such are produced.[88] The certification system is now being modified under Gorbachev, but the essence of the system remains unchanged: quality certification boards representing consumers, producers, and technical experts review products and certify their quality. Only the most important output of the system goes through this process. By 1983, 80,000 products were certified as being in the highest category.[89]

A plan indicator for ministries and therefore enterprises since 1971

87. The first *znak kachestva* was awarded on April 22, 1967, to an electric motor produced by the Vladimir Il'ich electromechanical factory in Moscow. Filippov, *Besedy*, p. 104–09, provides an account of this system.
88. I. Isaev, "Plan, standart, kachestvo" (Plan, standard, and quality), *Planovoe khoziaistvo*, no. 12 (December 1983), p. 15.
89. Filippov, *Besedy*, table on p. 105.

has been the share of highest-quality products in their mix, or the growth of goods with that certification.[90] Ministries also receive targets for producing new items.[91] In addition various schemes have been used in recent years to raise the prices that enterprises receive for products achieving the highest-quality certification.[92] Each enterprise has a quality control department charged with ensuring that enterprise output is up to state standards.[93] All of this is designed to ensure that enterprises will not meet their output indicators by reducing the quality of output.

Although this approach to quality control has not led to failure, neither has it led to success. Enterprises and ministries have naturally focused their efforts on the indicators, not quality per se, or the preferences of their customers for goods with particular qualities. Quality control boards are overloaded and not always staffed with the best specialists, and presumably are forced to rely on sellers' documentation and judgment to make a decision. The result has been an indeterminate, but presumably large, number of products that clearly fall short of world standards, and the introduction of "new" products that actually incorporate minor modifications of previous models.[94] Products that may have deserved certification in their prototype versions fall short of standards in serial production as the quality control departments in the enterprise allow them to slip through.[95]

Aside from the possibilities for enterprise maneuvers, another weakness of the quality control system is an inherent bias toward supply-side quality indicators. In those industries where competitive pressures are strong in Western countries, enterprises are constantly engaged in a search for goods and services that meet the needs of consumers. Many products that would surely be acceptable by the standards of quality in the Soviet system fail because consumers reject them for competing products. Because enterprises need to survive, they learn from that or

90. Jan Adam, "The Present Soviet Incentive System," *Soviet Studies*, vol. 32 (July 1980), p. 357; and Filippov, *Besedy*, p. 66.

91. Isaev, "Plan, standart, kachestvo," p. 11.

92. Bornstein, "Soviet Industrial Price Revision," p. 164.

93. These are the *Otdeli tekhnicheskogo kontrolia* (Departments of technical control). See, for example, V. Trapeznikov, "Eshche raz o kachestve, tekhnicheskom progresse i stimulakh" (One more time on quality, technical progress and stimuli), *Pravda*, October 2, 1985.

94. Isaev, "Plan, standart, kachestvo," p. 15.

95. The director of the quality control department (OTK) is paid premiums according to the same criteria as plant managers, which clearly places him in an awkward position. Trapeznikov, "Eshche raz o kachestve."

they fail. The result is a demand-driven, unforgiving, quality-control environment.

In the Soviet system the survival of enterprises is not the issue. Bonuses are, and the management focuses on the determinants of those: that is to say, it focuses on the plan targets for quality and output. Even a well-meaning Soviet manager could easily end up producing goods that precisely meet the quality targets, but fall short of what customers need.

The game over quality is an important, but not unique, example of the way that the reliance on quantitative indicators creates problems within the system. Other examples—such as energy conservation, which in reality has not occurred, or innovations in production processes that are in fact not innovations—merely provide additional evidence without adding to the basic story. The problem here is Soviet unwillingness to accept the costs of relying on a single and hard indicator such as profits. The fear runs deep that a firm solely interested in profits will be inclined to antisocial (and antisocialist) activities. The Soviet solution is to use a multiplicity of indicators and constantly try to perfect them, while accepting the antisocial consequences of that system as inherently less costly than the alternative.

A World of Special Deals

The formal system consists of a bonus schedule linked to targets and clear rules stating the link between bonuses and the economic activity of the enterprise.[96] Since the mid-1970s Gosplan has distributed bonuses to ministries according to criteria linked to the wage bill of the ministry and gross value of output. Ministries in turn negotiate with enterprises over the size of bonus funds. The basic negotiation is for a five-year-plan period, which determines the size of the bonus fund. Then the ministry specifies a set of performance indicators and a bonus schedule that will determine how the actual bonus fund will deviate from that planned, depending on actual performance. Those indicators must include the proportion of highest-quality output in total output and the growth of labor productivity. Other indicators, such as profitability, gross output, cost reductions, or the mastering of new technology, can also be included, the choice depending on what is appropriate for the branch. In addition

96. Unless otherwise specified, this paragraph relies on Jan Adam, "The Present Soviet Incentive System," pp. 352–57.

a number of specific indicators, as discussed above, are part of the plan. Some—the output of specific products or the fulfillment of delivery contracts—are a type of threshold indicator: if they are not fulfilled, then some portion of bonuses is lost.

Despite these elaborate procedures, there is evidence that in fact the relations between Gosplan and the ministries, and between the ministries and their enterprises, tend to dissolve into complex bilateral bargains, customized to suit the needs and requirements of each side. These deals, which contravene the formal bonus distribution procedures specified in numerous regulations, reflect a number of complex considerations, two of which stand out: (1) enterprises should somehow be able to cover their wages and a minimal amount of bonuses for the work force; (2) on the other hand, enterprises should not be able to do so well that they can offer bonuses and other privileges to their workers dramatically higher than those of other enterprises in the same branch. Basically the system operates to ensure that there is a tight safety net to prevent an enterprise from failing, and a rather low ceiling to prevent extraordinary success. It is, at an enterprise level, the reality of *uravnilovka* that many complain about and that Soviet leaders say they wish to do something about.

The existence of the safety net is clear from basic facts known about the Soviet economy. Enterprise failures are few. Mergers and management changes occur with frequency. Unemployment is typically voluntary. Unwanted products fill warehouses, but there are no dramatic consequences for the suppliers. Many of the plan corrections introduced during the year are no more than ratifications of enterprise failures. "Everyone knows," said Iurii Andropov,"the phrase 'correct the plan. . . . [but] if one speaks of the need to 'correct,' then it means reductions are being discussed. Production falls, but wages remain as before."[97]

The "ceiling" suppressing the incomes of the most successful enterprises is a direct result of the cross-subsidization necessary to support poorly performing enterprises. There are no aggregate data on the magnitude of these cross-subsidies; most of the evidence is anecdotal in the form of complaints from successful enterprises that funds from their economic stimulation accounts are being confiscated by their ministry—

---

97. "Vstrecha Iu. V. Andropova s moskovskimi stankostroiteliami" (The Meeting of Iu. V. Andropov with Moscow machinebuilders), *Ekon. gaz.*, no. 6 (February 1983).

in direct contravention of the rules governing the formation of those accounts—to subsidize weak enterprises.

One piece of direct evidence consistent with the existence of both the safety net and the ceiling comes from a study of 100 enterprises in the Russian Republic's light and food industries covering the years 1966 to 1974.[98] The basic conclusion of the study is that for the years in question there was no clear connection between the size of the material stimulation accounts in these 100 enterprises and the rules governing the formation of those accounts at the time. Whatever determined payments into the material stimulation accounts in those enterprises in those years, it was not the bonus regulations.

Aside from this circumstantial evidence that bonus rules are generally not de facto determinants of actual bonus payments to enterprises, that state of affairs makes intuitive sense. Ministries and enterprises are locked in a complex, constant game of wits in which each side needs the other. Enterprise performance is as much a result of central decisions on prices, investments, materials allocations, and regulations as it is a reflection of the skill of enterprise management and the workers. It is the operation of the entire central planning mechanism, with its some-times arbitrary consequences for a particular enterprise, that gives the manager of every large enterprise in the Soviet Union the right to argue that his enterprise should be an exception. But the all-encompassing nature of central institutions in the economy also gives the ministry the right to argue that any enterprise receiving an unusually large income flow is earning rents from mistakes in central controls, and therefore does not deserve the income. The result is a system in which special deals, not compliance with bonus regulations, are the norm.

One important consequence of this difference between the formal and de facto system is the fact that outsiders have great difficulty telling what performance indicators are actually used to judge enterprise performance and determine bonus account payments. Enterprise directors may have similar difficulties. Aside from obviously having to take into account output indicators, enterprise directors are living in a symbiotic relation-ship with their ministry in which the written rules rarely guide decisions and the unspoken rules can change without notice. This is yet another

98. See N. A. Vasil'eva, "Fond material'nogo pooshchreniia i fondoobrazuiushchie pokazateli" (The fund for material stimulation and fund-forming indicators), *Izvestiia sibirskogo otdeleniia Akademii Nauk SSSR*, no. 11, (1977), pp. 137–43, esp. p. 138. I am grateful to Vladimir Kantorovich for this reference.

example in which "working according to rule" would be a radical reform in its own right.

This network of special deals that defines the ceiling and the floor on enterprise results is the foundation on which economic security rests in the USSR. Workers need not fear for their wages or their jobs thanks to the special deals. Enterprises need not fear that they will fail if they do not satisfy consumers—or, for that matter, some of the minor wishes of planners. Although managers can, and do, experience the fear of personal failure, their enterprise and its workers are extraordinarily secure.

On the other side of the special deals, however, are the extremely truncated rewards for success. Enterprise management and workers know from long experience that even wildly successful commercial innovations in this system lead to positive, but modest, rewards. Regulations may tell enterprises that a burst in sales or profitability or productivity will bring a significant increase in bonuses. However, experience tells them that the gains will be short-lived, as they will be taken away in the next plan period through modified norms or more taut plans.

The ceiling and the floor are not coincident, and enterprises in the USSR can be found on both, as well as in between. The floor, however, takes away the fear of failure and hence one of the major incentives to innovation. The ceiling takes away the other key incentive: the knowledge that an extraordinarily good idea will bring large rewards. Together these factors amount to an institutional explanation for the tendency of civilian enterprises in the USSR to avoid innovation, or at best to simulate it in an effort to fulfill the indicators.

The Workers

Ultimately, the entire system of plan indicators and the elaborate bonus structure surrounding it are designed to induce Soviet workers to produce what the state wants, with maximal efficiency. Enterprise directors are on the front lines of this effort, and the special deals they negotiate (or are forced to accept) provide them with the funds to pay workers and obtain new capital equipment. Thus, the incentive for Soviet workers to work to fulfill plans is directly linked to the wage and bonus systems used within the factory.

The enterprise director's room for maneuver here is severely constrained. As discussed briefly in chapter 3, he must work within a six-tiered wage scale, with numerous possibilities to award special bonuses for particularly difficult work conditions, length of service in the factory, and the location of the work, as well as bonuses for overfulfilling particular plan indicators. Although this can, and does, lead to variations in the earnings of individual workers, the variance is relatively modest. The system as a whole is biased toward equality, so that it is difficult to penalize poor workers or adequately reward superior workers. The de facto impossibility of laying off workers for economic reasons, because of the safety net, is one of the strongest constraints.

It would be a mistake, however, to focus on the wage and bonus system as the sole, or even the major, problem with the incentive system linking workers to national economic goals. The general shortage of high-quality consumer goods is another factor contributing to weak incentives for high labor productivity. It may well be the major factor: even the most elaborate mechanism for redistributing rubles among workers within a Soviet factory will have little effect if the rubles will not buy commodities of interest to workers. "It is insufficient to improve the system of financial rewards for labor," said Iurii Andropov at the June 1983 party plenum; "one must also produce the necessary quantity of commodities which are in demand."[99]

It is in this sense that the macro performance of the economy and the performance of individual enterprises and individual workers are intertwined. Problems in worker productivity, which in turn contribute to (but are not the sole cause of) problems in enterprise performance, lead to poor performance in the overall economy. That, combined with planners' low priority for consumer goods and the very weak incentives for enterprises to produce consumer goods in demand, leads to persistent shortages of consumer goods. And those, in turn, affect worker productivity. This interconnected set of problems in the de facto system is what Soviet leaders have sought to address through economic reforms over the past quarter century. The only effective strategy is one that addresses all points on this vicious circle.

The De Facto System in Action

The logic of the de facto system is now analyzed in terms of how its actors (1) identify and respond to changes in supply conditions; (2)

99. "Rech' General'nogo sekretaria TsK KPSS tovarishcha Iu. V. Andropova" (Speech of the general secretary of the CC of the CPSU comrade Iu. V. Andropov), *Kommunist*, no. 9 (June 1983), p. 9.

identify and respond to changes in demand; (3) make investment decisions; and (4) stimulate technological progress. Each situation is discussed briefly and compared with the formal system.

Changes in Supply

As noted earlier, the formal system, when faced with a change in supply such as a secular rise in the cost of oil extraction, would have difficulty detecting the rising costs and handling quick, within-year changes in supply. The de facto system compensates somewhat for both of these weaknesses.

Signals that the costs of extraction are rising move through the system by means of Powell's numerous informal information mechanisms. Increased difficulty in procuring scarce products via formal channels or via *tolkachi* or increases in implicit prices (including bribes) tell users that the relative cost of the product is increasing and that they should substitute away from it if possible. This comes in addition to information of various types and quality gleaned in negotiations with the units of the formal system. If there are substitutes, the trend may be to substitute toward cheaper alternatives, as in a market economy, even though the official price for the product does not move.

The quick, within-year changes in supply cannot be accommodated in the formal system in any obvious way owing to the stability of annual plans. In the de facto system constant plan corrections in part respond to that problem. Shortages in a particular product may—if lags for increasing output are short—trigger within-year revisions in plan targets for producing ministries, and in turn for their enterprises. Simultaneously, if the product involved is under the central control of Gosplan or Gossnab, reductions in authorizations for purchase may be ordered. Furthermore, reductions in shipments to particular customers may be imposed automatically, without notice to those authorized to purchase the product, according to previously specified priorities in the event of shortage (first the military, then heavy industry, light industry, and agriculture).

The shadow economy will also play a role. Emerging shortages of a product increase demand via *tolkachi* and the party network for the scarce materials. The result may be to ferret out reserves that otherwise might not have been brought into circulation and thus to reduce the magnitude and effect of the shortage.

This is hardly a neat or simple way of identifying and reacting to changes in supply conditions. It is no match for a well-functioning price system. Even a price system hampered by regulations and high concentration of economic power is probably superior to the de facto Soviet system. Nonetheless, this is a workable arrangement, as has been proven over time, although it is probably more useful for identifying emerging shortages and triggering a response, than it is for noticing emerging surpluses and generating a response there. In a system oriented to increasing output, shortages are of far greater concern than surpluses, and that fundamental concern determines the shape of institutions in the de facto system.

Shifts in Demand

When there is a shift in demand for the intermediate products used in industry or agriculture, the concerns that arise in the formal system and the consequences for the de facto system are similar to those that involve supply-side phenomena. Emerging changes in demand show up through the informal information system, trigger the use of the shadow economy, may bring about plan corrections and other short-term adjustments in the material supply system, and eventually will work their way through the planning system.

For consumers, excess demand for many goods and services may reflect true priorities of planners; however, they are masked by the rhetoric of politicians. The planning system is not well designed to pick up signals of shortages or surpluses in consumer goods and services, and where it does the decision may be to allow them to persist. For the formal system the matter stops there.

In the de facto system persistent shortages trigger the second economy into action as individuals seek to fill gaps in the supply of goods and services in contravention of the law. The result is an essentially illegal, highly flexible system that identifies changes in demand and responds to them. It is primarily in the business of supplying services, but also some goods. This is a clear example of a way in which the de facto system is far more adroit at responding to changes in demand than the formal system would suggest.

Investment Decisions

It is true, as the formal system specifies, that Gosplan wields tremendous power in decisions on the level and structure of investment. Under the Politburo's guidance, Gosplan decides on a basic structural strategy for the system; Gosplan sets policy on the types of investments industry and agriculture will make; and Gosplan controls the materials that ultimately determine which investment projects will be completed irrespective of investment allocations. Yet there are unmistakable indications that in the de facto system Gosplan's control is diluted and that it has far less control over investment processes than the description of the formal system would lead one to expect.

Recall from chapter 2 that by virtue of the relationship between planned and actual investments in recent years, planners have been unable to hold down the growth of investment. This system must constantly be on guard against a seemingly insatiable hunger on the part of enterprises for investment funds.[100]

Ministries fully share that hunger, and thus, despite valiant efforts by central planners, the number of investment projects under way far exceeds the capacity of the construction industry, with the result that human and capital resources are dispersed over too many projects. In 1985, for example, the country's 4.1 million construction workers were busy on 350,000 investment projects; that meant an average of 12 workers per project.[101] This type of dispersion in construction resources contributes to long delays in project completion. In the 1980s close to a decade is needed to bring a factory from the design table to full capacity.[102] The logical response from planners of the five-year plans for the 1970s was an effort to increase the share of reconstruction in total investment. That was to have the double advantage of reducing demands on an overburdened construction industry and shifting emphasis away from building totally new factories for which there is no new labor. Yet, because ministries hunger for new enterprises, they have successfully resisted, and the share of reconstruction in investment has not risen.[103]

This record of weakness for a system in which the center has strong

100. In negotiations for the 1982 annual plan, for example, Gosplan received proposals for 2,000 projects, which it had to boil down to 385. See N. Baryshnikov and G. Galakhov, "Kapital'noe stroitel'stvo—reshaiuschchii uchastok sotsialisticheskogo vosproizvodstva" (Capital construction—a decisive part of socialist reproduction), *Planovoe khoziaistvo*, no. 3 (March 1982), p. 26.

101. T. Khachaturov, "Investitsionnaia politika" (Investment policy), *Sots. ind.*, July 20, 1985.

102. Dyker, *The Process of Investment*, p. 36.

103. See Boris Z. Rumer, *Investment and Reindustrialization in the Soviet Economy* (Boulder: Colo.: Westview Press, 1984), chap. 2.

formal powers over investment has some implications for several inter-connected portions of the de facto system. For large projects, enterprise directors receive investment funds in the form of grants from the center, and there is no direct requirement to repay, only a capital charge on all assets. At the same time, ministries and their enterprises are under constant pressure to produce more goods. That, combined with the safety net, means that investment is virtually a riskless proposition for an enterprise director and his minister, and the easiest way to eventually increase output. That also explains the profusion of investment starts, since delayed completions cause no problem owing to the safety net and the zero cost of the investment. Construction enterprises readily agree to accept more contracts than they can handle since their performance indicators reflect work in progress, not completion.

The preference for new factories arises from the desire of ministries and local party secretaries to have their empires grow, the fact that reconstruction is not as prestigious as building new factories, and the bias of construction organizations against reconstruction (it is harder to fulfill the same indicators).[104]

These considerations have a dual effect on Gosplan. On the one hand, its role as a financial intermediary, acting to curb the otherwise boundless appetite of enterprises for investment capital, becomes more important. Virtually everything in the de facto system tells enterprises and ministries to do their utmost to expand productive capacity; and virtually nothing save Gosplan tells them there are limits. Profits are not a constraint, the cost of the investment is not a consideration, risk is virtually nil, and banks are a source of easy money.

On the other hand, Gosplan cannot fully control the system and curb these demands. Enterprises know the game and play it well, underesti-mating the ultimate cost of their projects when they apply, and then revealing the true costs as the project gets under way and is hard to stop.[105] Investments are therefore a negotiated outcome between Gos-

104. See A. Stepun, "O ratsional'nom napravlenii kapitalovlozhenii v odinnadtsatoi piatiletke" (On the rational direction of capital expenditures in the eleventh five-year plan), *Planovoe khoziaistvo*, no. 10 (October 1981), pp. 34–41.

105. See, for example, V. Kirichenko, "O nekotorykh voprosakh dal'neishevo sovershenstvovaniia planirovaniia i upravleniia khoziaistvom" (On several questions concerning the further improvement of the planning and management of the economy), *Planovoe khoziaistvo*, no. 9 (September 1982), pp. 63–64. Kirichenko, who at the time was director of Gosplan's research institute, illustrates the point for the latter half of the 1970s during which authorized capital expenditures for projects in process rose 1

plan and the ministries and enterprises, which is a considerable departure from the formal system.

Technological Innovation

This system has chronic difficulties in bringing technological innovations into production processes and products, in part because of the way the entire de facto system operates. Technological change is a major consideration behind efforts to reform the system and a continuing source of frustration.

The formal system itself accounts for some of the barriers to technological progress. The innovative process is a prime example of an activity that resists quantification and therefore centrally set targets. It is too easy to fulfill any target the center might impose without actually introducing an innovation. Furthermore the urge to specify from above the organizational structure of the entire system and the internal workings of organizations dampens whatever entrepreneurial urges may exist in the system.

However, the major barriers to technological progress lie in the de facto system itself, as it has evolved in response to the formal system, the behavior of planners, and the incentives those two factors create. The same incentives that explain the hunger for investment in ministries and enterprises also explain their lack of appetite for innovation. Innovations in Western industries occur not because they are enjoyable or because they are ordered by the state. They arise out of a desire to survive and thrive in a competitive environment. The safety net in the Soviet Union takes away that incentive; and the ceiling takes away the possibility of large rewards for innovative effort. But things are even worse than that in this system, as Iurii Andropov once lamented: "The business leader who has taken a 'risk' and introduced in the enterprise a new technology, introduced or produced new equipment, not infrequently is a loser, while those who avoid that which is new lose nothing."[106]

This system favors expanding productive capacity, not improving it; expanding output, not improving it; and expanding the use of inputs, rather than conserving them. The formal system relies on quantitative

---

percent a year and their estimated costs were revised at a rate of 6.9 percent a year. This is one factor contributing to project stretch-outs.

106. "Rech' General'nogo sekretaria TsK KPSS tovarishcha Iu. V. Andropova," p. 7.

indicators to lean against those incentives, with very little apparent effect.

Even so, some products produced in the USSR are up to world standards and innovations occur. Soviet turbines for hydroelectric stations are up to world standards; the USSR leads in the development of long-distance high-voltage transmission lines; and it has a formidable military capability built primarily on the basis of Soviet technology. The question is, why? The system seems to be so stacked against innovations that it is difficult to understand when they occur. In answering that question, it is best to separate civilian industries from defense.

INNOVATION IN CIVILIAN INDUSTRIES. Successful innovations in civilian industries seem to be related to two factors. The most important goes back to the role of government and party organizations in forcing innovations. When the attention of the government and the party turns to a particular industry, product, or process, innovative activity quite naturally picks up. Limits exist even here, however, and the innovations tend to be easiest to elicit when the support of government and party organizations is long-term and the requirements for interdisciplinary research (across branches) are modest.[107]

The nuclear power industry illustrates both the potentialities and limits of long-term central support as a spur to innovation.[108] The sustained high priority accorded that industry has produced an impressive array of technologies based almost exclusively on Soviet research and development efforts; and that accomplishment is directly attributable to sustained central attention to the sector. Yet the problems in developing a manufacturing base for the equipment, which has involved the work of numerous sectors, and in building the power plants, have been difficult. In particular the transition to 1,000-megawatt reactors has been bedeviled with problems; and that is testimony to the limits to central attention in a sector where coordination among many sectors is involved. Of course the other eloquent testimony to the costs of central intervention is the Chernobyl' tragedy, where the Soviet Union's casual attitude toward nuclear safety cost it dearly.[109]

The second set of factors, intangible and difficult to evaluate, are

107. Amann and Cooper, eds., *Industrial Innovation*, p. 7.

108. See Robert W. Campbell, *Soviet Energy Technologies: Planning, Policy, Research and Development* (Indiana University Press, 1980), chap. 5, especially pp. 163–69.

109. On Chernobyl' see the special issue of *Soviet Economy*, vol. 2 (April–June 1986).

those "human" factors on which Mikhail Gorbachev has come to rely so heavily for the success of his efforts to turn the economy around. This includes the simple human desire to push through innovations, a result of pride in one's work. A complementary motivating factor may be the tradition of high-quality work in some institutions, which somehow is passed from one generation of managers and workers to the next and is in some sense a "culture" of quality. Finally, there is the possibility that some individuals, who are not risk averse, will seek to use the leadership's thirst for innovation to push an organization in ways it is not otherwise inclined to go to generate visible innovations, in the hope that the result will advance their, and their organization's, political and economic fortunes. Anyone who has traveled to the USSR has met individuals who show some combination of these motives or has visited organizations whose traditions value a quality of product uncommon in the system.[110] This system does not forbid such people to operate; indeed there are plan indicators for them to fulfill in spirit as well as in form. However, it is much harder to be an innovator than need be the case and much easier than it should be to avoid change.

INNOVATION IN DEFENSE INDUSTRIES. Defense products in the Soviet Union are different. The quality of Soviet conventional and strategic weapons rivals that of the U.S. weapons, and where it does not, Soviet designers have been clever in designing around their technological weaknesses. The general quality of defense goods is much closer to world standards than that of civilian goods. Innovations in Soviet weapons systems come with considerable regularity. The question is why, and whether the organization of the defense industries might offer ideas for a reform of civilian industry.

In many ways the formal system controlling the operation of the defense industries resembles that on the civilian side of the economy. The ministerial system and its links to parallel party and government institutions are essentially the same, except that here there is a Military-Industrial Commission with apparently considerable power over the nine defense machinebuilding ministries. As in the remainder of the system, ministries that oversee defense industries strive for self-suffi-

110. Julian Cooper ("The Civilian Production of the Soviet Defence Industry," pp. 44–45) suggests that the culture of production in defense industries carries over into their production of consumer goods, where, even though military quality control inspectors are not operating, the quality of output is regularly higher than the norm for the system as a whole.

ciency, fight for investment resources, and enjoy the protection of the safety net covering the remainder of the system. There is no similar commission on the civilian side, although the MBMW *biuro* created in 1985 may eventually evolve into a similar organization.

Each Soviet defense factory has senior military representatives (who are paid by the military) acting as quality control inspectors. These inspectors have no visible vested interest in the plant's fulfillment of plan indicators, and their career prospects depend on quality control.[111] This is an enormous improvement over the civilian side, where quality control is in the hands of factory employees who are judged by the same criteria as their director.

The arrangement for research and development is different in a way that favors innovation. Design bureaus are attached directly to production plants in defense and have experimental shops at their disposal.[112] This makes the entire R&D cycle much easier to complete than is the case in civilian industry, where design bureaus, prototype plants, and the serial plants are frequently separated by thousands of miles and considerable bureaucratic red tape.

Defense differs from other sectors in two additional important ways. First, the United States provides a constant and tough competitor that the Soviet military cannot ignore. Unlike civilian enterprises in the USSR, defense enterprises cannot continue to produce the same old goods and pretend they are better. Simulated battlefield tests are used by the military to verify the claims for the product and its capability against U.S. counterparts; and the resulting feedback keeps the innovative process going.

Second, the defense industries are the clearest example of the beneficial effects of a long-term high priority. It conveys a sense of urgency and importance to the work of the entire sector, clothed in an aura of patriotism, which is absent from the civilian sector. With that comes high priority in procurement of materials, investment, and access to talented labor.

As a result, the military industries, unlike their civilian counterparts, have the wherewithal and the incentive to produce high-quality products and to constantly search for ways to improve them. Whether or not this means that the defense industries are a useful model for a reformed Soviet economy depends on what proportion of the military success

111. Amann and Cooper, eds., *Industrial Innovation*, p. 35.
112. Ibid., p. 16.

arises from the organizational differences with the civilian economy, as opposed to the high level of attention and priority accorded the sector. To the extent that the last two factors play a role, they are scarce goods that can only be used effectively in the civilian economy if the priority of the military is reduced. It is possible, for example, to revamp civilian quality control by relying on inspectors who are paid by Gosstandart, as Mikhail Gorbachev has begun to do. But is the state willing to accept in the civilian economy a high level of rejects, and the cost associated with those?

Mikhail Gorbachev has decided that there is much to learn from the defense industries, so the issue is now very much alive. I return to it in later chapters.

CHAPTER FIVE

Khrushchev to Brezhnev: Previous Efforts at Economic Reform

IN THE post-Stalin era Soviet leaders have never been even close to fully satisfied with the performance of the economic system. The chronic tendency toward imbalance, unwillingness of enterprises to innovate, pervasive inefficiencies, and systemwide indifference to customers—all of these characteristics are constants that have nagged at Soviet leaders, and served as a continuous pressure for change. There is no year in which some change in the Soviet system is not introduced, some new experiment not begun that anticipates possible future changes. Reform in the USSR is a continuous process, which in the 1970s took on an almost routinized character as Soviet leaders sought "further perfection" (*dalneishee sovershenstvovanie*) of the economic system.

This constant tinkering with the system has never had the desired effect. As a result, the leadership has gone for a new reform package at fairly regular intervals, taking many elements from previous reforms and experiments, but possibly some new ideas also. These bursts of new reform activity, or waves, make up the peaks of the reform cycles that have characterized the post-Stalin economic history of the USSR and of Eastern Europe.

In the Soviet case there have been five identifiable peaks (dated according to the appearance of the key decree or decrees, not according to the period during which there were serious efforts to implement the reforms): (1) Khrushchev's 1957 *sovnarkhoz* reforms; (2) the Brezhnev-

Kosygin 1965 reforms; (3) the 1973 industrial reorganization; (4) the 1979 reforms; and (5) the Gorbachev reforms. In each of these reforms there are new elements, but much that is old and that represents a summary of previous experiments and partial reforms. They are all bound together by the common concerns that spawned them: balance, efficiency, innovation, and responsiveness to customers.

The Gorbachev reforms, now a subject of intense interest in the West and in the USSR, cannot be discussed until they are placed firmly in their historical context. Traditionally economic reforms in the Soviet Union have been a mixture of the old and the new, and the main issue has been a combination of the two. Previous efforts at reform, and their consequences, are therefore an invaluable indicator of how the Gorbachev reforms might fare, although they are far from an unambiguous indicator. The fact, for example, that the effort in 1965 to decentralize decisionmaking power to lower levels ultimately failed because the ministries reasserted their authority does not automatically guarantee that a similar effort in the 1980s is doomed. However, by understanding why those measures were ineffective in 1965, it is possible to ask some penetrating questions about Gorbachev's approach and to come away with a tentative answer.

At the same time, the prospects for Gorbachev's reforms are not completely tied to the uninspired history of previous efforts to reform the Soviet economy. This is a society in which the party leader's enthusiasm for a particular measure or set of measures is a precondition, although not a guarantee, of success. Brezhnev brought no such enthusiasm to the task of economic reform. Gorbachev is the first general secretary since Khrushchev to enthusiastically support, conceive, and implement reforms in the economy. He is a skillful politician who understands the utility of symbols and the importance of competent cadres in leading positions. Thus even if his reforms resemble measures in the past, he may succeed where others have failed.

The four reform efforts of the 1950s, 1960s, and 1970s are not equally interesting. Khrushchev's *sovnarkhoz* reforms, motivated in important ways by political rather than economic considerations, failed quickly. This episode is of only passing interest for what it has to say about the pitfalls of regionally decentralized planning for a highly industrialized economy with long-standing interregional economic ties. The reform efforts of the 1970s—the industrial reorganization beginning in 1973 and the decree of July 1979—both had minimal impact on the system. In many ways they are most interesting as indicators of Brezhnev's increasing frustration with the economic system and his muddled and ineffective strategy for changing things.

It is the 1965 reforms that are the touchstone for analyzing the Gorbachev reforms. The 1965 reforms were the only effort at a comprehensive reform in the USSR before Gorbachev. The debate preceding them covered many topics, which reappeared in the early 1980s when Andropov urged a new debate on the economy. The measures introduced contain much in common with Gorbachev's reforms. They affected, or sought to affect, many fundamental aspects of the system. Officially they were regarded as so successful that talk of reform disappeared for years, the issue being only the further perfection of an already acceptable system. In reality the reforms failed in their basic goals—which explains the two efforts in the 1970s to set things right. However, they did leave a tangible legacy within the system, so that an understanding of why they failed and why in some areas they had a positive effect is necessary for an understanding of the Gorbachev reforms.

Although 1965 is an important part of the story, the reform cycle itself is another important component. The 1965 reforms are easier to comprehend in the context of the problems with the *sovnarkhoz* reforms; the merger movement of 1973 is understandable as an attempt to patch up the 1965 reforms; and so on. Therefore I take the story in chronological order, but devote most attention to the 1965 reforms.

The *Sovnarkhoz* Reforms

In the first years after Stalin's death, the twists and turns of economic policy and the legacies of the excesses in the last years of Stalin's economy began to show up in problems in economic performance.[1] In the industrial sector, the dissatisfaction with the economic system that had begun to emerge after Stalin's death coalesced primarily around the substantial inefficiencies in the operation of enterprises. The ministries were judged to be the culprits. Their attempts to achieve autarky had led

1. Unless otherwise indicated, this section draws on Michael Kaser, "The Reorganization of Soviet Industry and Its Effects on Decision Making," in Gregory Grossman, ed., *Value and Plan: Economic Calculation and Organization in Eastern Europe* (Westport, Conn.: Greenwood Press, 1976), pp. 213–44, and Alec Nove, *The Soviet Economy: An Introduction,* rev. ed. (Praeger, 1966), chap. 2.

to highly variable, and generally high, production costs, as well as significant cross-hauls of identical, or similar, products.

Attempts to deal with the problems became intertwined with the struggle by Khrushchev's opponents to halt his consolidation of power. Those who opposed Khrushchev saw a double opportunity to improve economic performance and weaken his power base by strengthening control of the ministries and other central organs and by weakening control of the regional party and government organizations, where Khrushchev's power base lay.[2]

Early in 1957 Khrushchev responded to the economic and political challenge by proposing the devolution of power to control the economy to regional economic councils (*sovnarkhozy*). The result was what came to be known as the *sovnarkhoz* reforms, which were introduced beginning in 1957, in the aftermath of Khrushchev's successful defense against an attempt by the Antiparty Group to unseat him in June of that year. The changes, introduced in the second half of 1957 and the first half of 1958, resulted in a massive shift of power from a much reduced central apparatus to approximately 100 economic councils (*Sovety narodnogo khoziaistva*, or *sovnarkhozy*), which, under the supervision of the republican-level branches of Gosplan, directly controlled major enterprises in their territory.[3] The ministries supervising productive activities were virtually all disbanded, their powers spread among the *sovnarkhozy*.[4] Those central bodies remaining (the Ministry of Trade, of Finance, even Gosplan) had reduced powers. Gosplan, for example, still directly controlled only about 1,000 key commodities, all former "funded" items. Another 6,000 commodities formerly classified as centralized and funded were now managed by the republics' *gosplany* in which more than 80 percent of their output was concentrated; USSR Gosplan handled only the most critical national commodities and those centralized commodities whose production was dispersed.[5]

2. On the political struggles during this period, see Jerry F. Hough and Merle Fainsod, *How the Soviet Union Is Governed* (Harvard University Press, 1979), pp. 215–19.

3. Enterprises of local significance remained under local (for example *oblast'*) control.

4. The Ministry of Medium Machinebuilding (defense) remained: a set of five state committees was created to advise enterprises in branches of the defense industry; and one new state committee was created to advise on developments in the chemical industry. See Nove, *Soviet Economy*, p. 75.

5. Kaser, "Reorganization of Soviet Industry," p. 227.

Political considerations were obviously behind Khrushchev's support for these reforms, but legitimate economic considerations also played a role. The symbolism was as powerful in the 1950s as it is today: two enterprises in one city making products that the other needs. Yet, because they are supervised by different ministries, each enterprise ships its products to other enterprises in the same ministry, frequently in distant locales. In exchange it receives products shipped from afar that could just as well have been obtained "next door." Local authorities are powerless in the face of clear irrationalities in the operation of the large enterprises in their area.

The reform was designed to eliminate the "departmentalism" of the ministerial system, replacing it with a rational division of labor within and between regions that would lead to increased efficiency and reduced demands on an overburdened transportation system. The *sovnarkhozy* were instructed to evaluate the entire economy of their region and ascertain where efficiency could be increased by shifting production among the region's enterprises or even by discontinuing production, importing the needed product from other regions with more efficient producers. As an added incentive for enterprises to join enthusiastically in the search for ways to increase efficiency, the bonus system was given a major overhaul in 1959. Gross output, up to then the major performance indicator determining enterprise bonuses, became what might be called a gate-keeping target: if the target for the growth of gross output was not fulfilled, no bonuses could be paid. However, the major bonus-determining indicator became the target for cost reductions, usually measured per ruble of commodity production.[6]

Khrushchev was aware of the opposite danger of localism but seemed to feel that could be managed. As Berliner has observed, the way the system was designed makes it difficult to believe that anyone could reasonably expect to avoid a rapid replacement of departmentalism with localism, a notion that lends credence to the suggestion that politics played a major role in Khrushchev's decision to undertake these ill-fated reforms.[7] In fact localism soon began to assert itself as *sovnarkhozy* quite predictably favored their own enterprises over others, the result

---

6. Nove, *Soviet Economy*, pp. 161–73, discusses the changes in success indicators for enterprises in the late 1950s and early 1960s.

7. Joseph S. Berliner, "Planning and Management," in Abram Bergson and Herbert S. Levine, eds., *The Soviet Economy: Toward the Year 2000* (London: Allen and Unwin, 1983), p. 352.

Table 5-1. *Selected Macroeconomic Growth Rates, 1955–62*
Annual growth rate (percent)

Year	National income produced	Labor production in industry	Real income per capita
1955	11.9	9.5	0.9
1956	11.3	7.0	5.9
1957	7.0	6.6	8.7
1958	12.4	6.2	5.9
1959	7.5	7.4	1.8
1960	7.7	5.4	6.4
1961	6.8	4.4	1.6
1962	5.7	5.5	3.2

Source: Tsentral'noe statisticheskoe upravlenie SSSR, *Narodnoe khoziaistvo SSSR v 1967 g.: Statisticheskii ezhegodnik* (Moscow: Statistika, 1968), p. 59.

being a potentially disastrous move toward a fractionated, regionally based, autarky divided among 100 or so "economies."

It is difficult to identify variables that directly measure the impact of the reforms on economic performance since much of the reform was concerned with rationalization in intraterritorial specialization and production. However, Soviet leaders were clearly expecting efficiency gains that would have shown up in higher growth rates for national income and living standards. In the few brief years the *sovnarkhoz* reforms were in force just the opposite occurred, as can be seen in table 5-1. Growth rates for national income and labor productivity fell off dramatically, implying significant reductions in the efficiency with which productive factors were used. Real per capita consumption growth rates fluctuated in the late 1950s and early 1960s, but around a lower average than in the period immediately preceding the *sovnarkhoz* reforms.

The declining growth rate at the beginning of the 1960s is probably the reflection of many influences, of which the *sovnarkhoz* reforms are only one. From the political point of view, a reform that is correlated, however spuriously, with declines in national income and living standards is in trouble. In addition there was ample anecdotal evidence of the excesses of localism and the resulting damage to efficiency.

By the early 1960s the excesses attributable to the reforms were forcing a retreat, complicated by Khrushchev's struggle to retain his position as party leader. The most important milepost in the reversal of the *sovnarkhoz* reforms came in March 1963—less than five years after they were introduced—when the number of *sovnarkhozy* dropped by more than half to forty-seven, and an old economic body—the Supreme Council for the National Economy (VESENKA)—was resurrected to coordinate planning for economic activity at the union level.

Khrushchev was ousted in October 1964, and in September 1965 the new collective leadership—Leonid Brezhnev, Alexei Kosygin, and Nikolai Podgorny—announced a full return to the ministerial system and the introduction of a comprehensive set of economic reforms.

The *sovnarkhoz* reforms are justifiably treated as a brief and highly misguided effort, at least from the economic point of view. However, the problems they addressed were serious, and remain so today. Ministerial autarky seems as prevalent today as it was then, although there is no concrete way to measure that. Local authorities still must struggle with Moscow-based ministries to achieve even the most rudimentary forms of cooperation in the economic development of a region. Khrushchev surely went too far too quickly, but he did so in response to some pronounced enduring weaknesses in the Soviet economy.

The 1965 Reforms

After Stalin's death the relative relaxation in censorship allowed those disenchanted with the economic system to voice their concerns. The result was a debate on the economy that smoldered on into the early 1960s. The *sovnarkhoz* reforms did little to placate critics of the system, who were most concerned with fundamental flaws in the incentive system used to control enterprises. The reforms themselves were much more concerned with changing who supervised enterprises, and less with changing the system used by whoever had direct authority over enterprises.

By the early 1960s it was clear that the bonus system needed a major overhaul. Among other things, the new emphasis on cost reduction as the primary determinant of bonuses, subject to the fulfillment of gross output, assortment, and other indicators, was making it increasingly difficult for enterprises to earn bonuses. In particular, the share of bonuses to higher-level management was falling, and that decline weakened incentives for this important link in the system.[8] In addition,

---

8. Eugene Zaleski, *Planning Reforms in the Soviet Union, 1962–1966* (University of North Carolina Press, 1967), p. 67.

performance in the system had deteriorated sufficiently to call into doubt Khrushchev's entire approach to the economy.

Debates Preceding the 1965 Reforms

As a result, Khrushchev was forced to allow a fairly broad debate on the system, which was signaled by the publication in the September 9, 1962, edition of *Pravda* of Evsei Liberman's call for a new approach to the incentive system for enterprises.[9] Liberman emphasized that enterprises should be induced to (1) enthusiastically seek out and use their full productive capacities, (2) dramatically improve the quality of goods produced, and (3) curb their strong appetite for new capital and additional workers. In addition he advocated elimination of the ratchet, which would serve the other goals, and the elimination of unwarranted central interference in enterprise activities. Liberman proposed to achieve his goals by significantly reducing the obligatory plan indicators sent to enterprises to a relatively few indicators relating to product mix, deliveries, and profits.[10]

In this much simpler system bonuses to enterprise employees would be determined primarily by their ability to sell their output and the profitability of their operations. This greatly revised incentive system would shift the attention of enterprise management from the ministry to the customer (owing to the sales indicator), reduce the demand for inputs (the profitability indicator), and yet still guarantee the state the basic mix of goods judged socially desirable (the product mix indicators).

The ensuing debates included a continued discussion of Liberman's proposals, along with other proposals for ways to improve the enterprise incentive system. In addition, those discussions expanded into new topics that reflected a broad range of views, many of which were to reappear in the early 1980s.[11]

One vocal group, connected with the Central Economic-Mathematical

9. An English translation of the Liberman piece is available in Morris Bornstein and Daniel R. Fusfeld, eds., *The Soviet Economy: A Book of Readings,* rev. ed. (Homewood, Ill.: Irwin, 1966), pp. 352–58.

10. He did propose retaining many of the previously large number of indicators as obligatory for *sovnarkhozy,* assuming that enterprises would seek to aid in fulfilling those indicators in the most profitable way possible.

11. Unless otherwise indicated, this brief account is taken from Zaleski's excellent summary of the debates preceding the 1965 reforms. See *Planning Reforms of the Soviet Union,* chap. 4.

Institute in Moscow, advocated relying heavily on optimal planning techniques to generate meaningful prices, which would in turn drive the entire planning process from the center to enterprises that focus on minimizing the costs of producing planned outputs.[12] These proposals had quite radical implications, for the role of the price system would be enhanced, the way the planning process was to be conducted would be dramatically rationalized, and, in particular, control over the system would shift from bureaucrats to computers programmed by economists. Yet the tenor of these proposals was conservative since they recommended that the central planning system be retained, but that it be streamlined through the application of mathematical techniques harnessed to what would be drastically expanded computer power utilized by the state.

Others were less impressed with the promise of mathematical economics or the need for a vast hierarchy to control the system and attacked the central planning system itself. They argued that although the central planning of supply is justified by the existence of shortage, and therefore by the need for socially determined priorities to guide the allocation of scarce products, in fact the system contributes to shortage through mistakes. The solution, some argued, was a shift from planned allocations of key commodities to a wholesale trade system that would allow buyer and seller to determine the flows of those commodities, and, by implication, a reform of the wholesale price system.[13]

Although many advocated reform, a good number opposed it, or at least were concerned that the reforms would undermine the party's control over the system and weaken party support by diluting the economic security offered by the existing system. This group was particularly concerned about the loss of control over the structure of the economy, the greater risk of micro and macro imbalance, and the consequent danger of recession and unemployment.[14]

The debates over the enterprise incentive system spurred authorities to select certain enterprises to try out some of the more promising proposals enjoying wide support among those advocating reform. The most notable experiments took place at the Bol'shevichka and Mayak

12. For a summary of these proposals see Michael Ellman, *Soviet Planning Today: Proposals for an Optimally Functioning Economic System* (Cambridge University Press, 1972).

13. Zaleski, *Planning Reforms in the Soviet Union*, pp. 103–07.

14. Ibid., pp. 101–02; see also pp. 108–09.

clothing factories in Leningrad, which were allowed in mid-1964 to switch to a system based on a greatly simplified set of targets emphasizing profitability on sales, wherein sales were an outcome of contracts directly negotiated with retail outlets, without central interference. The experiment was expanded in 1965 to 400 consumer goods enterprises and a few plants in other industries.[15]

Basic Elements of the 1965 Reforms

At the September 1965 Plenum of the Central Committee Alexei Kosygin announced a set of measures that have come to be known as the 1965 reforms. They consisted of three basic measures: an administrative reform reinstituting the ministerial system, a complete overhaul of the enterprise incentive system, and a price reform. The initial decree was quite general, and it was clear at the beginning that the actual regulations necessary to implement the full program would take some time to draft and bring into force. But the anticipation was that the system would be in place and functioning well before 1979.[16]

THE ADMINISTRATIVE REFORM. Although the *sovnarkhoz* system was not itself a major focus of the debates preceding the 1965 reforms, it was clearly a principal source of concern for the leadership. The chaos, real or imagined, inherent in a dispersion of planning powers among regional authorities and the unquestioned loss of central control were both unacceptable to the leadership.

Thus an important feature of the 1965 reforms was a recentralization of power from the regional planning authorities to twenty-three newly constituted (in some cases reconstituted) industrial ministries. In addition, existing state committees—for example, Gosplan—assumed greater authority and responsibility as a result of the 1965 decree. Other committees critical to the subsequent operation of the system were created in the fall of 1965, or soon thereafter—most notably Goskomtsen (Prices), Gossnab (Material-Technical Supply), and GKNT (Science and Technology).

The clear purpose of these measures was to recentralize decision-making power to Moscow, a point worth emphasizing since Western commentary on the 1965 reforms frequently concentrated on decrees

15. Gertrude E. Schroeder, "Soviet Economic 'Reforms': A Study in Contradictions," *Soviet Studies,* vol. 20 (July 1968), p. 3.
16. Unless otherwise indicated, this account is based on ibid.

that called for a decentralization of some decisionmaking authority to enterprises.[17] It is also important to note the potential for chaos, or at least confusion, in the simultaneous dismantling of the *sovnarkhoz* system and the reform of the enterprise incentive system, with related reforms of the planning system. Various ministries and state committees were being asked to organize themselves and at the same time produce legislation overhauling the entire system. Not surprisingly, the result was both delay and confusion.[18]

THE ENTERPRISE INCENTIVE SYSTEM AND RELATED ISSUES. The second major decree in September 1965 called for a complete reform of the system of obligatory plan targets for which enterprises were held responsible and a change in the bonus system attached to the targets. Supervising authorities (now ministries and their departments [*glavki*]), which had previously been authorized to send down thirty-five to forty obligatory targets to individual enterprises, were limited to only eight:[19] output of principal products (in physical units), sales volume, total profits and the rate of profit on capital, total wage fund, the level of payments into the state budget, capital investments from centrally provided funds, specific tasks linked to the introduction of new technology, and allocations for the most important material supplies. The gross output indicator, the cornerstone of the previous system, was replaced by a target for sales volume; the targets for cost, briefly the main determinant of bonuses from 1959, were no longer a part of the obligatory targets.

The 1965 decree called for a new bonus distribution system built on stable norms[20] linking enterprise performance in the above indicators to

17. Fyodor Kushnirsky, an émigré economist who worked in Gosplan during the period of the 1965 reforms, quite rightly criticizes Western economists for missing the fact that the 1965 reforms in many ways represented a *recentralizing* reform. See Fyodor I. Kushnirsky, *Soviet Economic Planning, 1965–1980* (Boulder, Colo.: Westview Press, 1982), pp. 49–53.

18. Gossnab is a good case in point. It was constituted as the central organ controlling the materials distribution system, assuming powers and responsibilities previously held by many bodies—which in itself involved considerable struggle over bureaucratic "turf"—and at the same time was instructed to move toward a wholesale trade system, which would reduce the responsibilities of the newly formed organ and enhance the chances of economic chaos. For a discussion of the creation of Gossnab and the difficulties associated with that, see Gertrude E. Schroeder, "The 'Reform' of the Supply System in Soviet Industry," *Soviet Studies*, vol. 24 (July 1972), pp. 97–119.

19. Schroeder, "Soviet Economic 'Reforms,' " p. 4.

20. Much of the Soviet economic literature distinguishes between "normatives," which are constants linking two financial flows (as in the current discussion), and "norms," which are generally physical input-output relationships. Technically the 1965

bonus payments from profits into the Material Stimulation, Social-Cultural Measures and Housing, and Development of Production Accounts (see chapter 3).[21] Payments into both the Material Stimulation and the Social-Cultural Measures and Housing Accounts were financed out of profits, according to formulas linking those payments to enterprise profitability and the percentage increase in either profits or sales. Payments into the Development of Production Account were also linked to those indicators (although in a slightly different way), and in addition the account was fed by a portion of deductions in costs for depreciation of capital and all proceeds from sales of excess assets.[22]

Furthermore, a general rule was introduced stipulating that enterprises would pay from profits a 6 percent charge on all assets, fixed and circulating, in order to reduce excess demand for capital. Also, some enterprises would have to pay special taxes to skim off rents they were earning because of a special position that had nothing to do with their own decisions (for example, because they were situated on a particularly rich ore deposit that made it possible to keep mining operations significantly below average costs in the industry).

Finally, Kosygin's 1965 statement before the Central Committee indicated a desire to move ahead with the introduction of wholesale

decree was focused on normatives, but I do not make the distinction, and instead simply refer to "norms." See Morris Bornstein, "Improving the Soviet Economic Mechanism," *Soviet Studies,* vol. 37 (January 1985), pp. 1–30.

21. For a brief and clear account of this complicated system, see Robert Campbell, "Economic Reform in the U.S.S.R.," *American Economic Review,* vol. 58 (May 1968), pp. 547–58.

22. In the case of the Material Stimulation and Social-Cultural Measures and Housing Accounts, the general rule—if one assumes that the planned growth rate of sales and profits or the planned profit rate was just achieved—was that for each 1 percent increase in sales or profits, a sum equal to x percent of the wage account was deducted from profits and paid into the accounts, where x differs for the two accounts; and, in addition, for each 1 percent of profitability (profit net of interest payments and certain fixed charges paid into the state budget) a sum equal to y percent of the wage account is deducted from profits and paid into each fund, where y differs for the two funds. The wage accounts here are used only to determine the size of the payments; the source is profits. Payments into the Production Development Account are handled similarly when it comes to these two indicators, except that the scale factor is the size of the capital stock rather than the wage account.

If the enterprise was to over- or underfulfill targets for either sales (or profit) growth, or profitability, then the norms were to be discounted so that authorized bonus payments would not increase proportionately. This was designed to encourage enterprises to reveal ahead of time their best guess of their true possibilities by penalizing them for hiding reserves or being too conservative in an assessment of their production possibilities.

trade and the expansion of direct supplier-customer ties, a logical accompaniment to the expanded powers being granted to enterprises and an echo of the Bol'shevichka-Maiak experiments. The newly formed Gossnab had the task of devising the new wholesale trade system.

These measures were designed to make it more difficult for new ministries to interfere in enterprise operations and for ministries to strike particular deals with each of their enterprises. Ministries were legally bound to limit the obligatory indicators they built into enterprise plans. In addition their ability to treat enterprises on an individual basis was statutorily limited by the norms at the heart of the new incentive system. Enterprises that did well were statutorily entitled to retain the new bonuses; those that did poorly had to absorb the losses in their own bonus accounts.

However, the remaining eight indicators that ministries were authorized to pass on to enterprises left each ministry, and therefore central planners, with considerable influence over the details of enterprise activities. The combination of the obligatory targets for the output of key products and the central distribution of key material inputs meant that planners and ministries were still seeking to determine the production function for the enterprise centrally. The targets for capital investment out of central funds, which meant all important capital investments, and the targets for technical change gave higher authorities control over the enterprise's renovations and expansion of productive capacity. Thus the ministries enjoyed considerable power over the enterprise, which was enhanced by the fact that the ministry (along with local party officials) had full control over the careers and bonuses of top management.

PRICE REFORM. The third component of the 1965 reforms was a centralization of the mechanism for setting prices and a revision of the prices themselves, generally referred to simply as the industrial price reform.[23] The price-setting mechanism was centralized through the formation of Goskomtsen, which absorbed the duties of bodies that had operated in the Council of Ministers and Gosplan and that centralized the hitherto fragmented control of prices among many bodies throughout the system. This set the stage for a more uniform approach to setting prices and for determining and enforcing the rules on price determination for new products coming between price revisions.

23. See Gertrude E. Schroeder, "The 1966–67 Soviet Industrial Price Reform: A Study in Complications," *Soviet Studies*. vol. 20 (April 1969), pp. 462–77.

Goskomtsen moved quickly to introduce revised prices in 1966–67, the general goal being to restore the profitability of the majority of enterprises. That is the traditional goal of price revisions in the Soviet economy—in fact such a revision had been under discussion since at least 1960. This was more than a revision, however, for in the process of changing prices Goskomtsen built in capital charges on all products and rents on some primary products, thus linking the price system to the goals of the reform, which emphasized full accounting for costs. In addition, a special system was introduced for new products that allowed temporarily high profits to cover the costs of introduction.

The most striking aspect of the new price reform was the unquestioned assumption that prices were not to interfere with central plan directives. That was especially clear in the basic task set for the designers of the price system: at the end of the process virtually all industries and enterprises were to be able to operate profitably in the new price environment. There was no entertaining the notion that some Soviet industries and many Soviet firms might, and possibly should, start off being unprofitable in the new system and then work their way into profitability.

This "given" reflects the conservative approach of the reform, which implicitly assumed that it was possible to preserve the fundamental aspects of the economic security guarantee offered by the old system while introducing other measures that would improve performance. The idea was not to use the price reform to bankrupt a large segment of industry; in fact there was no statutory provision for the failure of an enterprise. To openly pursue such a strategy would have been politically risky and would have surely generated much more opposition to the reforms than actually materialized. Rather, the notion was that it was possible *on the margin* to induce enterprises to improve performance and to penalize them for failing to do so.

The "given" also reflects a basic problem that confronts reformers in any system, at any time—namely, the legacies of central planning.[24] When the leaders of a centrally planned economy set out to reform the system, all they have to work with at the outset is the physical and human capital inherited from the old system. Yet that inheritance reflects

24. This term, and the concept behind it was, to my knowledge, first suggested by Egon Neuberger, "Central Planning and Its Legacies: Implications for Foreign Trade," in Alan A. Brown and Egon Neuberger, eds., *International Trade and Central Planning* (University of California Press, 1968), pp. 349–77.

all the misguided decisions of the old system: the steel mills that should never have been built, the clothing factories designed to meet needs that consumers no longer have, and the consumer durables factories capable of producing only outmoded goods enjoying little or no demand. A price system that was solely forward looking, and ratified only what was justified under current demand and supply conditions, would shut down a significant number of factories and make their work force temporarily redundant; and many other factories might at best only be able to limp along with no profits but no losses.

Although such an approach would represent the quickest way to generate structural change in the system, with resulting efficiency gains, for a socialist government it has the distinct disadvantage that individuals would suffer, not because of something they themselves did, but merely because they happened to be in an enterprise that society thought should be built some thirty, forty, or even fifty years ago and that society had since decided was unprofitable. Ignoring parts of the inheritance is clearly unfair to those who are in those parts yet had little or nothing to do with constructing them.

The Soviet solution in the case of price reform was to ratify virtually all of the inheritance and count on decisions on the margin to gradually add efficient capital (human and physical) to the existing stock, at the same time making do with what the past has left the present. It is an evolutionary, rather than a revolutionary, approach to restructuring the system. The advantage is that no one feels unfairly penalized for mistakes of the past. The disadvantage is the virtual absence of pressure to work hard to improve the utilization of existing capital and labor.

Implementation of the Reform

The administrative reform replacing the *sovnarkhozy* with a resurrected ministerial system was the most rapidly implemented portion of the 1965 reforms. The general regulations were issued in October 1965 and by early 1966 the ministries as well as the new state committees were already deeply involved in establishing themselves and writing regulations for the reforms. The basic institutional structure that emerged still guides the Soviet economy in the 1980s.

Implementation of the reforms in the price system and enterprise incentive system did not begin until 1967. The task was assigned to a newly formed (1966) interdepartmental commission supervised by Gosplan and charged with overseeing the development of decrees and regulations needed to implement the reforms.[25] Its direct descendant is doing precisely the same for Gorbachev's reforms. The remainder of 1965 and all of 1966 were taken up with issuing the necessary decrees and regulations. When the implementation finally began, it moved slowly, and in some areas never moved ahead as originally intended.

Price reform began in October 1966 with changes in retail prices for light and food products. It continued with the issuance of additional retail price lists in January 1967 and then concluded with the introduction of new wholesale prices for heavy industrial products on July 1, 1967.

The first enterprises transferred to the new system in 1966 encountered difficulties, so that in August of that year a moratorium was placed on further transfers. Thus by the end of 1966 only 1.5 percent of industrial enterprises (which accounted for 8 percent of the volume of production and 16 percent of industrial profits) were operating under the new regulations. In 1967 the first serious efforts at implementation began, and by the end of that year 15 percent of industrial enterprises (which accounted for 37 percent of the volume of production and 50 percent of profits) were on the new system.[26] Obviously the strategy was to first add the most profitable enterprises in the system and leave to last those that would have the most difficulty financing bonus payments under the new rules. That criterion was most likely responsible for slowing down implementation in the late 1960s, so that by 1970—when all enterprises were to be in the new system—10 percent of the enterprises were still operating under the old rules.[27]

By other measures, implementation went even more slowly. One of the key provisions of the reform was that ministries and their departments (*glavki*) were to begin operating on a *khozraschet* basis; that is, they should as a rule be self-financing.[28] In fact by 1970 only Minpribor and a

25. Unless otherwise noted, the account of implementation is taken from Schroeder, "Soviet Economic 'Reforms,'" pp. 4–6; and Gertrude E. Schroeder, "Soviet Economic Reform at an Impasse," *Problems of Communism,* vol. 20 (July–August 1970), pp. 38–40.

26. The data are from Tsentral'noe statisticheskoe upravlenie SSSR, *Narodnoe khoziaistvo SSSR v 1967 g.: Statisticheskii ezhegodnik* (Moscow: Statistika, 1986), p. 186. (Hereafter *Narkhoz.*)

27. Schroeder, "Soviet Economic Reform at an Impasse," p. 38.

28. The term *khozraschet,* which literally translates as "cost accounting," is probably best translated as "businesslike management." *Khozraschet* entities are expected to keep cost accounts, find the most efficient means to fulfill their obligatory plans, and

few *glavki* were operating in this way on an experimental basis.[29] The idea has now surfaced again in the Gorbachev reforms.

Similarly, Kosygin's call for an expansion of wholesale trade bore little fruit. By 1969 the 460 small wholesale stores operated by Gossnab were handling 1 percent of wholesale trade in producer goods.[30] Gossnab delayed introducing a system of direct ties between enterprises designed to leave to buyer and seller most of the details of contracts settled according to very general central criteria. In April 1969 the Council of Ministers ordered Gossnab to move ahead with establishing direct ties during 1969–70, but to no avail.[31]

These delays reflect an impressive, ultimately successful, effort by the system as a whole to reject reforms. The ministries, and the *glavki* under them, were in the front lines, relying on a combination—to use Gertrude Schroeder's apt characterization—of procrastination, assimilation, complication, and regulation. Where they could, they delayed implementing the reforms, at least where implementation would discomfort them. In this they were helped immensely by the fact that they were responsible for drafting the regulations needed to implement the reform.

If delay was not possible, they sometimes "assimilated" new procedures into old bureaucratic procedures. This proved a relatively easy matter in the case of the 1965 reforms since the basic features of the prior system were retained (the planning of the output of key commodities, the allocation of materials by the center, and passive prices). All that was needed was to graft the new indirect levers (prices, taxes, and interest rates) onto the old system, a task that was completed by the end of the 1960s.

Complexity was the third line of defense, heavily used in the implementation of 1965 reforms. The basic decrees already constituted an "insanely baroque creation,"[32] reflecting a multiplicity of goals for the enterprise. Ministries used that multiplicity to further complicate the regulations and instructions they issued so that in the final analysis they were negotiating particular deals with each enterprise. The "normatives" linking bonus payments to enterprise performance were one of

remain solvent, unless there are specific plans calling for an operating loss. See Gregory Grossman, "Notes for a Theory of the Command Economy," *Soviet Studies*, vol. 15 (October, 1963), pp. 116–17.

29. Schroeder, "Soviet Economic Reform at an Impasse," p. 39.

30. Ibid., pp. 39–40.

31. Schroeder, "'Reform' of the Supply System," pp. 105–06.

32. Campbell, "Economic Reform in the USSR," p. 551.

the cornerstones of the reform. They represented an intention to establish publicly understood rules of the game that enterprises could adjust to and enjoy the resulting benefits or suffer the resulting losses. In fact the normatives lost all meaning and became rubber rulers that ministries manipulated constantly to ratify particular deals negotiated with each enterprise, or—in many cases—to simply impose a deal on an enterprise.

The final line of defense for ministries was simply to violate the statutes and persist in formal or informal continuation of more than the allowed number of obligatory indicators. When, for example, enterprises began to expand office staffs in legal fulfillment of their statutory duties, ministries simply declared these to be "undesired" results and imposed new targets. Some ministries and *glavki* confiscated financial assets of well-off enterprises to subsidize those in difficulty.

There were, and are, lasting legacies to the reforms of 1965, the most important being the ministerial system, reincarnated in 1965 and expanded since then. There were twenty-three industrial ministries in 1965; twenty years later there are more than twice that many. The Goskomtsen, Gossnab, and GKNT, all creations of 1965, are now enormously powerful bureaucracies in their areas of competence.

However, the reforms of the enterprise incentive system were never fully implemented, and the implementation that did occur was soon eroded and its impact short-lived. The highly centralized system controlling intra-enterprise transactions through obligatory plans, with each enterprise locked in a highly complex special deal with its ministry, remained intact; the reform, never a terribly vibrant affair, was dead by the early 1970s.

Impact on Economic Performance

Because the reforms were implemented, albeit not fully, the question arises, what, if any, impact did they have on the macroeconomic performance indicators of interest to planners and Soviet leaders? As with the *sovnarkhoz* reforms, I assume that Soviet leaders are most interested in the growth rate of national income, of labor productivity (which is closely related), and of living standards. The rate of technical progress, improvement in the satisfaction of customer demands, or improvements in product quality are also important, but difficult to measure. The first of these three should show up in the growth rates; the

Table 5-2. *Selected Macroeconomic Growth Rates, 1961–72*
Average annual growth rates (percent)

Variables	1961–65	1966–72
National income produced	6.5	6.9
Industrial output	8.6	8.1
Labor productivity in industry	4.6	5.8
Real per capital income	3.5	5.5

Source: Tsentral'noe statisticheskoe upravlenie SSSR, *Narodnoe khoziaistvo SSSR v 1975 g.: Statisticheskii ezhegodnik* (Moscow: Statistika, 1976), p. 56.

other two, probably not. At best it is possible only to measure crudely the effects of the reforms on performance.

A second difficulty concerns timing. Although the reform decrees date from 1965, the implementation does not begin in earnest until 1966 for the new ministerial system, and later for the enterprise incentive system. In fact the system was not operational in most of industry until the late 1960s. The ending date is also problematic. Theoretically it could be the present, under the argument that the reform is still essentially intact in the formal system. I have chosen to end in 1972, thus limiting the search for macroeconomic effects to those years preceding the next reform effort. For the pre-reform reference period, I use 1961–65.

Table 5-2 reports the results for the same three variables used to evaluate the *sovnarkhoz* reforms: national income produced, labor productivity in industry, and real per capita income. These results suggest that, in the period during and immediately following the implementation of the 1965 reforms, economic performance was somewhat improved over the immediate past. National income growth rates were slightly higher, even though industrial output had fallen somewhat; the significant fact here for Soviet leaders may have been that national income growth rates had not fallen. More significant was the marked improvement in labor productivity growth rates in industry and the dramatic improvement in the growth rate of real per capita incomes.

However, these data must be interpreted with caution, particularly in view of references in the current Soviet literature to a burst of hidden inflation during 1966–70 occasioned by the new price regulations favoring new products. If that is indeed the case, then these improvements in economic performance could, in part or in total, be an illusion.[33] Even to the extent that there was an improvement in performance, it might

33. Vasilii Seliunin and Grigorii Khanin, "Lukavaia tsifra" (Cunning figures), *Novyi Mir*, no. 2 (February 1987), especially p. 194.

have nothing to do with the reforms, but rather reflect the benefits of the restoration of economic order after the chaos of the Khrushchev years.

Whatever judgment one might finally reach on the effects of the reforms, the leadership was obviously dissatisfied and felt it necessary to come back to the problem in the 1970s.

The Mistakes of the 1965 Reforms

If a "death certificate" were issued for the 1965 reforms, it would read "ministerial interference, aided by the lack of attention by the obstetrician (L. Brezhnev)." Less obvious is why the ministries felt compelled to oppose the reform. Surely one of the motives was a simple desire to preserve their position in the system; a successful radical reform could render them redundant. A look at the design of the 1965 reform suggests that there was more to it than that. The actions the ministries took were the natural outcome of mistakes in the basic design of the reform.

Those design flaws do not exhaust the list of mistakes leaders made in the 1965 reforms. It is clear in retrospect that the leadership sought to control more variables than was feasible. That led to inevitable disappointment and pressure to resort once again to more direct controls. The leadership, having little tolerance for those pressures, moved fairly quickly to dilute reform measures without giving them a decent chance to work.

THE IMPOSSIBLE TASK FOR MINISTRIES. The 1965 reforms placed the newly created ministries in a basically impossible position. On the one hand, the fact that norms were set for five-year periods and the obligatory plan indicators were reduced from 35–40 to 8 implied that the ministries should reduce considerably their interference in enterprise affairs. Their task was to use the norms to set the general parameters for the five-year period, counting on those and the eight indicators to induce the enterprises to do what was best for the state.

On the other hand, each ministry was directly responsible for the performance of "its" enterprises over a wide range of performance indicators, including gross output. If planned outputs of centrally planned commodities fell short of the target, the ministry was responsible. If innovative activity lagged in some enterprises, their ministries were to blame. If some enterprises in a sector were ailing, the ministry would be expected to cover, which in many cases probably meant confiscating funds from successful enterprises.

Although the eight obligatory indicators left to ministries did give them some control over enterprises, the temptation to pile on more indicators would still be irresistible, even if it were misguided. The entire "culture" of the economic system under Stalin involved direct supervision of enterprises, the philosophy being that things only get done if enterprises are told to do them. A minister who rejected that culture and "worked according to rule" under the 1965 reforms might well find himself in the uncomfortable position of explaining to Gosplan that his enterprises had used their statutory power to reach decisions that made it impossible for the ministry to fulfill its obligations to Gosplan.

This contradiction in the basic design of the system suggests that, even in the absence of any motives on the part of ministries to preserve their power or any misguided overestimate of their contribution to the operation of the economy, this system was still programmed to create a dilemma for even the most well-intentioned minister: either he had to violate the spirit of the 1965 reforms and interfere in the operation of his enterprises, or he had to risk disappointing his superiors. Understandably, ministries chose to intervene, hoping that the law would be either ignored or changed, both of which occurred.[34]

UNREALISTIC EXPECTATIONS FOR ENTERPRISE PERFORMANCE. The tendency for targets to proliferate in this system is a consequence of the constant effort by Soviet leaders and central planners to control more variables than they can possibly control, the result being a profusion of targets that frequently contradict each other.

Some of these contradictions are readily apparent in the 1965 regulations. The wage fund, multiplied by the norms—those in turn being linked to sales or profit growth and the profit rate—determines the authorized bonus payments out of profits. If an enterprise then economizes on labor and lowers wages, that reduces available bonuses. Or, enterprises may be told to make choices that maximize sales growth and profit rates, while the ministry orders them to introduce specific new technologies and thereby gives them less room in which to maneuver.

The fact that planners had preferences for too many variables in the system is probably an accurate reflection of the expectations the leadership set for them. It was not enough to tell enterprises to maximize

---

34. Berliner, "Planning and Management," p. 354, makes this very important point.

profitability. The growth of sales had to be planned or else enterprises might figure out ways to increase profits yet reduce the volume of supplies to the system. Then the enterprises had two targets to play off against each other—the growth of sales and profitability—which implied it might be possible to achieve very high growth by allowing wages to grow, even though profits fell. Hence the wage bill target, which was also needed to control aggregate demand for consumption goods. However, given the passive nature of the price system, there was no way that enterprises guided by profit could be counted on to choose the products the economy actually needed. Hence the need to specify the mix of products, a requirement that also flowed from the decision to retain central control over the distribution of key products. And so on.

The basic philosophy built into these indicators, already full of contradictions before they traversed the treacherous halls of the ministries on their way to enterprises, speaks eloquently of the Soviet approach to an incentive system for enterprises. Soviet planners are concerned not only about the final results of enterprise activities (the outputs of key products and the efficiency with which those products are produced) but also about the way in which enterprises achieve those results (the specific innovations they undertake, the amount of labor they use, the specific material inputs they use, their wage and bonus schemes, and their organizational structure). Planners in the Soviet Union define planning in terms of both the "what" and the "how" of each enterprise's activity. The logic of that approach gives rise to a profusion of obligatory indicators in enterprise plans. If enterprises are allowed to rely on any single or small set of indicators, this inevitably gives them space to maneuver and produces results that planners cannot accept.

A second important factor in the 1965 reforms was the decision to retain the information system essentially in its previous form, with a price system so crippled that it could carry little information on supply and demand. Thus the planning system was expected to take over the coordinating function. That meant using a material-technical supply system and obligatory plans for the detailed outputs and inputs of each enterprise. All of this was to be handled through the ministries, which were supposed to refrain from interfering in the activities of their enterprises.

The interesting question is what is the minimum number of indicators that will serve planners' basic needs? The 1965 reforms were intended to answer that, since they represented a partial attempt to limit obligatory indicators to those of greatest importance to planners, leaving to enterprises those indicators of secondary importance. The implicit theory was that, by focusing on sales growth and profitability, the enterprise would automatically generate efficiency gains and output quality that would satisfy planners' goals.

It was clear early on, however, that the changes to the incentive system were the wrong answer for planners. By the early 1970s, when most enterprises were formally working under the 1965 system, planners, ministries, and enterprises found themselves deeply engaged in a game that led to a steady increase in the number of obligatory indicators imposed on enterprises. When planners saw the consequences of a relatively uncontrolled determination of bonus funds in the economy, they reinstituted (in 1971) a system for distributing bonus funds among ministries that was based on their wage bill in the previous five-year period and the proportion of white-collar workers in the total ministerial work force.[35] As it became clear that the new incentive system was failing to stimulate improvements in product quality, planners introduced in 1972 a new indicator authorizing a 2 percent increase in the planned level of the Material Incentive Account for every 1 percent increase in the planned share of highest-quality goods in the total output.[36] When, for example, enterprises found that it paid (in terms of bonuses) to push for high sales growth even if labor productivity suffered, an obligatory labor productivity target was introduced (in 1973).[37] When planners found that the existing incentive system was providing insufficient incentives to hold down costs, they applied more norms that specified the use of particular inputs per unit of output; this marked a return to detailed planning of input-output relationships, which persists to this day.[38] When enterprises began to use their statutory right to determine the composition of their staffs, particularly to increase office staffs to handle the higher administrative load associated with their new autonomy, the ministries imposed ceilings on administrative and managerial staffs.[39]

35. Jan Adam, "The Present Soviet Incentive System," *Soviet Studies,* vol. 32 (July 1980), p. 352. Adam discusses other complications introduced for 1971–75, but they are not of a fundamental nature and will not be discussed here.

36. Ibid., p. 357.

37. Kushnirsky, *Soviet Economic Planning,* p. 18.

38. Ibid., p. 19.

39. Schroeder, "Soviet Economic Reform at an Impasse," p. 43.

By the second half of the 1970s the ministries were authorized to assign more indicators as planners became concerned that the existing incentive system was not pressuring enterprises to increase labor productivity or the quality of output. Therefore they authorized ministries to use indicators for those two variables as two of the four that they were to rely on to distribute bonuses to enterprises.

The Legacy of the 1965 Reforms

Of the three parts of the 1965 reforms—the administrative recentralization, the price reform, and the reform of the enterprise incentive system—the administrative recentralization had the most lasting impact. It reintroduced a decisionmaking hierarchy that Stalin had used to manage the economy, in the process expanding the numbers of ministries and state committees. Since 1965 that ministerial hierarchy has steadily expanded in scope in a constant effort by successive Soviet leaders to administer the increasingly complicated system.

The price reform was first of all part of the effort to centralize economic administration as Goskomtsen was given the task of bringing order to a fragmented price control system. Although the price reform did reflect some changes in price-determination principles, the fundamental system of basing the prices on costs and ensuring the profitability of virtually all enterprises remained intact. After the reform this was still a fixed-price, supply-oriented price system unresponsive to changes in demand, or even to changes in domestic costs.

The reform of the enterprise incentive system, which is in fact the measure most frequently associated with the 1965 reforms, was never fully implemented, and the few measures that were introduced were neutralized first by ministries and then by new regulations. To be sure, traces of the incentive system reform still remain, but these sorts of legacies primarily affect the formal system. The de facto system remains one in which outputs are the key determinant of bonuses, and other indicators—although they are the subject of obligatory targets—are of secondary importance.

The failure of the 1965 incentive system reforms served as the background for two further efforts to improve the system in the 1970s, first by a merger movement begun in 1973 that was designed to reduce the number of administrative units and enhance the efficiency of their operation, and then by the move in 1979 to once again rely on normatives to guide economic activity at the enterprise level.

The 1973 Industrial Reorganization

Aside from tinkering with the incentive system, Brezhnev attempted—in two decrees announced in March 1973—to remake the decisionmaking hierarchy by streamlining the administrative apparatus of ministries and merging enterprises into production associations (*proizvodstvennie ob"edinenie*).[40] Those associations became the basic decisionmaking unit in the system.[41] This effort qualifies as a reform since it was designed to alter the decisionmaking hierarchy. However, it was a partial reform even at inception, and in the event it had little tangible effect on the de facto decisionmaking hierarchy.

The 1973 Reforms

The basic purpose of the 1973 reforms was to reduce the size of the administrative hierarchy in industry and increase the efficiency with which industrial enterprises were managed by the center. It was in the spirit of the centralizing, not the decentralizing, components of the 1965 reforms. The basic tool was to be mergers conceived and supervised by the ministries. These mergers were to place many enterprises under one decisionmaking authority and then allow that authority to shift production tasks and input allotments from the least to the most efficient enterprises. The notion of increased efficiency through mergers may, in

40. Unless otherwise indicated, this section is based on Alice C. Gorlin, "Industrial Reorganization: The Associations," in U.S. Congress, Joint Economic Committee, *Soviet Economy in a New Perspective*, Joint Committee Print, 94 Cong. 2 sess. (GPO, 1976), pp. 162–88; and William J. Conyngham, *The Modernization of Soviet Industrial Management: Socioeconomic Development and the Search for Viability* (Cambridge University Press, 1982), chap. 6.

41. The March 2, 1973, decree ordered ministries to draw up plans for administrative reorganization according to one of several models, all of which were designed to reduce the number of intermediate links between the ministerial apparatus and the enterprise or production association, and all of which were built around all-union industrial associations (*vsesoiuznie promyshlennie ob"edinenie*) that were to replace the *glavki*, and operate on *khozraschet*. The March 2, 1973, decree specified the rights of the production association, essentially giving it the rights formerly accorded to enterprises. Conyngham, *Modernization of Soviet Industrial Management*, p. 220.

part, have been an outgrowth of Soviet readings of the U.S. experience. In addition, as with most reforms in the USSR, there were precedents going back to the late 1950s that suggested this was a promising way to achieve efficiency gains, and in the 1960s a considerable number of mergers occurred.[42] The steps taken in 1970 on an experimental basis in Minpribor (Instrument-making, Automation, and Control Systems), Minneftprom (Petroleum), Minugleprom (Coal), and Minkhimprom (Chemicals) were, in restrospect, an accurate predictor of the 1973 measures.[43]

Brezhnev clearly intended to redirect each ministry's efforts away from the daily management of enterprises toward long-range planning and technical progress in the sector as a whole. The 1973 measures therefore called for the total replacement of the old *glavki*—the divisions within ministries that supervised all enterprises involved in closely related products within each ministry—with all-union industrial associations (*vsesoiuznie promyshelnnie ob"edinenie*, VPOs), whose authority would in general cover similar enterprises throughout the USSR. These would now control the production associations the way the *glavki* had controlled the enterprises, but with several crucial differences. The VPOs were to be much more independent of the ministry than the *glavki* had been as they were to operate on a *khozraschet* basis and finance their activities out of small deductions from members' profits. Their job was to actually supervise the operation of the production associations and enterprises; the ministry was no longer expected to be involved in those matters. Also the VPOs would include in their membership, in addition to production associations and enterprises, research and design organizations and technical institutes.

The hope was that through the mergers some of the most blatant cases of ministerial autarky could be eliminated, since similar enterprises that

42. For example, in the late 1950s the Lvov *sovnarkhoz* began to group together small and medium-sized enterprises that produced footwear into what were called *firmy* or, in some cases, *ob"edineniia*. These associations of enterprises operated under a general director, who in some cases had powers equivalent to a super-enterprise director, whereas in other cases the enterprises retained their autonomy. Although the merger movement was not the subject of an economywide program in the 1960s, mergers continued to occur throughout that decade. Already by 1964 there were 370 *firmy* in existence throughout the USSR. Nove, *Soviet Economy*, pp. 72–73. By 1970 there were 608 production associations (many probably renamed *firmy*) that encompassed 2,564 production units and accounted for 6.7 percent of industrial output. *Narkhoz 1982*, p. 110.

43. Conyngham, *Modernization of Soviet Industrial Management*, pp. 216–17.

had previously operated under the supervision of different *glavki*, or different ministries, could now be combined under one production association, and production associations producing similar products under one VPO. Previous geographical or territorial boundaries were to be ignored in the proposals for mergers.

The Soviet leaders also hoped that through the reform they could create special production associations that combined under one organizational organ all the necessary components to conceive, design, and produce new technologies. These were to be the scientific-production associations (*nauchno-proizvodstvennie ob"edinenie, NPOs*), which were to include their own research and design institutes, with accompanying factories capable of producing and testing prototypes, all attached to one or more major entities engaged in serial production of related products.

Implementation

The government ordered ministries to draw up the merger plans, submit them to the Council of Ministers for approval, and then implement them upon their approval. Many of the preliminary plans submitted by ministries were rejected as being too conservative and reflecting a general reluctance to promote far-reaching mergers or to give up direct control over enterprise activities.

Continued pressure from the government finally bore fruit in a massive merger movement in industry. In 1970 the number of production and scientific-production associations was 608, which accounted for 6.7 percent of industrial output. By 1975 that number had almost quadrupled to 2,314, which accounted for 24.4 percent of industrial output. Those figures continued to climb in the second half of the 1970s, stabilizing in the early 1980s at approximately 4,200 production and scientific-production associations, which accounted for one-half of industrial output.[44] The other half of industrial sales is still accounted for by independent enterprises, most of which are supervised directly by VPOs.

Even the raw numbers indicate that the mergers were far from all-encompassing. Furthermore, there is ample evidence that many of the mergers were pro forma and had little or no effect on the actual

44. *Narkhoz 1984*, p. 128.

decisionmaking of the member enterprises.[45] And, since all of the production associations were formed within ministries, ministerial autarky was preserved, a totally predictable outcome of the decision to put the ministries in charge of planning and executing the mergers.

Also predictable was the ministries' unwillingness to give up the VPOs' direct control over the enterprises or production associations. Like the 1965 reforms, the 1973 mergers were not accompanied by any change whatsoever in the central planners' expectation that ministries would be held responsible for providing the economy with reliable supplies of "their" products produced by "their" enterprises or associations. There was therefore no incentive for the ministries to empower the VPOs with new authority. Instead the VPOs basically acted in the way the *glavki* before them had acted; and they, together with the ministries, continued to control enterprise behavior as in the past.

Legacies and Lessons of the 1973 Merger Movement

The industrial reorganization begun in 1973 was an attempt to concentrate power in the center of the decisionmaking hierarchy, simultaneously drawing power away from the ministries to the VPOs and away from the enterprises to the production and scientific-production associations. Ultimately it had virtually none of the consequences the leadership had hoped for. Ministries managed to protect their authority over production units and their empires by assimilating the new measures into the existing de facto system.[46] For the most part, enterprises managed to avoid efforts to intermingle their administrative staff (and the resulting decisionmaking process) with other enterprises putting out similar products. The efficiency gains, if any, were probably significantly

45. This is clear from the data. The 4,295 production and scientific-production associations existing in 1984 supervised 18,507 independent units, of which 8,415 were still on "independent balance," which signifies that they are still separate entities participating in the planning process, despite their membership in the association. Ibid.

46. This is in fact the Soviet assessment of these reforms. See, for example V. Kirichenko, "O nekotorykh voprosakh dal'neishego sovershenstvovaniia planirovaniia i upravleniia khoziaistvom" (Concerning several questions on the further improvement of planning and administration of the economy), *Planovoe khoziaistvo,* no. 9 (September 1982), p. 58. He concludes that many of the mergers were mere formalities and that the ministries managed to protect their existing arrangements. The one example he gives, possibly atypical, is the Ministry of Construction, Road and Communal Machinebuilding, which created twenty-six associations out of forty-four enterprises, leaving thirty-two other enterprises with total juridical independence.

diluted by the additional administrative burden of the production association staffs.

Although this reform was far more modest in its goals than those of 1965, it was in the nature of an "aftershock" designed to accomplish some of the goals that the 1965 reforms had not addressed. The underlying assumption was that, no matter what the incentive system, the enterprises could not be trusted to behave correctly; hence the need for mergers into a fewer number of larger, more efficient, more easily controllable units.[47]

To an outsider the failure of the reform would seem to carry two messages. First, it is naive to give to ministries the duty of designing and implementing a reform that would reduce their powers, not only because they still have the same detailed responsibilities to the planning system as before, but also because of simple considerations of bureaucratic politics. A serious effort at reform would have required a tough extra-ministerial body that assumed from the outset that the ministries would try to protect their bureaucratic domains. The Council of Ministers was theoretically set to play that role, but did not actually do so.

Second, the wholehearted embrace of mergers as a panacea for efficiency problems in the system testifies to the tendency of Soviet leaders to look to supply-side solutions to their problems and to ignore the demand-side consequences. The fact that the mergers would enhance the already high concentration of Soviet industry and increase the power of suppliers seemed to be virtually irrelevant to those who designed this reform. In ignoring this issue, they perpetuated, and possibly worsened, a situation already clear in the implementation of the 1965 reforms, where the extraordinary power of suppliers eviscerated any potential incentive effect in the switch to the growth of sales as an important bonus-forming indicator.

Finally, the Soviet approach of ordering mergers from the center is yet another example of the central planners' conviction that they know best for all economic units in the system. In Western economies mergers have, at times, increased efficiency, particularly when enterprises in different parts of industry have combined, to seek efficiency gains and synergistic effects. The fact that such mergers are driven by a search for increased profits usually—although far from always—implies increased efficiency. In the Soviet case the central control of mergers implied

47. Berliner, "Planning and Management," p. 357, makes this point.

bureaucratic, not efficiency, criteria, so that in many cases the mergers were probably ill-conceived. The potentially far more powerful approach of allowing the principals to conceive mergers for primarily economic reasons was almost forbidden by the rules of the 1973 reforms, as it is today. Thus the Soviet leaders erected, not for the first time, a facade suggesting change. Behind it the system continued to operate as in the past.

The July 1979 Decree

Throughout the 1970s complaints could be heard about the results of previous reform efforts and the fact that they had not been fully implemented. Those concerns, along with the rapid deterioration in economic performance in this period (see chapter 2), provided new impetus to further reform efforts. Planners had attempted in the Tenth FYP (1976–80) to cut the growth rate of investment but speed up the rate of project completions in order to economize on new investments without affecting the rate at which new productive capacity was being introduced. The maneuver failed and was probably a major cause of the growth slowdown, although other factors—including bad weather— probably played a role.[48] Whatever the causes of the slowdown, the fact that it occurred was taken as evidence of the need for further reform.

As a result yet a third effort was made to implement reforms in the spirit of 1965. Although the July 1979 decree fell short of the comprehensive nature of the 1965 reforms, it proposed substantial changes, most of which were somehow related to the incentive system.[49] This decree in many ways represented an extraordinarily complex compilation of measures announced since 1965 but not implemented: stable norms linking enterprise performance to bonus funds, stable plans, and the use of bonus-forming indicators that avoided direct use of gross output and the spread of *khozraschet* conditions up the hierarchy. However, it also

48. For a discussion of the growth slowdown in industry, see Gertrude E. Schroeder, "The Slowdown in Soviet Industry, 1976-1982," *Soviet Economy*, vol. 1 (January– March 1985), pp 42–74.

49. "Ob uluchshenii planirovaniia i usilenii vozdeistviia khoziaistvennogo mekhanizma na povyshenie effectivnosti proizvodstva i kachstva raboty" (On the improvement of planning and the strengthening of the action of the economic mechanism on increasing the effectiveness of production and the quality of work), *Ekonomicheskaia gazeta,* no. 32 (August 1979).

sought to introduce some new ideas (at least new on a systemwide basis), most notably a reliance on a calculated value-added index as the primary bonus-forming indicator for enterprises.

Coming as it did at the end of an increasingly ineffective rule by Leonid Brezhnev, the July decree seemed bereft of new ideas and enjoyed little support from the center in its implementation. As a consequence, many of the measures were at best only partly implemented; and many were not implemented at all. If the measures in this decree left any legacy, it is in their individual contributions, or in their impact on present thinking about the Gorbachev reforms. I focus only on the most important measures that fit one of those criteria.

A Brief Overview of the Decree

The agenda motivating the 1979 decree was a familiar one: to induce enterprises[50] to operate as closely as possible to their full productive capacities by increasing the efficiency of their use of human and physical inputs, all applied to the production and timely delivery to customers of products actually in demand in the system.[51]

The measures introduced fall broadly into two categories: planning and supply, and performance indicators. Each included a number of detailed measures, but only the most important are discussed here. In addition, several measures in other areas were important, at least for legacies in the 1980s.

PLANNING AND SUPPLY. One of the important goals of the decree was to enhance the role of five-year plans by relegating annual plans to their originally intended role as an elaboration of, but not typically a major revision of, five-year plans. The five-year plans, in turn, were to be based on ten-year plans setting out the main directions of economic and social development and twenty-year plans outlining the main directions of

50. I continue to refer to "enterprises" from here on, even though many of the basic economic units are formally associations. For the associations that are actually functioning as one economic unit, they are in effect enterprises; for those that are not, the individual enterprises are the important decisionmaking unit in any event.

51. There are several useful analyses of the most important aspects of the July 1979 decree: Bornstein, "Improving the Soviet Economic Mechanism," pp. 1–30; Philip Hanson, "Success Indicators Revisited: The July 1979 Soviet Decree on Planning and Management,"*Soviet Studies,* vol. 35 (January 1983), pp. 1–13; Gertrude E. Schroeder, "Soviet Economic 'Reform' Decrees: More Steps on the Treadmill," U.S. Congress, Joint Economic Committee, *Soviet Economy in the 1980s: Problems and Prospects,* Joint Committee Print, 97 Cong. 2 sess. (GPO, 1982), pt. 1, pp. 65–88.

technological progress. That would provide a hitherto absent stability to the entire planning system and a much-needed long-term outlook by allowing enterprises to plan further in advance; it would also eliminate the ratchet, and therefore an important incentive for enterprises to hide reserves. To promote that stability and push for greater efficiency the decree called for a substantial increase in the use of input-output norms in the planning process so that permissible input would be spelled out to enterprises and they would be pressured to use physical inputs more efficiently.[52]

The decree also called for heavier use of counterplanning, an add-on to the incentive system first introduced for the 1971–75 plan. This is a mechanism by which enterprises are rewarded for adopting annual plan targets more ambitious than those in the initial five-year plan sent down from the ministry. Although this represents an effort to induce enterprises to ignore the ratchet, it has had virtually no effect on enterprise behavior for the simple reason that whatever short-term rewards an enterprise might receive by being more ambitious than its superiors would quickly evaporate when a more ambitious annual plan comes down the next year from those same superiors.

PERFORMANCE INDICATORS. Possibly the most innovative step taken was to make "normative net output" (*normativnaia chistaia produktsiia;* hereafter, NNO) the main indicator for enterprise activities. NNO measures value-added by the enterprise by using quantities of actual outputs multiplied by a branchwide average of the value-added in producing each product. Thus an enterprise that uses more labor than the branch average would not be rewarded for doing that and would have to accept the normative rather than its actual value-added; an enterprise

52. A typical norm would, for example, specify the amount of coking coal that it should require to smelt a ton of iron ore. That norm was to be used, in concert with a ministry's or enterprise's output plan, to specify permissible coking coal utilization. The data underlying the norm would be actual input-output ratios, but could be based on the more efficient users of the input, which yields so-called progressive norms. The norm would probably decline slowly over the plan period in order to stimulate economies in coking coal use. Gosplan at the all-union and union-republic level, along with numerous other institutions, was instructed to compute the relevant norms for use in deriving five-year supply distribution plans for ministries and their enterprises.

The main focus here was on raw material and fuel use, and in 1980 Gosplan announced an ambitious program to revise and expand norms for the use of those materials. As a result, Gosplan—which up until the Tenth FYP (1976–80) had constructed distribution plans for no products in the five-year plans—constructed distribution plans for 331 products. See Schroeder, "Soviet Economic 'Reform' Decrees," pp. 71, 75.

using less than branch average labor inputs would be rewarded.[53] The value-added weights that go into the calculation were set by Goskomtsen and issued in 1981, along with new price lists to take effect in 1982. NNO was to be used in the calculation of the two primary bonus-forming indicators for enterprises: labor productivity and the proportion of highest-quality goods in total output (both previously calculated by using gross output).[54]

The NNO indicator was not a new idea; experiments with similar indicators go back at least to the early 1960s.[55] NNO was used primarily to enhance incentives for enterprises to economize on material inputs by eliminating any payoff from increasing the value of purchased inputs in order to increase the value of outputs. Under the 1965 reform an enterprise could earn bonuses by increasing expensive inputs in a product, passing those through with a new higher price (justified, presumably, by calling it a new product) and therefore increasing sales. Under this system that should not work.

Unfortunately other things will work for the enterprise and can be counterproductive, or at least ambiguous, for the general economic interests of the system. Under this system, for example, it pays an enterprise to increase the output of labor-intensive products, since those have higher NNO weights per unit of output. On the other hand, having chosen the most labor-intensive product mix feasible for the enterprise, it pays to minimize actual value-added (labor input) in producing that product. That, in turn, indicates a possible incentive to try to get away with low-quality products that customers will nevertheless accept. Because of the high concentration of industry and consequent monopoly position of most producers, it is fairly easy to sell low-quality goods to customers with few, if any, alternatives. There are other possibilities for games with the indicator, but this example suffices to show the source of what turned out to be considerable problems with the indicator.[56]

53. I am simplifying a rather complicated calculation here. For details, see Bornstein, "Improving the Soviet Economic Mechanism," p. 9; and Schroeder, "Soviet Economic 'Reform' Decrees," p. 72.

54. It was not universally introduced, the widest application being in those intermediate production processes that utilized material inputs to produce manufactured goods. Bornstein, "Improving the Soviet Economic Mechanism, " pp. 9–10.

55. The Tartar *sovnarkhoz* experimented with such a system in the early 1960s. See Jere L. Felker, *Soviet Economic Controversies* (MIT Press, 1966), p. 58; and Gregory Grossman, "Notes for a Theory of the Command Economy," in Morris Bornstein, ed., *Comparative Economic Systems: Models and Cases* (Homewood, Ill.: Irwin, 1965), pp. 135–56.

56. For a frank discussion of the positive and negative aspects of the NNO, see V.

Problems can arise not only in using NNO to calculate the main bonus-forming indicators—labor productivity growth and the growth of output of products in the highest-quality category—but also in measuring quality. The bonus-forming indicator for the proportion of highest-quality goods gave the enterprises a strong incentive to simulate new, higher-quality, products in the pursuit of bonuses. Not surprisingly, this led to perpetual games between suppliers and the quality control boards, with the enterprises holding a definite advantage.[57]

Although two prime determinants of bonus payments were specified in the 1979 decree, ministries were also allowed to include in enterprises' plans eighteen other indicators, the most important being the production of principal products in physical units, normed wages per ruble of output, the number of employees, the commissioning of new capacities, and goals for production costs. Some of these had to be fulfilled before the enterprise could pay out bonuses (for example, the physical output targets, or at least a 97–98 percent fulfillment of the volume of delivery contracts); and others had relatively small bonuses attached to them.[58]

Clearly there was no attempt, even in the decrees, to substantially reduce the number of obligatory indicators governing enterprise activities. The July 1979 decree was an attempt to improve upon central control over microeconomic decisions, but in no fundamental way did it

F. Filippov, *Besedy o khoziaistvennom mekhanizme* (Conversations on the economic mechanism) (Moscow: Politizdat, 1984), pp. 83–88. Some aspects of the indicator are potentially ambiguous in their implications for the system. For example, it pays an enterprise to maximize its acquisition of inputs from other enterprises, rather than make them itself, since that would minimize actual value-added in a particular product, freeing up labor for other uses without affecting value-added calculated for bonus purposes. To the extent that this stimulates enterprises to reduce some of the inefficient production apparently so common in the USSR, it is a positive development; but if it encourages enterprises to go too far in the other direction, by maximizing input purchases in an effort to maximize bonuses, those opposite excesses would also cost the system.

57. Under the 1979 decree matters other than bonuses rode on the judgments of these quality boards. All products that were certified as being in the highest-quality category are eligible for a profit rate between 50 percent and 125 percent of the standard profit norm for that category of output, the actual amount being determined by the cost savings to the customer represented by using the new product. On the other hand, second-category goods would have their profit rate reduced by 50 percent up to the date the product was scheduled to be discontinued, after which no profits were authorized. However, these fluctuations in profit rates have a small influence on price, which is generally washed out by other considerations the producer must take into account. For the details, see Bornstein, "Improving the Soviet Economic Mechanism," pp. 12–14.

58. For the full list, see Schroeder, "Soviet Economic 'Reform' Decrees," pp. 84–85.

seek to alter that control. In particular all signals indicated that the center would continue to enforce its wishes with regard not only to the final results of enterprise activity, but also to the methods used to obtain those results.

Even the few measures that were taken to improve on the old system were half-hearted. Although NNO was the official aggregate measure of enterprise activity, for example, enterprises were still required to report gross output and sales. More important, the fact that some of the obligatory enterprise indicators were still calculated by using gross output presented the distinct possibility of a conflict between the old gross output and the new NNO indicators.[59]

The Fate of the Decree

There was never a serious effort to implement the 1979 decree, which was probably just as well, given its lack of coherence. The decree was primarily an indicator of the leaders' continued concern about the performance of the system and their inability to conceive of new approaches to dealing with the system. However, it is also interesting for what it says about mainstream thought in the USSR concerning the proper approach to organizing an economic system.

Common Elements in the History of Reforms

The underlying philosophy of the 1979 decree is unmistakably linked to the Stalinist approach to managing the system and to previous efforts to improve on that system. The basic tool is the plan, construed as a detailed blueprint for microeconomic decisions in the enterprise and devised and enforced by the ministries. Its basic feature is the joint system of plan indicators and bonuses, which simultaneously specifies the most important indicators of enterprise performance and pays enterprises to do their best to conform with those indicators. Improvements to the system take the form of new incentive systems and new indicators; the devotion to a centrally determined blueprint for micro-economic decisions remains.

59. For example, the indicator for fulfillment of delivery contracts was calculated by using gross output, and enterprise input requirements were still calculated by norms linked to gross output. See Hanson, "Success Indicators Revisited," pp. 3–4.

All of this comes together in the critical area of quality control, an increasingly important consideration as the Soviet economy has grown into a mature industrial power, but nevertheless one that is patently unable to compete with the rest of the industrialized world in fast-paced markets for manufactured goods characterized by a close link between science and production. In Western countries, enterprises innovate as a consequence of the struggle for markets. How they manage quality control is one of the determinants of their success; but there are many other factors, including the care with which they ascertain and attempt to meet the needs of their consumers. The final judgment on how well a firm does in these matters is the markets; firms with what appear to be up-to-date, high-quality products may fail if for some reason they have misread their customers.

Soviet leaders want the high quality they see in manufactured goods produced in the West—indeed, they would like Soviet enterprises to compete in those markets—but they are not inclined to use the world market to discipline their firms. They fear the loss of control and the potential chaos that could result from such an approach.

Instead they have tackled the problem with familiar techniques—by relying on new plan indicators and bonuses. The 1979 decree represented a new dedication to that approach in specifying that bureaucratically determined quality judgments were to be the basis for constructing one of the major fund-forming indicators. Moreover, the notion that the obligatory planning system can be modernized to manage the increasingly important issue of quality control still finds considerable support in the Soviet economic literature, and within the top Soviet leadership.

The Soviet approach to other aspects of operating the economic system has been no different. If planners have a problem with enterprises using inputs inefficiently, then the answer is new targets linking enterprise outputs to inputs and bonuses for their fulfillment. If the problem is overstaffing, then the answer is new indicators and new bonuses. If the problem is insufficient enthusiasm in enterprises for new technology, the answer is targets and bonuses focused on the requisite activities.

The Soviet Union entered the 1980s with its worst economic performance of the postwar period. It was clear that the efforts in the past to reform the economy had failed in their primary task and that a new approach was necessary. That became a major issue in the prolonged transition from Brezhnev to the new generation represented by Mikhail Gorbachev.

CHAPTER SIX

Setting the Stage
for Gorbachev:
Andropov, Chernenko,
and the Debates

In general, comrades, there are many unresolved problems in the economy. I have, I should say, no fixed prescriptions for their resolution. It falls to all of us—the Central Committee of the Party—to find answers. I wish to emphasize that these questions are of the first order, and of vital importance to the country. If we resolve them, the economy will continue to develop, the welfare of the population will increase.
      —Iurii V. Andropov, speech at Central Committee Plenum, November 22, 1982

L EONID BREZHNEV'S death created a long-awaited opportunity for the Soviet elite to rethink their approach to the economy and introduce new reforms in an effort—to use an apt phrase from American politics—"to get the country moving again." The impetus to do so lay not only in the continued deterioration in Soviet economic performance that threatened the party's ability to respond to the increasingly sophisticated demands of the population. In addition, the links between the Soviet economic system and Soviet national security—always a consideration for any Soviet leader—took on a new urgency in the face of President Ronald Reagan's formidable challenge to the Soviet position as a superpower.

In November 1982 Brezhnev's successor, Iurii V. Andropov, turned immediately to Soviet economic problems, devoting much of his first public speech as general secretary to the economy. In that, and subsequent public statements, he left no doubt of his dissatisfaction with the performance of the economy, his openness to innovative solutions, and his desire for a public debate. But Andropov's time was too short to do much more than register dissatisfaction. The significance of the brief Andropov period lay not in substance, but in the tone he set for his successors.

Konstantin U. Chernenko, during his even shorter one-year term as general secretary, acted as a caretaker, making no new contribution to the debate on the economy, but making no effort to stop the debate. During that period Gorbachev's influence increased, so that even before he assumed the post of general secretary in March 1985, he was deeply involved in economic affairs.[1]

It was to Mikhail Sergeevich Gorbachev that the party turned in March 1985, passing on to him the legacy of several decades of failed economic policies, charging him with the task of setting things right. Gorbachev's strategy for dealing with the economy and the actual measures he has taken to date are the subject of chapters 7 and 8. This chapter sets the stage for that discussion. The story begins with Andropov, for he sounded many of the themes underlying Gorbachev's approach to the economy, and it continues with Chernenko, for under him the debate about economic reform rapidly expanded and paved the way for Gorbachev's reforms.

Andropov and the Economy

Andropov's complaints about the economy were the familiar ones.[2] Labor productivity growth rates were too low, and declining. The

1. Gorbachev played the pivotal role in the construction of the Twelfth FYP, beginning early in the Chernenko period. See Ed A. Hewett, "Gorbachev's Economic Strategy: A Preliminary Assessment," *Soviet Economy*, vol. 1 (October–December, 1985), pp. 286–87. His influence on the reform discussion is also apparent early in the Chernenko period, for example, in the tone and some of the substance of the April 26, 1984, Politburo meeting devoted to a wide-ranging discussion of economic reforms.

2. In addition to the speech quoted at the beginning of the chapter, a sampling of Andropov's major statements on the economy can be found in the following sources: "Uchenie Karla Marksa i nekotorye voprosy sotsialisticheskogo stroitel'stva v SSSR" (The teachings of Karl Marx and several issues of socialist construction in the USSR), *Kommunist*, no. 3 (February 1983), pp. 9–23; "Tekst vystupleniia General'nogo sekretaria TsK KPSS tovarishcha Iu. V. Andropova" (Text of a speech by the general secretary of the CC of the CPSU, Comrade Iu. V. Andropov), *Kommunist*, no. 1

extensive and wasteful use of material and capital inputs persisted despite efforts by the center to promote efficient production operations. Suppliers showed disdain for the desires of customers. Innovators encountered difficulties in the system as bureaucrats set the tone. The ease with which enterprises paid wages irrespective of their performance led to imbalances in the supply of and demand for consumer goods. Efforts at reform were of minimal, if any, consequence.

Although the concerns were familiar ones, the rhetoric and the proposed solutions were not. Not only was Andropov dissatisfied with the performance of the economy, he was offended by it. "Now the situation at times is simply offensive," he said. "The starting materials are good, but the production is such that people prefer to overpay speculators for good, tastefully manufactured commodities."[3] In openly discussing and ridiculing these facts of everyday Soviet life, Andropov set himself apart from the Brezhnev leadership. Economic reforms, which hitherto had been almost routinized and in the process trivialized, became an issue of national pride, a symbol of modernity.

Andropov also departed from previous leaders in his willingness to talk frankly to the people about the fact that they themselves were the ultimate source of Soviet economic difficulties and the ultimate source of the solution. In one of his first appearances among workers in factories he spoke of shortages of consumer goods not as some abstract problem to be fixed with reforms, but as a problem that they would have to address, for "miracles, as they say, do not happen in the world. You yourselves understand that the state can give commodities equal only to those produced."[4]

Finally, he constantly stressed that the solution to Soviet economic problems ultimately lay in increased discipline, in the party, in the government, and in the workplace. When Andropov talked of discipline, he had a very broad notion in mind of improved discipline throughout the system. In the economy, he saw that discipline required tight links between economic performance and rewards to enterprises and individuals. This lay behind his attack on *uravnilovka*, the tendency toward

(January 1984), pp. 4–11; and "Rech' General'nogo sekretaria TsK KPSS tovarishcha Iu. V. Andropova" (The speech of the general secretary of the CC of the CPSU, Iu. V. Andropov), *Kommunist*, no. 9 (June 1983), pp. 4–16.

3. "Rech' General'nogo sekretaria," *Kommunist*, no. 9 (June 1983), p. 9.

4. "Vstrecha Iu. V. Andropova s moskovskimi stankostroiteliami" (The meeting of Iu. V. Andropov with Moscow machinebuilders), *Ekonomicheskaia gazeta*, no. 6 (February 1983), p. 3. (Hereafter cited as *Ekon. gaz.*)

equality in wages, in incomes, and in the positions of various enterprises. His opposition to *uravnilovka* was firmly rooted in the Marxian notion that in socialism, unlike full communism, each contributed according to his capabilities and received rewards commensurate with those contributions.[5] In this Andropov had identified one of the roots of Soviet economic problems and one of the important roots of popular support for the existing system.

Although Andropov had no time to devise a complete reform program for the system, he did move quickly to work on the most obvious problems in the enterprise incentive system. In his November 22, 1982, speech he called for greater independence for enterprises and farms. He ordered the Council of Ministers and Gosplan to experiment with ways to realize that goal and in so doing to study the experience of other socialist countries.[6] A commission under Gosplan, chaired by Nikolai Baibakov (then Gosplan's chairman), was charged with that task and apparently became a source of considerable information on reforms in other socialist countries, including China.[7]

The Andropov Experiment

Andropov's desire to give more autonomy to Soviet enterprises led to a July 1983 decree calling for an experiment with a new set of plan indicators and incentives, to be introduced on January 1, 1984, in all enterprises in two all-union ministries, Mintiazhmash (Heavy and Transport Machinebuilding) and Minelektrotekhprom (Electrotechnical Industry), and three republican ministries, Minpishcheprom (Food Industry) in the Ukraine; Minlegprom (Light Industry) of Belorussia; and Minmestprom (Local Industry) of Latvia.[8] Although I follow the general

5. Andropov, "Uchenie Karla Marksa," p. 15.
6. Andropov, "Rech' General'nogo sekretaria."
7. Oleg Bogomolov, director of the Institute on the Economics of the World Socialist System, was a member of the commission. His institute (Institut ekonomiki mirovoi sotsialisticheskikh stran) is dedicated to the study of other socialist countries, and is the source of high-quality, extensive research on those systems.
8. "V Tsentral'nom Komitete KPSS i Sovete Ministrov SSSR. O dopolnitel'nykh merakh po rasshireniiu prav proizvodstvennykh ob"edinenii (predpriiatii) promyshlennosti v planirovanii i khoziaistvennoi deiatel'nosti i po usileniiu ikh otvetstvennosti za rezul'taty raboty" (In the Central Committee of the CPSU and Council of Ministers, USSR. On additional measures for expanding the rights of production associations [enterprises] of industry in planning and economic activity, and in the strengthening of their responsibility for the results of their work), *Ekon. gaz.*, no. 31 (July 1983).

practice of referring to this experiment as Andropov's, it is quite likely that Gorbachev—given his increasing prominence under Andropov—played a major role in devising the provisions and supervising implementation. In addition, many other party and economic officials subsequently promoted under Gorbachev were closely associated with the design and implementation of the experiment.[9]

THE BASIC APPROACH. The experiment was not a radical departure from the past, but more a reaffirmation of the need to address the implementation of past approaches more vigorously. Once again the basic approach rested on stable five-year norms linking worker and managerial remuneration to enterprise performance. Ministries were ordered to respect the norms. Successful enterprises would not be "taxed" to support enterprises in difficulties, and poorly performing enterprises would be forced to face up to the consequences of poor management. The number of plan indicators that ministries could send to enterprises was strictly limited. Although both the 1965 and 1979 reforms embodied similar measures, the experiment departed from the past reforms in the specific indicators used and in the new efforts by planners to compel enterprises to improve their performance.

Soviet planners' highest priority in designing the experiment was to penetrate the indifference of Soviet enterprises to customer needs. The simple sales indicator introduced in 1965 had not worked; enterprises found it easy to produce and sell goods that in some cases customers had not actually ordered and did not want. The experiment tightened up the sales indicator by stipulating that only sales that actually fulfilled contracts would be counted. In order to interest workers in fulfilling contracts, the Material Stimulation Account was to be increased by 15 percent if contracted sales were all fulfilled; for every 1 percent shortfall in sales according to contract, the Material Stimulation Account was to be reduced by 3 percent.[10] Top managers' interest in the indicator

9. Nikolai Ryzhkov, CC secretary for industry and chief of the economic section at the time, generally supervised the experiment's implementation. Alexei Antonov, one of the few deputy chairmen of the Council of Ministers to survive the Gorbachev succession supervised on the government side. The experiment was implemented and managed by Gosplan under the supervision of L. A. Voronin, then Gosplan first deputy chairman, and now chairman of Gossnab, and S. A. Sitarian, then deputy, and now first deputy, chairman of Gosplan.

10. The sales according to contract indicator was actually introduced in 1974, but enterprises generally resisted calculating it. Dmitrii Valovoi, "Dogovor" (The contract), Pravda, September 12, 1983. Precisely how this indicator was calculated during the

was secured by eliminating any bonus payment to them unless the indicator measuring sales according to contract was at 100 percent.[11]

The experiment was also designed to reward workers directly for increased efficiency. The Material Stimulation Account was formed primarily as a function of cost reductions per unit of commodity output. A second, related incentive was provided by tying formation of the Social-Cultural Measures Account (from which housing was financed) directly to the growth rate of labor productivity (calculated using normative net output [NNO], which was a direct link to the 1979 decree). These two provisions signaled to workers that improved housing and bonus income would come directly from productivity increases and other cost decreases.

A third and venerable concern to planners was that enterprises might reduce costs and fulfill contracts by cutting output. To insure against that, planners used the powerful tool of a norm linking the formation of the wage fund to the growth rate of NNO. Now, in a major departure from the past, the growth rate of enterprise output and the enterprise wage fund were locked together. This arrangement ended (at least formally) any possibility that an enterprise could meet its wages irrespective of its output performance.

These key indicators and their connections to enterprise bonus accounts represented the practical manifestation of Andropov's determination to increase discipline in the economy; that discipline would touch everyone from the highest level of management to the individual worker.[12] The stability of norms was meant to eliminate "planning from

---

experiments is not clear, but the procedures were most likely those laid out in 1974; that is, the indicator is a ratio in which the denominator is the value of total deliveries and the numerator is the value of total deliveries minus the value of all deliveries not made according to schedule, required assortment, or agreed-upon quality. See Fyodor Kushnirsky, *Soviet Economic Planning, 1965–1980* (Boulder, Colo.: Westview Press, 1982), p. 24).

11. A. I. Maiorets, "Otrasl' v ekonomicheskom eksperimente" (The sector in the economic experiment), *Ekon. gaz.*, no. 9 (February 1984). Maiorets was at the time the head of Minelektrotekhprom.

12. This search for discipline motivated the centrally directed move into brigade forms for organizing payment of workers. Under this system workers are organized into small groups of twenty or so individuals, and the group is compensated according to a fixed norm linking their work to indicators important to factory management. Payment within the brigade is determined more subjectively, allowing individual members to judge each other's contribution in a situation where they know what that contribution was. See, for example, A. I. Maiorets, "Povorot k potrebiteliu" (Turn toward the customer), *Sotsialisticheskaia industriia*, June 12, 1984. (Hereafter cited as *Sots. ind.*)

the achieved level," the "ratchet" principle, which almost uniformly discourages enterprises from revealing their productive potential. The stability of the norms would mean that enterprises would know the rules and could be sure they would not change.

And the rules would be strict. The direct link between bonuses and enterprise performance was intended to leave enterprises with no viable alternatives except to increase efficiency and satisfy customers. To justify this much tougher approach to enterprise performance, it was necessary to convince enterprises and their workers that they had a plausible chance at doing well, even when the remainder of the economy was working under the old system. Enterprises in the experiment were therefore given special priority in procuring needed inputs, the hope being that enterprises would be deprived of their favorite excuse for poor performance in fulfilling contracts: the failures of the material-technical supply system.[13]

In addition to introducing the three indicators—sales according to contract, labor productivity, and cost reductions—planners authorized ministries to set obligatory targets for new technology introduced into the enterprise and for the share of highest-quality goods in total output.[14] Ministries also set the norms linking these performance indicators to enterprise accounts. Otherwise the ministries were to leave enterprises to their own devices, refrain from the petty tutelage (*melochnaia opeka*) of the past, and do their best to see that the enterprises operated in a stable environment according to clearly specified rules for success and failure. Enterprises were to be allowed to make their own decisions on the use of the Production Development and Depreciation Accounts and were to be given access to capital and materials needed for small renovations. Finally, enterprises were given wide powers to use their bonus accounts to stimulate higher productivity within the enterprise.

IMPLEMENTATION. The five ministries involved in the experiment were

13. Enterprises under the experiment were actually given a special *nariad* with the word *experiment* stamped on it, assuring them in theory of first priority in their orders for centrally controlled commodities, when such orders were authorized in their annual plans. Interview with L. A. Voronin by *Izvestiia* correspondent V. Sukhachevsky, "Economic Experiment: Advantageous to the Plan—Advantageous to the State," in Foreign Broadcast Information Service, *Daily Report: Soviet Union*, January 9, 1984, pp. S1–S4. (Hereafter cited as *FBIS-SU*.)

14. These last two also had bonuses attached to them. For example, managers could lose at least 25 percent of their bonuses if they failed to fulfill plans for introducing new technology. Maiorets, "Otrasl' v ekonomicheskom eksperimente."

charged with drafting implementing decrees by January 1, 1984, when the experiment was to begin. The entire process was managed by a Gosplan commission, which had its counterparts in each ministry and state committee involved in the experiment.[15]

Problems emerged early on as the ministries found it difficult, or chose to find it difficult, to meet the deadlines set for drafting the decrees. In early December a Politburo meeting devoted solely to considering progress in preparing for the experiment reprimanded the two all-union ministries and their ministers for delaying implementation. The three republican ministries were enjoined to draw the proper conclusions from this dressing down. This was the beginning of a now-familiar battle between the ministries and the center over the implementation of decrees designed to reduce ministerial influence over the operation of the economy.[16]

Somehow the ministers did manage to introduce the reforms on schedule, whereupon 700 enterprises were transferred to the new system. However, many enterprises were unprepared and found it difficult to meet their delivery targets.[17]

As the experiment began to operate in 1984, complaints of ministerial interference appeared with increasing frequency. The ministries and their all-union industrial associations—*vseoiuznie promyshlennie ob''edineniia* (VPOs) continued their previous practice of sending plans down to enterprises at the last minute and then changing them frequently, thus forcing the enterprise to chase a "moving target."[18] Ministries

15. *Komissiia po obshchemu rukovodstvu provedeniem eksperimenta* (Commission for the Overall Leadership of the Conduct of the Experiment). The commission's chair was Lev A. Voronin, first deputy chairman of Gosplan. For a brief discussion of the work of the commission, see Voronin, "Ekonomicheskii eksperiment—pervye itogi i puti razvitiia" (The economic experiment—first results and the path of development) *Planovoe khoziaistvo*, no. 12 (December 1984), p. 17.

16. See "V Politbiuro TsK KPSS" (In the Politburo of the CC of the CPSU), *Pravda*, December 10, 1983.

17. The figures for the number of enterprises under the experiment are taken from Tsentral'noe statisticheskoe upravlenie SSSR, *Narodnoe khoziaistvo SSSR v 1984 g: Statisticheskii ezhegodnik* (Moscow: "Finansy i statistika"), p. 130. (Hereafter cited as *Narkhoz*.) On the poor preparation for the experiment, see, for example, V. Gaevoi, "Pervye uroki" (First lessons), *Sots. ind.*, September 22, 1984.

18. The head engineer at one of Minelektrotekhprom's factories complained that the financial plan for his enterprise (which included authorized use of internally generated investment funds) was changed eleven times in the first quarter of 1984, six times in March alone. See Iu. Usol'tsev, "Krepnut' rostkam samostoiatel'nosti" (Strengthening the shoots of independence), *Sots. ind.*, May 26, 1984. In a survey of Siberian enterprises

wrote regulations that appeared to exceed the limits set by the July 1983 decree on obligatory indicators. In any event the ministries generally treated all indicators, whether formally obligatory or not, as obligatory for the enterprise.[19] Many enterprises complained that, contrary to the provisions of the experiment, the ministry prevented them from using the investment funds that were rightfully theirs and in some cases confiscated the funds of some enterprises to subsidize investments in others.[20] The stable norms, the core of the experiment, were consistently violated, so that the rules for winners and losers were not as clear as Andropov had hoped they would be.[21]

Thus the old behavior persisted, as is illustrated by the effort of the director of Iuzdizelmash, a Mintiazhmash enterprise, to bring into production a new 600-horsepower diesel of the enterprise's design,

---

in the two all-union ministries participating in the experiment R. G. Karagedov found numerous complaints of multiple corrections to the annual plan. One firm complained that during the first quarter of 1984 it received an average of one major plan revision per week. See R. G. Karagedov, "Pervye itogi, problemy, perspektivy" (First results, problems, and perspectives), *EKO*, no. 5 (May 1985), pp. 80–99.

19. Although the July 1983 decree was vague on the list of obligatory targets to be permitted in the experiment, it seemed to specify that the main indicators that ministries could oblige enterprises to fulfill would be limited to targets for the volume of sales in fulfillment of contracts, scientific-technical progress, labor productivity growth, the share of *znak kachestva* products in total output, and cost reductions per unit of commodity production. Yet when the "methodological instructions" regarding which plan indicators ministries would be permitted to send down to enterprises were published, those five indicators were augmented by seven others: output in natural units, including subdivisions for products embodying new technology and items destined for export; profits; wages for nonproduction personnel; limits on centralized state capital expenditures and construction work, and within those, targets for the installation of new capital stock; funds available for basic types of material-technical resources, a norm for contributions from calculated profit into the state budget; and targets for decentralized capital expenditures out of both the Production Development Account and the Material-Cultural Measures and Housing Account. See "Uverennost' v eksperimente" (Confidence in the experiment), *Ekon. gaz.*, no. 15 (April 1984).

On the tendency for ministries to treat nonobligatory indicators as obligatory for enterprises, see Karagedov, "Pervye itogi."

20. Editorial, "The Experiment Continues," in *FBIS-SU*, January 11, 1985, p. S1. This was, for example, the subject of an important meeting of the commission overseeing the experiment. "V Komissii po obshchemu rukovodstvu ekonomicheskim eksperimentom" (In the Commission for Overall Leadership of the Economic Experiment), *Ekon. gaz.*, no. 3 (January 1985).

21. Karagedov, "Pervye itogi," pp. 88–89. During 1984, for example, Mintiazhmash revised four times the norm linking wage funds to performance in the Sibtiazhmash Production Association, and this norm was to be stable for five years. See *FBIS-SU*, January 11, 1985, p. S1.

named the Tokmak diesel (after the town in which the enterprise is situated).[22] The enterprise needed 20 million rubles to develop the Tokmak (which managers thought could easily be earned in the first year's returns), but it had only 2.8 million rubles in its Production Development Account. The State Committee for Science and Technology and the enterprise's supervising VPO were excited about it, but could offer no financial assistance. The department in Gosplan directly responsible for production in this sector offered little help in financing or in finding customers for the new engine. When the enterprise suggested that it cut the production of older products to finance the new diesel, Gosplan forbade it, saying that those products were "very much needed by the country." Various ministries interested in buying the diesel, which was far more efficient than the machine it would replace, offered no help in the financing either, arguing that, although they would indeed be the final users, Gosplan had to issue the order. In the end the diesel was apparently never introduced into serial production.

In sum, it was clear at the outset of the experiment that the ministries, their VPOs, and the central planning organs were continuing their familiar pattern of overbearing interference in all aspects of enterprise activities and were sabotaging efforts to change the system.[23] In this important sense, the failures of 1965, 1973, and 1979 had emerged once again, despite Andropov's determination to implement previously unimplemented measures. Moreover, the notion that a "psychology" was tacitly supporting the old system took on a significance that Mikhail Gorbachev has emphasized in his approach to reforming the system.

RESULTS OF THE EXPERIMENTS. The political judgment on the experiments, rendered at an August 23, 1984, Politburo meeting, was that they were a qualified success. Contract fulfillment in the five ministries had risen significantly, and labor productivity growth rates were higher.[24] In addition, the brigade system had moved ahead formally, although in fact it had little effect on compensation within the factory. In other important

22. A. Nikitin, "Plan s mnogotochiem" (A plan with many omissions), *Pravda*, April 20, 1984.

23. See, for example, the interview by correspondent O. Mikheev with one of Gosplan's deputy chairmen, S. A. Sitarian, "Poisk prodolzhaetsia" (The search continues), *Pravda*, October 2, 1984.

24. L. Abalkin, "Vzaimodeistvie proizvoditel'nykh sil i proizvodstvennykh otnoshenii" (The interrelationships of productive forces and production relations), *Voprosy ekonomiki*, no. 6 (June 1985), pp. 21–22; interview with Sitarian, "Poisk prodolzhaetsia"; and "Polgoda eksperimenta" (Half a year of the experiment), *Sots. ind.*, July 18, 1984.

areas, however, the impact of the experiment was judged minimal. There had been no significant boost to technological progress or product quality, and the ministries and other central authorities had been virtually untouched by the reform measures.[25]

Still, the successes were sufficient to induce the Politburo to extend the experiments—with some modification—to another 1,600 enterprises during 1985 (bringing the total to 2,300 enterprises) in an additional twenty all-union and republican ministries, including five more of the civilian machinebuilding ministries (bringing the total civilian ministries under the experiment to seven out of eleven).[26] The modifications introduced in 1985 were designed to motivate enterprises to increase the quality of their output and to give them somewhat more control over their internal operations.[27]

25. A. Aganbegian, "The Course is Toward an Economical Economy: The Experiment and Financial Autonomy," *FBIS-SU*, August 30, 1984, p. S3.

26. The figures on the number of enterprises operating under the experiments in 1985 are from *Narkhoz 1984*, p. 130. Report of the Politburo meeting of August 23, 1984, is taken from "V Politbiuro TsK KPSS" (In the Politburo of the CC of the CPSU), *Pravda*, August 24, 1984.

The five all-union ministries added to the experiment in 1985 were Minenergomash (Power Machinebuilding), Minneftekhimmash (Chemical and Petroleum Machinebuilding), Minstankoprom (Machine Tool and Tool Building), Minpribor (Instrument-making Automation, and Control Systems), and Minsel'khozmash (Tractor and Agricultural Machinebuilding). In addition, the operation of selected enterprises in Minchermet (Ferrous Metallurgy) was to be switched to the rules of the experiment. These changes brought all but four of the eleven civilian machinebuilding ministries under the experimental system.

The remaining ministries, all republican, were Minpishcheprom (Food) of Belorussia, Azerbaidzhan, Moldavia, Latvia, and Estonia; Minlegprom (Light), of Lithuania, Moldavia, Latvia, Armenia, and Estonia; Minmiasomolprom (Meat and Dairy) of Belorussia; Minrybkhoz (Fishing) of the RSFSR; and selected enterprises of Minmestprom (Local Industry) of the RSFSR and the Ukraine. The list of ministries is from *Narkhoz 1984*, p. 130.

The initial discussions of the extension of the experiments in 1985 also listed enterprises in the *Ministerstvo bytovogo obsluzhivaniia naselniia* (Household Services) of Latvia, Lithuania, Belorussia, and Estonia as switching to the new system. See interview with Sitarian, "Poisk prodolzhaetsia." However, it would appear that these ministries did not participate.

27. To strengthen the pressure for increased quality, the rules of the experiment were altered so that all products in machinebuilding would become subject to state certification, and not just the *znak kachestva* products, as had been the case under the 1984 rules. State standards were changed to raise quality demands. The machinebuilding ministries operating under the new system were authorized to switch to a "Leningrad"-type payment scheme for engineers involved in designing machinery and equipment, an experimental system first tried in Leningrad-area enterprises in which design bureaus

However, further scrutiny of the 1984 experiments suggests a far less sanguine interpretation of the results. The ratchet seems to have survived intact. The improvement in plan fulfillment may be an illusion. Most important, some contradictions that crippled previous reform efforts remain unresolved, even unaddressed, in the experiment.

The ratchet. The emphasis on long-term norms in the experiment reflected a desire to eliminate the pervasive influence of the ratchet and the consequent incentive for enterprises to hide their production possibilities from the center. Yet the very design of the experiment institutionalized a new, particularly perverse, version of the ratchet. Because of *uravnilovka,* enterprises producing approximately the same profile of products began the experiment with approximately the same level of wages and other compensation, irrespective of their previous performance. However, when all enterprises began operating under the experiment, those with reserves implicit in poor previous performance were able to raise wages and bonuses most rapidly—a function of norms linking bonuses to cost reductions, productivity increases, and output growth—whereas the enterprises that had performed well before the experiment encountered enormous difficulties in raising worker compensation. As a result, the enterprises that were the most efficient at the beginning of the experiment soon became the low-wage enterprises in the sector, even though they continued to be the most efficient producers.[28]

The immediate cause of the problem was the persistence of planning on the margin, a sign of planners' ignorance about actual production possibilities. Planners could only know which firms had excess reserves if they knew the production possibilities of each enterprise; since they could not know those, they had to resort to simple rules of thumb. A

---

were allowed to reduce staff and keep most of the wage-bill savings for distribution among the remaining staff. New bonuses were introduced to reward increased exports of manufactured goods. Finally, increased norms linking labor productivity increases to the Social-Cultural and Housing Account were introduced in order to increase enterprise funds available for housing. See interview with Sitarian, "Poisk prodolzhaetsia;" and P. G. Bunich, "Eksperiment na distantsii" (The experiment at a distance), *EKO,* no. 2 (February 1985), pp. 5–7.

28. That was the case, for example, in the wool industry, where one of the worst enterprises and one of the best began the experiment in 1984 by paying essentially identical wages of approximately 177 rubles a month. Six months into the experiment, the worst factory was paying wages averaging 197.3 rubles, while the best had managed to raise wages only 1.6 rubles per month. See P. Bunich, "Pooshrenie za effekt" (Stimulus for effect), *Sots. ind.,* February 12, 1985.

related problem was the lack of a reliable price system and planners' unwillingness to introduce such a system and then use it. The experiment was therefore infused with an aura of arbitrariness from the very beginning, which provided fertile ground for the emergence of special deals between the ministries and their enterprises.

As enterprises began to improve their performance, they discovered that the ratchet was also quite alive in its old form. Ministries did not hesitate to change plans frequently—in direct contravention of both the letter and the spirit of the experiment. As a consequence, an enterprise director had to be incredibly naive, and rather dense, to believe that the ratchet died when the experiment began. Not surprisingly, the incentive for an enterprise director to hide his enterprise's true production possibilities remained strong under the experiment as it was actually implemented.

The contract fulfillment indicator. The fact that more delivery contracts were fulfilled may signal less than appearances suggest. The Soviet economy is populated by powerful suppliers and weak customers, so that if suppliers are required to fulfill all contracts, they will naturally refuse contracts they do not want to try to fulfill. This is precisely what appears to have happened as suppliers used various technicalities to postpone or reject orders they wished to avoid. Even those who fulfilled all orders were helped immensely in the game with the center by the rule that a commodity would be counted as delivered for bonus purposes the moment it was loaded for shipment. If the shipment was later rejected, bonus funds were generally not affected.[29]

There is yet another way in which the practice of fulfilling all contracts is not automatically good for this system. Enterprises as buyers know that they cannot fail financially, but that they can get in bureaucratic trouble if they are unable to meet the plan. Furthermore, enterprise managers know that "the" plan is constantly changing and thus have a strong incentive to hoard inputs for any eventuality. The result is a virtually insatiable demand for all inputs, which, in too many cases, can mean that an enterprise buys a machine and leaves it in inventory for an inordinately long period of time, where it may suffer damage if storage is poor. Because far from all demands in this economy are rational or economically justified, 100 percent contract fulfillment could well tie up

---

29. N. Petrakov and E. Iasin, "Zakaz—v osnovu plana" (The order—at the foundation of the plan), *Sots. ind.*, January 25, 1985.

all productive capacity in the satisfaction of demands, only some of which are justified at the time.[30]

Yet a third factor to consider in evaluating the improvement in contract fulfillment is the special treatment given to the 700 enterprises participating in the experiment in 1984. The special *nariady* of the experiment reduced the uncertainty enterprises normally face in obtaining input supplies and improved their chances of fulfilling their contracts. That says something about what would happen if supply difficulties were less severe in this system; but it confounds the issue of what the effect would be of simultaneously converting all of industry to the new system.[31]

Unresolved contradictions. The design of the experiment was such that enterprise managers were encouraged both to seek high output growth rates and to improve the quality of output. Yet, not infrequently, enterprise managers must choose between quality improvements that would enhance customer satisfaction and high growth of output via the existing output mix, which would boost bonus-forming indicators.

The experiment's incentive system implicitly favored high growth over quality improvements, although planners seemed to want enterprises to achieve both. The dominance of the supplier in the system makes it relatively easy to fulfill contracts without straining to improve quality. Also, newer products tend to have higher labor costs per ruble of sales; therefore a shift to newer products can reduce sales growth (with a fixed labor force) and thereby reduce authorized growth of the wage bill.[32] In addition, the ministries were under pressure from Gosplan to guarantee increased output of important products, thereby institutionalizing their interest in high growth. To be sure, the ministries and

30. This issue is discussed with particular force by Vasilii Seliunin in "Eksperiment" (Experiment), *Novyi mir*, no. 8 (August 1985), pp. 173–79. He notes that in Minenergo (Electric Power) the value of uninstalled equipment has tripled in just the last eight years. Ibid., p. 174. A *Stroibank* study concluded that, on the average, nuclear power stations under construction by Minenergo installed their equipment three to four years after receipt of shipment. Seliunin's check of Minenergo's records showed that approximately half of the equipment on order was not even for stations scheduled in the current five-year plan; indeed that equipment was for stations yet unscheduled to begin construction. Ibid., p. 175.

31. Bunich, "Eksperiment na distantsii," p. 12, suggests this is a factor in the high contract fulfillment indicators for 1984. However, others indicated that supply difficulties continued to be an important factor even for enterprises operating under the experiment. Karagedov, "Pervye itogi," pp. 89–90. It was probably the case that some enterprises were better off and none were worse off, so that the "hothouse" conditions of the 1984 experiment did contribute to the improved contract fulfillment indicators.

32. Seliunin, "Eksperiment," p. 182, makes this point.

the enterprises also had targets for *znak kachestva* products, but it is easier to simulate higher quality (since quality is certified through bureaucratic procedures, and not through the much more unforgiving competitive market) than to simulate higher growth.

In a broader sense, the ministries were the focus of the most damaging contradiction built into the experiment, which had clear antecedents in previous reforms. Although the ministries were enjoined in the experiment to restrict the number of obligatory indicators sent to enterprises and to respect the stability of those indicators, the demands they faced from the center were not materially different from those of the past. They were still responsible for all the same indicators, but were asked to have faith that the new system would induce enterprises to try to fulfill those indicators. Furthermore, the number of indicators Gosplan sent to the ministries was formidable even for those ministries participating in the experiment.

Consider the account of the head of the planning-economic directorate in Minpribor, one of the ministries that began operating under the experiment in 1985: "Here if you please—brandishing a ponderous book—46 pages! 208 positions on nomenclature! This is the plan for production, which we send to the VPO on the basis of indicators sent to us from Gosplan. And the VPO, in its turn, sends them to the enterprises. In those goals there are already up to 200 pages. And what are they full of? Look: 'welded metal structures' (!) which the enterprise makes only for itself. Or here,—Vasilii Antonomvich angrily flips the pages— stampings. One or another on one press, on another. . . . Cast iron castings. . . . Nonferrous metal castings!"[33] These rantings of a very frustrated bureaucrat eloquently express a basic consideration that Soviet leaders seem unwilling to grasp: ministries will impose on lower levels targets that are no less detailed than those the center imposes on them, irrespective of the formal regulations.

The Limits to the Andropov Experiment

The links between the experiment and previous reforms, particularly the 1965 reforms, are obviously strong. In both systems the basic goal was to departicularize the relationship between ministries and enter-

33. E. Panov, "Otrasl' delaet vybor" (The sector makes a choice), *Sots. ind.*, July 19, 1985.

prises and interpose fixed norms that would create a stable environment in which winners and losers would be impartially chosen via publicly announced criteria. In both schemes the emphasis was on the enterprise incentive system, which favored a sales indicator designed to satisfy customers' needs. Both in 1965 and 1984 the central planners retained a relatively comprehensive number of obligatory indicators designed to retain central control over output of the most important products and over the major details of the internal operation of enterprises. Furthermore, in both periods the multiple indicators reflected multiple leadership goals and thus created tensions that were left to the enterprise and the ministries to work out. Soviet leaders, unable to accept the limited capacity of the system to serve multiple centrally set goals, persist in asking too much, then in trying to counteract the antisocial behavior of the system.

The innovations of 1984 were in details, not philosophy. For example, enterprises were judged by compliance with sales contracts in lieu of a simple sales indicator so as to strengthen the weak hand of the buyer. Wage funds, previously set centrally, were linked directly to enterprise output. Bonus funds, previously linked to sales and profitability, became a function of efficiency measures. Housing provided by enterprises through the Social-Cultural Measures Account, formerly linked to sales and profitability, were linked directly to worker productivity. These measures seem to reflect an effort to develop much more carefully targeted indicators and to reduce the room for maneuver that previously had allowed enterprises and their workers to fulfill indicators without actually doing what the center wished them to do.

On a more general plane the 1965 reforms and the 1984 experiments share in common a modest scope. In both the traditional planning system remained intact; the price system remained a mere shadow of its namesakes in Western industrialized countries. In both the barriers to imports were extraordinarily high and provided comfortable protection against competitive pressures from abroad. Both provided a safety net that safeguards against failure; if anything, it is there because no procedure has been established for dealing with the failure of an enterprise.

In sum, the Andropov experiment should be viewed, not as a new approach to the economy, but as an experiment with new tactics for pursuing previous approaches to the economy. It was meant as a serious effort to reform and implement the many decrees that had languished, for lack of attention or will, unimplemented under Brezhnev. It was as conservative and limited in scope as previous decrees, and in many ways just as myopic in refusing to acknowledge the necessity of choosing among multiple goals and in neglecting to anticipate and resolve contradictions within the decisionmaking hierarchy.

Iurii Andropov may have regarded these experiments as a stopgap until far more ambitious reforms could be developed and implemented later on.[34] His time ran out before such notions could be pursued, and the task of working out the strategy for a more comprehensive reform fell to Chernenko, and then to Gorbachev.

Chernenko's Year

Politically and economically, Konstantin Chernenko was a caretaker. His close links to Brezhnev and modest capabilities as a leader suggested that he would not go beyond what Andropov had begun. Indeed when Chernenko assumed office, the most optimistic assessment appeared to be that he would not try to reverse the embryonic debate on the economy begun under Andropov.

In fact he turned out to be a very acceptable caretaker. It fell to him to oversee the implementation of the experiments in 1984 and to go through with plans for their modification and expansion in 1985. In all of this he was most likely a facade behind which Gorbachev worked, but he served that role well.

In his speeches he continued to raise serious issues regarding the performance of the system in ways that sustained political support for a debate on the economic system.[35] He stressed consumer welfare issues, giving attention to general living standards, particularly to the extreme shortage and variable quality of housing. His emphasis on social justice and the need to strengthen the prestige of the common worker suggests

34. In the last speech attributed to Andropov, in January 1984, he discussed briefly the need for a comprehensive improvement (*sovershenstvovanie*) of the entire economic system, but he did not elaborate on what might be involved. "Tekst vystupleniia General'nogo sekretaria TsK KPSS tovarishcha Iu. V. Andropova," pp. 4–11.

35. A sampling of Chernenko's statements on the economy can be found in his speech to voters during the campaign for the Supreme Soviet, "Narod i partiia ediny" (The people and the party are united), *Ekon. gaz.*, no. 11 (March 1984); and his speech to workers at the Serp i Molot Factory "Rech' tovarishcha K. U. Chernenko," *Pravda*, April 30, 1984.

that he was less enthusiastic about attacking *uravnilovka* than Andropov had been, but he showed sympathy for the notion that wages had equalized excessively in recent years. In addition his statements touched on general themes regarding the unacceptably low rate of technical change, the relative inefficiency of the administrative apparatus, and the general need to improve the management system. He seemed much more inclined to find solutions in increased discipline than in reforms per se, but he at least did not openly oppose further discussion of more radical reforms than were implied by the experiment.

In the end Chernenko was somewhat of a pleasant surprise, mainly because of what he did not do. His close association with Brezhnev suggested that he might try to pull back on some of the more dramatic, and possibly disconcerting, aspects of Andropov's new style. However, it seems that even Chernenko recognized the need for a significantly different approach to managing the economy. At least he seemed sufficiently convinced that he did not get in the way of further discussion and debate; in fact some of the most far-reaching proposals for economic reforms were published, or approved for publication, while Chernenko was general secretary.[36] Much more important was his willingness to allow Gorbachev to gain influence. Thus he smoothed the transition in March 1985 to the fourth, but probably the last, general secretary in the 1980s.

Debates on the Economic System

In his first speech as general secretary Andropov openly invited debate on the economy. The response was a virtual explosion of views on how to solve Soviet economic problems. The debates continued under Konstantin Chernenko, and since then, under Mikhail Gorbachev, their scope and import have begun to expand well beyond what in hindsight appears to be the modest nature of the debates in 1983–84. Even though Gorbachev began to introduce reforms in 1986, he has encouraged the debate to continue, so that the dialogue between the

36. The debates are discussed below. Quite radical reform proposals such as those of Kurashvili and fairly frank and tough-minded analyses such as those of Abalkin were either published while Chernenko was in power or approved for publication. More generally, Philip Hanson has concluded that there was an effort by conservative economists to put down reform economists during Chernenko's time in office, and they were rebuffed. See Philip Hanson, "Economics, Economic Advisers, and the Gorbachev Leadership," *Radio Liberty Research Bulletin*, RL 308/85, September 16, 1985.

leadership and the population about a strategy for economic reform is becoming increasingly interesting.

To do justice to those debates would require a book in itself and would be far beyond the scope of this volume. Nonetheless, it is possible to sketch out some of the major themes that are either important in themselves or have had some bearing on the Gorbachev reforms.

The debates have revealed a strong consensus on the unsatisfactory nature of Soviet economic performance and a wide range of sometimes deeply held viewpoints concerning what should be done about it. Some conservatives believe the current system is unsatisfactory only because of the backsliding from the basic, and sound, principles of a planned economy. For them the solution is to return to the no-nonsense, disciplined approach to central planning of the Stalin era. In contrast, some radicals envision a Soviet economy similar to that of Hungary, which has no obligatory plans, an active price system, and ministries with far more modest functions than those in the USSR. The majority of economists are in the middle: they see that something serious must be done, but are unwilling to contemplate a leap into the unknown of a truly comprehensive reform.

During 1983–85 the range of views did not differ significantly from the range observed in 1962–64, in the debate preceding the 1965 reforms. By 1986, however, some economists had begun to strike out on what, publicly at least, was new ground, as they began to probe deeper into the roots of the reform dilemmas. Another new element in this debate relative to past debates, and a sign of some learning, is the emerging theory of reform strategy, which is concerned with the forces arrayed against reforms and emphasizes the need to neutralize that opposition while seeking support from groups that will benefit from reforms. Also implicit is an as yet embryonic theory of the political preconditions for successful reform.

I begin this brief review of the debates by discussing the Soviet theory of why past reforms failed, since it has some bearing on the current overall debate. I emphasize that these are the views to which Gorbachev has easy access. His own views, to be discussed in a subsequent chapter, reflect some, but not all, of what has emerged in the debates.

The Theory of Reforms

In their totality, economic reforms imply a theory, quite possibly not consciously articulated, concerning the nature of the problems, the systemic changes needed to fix the problems, and the best strategy for bringing about those changes. In the history of Soviet reform efforts, most of the leadership's attention has been focused on the first two components of the theory: what's wrong, and what's the fix? The strategic issue has not been addressed openly, and implicitly the approach has been rather simpleminded: the bureaucracy will, in good faith, design and implement decrees conforming to the wishes of the party.

However, the modest results of previous reform efforts have gradually stirred up interest in the strategic issue, with the result that a rather simple, widely held theory has emerged that previous reforms failed primarily because of bureaucratic resistance centered in the ministries.[37] The diagnosis of the problem is fine, so this reasoning goes, and the solutions are basically sound, but the ministries are saboteurs, driven by a desire to protect their considerable power in the system.

As the discussion of previous efforts shows, this view is not wrong, but it is incomplete and superficial. Even as an analysis of the bureaucratic impediments to reform, it fails to take into account the flaws in reform design that create incentives for ministries to preserve controls over enterprises. Furthermore, it assumes that other elements of the system are anxious for the reforms to work, but the ministries are standing in the way. It uses the ministries as scapegoats, loading the explanation for a very complex phenomenon on the back of a very small part of the problem. Most important, this simple view of the impediments to reform ignores the large and important political issues that affect in a fundamental way the choices made in the design of reforms and the fate of the resulting decrees.

What is significant in the debate since 1982 is the development by a few scholars of a much more nuanced and believable understanding of the impediments to reform, and—by implication—the requirements for the successful implementation of a reform. The most prominent of those few scholars is Tat'iana Zaslavskaia, an economic sociologist based in Novosibirsk, who has put forth in numerous publications a frank and

37. Many of the leadership speeches and a number of the decrees under Gorbachev eloquently testify to the widespread acceptance of the theory. During Gorbachev's first year in power I had the opportunity during a visit to Moscow for a lengthy discussion with one of the USSR's most thoughtful advocates of radical economic reforms. When I asked him why previous reforms had failed, he replied with no hesitation and great conviction: "the ministries!"

important analysis of the need for reform, the impediments to it, and the requirements for a strategy to implement it.[38] Zaslavskaia stresses three points: that the old system is an anachronism, that changing it will inevitably affect the interests of certain social groups and therefore require a carefully thought-out strategy to neutralize opposition and build support, and that the leadership must get its priorities right so that the reform is as free as possible of contradictions.

Zaslavskaia's contention that the old system is an anachronism rests not so much on the inability of economic institutions to cope with the demands of a modern industrialized economy—although she would not dispute that—as on the political point that the population is far better educated and more mature than it was in the 1930s when the system was conceived. The uneducated peasants drawn into the factories in the 1930s may have welcomed, and may have required, a highly centralized system that treated them as cogs in a machine. They needed work, and they were living close to subsistence, so whatever wages and goods they received were welcome. Soviet citizens in the 1980s are much better off, much better educated, and increasingly impatient with a system that treats them as if they were still uneducated peasants. The system capable of coordinating the actions of this much more mature population is not the one in place currently, which has its roots in the 1930s.

Zaslavskaia notes that in reforming the system the leadership must take into account the identifiable social groups in this system and their behavior patterns, which are conditioned by a number of factors. The state cannot control all aspects of that behavior, nor should it want to. The state should seek to control only those key aspects of behavior that directly affect social interests. The best instruments for doing that are the indirect ones, which influence incentives, which in turn influence individual behavior.

However, any major restructuring of an economic system will affect different social groups in different ways: some will gain, others will lose. In consequence, a reform is not simply a program worked out and implemented by professionals, but rather a "complex process of mutual

38. Zaslavskaia came to the attention of Western observers in the summer of 1983 when an untitled paper she had presented at a secret seminar in Moscow was summarized in the Western press and then made available in full version. See "The Novosibirsk Report," *Survey*, vol. 28 (Spring 1984), pp. 88–108. Since then she has enumerated most of the points in that paper in print, in the USSR. See, for example, T. I. Zaslavskaia, "Ekonomika skvoz' prizmu sotsiologii" (Economics through the prism of sociology), *EKO*, no. 7 (July 1985), pp. 3–22; and her interview in *Izvestiia*, June 1, 1985.

interaction of social-economic groups, occupying different positions in social production and following contradictory interests." That complex process is what has led to reform cycles in the past (my words, but clearly her meaning).[39] A successful reform involves a well-thought-out strategy that identifies potential winners and losers, enlists the winners in support of reforms, and neutralizes the losers. Zaslavskaia readily admits that the losers include the middle levels of the bureaucracy—the ministries and their departments. But the potential opposition to the reforms runs far deeper than that: throughout the system from top to bottom the less qualified workers are fearful of reforms and will oppose them. She does not actually identify social groups that oppose reforms, but the implication seems to be that opposition in the blue-collar work force could be significant. She would presumably agree with those who have suggested that managers too are far from enthusiastic about reforms.[40] Her conclusion on this issue is simultaneously a criticism of previous leaders and an admonition to the current leadership: "For success in improving productive relations it is necessary to have a well-thought-out social strategy, capable, on the one hand, of consolidating groups truly interested in intensification of the economy and a corresponding restructuring of the methods of management; and on the other hand, blocking the actions of groups disposed to impede decisions of the critical questions."[41]

For Zaslavskaia, an important component of the strategy is clearly defined priorities, which must be established before deciding on the actual design of the reform. If economic performance alone is emphasized, in particular high growth and higher-quality goods and services, the logical decision may be to increase the role of private economic activity in the system. Along with that, however, comes higher incomes for some, but not for others, in potential conflict with important social goals. These conflicts must be resolved ahead of time, to the extent that

39. Zaslavskaia, "Ekonomika skvoz' prizmu sotsiologii," p. 19.

40. Leonid Abalkin, a liberal economist who in 1986 was the director of the Political Economy Department of the CC's Academy of the Social Sciences and has subsequently moved to the directorship of the Academy of Science's Institute of Economics, was asked in an interview in *L'Unità* if the ministries were the major source of opposition to reforms. He answered that this was the general impresson, and also his, until he saw the results of the 1984 experiment in which "suddenly the industrial leaders, who had always claimed to have too few rights, said that they no longer wanted them. The basic reason is simple. Hand in hand with rights came responsibility." See *FBIS-SU*, November 12, 1985, p. S2.

41. Zaslavskaia, "Ekonomika skvoz' prizmu sotsiologii," p. 22.

is possible, by being clear on which is the higher priority, economic performance or social goals.

Zaslavskaia's understanding of the reform process as a social and political phenomenon clearly is a more powerful and useful approach than the monochrome view that focuses solely on opposition from mid-level bureaucrats. Still, there are gaps in her public writings. She sees the need for a strategy, but does not expand on what precisely the strategy might be. She obviously senses the growing political sophistication of the Soviet population but does not, or chooses not to, make the connection between economic reform and the need for increased political participation in the entire process. She is advocating further economic reforms, yet says little on what those might be.

That in no way diminishes the importance of Zaslavskaia's views and the fact that they are now in the public domain. Her work is a giant stride in the direction of raising the quality of discourse on the reform process. And, most important, her propositions are in print and therefore are legitimate subjects for discussion. Zaslavskaia's work is but one example of many illustrating the fact that the Soviet leadership is encouraging a far more frank and broad discussion of views than has been seen in this society since the late 1920s.

Debates on Reforms

The reform debate itself serves as a major indicator of the considerable loosening of the limits on public discussion dating from the Andropov period, but considerably expanded under Gorbachev. Beginning roughly in 1984 the entire tone of public discussion of the Soviet economy and economic reforms began to change, and under Gorbachev the change has accelerated. Subjects previously taboo, such as bankruptcy or the social functions of transitional unemployment, are now actively debated in the press. Subjects previously considered resolved (for example, the appropriate role for private economic activity and the acceptable spread in the income distribution) are now being given a fresh look.

These unfolding debates react in complex ways with Gorbachev's evolving views on the economy and with the measures he is introducing. Issues explored in major national publications give an indication of views that Gorbachev and his appointees are willing to listen to, even if they do not fully agree with them. The airing of some views may in fact represent trial balloons by Gorbachev or those close to him. A proposal for a new incentive scheme or new rules for private economic activity may be initiated by economists close to the leadership in an effort to take a reading on the possible opposition to such measures. Zaslavskaia's careful strategy would require such tactics.

For these reasons the debate is a useful indicator of what is possible. However, it is not always an accurate predictor of what will occur, since it is primarily a debate among professionals about reforms, and—as Zaslavskaia reminds us—the actual outcome of a reform has more to do with political and social processes than it does with the views of professionals.

Finally, the debate has undoubtedly had an influence on the views of the leadership. Gorbachev appears to be a curious man, who—like Andropov—has emphasized that he does not have a fully articulated plan for reforming the system. As the debate generates new ideas about possible approaches to the economy, Gorbachev may build those into his program. Also, as the measures he introduces come into force and the debate about them proceeds (if he encourages that), this too can influence the measures he introduces.

In sum, while Gorbachev and those who advise him are developing a concept of how the reform should proceed and are drafting the decrees that will constitute the reform, the debate is being influenced by, and is influencing, what they do. Thus the two processes—the debate and the reforms—are best discussed as one. In preparation for that it is useful to outline briefly the basic positions that have emerged.

The views of Soviet social scientists and politicians form a rich and wide spectrum, ranging from very conservative to very radical views. That spectrum can be said to consist of three clusters around general propositions. The neoconservatives make up one cluster. They advocate a return to the basic principles of central planning of the Stalin years, but without the political repression of those years. The second, and by far the largest, group I call—for want of a better phrase—the moderates. Those who fall into this group accept the system as a whole, but have various ideas on how it could be improved upon; sometimes they recommend a significant departure from particular features of the current system. These individuals have had their views published throughout the post-Stalin period, but they are becoming somewhat more radical under Gorbachev.

The radical reformers fall into a third category. Unlike the moderates, they advocate systemwide reforms; unlike the neoconservatives, they want to see the management of the system greatly decentralized.

The people in these three categories would all agree that Soviet economic performance is marred by significant weaknesses, which must be addressed: declining growth rates, imbalances, low rates of technical change, persistent quality problems, and a failure to meet customer demands. They disagree on the source of these problems, and therefore on the solution. Of course in reality these three categories are not terribly neat: particular individuals may hold views that fall into two or even three categories. Nevertheless, the three categories provide a useful device for abstracting the essence of what is in fact an enormously rich and diverse debate on the economy.

THE NEOCONSERVATIVES. Those whom I characterize as neoconservatives attribute the problems in economic performance to the fact that the system has drifted away from the basic, and sound, principles established by Stalin for administering an economy. These individuals count in their ranks many who were in high positions at the time Mikhail Gorbachev became general secretary. For them the glorious years were those of World War II, when the system was run from the center, and run well. They believe that it is not only possible, but advisable, to return to those first principles. However, the leadership must be willing to use a firm hand to reintroduce discipline throughout the system, reducing the chaos of the involuntarily decentralized system of today. In such a system, the penalty for not fulfilling indicators would be far more severe than it is today; thus directives from above would be reinstituted as something to be taken quite seriously.

A prominent advocate of that view is Nikolai Baibakov, who was in his twentieth year as chairman of Gosplan when Gorbachev retired him in 1985. A few months before he was retired he wrote a piece celebrating the approach to the economy in those years.[42] Baibakov is particularly impressed by the fact that during World War II the ministries (then called People's Commissariats) were not the channel used to send obligatory plans to enterprises. Rather, enterprises received their orders directly from the State Defense Committee, and enterprise managers did their best, under terrible conditions, to fulfill those orders. That form of direct central commands, which enterprise managers regard as obligations, is what Baibakov understands to be the only possible form of true central planning. For him, central planning is "one of the most important accomplishments and advantages of the socialist economic sys-

42. N. Baibakov, "Sovetskaia ekonomika v godu velikoi otechestvennoi voinu" (The Soviet economy in the years of the great patriotic war), *Planovoe khoziaistvo*, no. 5 (May 1985), pp. 3–14.

tem . . . [which] has stood the test of time and guaranteed the resolution of those tasks which were historically placed before our state.''[43]

By implication this view proposes that the de facto system return to the principles of the formal system. The plan should be the heart of the resource-allocation system and probably rely even more than at present on quantitative indicators in natural units. Prices are to be passive, supporting, and not interfering with the plan. Similarly, money is no more than a means of account. The foreign trade monopoly remains a mainstay in the defense against the chaos of the world capitalist system.

Baibakov's viewpoint is important for several reasons. First, although it is not articulated with any frequency now that Gorbachev has set out a fairly ambitious reform program, it is still probably held by many, particularly in the older generation. They recall with some nostalgia simpler times when the Soviet Union, faced with a deadly external threat, responded with an effort of heroic proportions, the success of which was—in their minds—directly attributable to the centrally guided economic activity. They are unconvinced by arguments that this is a different economy and these are different times.

Nonetheless, this view, in some form, probably has the support of far more than simply those who are of the older generation. Although it is difficult to document, anyone who has had the opportunity to discuss the economy with Soviet economists discovers an almost visceral fear of the economic chaos that might result from allowing individuals and single enterprises to make major economic decisions without direct central guidance. It is the obverse of the conviction—obvious in the design of the system—that enterprises will at most do what they are told, and if they are not guided by targets, then who knows what they will do?[44] Second, by hearkening back to World War II, neoconservatives

43. Ibid., p. 10.

44. Filippov, when discussing the possibility of instituting a system in which enterprises are subjected to a profit tax and then allowed to retain the remainder of their earnings—a system that has gained widespread support in the form of the SUMY/VAZ experiments—objects by asking what might happen if the enterprise earned more profits than originally planned. "Where will those means be applied? Should the enterprise retain them under all circumstances? Should they be set free in circulation?" V. F. Filippov, *Besedy o khoziaistvennom mekhanizme* (Conversations on the economic mechanism) (Moscow: Politizdat, 1984), p. 152. His answer was the traditional one: control the amount of profits the enterprise can retain, and confiscate the rest.

Or, consider the response of a Gosplan official to the question of whether wholesale markets might not resolve some of the deficits prevalent in the material-technical supply system. His reply: don't overestimate those markets. They can't account for the level

are inviting an analogy between those times and the current situation in which the threat comes not from Germany but from the United States. This view does not deny the existence of some degree of chaos in the economy; it highlights it. But it goes on to say, implicitly, that such chaos is a luxury that the USSR, in the current "historical circumstances," can ill afford.

There is a natural link between this group and those economists who advocate increased computerization of the system in order to enhance the quality of information and planning decisions handled by the center. The dream of the neoconservatives is that the so-called *avtomaticheskaia sistsema upravleniia* (automated management system) will be successfully installed in the economy. With this system, central planners will be able to keep tabs on each enterprise, each association, and each ministry. Moreover planners' orders to all of them will be based on accurate information concerning their production possibilities.[45] For the neoconservatives the computer is the vehicle through which the Soviet Union can recreate the efficiently run, centralized system of the 1940s.

At the core of the neoconservative position is the belief that discipline needs to be restored, which is also at the core of Gorbachev's approach to the economy. However, that belief unites virtually all of the participants in the debate. The question is not about the need to increase discipline, but the means. To what extent should markets—a harsh disciplinary force—be utilized to supplement planners in imposing discipline on the economy? The neoconservatives approach this issue with a nostalgia for past methods. Gorbachev, it would appear, does not share that nostalgia. Those holdovers from Brezhnev's years who are most strongly associated with the view have retired (presumably not all voluntarily).[46] Many who may still hold those views are, wisely, either being silent or paying homage to Gorbachev's approach to the system, waiting for a failure and an opportunity to reassert their views. It is

of development, state price policy, or the growth of incomes. In any event, you need a state plan to avoid the unpredictable influences from what are at times the subjective opinions of individual buyers, which are capable of creating new deficits. Interview with M. Darbinianom, *Sots. ind.*, June 18, 1984.

45. See, for example, S. E. Goodman, "Computing and the Development of the Soviet Economy," in U.S. Joint Economic Committee, *The Soviet Economy in a Time of Change*, Joint Committee Print, 96 Cong. 1 sess. (GPO, 1979), vol. 1, pp. 540–45.

46. Nikolai Baibakov was removed as head of Gosplan in 1985. N. Patolichev, former head of Minvneshtorg (Foreign Trade) and a staunch defender of the monopoly of foreign trade, was removed in 1985; N. Glushkov, former head of Goskomtsen and an opponent of reforms, was removed in 1986.

Gorbachev's intolerance for these views that has effectively muted the public expression of the neoconservative view. But that should not be allowed to obscure the fact that there must be many who still subscribe to such views.

THE MODERATES. In the middle of the spectrum are the moderates, who account for the vast majority of Soviet economists and many in the Soviet leadership. By definition, this is a diverse and diffuse collection of people whose viewpoints range from concurrence with some, but not all, of the neoconservative propositions to support for decentralization of the decisionmaking authority, short of a radical reform. Some in this group focus on partial reforms that would respond to particular problems in the economic system without devoting a great deal of attention to the system as a whole. Some call for "comprehensive restructuring," but in fact propose no more than an aggregation of partial reforms, which in some cases contradict each other. Some do have a complete conception of how the system would look after a "restructuring" that would leave the fundamentals intact, but sometimes differ significantly from the system of the mid-1980s in the details. In the interest of brevity, I discuss only a few of the most prominent views of this group, the majority of Soviet economists.

In general, the moderates regard the Andropov experiment (as it was intended and not necessarily as it was implemented) as an important step in the right direction.[47] Most of them believe that enterprises should not be subjected to petty interference from superiors, but that strict central control should be maintained over the important decisions, most notably all those associated with significant expansion in productive capacity. This implies support for the expanded use of norms and increasing reliance on stable five-year plans to guide individual enterprises and the system as a whole. Some advocate overhauling the enterprise system by increasing the number of scientific-production associations and encouraging mergers across ministerial lines. These enterprises, it is argued, should be operated according to full (*polnyi*) *khozraschet*, which means they should be self-financing and should

47. See, for example, E. Kapustin, "Sovershenstvovanie upravleniia narodnym khoziaistvom" (Improvement in the management of the economy), *Voprosy ekonomiki*, no. 12 (December 1984), pp. 25–36, for what appears to be a summary of the views of the Academy of Sciences Institute of Economics, which he directed at the time and which generally has been associated with eclectic views on reform. A somewhat briefer and more coherent statement of the eclectic view by someone not necessarily sympathetic with it can be found in Karagedov. "Pervye itogi," pp. 91–92.

cover all current costs and the capital costs for renovations out of their own funds. They should only be offered state help, probably on a loan basis, for large projects.

The price system consistent with this approach would still serve the plan, not influence it.[48] Prices would be set by strict rules, uniform for the economy as a whole, designed to reflect the full socially necessary cost of a product (which would in reality be no higher than the average cost of a product, and perhaps even below the average). They would be more flexible than the current prices, in order to capture changes in costs over time, but they would be centrally set (although some of the moderates would not apply that dictum to all sectors) with the aid of an expanded system of norms to guide price-setters in their task. With improved prices, it would be possible to reduce the number of commodities under direct control through the material-technical supply system, by increasing the reliance on wholesale trade for less than critical commodities.

The moderates apportion some of the blame for the poor performance of the system, and in particular the existence of imbalances, to mistakes of the planners themselves. Thus they want to see substantial improvements in the efficacy of the planning process, and therefore in the quality of plans, the notion being that plans designed to search for balance a priori will be more stable and will provide enterprises with an environment in which they will be motivated to take a longer-term view.

The ministerial system is regarded by the moderates as a necessary, indeed important, component of the system. However, its current form, with the resulting "departmentalism" and its tenacious hold on power over the enterprises, is widely condemned. The solution many seem to favor is either superministries formed by the merger of related ministries or at least supraministerial organs that would coordinate the work of related ministries and make the critical strategic decisions.[49] Whichever

48. In addition to Kapustin, "Sovershenstvovanie upravleniia narodnym khoziaist-vom," p. 31, see A. A. Deriabin's outline of a price reform in his contribution to a discussion on the Twelfth FYP, "Obsuzhdenie proektov novoi redaktsii programmy KPSS i osnovnykh napravlenii ekonomicheskogo i sotsial'nogo razvitiia SSSR na 1986–1990 gody i na period do 2000 goda" (A discussion of the draft of the new edition of the program of the CPSU and the basic guidelines for the economic and social development of the USSR during 1986-1990 and to the year 2000), *Voprosy ekonomiki*, no. 1 (January 1986), pp. 95–96; or, more recently, A. Deriabin, "Tsena: stimul ili tormoz?" (Price: stimulus or brake?), *Sots. ind.*, March 18, 1987.

49. R. G. Karagedov, "Ob organizatsionnoi strukture upravleniia promyshlennos-

form is used, the ministries would work with reduced staffs and be expected to focus on the larger issues, leaving to the enterprises (on full *khozraschet*) the more detailed decisions. The smaller number of ministries, or the few supervisory bodies over the ministries, would considerably reduce the strong departmental barriers and lead to increased cooperation and specialization within the industrial sector; that in turn would help to accelerate technological change. The streamlined ministerial system is also expected to improve central control over the variables that matter in the system.

This view implies a tougher approach to enterprises, which would be forced to absorb losses, but allowed to keep part of the proceeds flowing from their successes. That suggests a much tougher stand on wages that calls for moving away from the system in which—irrespective of enterprise performance—the enterprise work force receives its full wage.

An increasingly popular notion among some moderate economists is that this approach could be modified somewhat by organizing the economy into a few major complexes. According to one proposal, only three would be necessary: fuels and raw materials; machinebuilding and metalworking, and related sectors; and consumer goods.[50] Each of these complexes would presumably be administered by a supraministerial organ, and each would be organized somewhat differently from the other. In the fuels and raw materials complex, the traditional planning techniques and traditional hierarchy would prevail, presumably with the continued reliance on centrally determined prices fixed for long periods of time. The complex consisting of machinebuilding and metalworking and related sectors would rely more heavily on *khozraschet* methods, and somewhat more on the banking system. Still, planners would retain full control over the structure of investment and presumably some control over the price level.

In the third complex, covering light industry, which presumably includes agriculture, decisionmaking would be much more decentralized than in the other two complexes. Investment would be guided solely by consumer demand, and thus the banking system would become more

---

t'iu" (On the organizational structure of the management of industry), *EKO*, no. 8 (August 1983), pp. 50–69; or V. Kirichenko, "O nekotorykh voprosakh dal'neishego sovershenstvovaniia planirovaniia i upravleniia khoziaistvom" (On several issues concerning the improvement of planning and management of the economy), *Planovoe khoziaistvo*, no. 1 (January 1982), pp. 57–65.

50. See L. Evstigneeva, "Ekonomika: vospriimchivost' k nauchno-tekhnicheskomu progressu" (The economy: receptiveness to scientific-technical progress), *Pravda*, June 28, 1985.

active. Prices would presumably be free to fluctuate, although it seems likely that some prices for socially important goods would somehow remain fixed (possibly through subsidies for variables).

This view of a differentiated approach to organizing the economy, now increasingly apparent in Gorbachev's reform program, is the understandable outcome of a continued conviction that the economy needs to be controlled from the center, combined with an increasingly sophisticated understanding that the priorities of the leadership may permit different levels of control in different sectors. For raw materials and fuels, critical to the entire system, central control makes much more sense—and is much easier to enforce—than it does for consumer goods. In the latter the planners can allocate investments to the complex and then allow consumers to drive the enterprises' decisions about what precisely to produce, all without violating in any significant way planners' or Soviet leaders' most important goals for the system.

Although the overall views of the neoconservatives and the moderates differ significantly, they also overlap in some areas. Both see a need to strengthen a weak center; both regard as a "given" continued central control over the economy, particularly control over the process by which capital is generated and distributed. Neither the neoconservatives nor the moderates would seriously contemplate relinquishing control over the investment process and allowing consumers to drive it by means of their savings choices and their demand for particular products. Neither group gives much thought to the role of foreign trade in the system; for example, neither would want to reduce the high import barriers that now protect Soviet industry. Both would like to continue relying on relatively few, very large enterprises to facilitate central control over economic activity.

One of the basic differences between the two is that the neoconservatives believe it is still possible to rely on administrative methods to achieve those goals, whereas the moderates are no longer convinced that such an approach is advisable or necessary. Some see those methods as primarily applicable to the early stages of the production cycle, which involve raw materials and fuels. In manufacturing the moderates would give somewhat more power to the individual enterprises than the neoconservatives would. At the same time the moderates would hold enterprises more accountable for their mistakes, implicitly generating shifts in the income distribution that might offend the generally egalitarian preferences of the neoconservatives.

THE RADICALS. Under Leonid Brezhnev the word *reform* virtually dropped from use, for the simple reason that the 1965 reforms had, according to the official version, been successful. What was needed was not another reform, so the reasoning went, but a further improvement (*dalneishee sovershenstvovanie*, literally, further perfection) of the existing system. When Iurii Andropov called for a debate on the economy without signaling his preference for a particular solution, he opened the door partway for the public discussion of more radical reforms.

However, it was Mikhail Gorbachev who threw the door wide open, encouraging a broad public discussion of subjects heretofore considered taboo. "Economic management is in need of constant improvement" (*sovershenstvovanie*), said Gorbachev at the Twenty-seventh Party Congress in February 1985. "But now the situation is such that it is impossible to simply limit our measures to partial improvements—what is needed is a radical reform."[51] Such words, never spoken and virtually never written from the late 1960s until Brezhnev's death, sent a clear signal to political leaders and the academics that this leader was looking for radically different solutions to Soviet economic problems.

The result has been the public articulation of a radical position on reform, which has taken two forms. Some authors have put forward proposals for comprehensive economic reform, usually following either the Hungarian model or the closely related model of the New Economic Policy (NEP). Other economists are generally sympathetic with that approach but have not outlined an entire system. Instead they have focused on the most sensitive issue in constructing such a system: the inextricable ties between Soviet economic problems and the extraordinary economic security for the population under the current system.

Comprehensive reform proposals. For some time a few voices in the USSR have been publicly calling for radical economic reform. Some have used the New Economic Policy of the 1920s as their model, the most prominent being Fedor Burlatskii, A. P. Butenko, and E. A. Ambartsumov.[52] Others have been more influenced by Hungary, al-

51. *Materialy XXVII s"ezda kommunisticheskoi partii Sovetskogo Soiuza* (Moscow: Politizdat, 1986), p. 33.

52. Fedor Burlatskii, "Lenin i strategiia krutogo pereloma" (Lenin and the strategy of a sharp turning point), *Literaturnaia gazeta*, April 16, 1986; A. P. Butenko, "Protivorechiia razvitiia sotsializma kak obshchestvennogo stroia" (Contradictions of the development of socialism as a social system), *Voprosy istorii*, no. 10 (October 1982), pp. 16–29; and E. A. Ambartsumov, "Analiz V. I. Leninym prichin krizisa 1921 g. i putei khoda iz nego" (An analysis by V. I. Lenin of the reasons for the crisis of 1921 and ways to resolve it), *Voprosy istorii*, no. 4 (April 1984), pp. 15–29.

though they are undoubtedly aware of the NEP analogy Among the latter, one of the earliest and most articulate advocates of radical reforms is B. P. Kurashvili, of the Institute for State and Law in Moscow, who has outlined what by Soviet standards is a bold departure from the existing system.[53] His inspiration is the Hungarian economic reforms of 1968, which eliminated obligatory plans to enterprises, simplified the ministerial system, and sought to reform the price system by allowing customers and their suppliers to exchange much more information on changing trends in supply and demand than was permitted in the past. However, his argument is not purely derivative of the Hungarian design; it is consciously tailored to meet the special needs of the Soviet economy. I focus on his work here as a broad example of the viewpoint expressed by those in the Soviet Union who support the radical alternative, whether or not they have chosen to write about it.[54]

Kurashvili regards the ministerial system, and the obligatory plans conveyed through it, as the most important source of Soviet economic problems. In particular he highlights the ministerial autarky discussed in chapter 4, which results in a "semi-cottage" type of industrial base. Kurashvili argues that this system creates barriers to the intersectoral cooperation necessary for rapid technological change and is responsible for many of the USSR's economic problems.

He concludes that any design that retains the ministerial system is doomed. The "command style . . . is in their blood, and it is difficult to conceive how they can change their nature."[55] Any reforms that preserve that system and actually submit plans for reform to the ministries for their opinions simply invite continued inertia. The old system has served its purpose, concludes Kurashvili, and now must give way to a different

53. B. P. Kurashvili, "Sud'by otraslevogo upravleniia" (The fate of sectoral management), *EKO*, no. 10 (October 1983), pp. 34–57; and B. P. Kurashvili, "Kontury vozmozhnoi perestroiki" (The contours of a possible restructuring), *EKO*, no. 5 (May 1985), pp. 59–70. Both of these articles are footnoted as "v poriadke obsuzhdeniia" (for purposes of discussion), an indication that the piece is regarded as potentially controversial. By 1987 such articles had become much more common.

54. Others holding similar views include Seliunin, "Eksperiment"; R. Belousov, "Tsentralizm i samostoiatel'nost'" (Centralism and independence), *Sots. ind.*, April 24, 1986; Karagedov, "Pervye itogi," pp. 93–99; S. Shatalin and E. Gaidar, "Uzlovye problemy reformy" (Key problems of reform), *Ekon. gaz.*, no. 29 (July 1986); S. S. Shatalin, "Effektivnoe ispol'zovanie resursov: interesy i stimuly" (The effective use of resources: interests and stimuli), *EKO*, no. 12 (December 1986), pp. 3–22; and N. Petrakov and E. Iasin, "Ekonomicheskie metody upravleniia" (Economic methods of management), *Ekon. gaz.*, no. 47 (November 1986)

55. Kurashvili, "Sud'by otraslevogo upravleniia," p. 38.

system that is suitable for managing a modern economy in which technological change is at the top of the agenda.

Kurashvili's solution is a "self-regulating economic mechanism" (*mekhanizm ekonomicheskogo samoreguliatsii*) in which the government focuses primarily on manipulating indirect instruments that influence economic activity (prices, taxes, subsidies, interest rates)—what he calls "economic planning"—while enterprises operate according to the principles of full *khozraschet* and make most decisions without interference from above. The system of approximately fifty union-level branch ministries would be compressed into seven ministerial-level bodies.

—The Ministry of the Economy (*Minnarkhoz*) would supervise much of the economy with a much smaller staff than the staffs in the approximately thirty ministries whose authority would be subsumed under this new body.[56] This ministry would not issue obligatory plans, but would focus instead on demand forecasting; planning material production, using aggregate indicators; setting the rules of the game; and setting policies on pricing procedures, standardization, and quality control.

—A Ministry of the Fuel and Energy Industry would manage production of those commodities, probably by relying on the traditional system of obligatory planning, and cost-plus pricing.

—A Ministry of Communal Economy and Communications would handle matters such as housing construction.

—A Ministry of Transport would supervise transport.

—The Ministry of Supply, Procurements, and Trade (*snabzhenie, zagotovok, i torgovlia*) would take over the remaining central functions of Gossnab, which would involve general management of wholesale and retail trade, but not detailed planning of deliveries.

—Gosplan would remain, but its primary duties would be long-term planning and the management of complex programs important to the entire system, such as energy and regional development.

—A State Committee on Defense Production would remain, probably a close relative of the current Military-Industrial Commission, which

56. Kurashvili does not go into details in this brief piece on which ministries would be subsumed under Minnarkhoz, but presumably he has in mind at least the eleven civilian machinebuilding ministries, the eight ministries managing construction and construction materials, probably the six ministries supervising agriculture and food, and probably several others. See Kurashvili, "Kontury vozmozhnoi perestroiki," pp. 75–77.

supervises the nine defense machinebuilding ministries (which might themselves be merged, although Kurashvili does not discuss this possibility).

Kurashvili's argument that some features of the traditional central planned economy should be retained in selected sectors links him to the moderates. The prices of fuels and raw materials, and presumably some necessities in the consumer basket, would be set by the state. The defense sector would remain a separate part of the system and presumably be shielded from any potential uncertainties that could accompany heavier reliance on markets.[57] Although he does not mention foreign trade, presumably the state monopoly over foreign trade would be retained.

The manufacturing sector, the core of the economy, is the target of Kurashvili's suggestions for far-reaching changes. Enterprises there would be given considerably more autonomy than past experiments granted. Enterprises would be primarily responsible for drawing up plans, although Minnarkhoz might specify some fairly aggregate constraints (for example, the proportion of output in various output groups), and it would review enterprise plans to check for general consistency with its overall demand projections. In addition Minnarkhoz would signal to enterprises what products or projects it favored (by means of taxes, credits, and other devices). Enterprises would enjoy full control over the wage fund and the level of employment (the latter two seemingly controlled by the workers as a whole), both determined primarily by the fact that the enterprise would be on full *khozraschet*, which would be strictly adhered to. Prices would be set in contracts under the close supervision of the state, supplemented by some state-set prices. In

57. Vasilii Seliunin, a frequent contributor to the economic press who advocates radical reform, outlines in a less systematic fashion a reform similar to that discussed by Kurashvili. In his brief discussion he is careful to note that, although relatively free domestic trade would be the norm, the state could set aside key commodities for "preferred institutions," of which he mentions hospitals and schools, but which presumably also include the defense industries. See Seliunin, "Eksperiment," p. 179.

By 1986 most of those advocating radical reform had in mind a system of "state orders" guaranteeing state access to the most important products and those in deficit. Aside from providing some assurance to conservatives and moderates that radical reform will not lead to chaos, this presumably is also a message to the military that its preferred access to the nation's products will remain. See, for example, Petrakov and Iasin, "Ekonomicheskie metody"; or P. Bunich and V. Moskalenko, "Samofinansirovanie: rezul'taty i problemy" (Self-finance: results and problems), *Kommunist*, no. 14 (September 1986), p. 36.

addition, state controls would consist primarily of a minimum wage, and possibly some controls on bonus schemes. No wage maximums would be set, but the enterprise would face a progressive wage tax.

Kurashvili's approach would entail a far-reaching price reform, which he does not discuss in any detail, an understandable omission for someone trained as a lawyer. Others advocating economic reform, particularly Petrakov and his colleagues at the Central Economic-Mathematical Institute, have devoted much more attention to how such a reform might work.[58] They have argued for a two-stage price reform, beginning with major price revisions in order to rationalize relative prices, for example, by introducing full rent charges into the prices for raw materials and fuels. For the longer term they advocate shifting toward decentralized price setting through wholesale trade.

This system will not work and the economic instruments used by the authorities will not have a significant effect unless competitive pressures are present to force enterprises to strive to increase their efficiency and satisfy their customers. Kurashvili does not focus on that point; but others are beginning to pay more attention to it. It is clear, for example, that a major November 1986 meeting on economic reform heard a rather strong statement from Institute of Economics representatives favoring increased competition in important spheres (including finance).[59] Petrakov and his colleagues make a similar point, but with the interesting addition of competition through imports as an important source of pressure.[60] In a country where appreciation for the economic benefits of competitive imports is rare, that is a potentially important new feature of the debate.

Kurashvili addresses directly the potential objection that such a system would result in layoffs and dislocations. "It would be strange," he notes, "if the absence of unemployment in socialism was based on enterprises keeping excess labor and giving little thought to technological

58. N. Petrakov, V. Volkonskii, and A. Vavilov, "Tsena: nuzhny krutye izmeneniia" (Price: fundamental changes are needed), *Sots. ind.*, April 3, 1987; and Petrakov and Iasin, "Ekonomicheskie metody."

59. See L. Abalkin, "Proizvodstvennye otnosheniia i khoziaistvennyi mekhanizm" (Production relations and the economic mechanism), *Ekon. gaz.*, no. 46 (November 1986). This is a summary of some (presumably from the Institute of Economics) papers given at a conference sponsored by *Ekon. gaz.* and the Board of the Scientific-Economic Society on the issue of economic reform.

60. Petrakov and Iasin, "Ekonomicheskie metody." This is also a summary of a set of papers, presumably those of the Central Economics-Mathematics Institute.

progress."[61] The solution, he goes on, is not to retain the old system, but to expect layoffs and to set up a system capable of finding new jobs for the laid-off workers. Kurashvili also advocates complete freedom for enterprises to merge, the state's only function here being vigilance that monopoly situations do not develop.

Kurashvili also suggests a basic change in the approach to territorial control over economic activity in an effort to capture the "rational grain" of the *sovnarkhoz* system without repeating all the mistakes, in particular without weakening central control.[62] He would create a Minnarkhoz in each republic, with local organs under the dual supervision of the republican organ and the local *sovet*. This would give every enterprise a local representative of the Minnarkhoz and would give local authorities the chance to assert their interests in decisions taken at the national economic level.[63]

The debate over economic security. Kurashvili's reference to the irrational foundations on which full employment now rests in the USSR is one example of an increasing frank public reconsideration of the basic foundations underlying economic security in the USSR. Aside from unemployment, the main issues under discussion are bankruptcy, income inequality, and—a closely related issue—the proper role for private economic activity in a socialist country. Taken together, the statements on various components of the economic security framework constitute the first hints of a rethinking of that framework as a prerequisite to a successful reform.

The evidence is now fairly strong, although still for the most part circumstantial, that some people in the Soviet Union are now willing to argue openly that the threat of unemployment provides a useful, possibly indispensable, tool that Soviet enterprises might use to increase the productivity of those workers who are not working anywhere near their potential. No statements in the published literature are formulated precisely in that fashion, but it does not take much imagination to come to the author's meaning. For example, Vasilii Seliunin observes that in the West there are Sonys and Grundigs, whereas in the Soviet Union there are only simple phonographs. True, the Soviet models are two to three times cheaper, but the quality is also worse. He continues: "[In

61. Kurashvili, "Kontury vozmozhnoi perestroiki," p. 69.
62. Kurashvili, "Sud'by otraslevogo upravleniia," p. 46.
63. How this would work is not specified, and not clear in Kurashvili's brief account. Ibid.

the West] they have unemployment, excess people in the full sense of the word, but on the other hand sweat is extracted from those who have to work [*vyzhimanie pota iz tekh, kto rabotu imeet*]. We have forgotten about unemployment, but is it good that we work at times at half strength?''[64] In a similar vein, Leonid Abalkin notes that both feudalism and capitalism had or have distasteful, but nevertheless effective, mechanisms for disciplining labor. It is socialism that has not yet solved the problem of finding an effective, but more humane, form of discipline.[65]

Those who hold this view are not in any way implying that they advocate or believe in the necessity of long-term unemployment as an underpinning to an efficiently operating economic system. What they do seem to be saying is that the current level of job security in the USSR is excessive, and directly linked to low labor productivity and the low quality of goods produced in the system. "After all," said S. Shatalin of the newly created Institute of the Economics and Prognosis of Scientific Progress (a spin-off of the Central Economics-Mathematical Institute), "socialism is no welfare society where each worker practically automatically is allowed to occupy a job which he by no means always fulfills."[66] Their argument, like Kurashvili's, implies that a successful reform will inevitably create transitional unemployment, which will require much improved facilities for enhancing labor mobility and retraining.

Although it is not clear that Soviet leaders have moved to improve those institutions, they have already begun to warn the population that widespread layoffs in manufacturing may be coming and that they may precipitate a flow of labor into services. In a frank and revealing discussion published in early 1986 in the national circulation journal *Sovetskaia kultura*, V. Kostavkov noted that the labor productivity targets for material sectors indicate that the number of people employed in those sectors is expected to decline by 13–19 million by the year 2000. He warned that many young people would have to be willing to make their living in service industries and that those now employed "all have

64. Seliunin, "Eksperiment," p. 173.
65. L. Abalkin, "Razvitoi sotsializm i formirovanie sovremennogo ekonomicheskogo myshleniia" (Developed socialism and the formation of modern economic thinking), *Kommunist*, no. 18 (December 1984), p. 67. *Kommunist* is the main theoretical journal of the Central Committee of the CPSU; hence the article was meant to receive prominent consideration. Professor Abalkin, at the time on the faculty of the party's Institute of the Social Sciences, was promoted in 1986 to the directorship of the Institute of Economics in Moscow.
66. Shatalin, "Effectivnoe ispol'zovanie resursov," p. 8.

to work with an intensity of which—it must be confessed—so far we have a purely speculative idea." He went on: "The necessity to seek work—a necessity which many now working in the sphere of material production and in the services sphere will certainly face—may also be new and unaccustomed for us. We have become used to exactly the reverse—work seeking out the individual."[67] In 1987 Kostakov made a similar point in *Kommunist*, the party's most prestigious journal, calling for an overhaul of the *trudoustroistvo* (literally, "work arrangement") system for handling laid-off workers.[68]

If the threat of unemployment is to become a reality for the Soviet work force, then, logically, so must some form of bankruptcy. There should be a clear rule defining success and failure, and enterprises should know that if they fail, there will be no possibility of an ad hoc rescue by the ministry. That, in turn, will force the enterprise to carefully calculate its needs for labor and other inputs and could thus lead to layoffs.

Of course, in a socialist society, bankruptcy itself makes little sense since the assets are state owned. But firm criteria defining enterprise failure, followed by a closedown or at least a reorganization, make a great deal of sense, and some Soviet economists have hinted at an interest in the issue, which can be detected in a piece by V. Trapeznikov published in *Pravda* in 1985.[69]

In discussing the source of high rates of technological change under capitalism, Trapeznikov identifies market pressure on the firm as the main mechanism; he calls it the stimulus of "to be or not to be." He also points out that in the USSR the "to be or not to be" atmosphere worked with full force only in World War II, and currently operates only in the defense industry. As a result, he notes, Soviet defense technology is superior to Soviet civilian technology. He suggests that the experience of the defense industry should be applied to the civilian side, the implication being that "to be or not to be" should also be applied there. In a similar vein, R. G. Karagedov defines full *khozraschet* to include the possibility that poorly run firms might have to face a threat to their "continued existence."[70]

In effect, the debate over permissible, or advisable, levels of unem-

67. V. Kostakov, "One for Seven," in *FBIS-SU*, January 13, 1986, pp. S2–S3.

68. V. Kostakov, "Zaniatost': defitsit ili izbytok?" (Employment: in deficit or surplus?), *Kommunist*, no. 2 (January 1987), p. 86.

69. V. Trapeznikov, "Eshche raz o kachestve, tekhnicheskom progresse i stimulakh" (One more time on quality, technical progress, and stimuli), *Pravda*, October 2, 1985.

70. Karagedov, "Pervye itogi," p. 96.

ployment and over enterprise failure is about the trade-offs between
equity and efficiency. Although the threat of enterprise failure and the
threat of unemployment, for example, might serve to increase efficiency,
they would do so at what is at least the temporary expense of the jobs
and incomes of particular individuals. If the system is working perfectly,
then those who suffer deserve it; but in the likely event that the system
is imperfect, not everyone will be treated fairly. In any case, to rely on
impersonal market forces in the search for higher efficiency is to risk
increases in inequality. That, for many in the USSR, would represent a
departure from socialist principles.

The issue of the equity-efficiency trade-off emerges most clearly in
the rapidly changing debate on private economic activity and the "just"
income distribution, which began under Andropov and has blossomed
under Gorbachev in the debates over new laws on individual and
cooperative economic activity (see chapter 7). There is no doubt that
the expansion of private and cooperative economic activity in the USSR
would, if it is encouraged by the state, lead to a considerable improvement
in the supply of goods and services available to the population. The issue
now at the center of constant debate in the Soviet Union is that some
persons, because of particular skills, intelligence, or simply luck, could
earn very high incomes in the process (that is, if tax rates are not
confiscatory, since if they are, there will be no expansion in private or
cooperative economic activity). Such incomes would give rise to a class
of relatively well-off people, which many Soviets would regard as yet
another departure from socialism.

The new laws on cooperative economic activity have set the stage for
a test of the leadership's, and the population's, willingness to tolerate
such consequences. The debate preceding and accompanying the introduction of these laws suggests that social support for their full implementation may be difficult to achieve. There are those who argue that
private economic activity only appears to be relatively profitable now
because it enjoys hidden subsidies: free land, no taxes or other social
contributions (for those who sell produce from private plots), and
something close to a monopoly position in the goods private producers
sell.[71] The main conclusion here is not that private economic activity
should be abolished, but that much of the current income from those

71. A. Kostiukov, "Reflections on Letters: From Sector A to Sector B," in *FBIS-
SU*, February 3, 1986, pp. S1–S2. See also A. Shokin, "Otkuda berutsia netrudovye
dokhody" (Where do nonlabor incomes come from?), *Ekon. gaz.*, no. 15 (April 1986).

activities constitutes economic rents or implicit state subsidies, both of which should be somehow extracted from incomes through taxes or new charges. The corollary is that any future expansion of private economic activities should be approached carefully to ensure that the incomes deriving from those activities are no more than those justified by the effort and special skills that go into those activities.

So stated, such a principle seems easy to accept, East or West. However, in practical terms the issue is whether, given the fact that not all rents can be identified and taxed away, it is better to err on the side of efficiency, by strongly favoring private producers and accepting the fact that some will make unearned incomes, or to err on the side of equity, by strongly controlling private producers to minimize rents, even if that tactic affects the supply of goods and services. The tone of discussion in the USSR suggests that economic rents are far more broadly defined there than in much of the West, and that they are regarded with far more seriousness.

If someone manages to grow an otherwise scarce flower, then stands on a street corner in Kiev and sells it for five times the cost of producing it, the general view would probably be that this individual is a "speculator" and is receiving income that should be taxed away. In market economies, the solution is to guarantee free entry, which will drive the price down.[72] Or, to take a real case cited in the debate, if someone who owns property close to a major resort rents it out at high prices, he is receiving economic rents that should be taxed away. In addition, such a situation suggests to one Soviet author the need for a progressive inheritance tax to rid the country of such "parasitism."[73]

This tendency toward a broad definition of economic rents and a consequent inclination to extract them, even if the economic activities involved are seriously curtailed, may well change under Gorbachev. We should find out soon as experience accumulates in this area of his reforms.

LACUNAE IN THE DEBATES. The radical position has raised many new

72. There are Soviet authors who advocate a similar position. See, for example, Fedor Burlatskii, "Implement the 27th CPSU Congress Decisions: Conversation without Equivocation," in *FBIS-SU*, October 8, 1986, pp. R6–R19. This is a fascinating account of an imaginary discussion between an incoming *obkom* first secretary appointed by Gorbachev and a former second secretary (now acting first secretary) appointed under Brezhnev, regarding the precise meaning of the new era. Incomes from private activity and how one defines speculators form the most important topic.

73. Shokin, "Otkuda berutsia netrudovye dokhody."

issues and has recast some issues in a newer and much franker way than in the past. At the same time, it has avoided some fundamental points that must be addressed if a comprehensive reform is to be successful.

First, there is the issue of how enterprise autonomy will be defined relative to the government (ministries) and the party (in particular, local first secretaries). Enterprises, local party officials, and the ministry are currently intertwined in a set of rules that subject the enterprise to considerable outside interference in its affairs and oblige the party and government to provide compensation and understanding for the failings of the enterprise. A radical reform that tightens the criteria for success and failure and that links enterprise performance to the fate of the enterprise and its work force eliminates some of the obligations the party and government have toward the enterprise. To be workable, however, the reform must also revise the obligations the enterprise has to the ministries and party officials.

It is untenable, for example, to hold enterprises responsible for their success in satisfying customers and at the same time permit local party officials to tax the enterprise by using its labor force, without compensation, for the harvest or other local projects. Such practices give enterprises an excuse to argue for special considerations, and they give party officials an incentive to lobby for them. Likewise, it will be difficult to tell workers that their wages could be cut or their jobs could disappear if the enterprise does not fare well if, at the same time, ministries are still permitted to appoint managers and impose plans on them from above.

Put briefly, a system that unambiguously links the income and fate of enterprises to their performance must—to be politically sustainable—provide equally unambiguous decisionmaking authority to those enterprises and their workers. Although this point is implicit in the reform debate, it has not received adequate attention. Most notably, there has been almost no discussion of the role of the party in a reformed system and very little discussion of how the ministries can, in a reformed system, exercise the rights of ownership while preserving incentives for the management of an enterprise to operate efficiently. No socialist country has yet faced up to the question of the party's role, for understandable reasons.

A related and critical question is how capital will move around in the new system. One of the strengths of Western economic systems that makes innovation possible is the ease with which capital moves within and between countries. Firms with high profits may choose to expand production in the areas in which they are involved; they may move into totally different activities (either as a direct or portfolio investor); or they may simply rent their money to financial intermediaries.

In the traditional Soviet system capital moves around through the planning process, and banks play primarily an accounting role. The logic of the new approach is that enterprises must finance their own investments, or borrow. But what about enterprises with high profits? Will there be ways for them to invest their funds outside their normal product lines if they wish, or ways for them to loan them to financial intermediaries? The answer to this depends in part on whether the right to create new enterprises will remain solely with the state authorities, or whether enterprises will also have that right.[74] Even if the right to found enterprises remains with the state (in the form of ministries and local authorities), other questions remain. How will banks work? How will they raise capital? What criteria will they use to make loans? And, in particular, how will the interest rate be determined? The Soviet reform debate has given some attention to banking and financial reform in which interest rates are used to attract deposits and allocate available investment funds.[75] However, the treatment has been fairly superficial, and the major focus has been on self-finance rather than on moving capital around. Thus capital would probably stay with profitable enterprises, irrespective of where the best opportunities were.

The role of foreign trade in the reformed system receives virtually no attention in the debate, even from the radicals (with the exceptions mentioned earlier). This accurately reflects the general tendency in the USSR to downgrade the role of foreign trade primarily to a source of noncompetitive imports. As a consequence, the debate ignores what surely has been a vital component of the "to be or not to be" environment in which modern multinationals operate and thus ignores the fact that in the absence of import competition Soviet enterprises will have only weak incentives to develop products truly up to world standards.

However, these lacunae merely indicate that the debate has been going on for only a short time and that the participants lack experience in operating a reformed system. If Gorbachev encourages them to continue the dialogue, these issues will no doubt receive increasing attention. Nevertheless, they are important to keep in mind. At best, political leaders determined to implement a comprehensive reform will

74. As they do now in Hungary.
75. See, for example, Petrakov and Iasin, "Ekonomicheskie metody."

draw on the ideas in these debates without improving on them. Thus what the debates ignore, the politicians seem sure to ignore.

How Reforms in Other Socialist Countries Have Influenced Debates in the USSR

The debates about how to proceed with reform in the Soviet economy touch on many issues that Eastern European and Chinese leaders have been grappling with for some time. The first major discussions of comprehensive reforms surfaced in Eastern Europe in the second half of the 1950s, notably in Poland and Hungary, where blueprints for the reforms of the 1960s were already in outline form. The reforms of the 1960s, particularly those in Hungary, went far beyond the Kosygin reforms in their design and implementation and provided potentially useful information on which Soviet economists and leaders could draw in their efforts to design a reform.

Soviet leaders have tracked those efforts through a number of channels: the aforementioned Baibakov Commission, which was specifically organized for this task; the *Institut ekonomiki mirovoi sotsialisticheskikh stran*, directed by Oleg Bogomolov; frequent contacts with Eastern European officials and economists via CMEA (Council for Mutual Economic Assistance) standing committees and state visits; and other means.[76] Nevertheless, the extensive information available in the Soviet Union on other socialist economic systems has not greatly influenced the debate on economic reform in the USSR. To be sure, the experience of other socialist countries—most notably Hungary and East Germany— constitutes part of the evidence used by some Soviet economists to argue for a particular reform position. East Germany's apparent success with a streamlined administrative structure built around *kombinate* is often

---

76. The Bogomolov institute includes by far the largest and best trained staff of professional Eastern European specialists in the world. They know the languages of Eastern Europe, travel there frequently, and are well read in the economic literature of those countries. The institute does not have its own journal, but the research output is widely disseminated among the public through numerous books and articles in major Soviet economics journals. From time to time this institute is also asked to provide briefing papers to the government and party on key Eastern European issues. Finally, the institute has established the precedent of stationing at the Soviet embassy in each socialist country one of its specialists, whose job is to follow closely economic events and debates in the country. I had occasion to spend some time with one such specialist in an Eastern European country several years ago and was impressed with the scope of his contacts and the sophistication of his understanding of developments in the country.

mentioned in Soviet discussions on the economy and is one source of inspiration for the continual push for additional mergers and superministerial-type organs. Hungary's successes in the agricultural sphere, particularly in improving efficiency in the cooperative sector, are another source of sustained attention in the USSR. China's general approach to reforms is a phenomenon of more recent, but apparently quite genuine, interest.[77]

Yet, even those who refer to models from another socialist country tend, at best, to take a "cafeteria" approach: a little here from Hungary, a little there from East Germany, and so on. That has a certain appeal and, handled correctly, could well work in some limited way. However, the Eastern European experience is potentially the most informative in the areas of reform design and strategy, precisely the areas that Soviet economists and Soviet leaders seem to ignore. For example, the Hungarian experience in the 1970s clearly demonstrated that enterprise autonomy is difficult to extend if ministries have the right to choose the top management of an enterprise and to set its compensation. This was the case even though the ministries no longer received obligatory targets from above. It is only in the 1980s that the Hungarians have begun to deal with that problem by allowing workers to select enterprise managers in all but the largest enterprises and by using a public competitive procedure for selecting management in the largest enterprises.[78] There was virtually no discussion of this issue in the USSR until Mikhail Gorbachev introduced the notion of worker-elected management in the January 1987 plenum (see chapter 7). Even after that, the apparent conflict between the still powerful ministries and the enterprises has received little attention.

The more general lesson of the Hungarian experience is that systemic reform is terribly difficult to carry out successfully, even when the central leadership is strongly in favor of it. The most important lesson is that careful preparation is essential. This includes a close study (as Zaslav-

---

77. For a typical statement from someone who follows Eastern European developments closely and who has influence with the Soviet leadership, see O. Bogomolov, "Obshchee dostoianie" (Common property), *Pravda*, March 14, 1983. For recent discussions of the Chinese reform strategy, see Fedor Burlatskii, "Conversations about Economic Reforms in China," in *FBIS-SU*, June 18, 1986, pp. B1–B9.

78. See Paul Marer, "Economic Reform in Hungary: From Central Planning to Regulated Market," U.S. Joint Economic Committee, *East European Economies: Slow Growth in the 1980s*, Joint Committee Print, 99 Cong. 2 sess. (GPO, 1986), vol. 3, p. 254; and interview material.

skaia has suggested) of the potential pockets of resistance in order to devise a strategy to neutralize them. None of these points have been developed in the Soviet literature, in part because the Soviet approach to borrowing is based on the cafeteria model, rather than on a thoughtful analysis of the main lessons and of the social-economic process as a whole.

All of this applies also in the case of China, although China's experience is in many ways particular and probably of limited use to the Soviet Union. However, the general strategy of rural areas first, including not only agriculture, but also rural industry, seems to be working quite well in China and is applicable to the Soviet case. Here again the strategy itself is the main lesson of interest; and here again there is no extensive discussion in the Soviet press.

The Eastern European and Chinese reform experience seems to have had only limited influence on Soviet thinking in regard to reform strategy. Soviet economists and Soviet leaders seem far more inclined to draw on their own history of reform efforts in devising new policies, and even there do so selectively. This reluctance to exploit the experience of other countries may in part stem from the belief that Soviet economic problems are unique. It may also be a matter of pride: some may think that the first socialist country has little to learn from more recent entrants. Another contributing factor is the traditional reluctance of the Soviet leadership to discuss, or even think through, the large political and social issues associated with economic reform. That attitude may be changing under Gorbachev, and if it is, observers may soon see a more careful and deeper examination of the overall reform experience in other socialist countries.

CHAPTER SEVEN

The Gorbachev Reforms

MIKHAIL S. GORBACHEV rose rapidly in the Soviet hierarchy. In 1978, after a twenty-year career as a local politician in Stavropol, he came to Moscow as the party secretary for agriculture. By 1980 he was a full member of the Politburo, which marked the beginning of his regular exposure to the full range of national issues. By 1984, in his position as second secretary to Konstantin Chernenko, he was already deeply involved in the management of the economy, and in foreign affairs. On March 11, 1985, he assumed the post of general secretary.[1]

The economy was then, and remains, the top item on his policy agenda.[2] Already under Konstantin U. Chernenko, Gorbachev's public statements indicated an ongoing effort to understand the roots of Soviet economic difficulties and to formulate an effective economic strategy that would lead to an *uskorenie* (acceleration) of social-economic development. After assuming the post of general secretary, his first speeches on the economy combined blunt language on economic failures reminiscent of Andropov's short tenure, with the barest outline of a clearly ambitious, but ill-defined, economic strategy.

Gorbachev's economic strategy took shape in the course of the debates over the Twelfth Five-Year Plan, for 1986–90. These debates began while he was still second secretary under Chernenko, then intensified during 1985 after he assumed the post of general secretary.[3] The

---

1. For an account of Gorbachev's career before he assumed the post of general secretary, see Archie Brown, "Gorbachev: New Man in the Kremlin," *Problems of Communism*, vol. 34 (May–June 1985), pp. 1–23.

2. The only close rival is the related issues surrounding a new Soviet foreign policy.

3. See Ed A. Hewett, "Gorbachev's Economic Strategy: A Preliminary Assessment," *Soviet Economy*, vol. 1 (October–December, 1985), pp. 285–305.

foundation of the strategy rests on economic reform, but other elements—investment policies supporting the modernization of machinebuilding, a special focus on housing, extensive changes in personnel,
and a new wage policy that increases incomes for high-skill groups, to
mention just four—play an important role. In the second half of the
1980s, while economic reforms are still being developed, these other
measures are the primary impetus behind what Gorbachev hopes will be
a revival in economic performance. Moreover, Gorbachev's broad
approach to remaking Soviet society—symbolized by his anti-alcohol
campaign, a new emphasis on discipline, *glasnost'*, and democratization—has guided his economic strategy. In brief, economic reforms are
the cornerstone of Gorbachev's economic strategy, but far from its
totality.

Yet, as the remainder of the strategy took form in 1986, the design of
the economic reform remained distinctly ill-defined. Behind Gorbachev's ringing call in February 1986 at the Twenty-seventh Party
Congress for a *radikal'naia reforma* stood a vague, incomplete set of
generalities of little use in constructing actual reform legislation.

Despite the lack of any more than a vague notion of how the reform
might work, Gorbachev threw himself into introducing reforms from the
very beginning. The years 1985 and 1986 saw a virtual flood of new
policies and reforms, some of which were distressingly similar to failed
measures of the previous two decades. During this period, which
extended into early 1987, it was as if Gorbachev was driven by a political
clock to be seen doing *something*, even if what he did would soon have
to be reversed by further, more radical measures. But it also seemed
that Gorbachev had not yet grasped the full implications of his ambitious
economic goals and his very general commitment to economic reform.
As a consequence, throughout 1985 and 1986 Gorbachev's rhetoric and
Soviet reality were on different courses; the vision of a radical reform
began to take on a tinge of delusion.

During 1986 Gorbachev strengthened his political position, and, at
the same time, showed increasing dissatisfaction with the indifference
and the resistance he was encountering in his efforts to reform the
system. Gorbachev knew precisely what he wanted: an acceleration of
economic development, broadly defined. He knew generally that radical
changes would be involved. But he was still searching for the right
combination of policy changes and reforms to actually get the acceleration going. The radicals, emboldened by Gorbachev's obvious sympathy

with their position, grew more vocal, and Gorbachev clearly listened to them as he continued his search for a way to realize his vision.

As we look back on Gorbachev's first years, we will probably come to view late 1986 and early 1987 as a turning point in which Gorbachev increasingly dissatisfied with the results of his first two years—was driven not to retreat, but to plunge ahead into a full-scale reconsideration of the roots of Soviet socialism. The result was two historic party plenums: the January 1987 plenum on cadres, which outlined democratization reforms in the choice of personnel, and the June 1987 plenum on the economy, which outlined a radical economic reform. These two plenums, the culmination of months of internal debate and negotiation, were important victories for Gorbachev, and testimony of his growing power.

The June 1987 plenum set the stage for the next battle over the economy and the next reform cycle. It is already clear that the length of the cycle and its implications for the economy will both rival, and probably surpass, the Kosygin reforms of 1965. Aleksei N. Kosygin was a prime minister pushing reforms in an inhospitable environment created by an indifferent general secretary (Brezhnev); Gorbachev is an increasingly powerful general secretary, and these are his reforms. But the venerable centrally planned economy and the culture that accompanies it are deeply entrenched in this society; even Gorbachev's own approach shows evidence of a struggle between past approaches and a compulsion to break out of the stifling bonds they have created.

It would be premature to attempt to predict the outcome of this new reform cycle. Too much remains to be revealed concerning the depth of political support for a radical reform, the design of the reform, and the skill and dedication that Gorbachev and his allies are bringing to the implementation of the reform. The June 1987 plenum gives Gorbachev a license to battle for reform, guided by a document that outlines the gross parameters of the campaign. But it will take years for the battle to play its course.

Nevertheless, it is possible, drawing on the lessons of previous reform efforts in the USSR and elsewhere, to identify the most important considerations that will determine the degree of success of Gorbachev's reform efforts. Beyond the indispensable requirement that the general secretary hold a genuine commitment to radical reform, there are many other important hurdles regarding the design of the reform, the strategy for its implementation, and the depth of leadership commitment to enforcing the laws, once they are introduced. These considerations provide guidelines on what to watch for in this reform in order to judge its chances of truly transforming the Soviet economy.

Gorbachev's Goals for the Economy

Gorbachev is searching for a formula that will bring Soviet economic performance up to the standards set by the most developed countries—Japan, the United States, and those in northern Europe. Aside from the strong political motivations for those ambitions, there is an obvious national security concern. Gorbachev knows full well that military and economic capabilities are intertwined, all the more so in a world in which the United States drives the arms race through the exploitation of its enormous innovative capacity. For Gorbachev, a dramatic improvement in Soviet economic performance is not only good politics; it is an important component of his approach to Soviet national security.

His aspirations for the economy are embodied in the concept of an *uskorenie* of social and economic development. *Uskorenie* expresses not only the rather narrow goal of higher national income growth rates, but also the general ambition to accelerate the development of Soviet society and the economy via innovative activity, economic institutions, and, most important, changes in the mentality of the population concerning the economy and society. "The acceleration of the social-economic development of the country is the key to all our problems: near-term and long term, economic and social, political and ideological, internal and foreign," Gorbachev told the Twenty-seventh Party Congress.[4]

Mikhail Gorbachev first gave a quantitative expression to his goal of *uskorenie* in the draft of the Twelfth Five-Year Plan, covering the years 1986–90. His role in the drafting of this plan began under Chernenko, and by the time it emerged in preliminary form in late 1985 it could fairly be labeled "Gorbachev's five-year plan."[5] The initial targets in the plan

4. "Politicheskii doklad Tsentral'nogo Komiteta KPSS XXVII S"ezdu Kommunisticheskoi partii Sovetskogo Soiuza" (The political report to the Central Committee of the CPSU to the 27th Congress of the Communist party of the Soviet Union), in *Materialy XXVII S"ezda Kommunisticheskoi partii Sovetskogo Soiuza* (Moscow: Politizdat, 1986), p. 22.
5. Hewett, "Gorbachev's Economic Strategy," pp. 286–87.

(table 7-1, col. 7), published in November 1985, were extremely ambitious. Even at the low end of the range they called for a reversal of the downward trend in growth rates in all major output categories. In general, the final version of the plan (col. 8), published in June 1986, reflects the most ambitious variant of the initial targets. National income is targeted for an average growth of 4.1 percent, which is, in essence, a return to growth rates of the early 1970s. Labor productivity, which must carry the burden of the acceleration, is set to grow at 4.6 percent, a rate not attained since the early 1970s. Real per capita income growth rates are to average 2.7 percent, which is considerably below the growth rates of the early 1970s, but significantly above those in recent years.

In the 1990s the acceleration is to be more pronounced, although there are few numbers to indicate what Gorbachev hopes for here. National income is to double by the year 2000. Given the target of 4.1 percent for 1986–90, that implies an average of 5 percent per annum in the 1990s. Total labor productivity in material production, which grew at 3.1 percent during 1981–85, is to grow at approximately 4 percent during 1986–90, and 6.5–7.4 percent in the 1990s. Real per capita income growth will move from 2.7 percent in 1986–90 to 3.4–4.7 percent in the 1990s.[6]

These dramatic increases in factor productivity can only be realized on the basis of a massive, across-the-board improvement in the quality of goods and services produced in the system. For machinebuilding, which by the Soviet's own estimates currently matches world standards in only 29 percent of its serially produced output, the ratio is targeted for 80–95 percent by 1990. This amounts to a huge leap into state-of-the-art technologies, which will serve as the foundation for replacing industry's old capital equipment with modern machinery and equipment, primarily of Soviet design and manufacture.[7]

This is an extraordinarily ambitious plan for at least two reasons. First, the turnaround in the secular decline of the last several decades begins before radical economic reforms are implemented. Gorbachev is counting on all of those measures aside from reforms to take hold

6. The figures given here are from table 2-3, p. 52.
7. In addition, Soviet planners are apparently counting on Eastern Europe for additional machinery and equipment for the modernization program, although it is not clear how seriously they take this possibility. For a discussion of the strategy, including mention of Eastern Europe, see the interview with G. Stroganov, deputy chairman of Gosplan, "Otvechat' dukhu vremeni" (Responding to the spirit of the times), *Sotsialisticheskaia industriia*, October 2, 1985. (Hereafter *Sots. ind.*)

Table 7-1. *Soviet Economic Performance and Plans, 1971–90*

Average annual growth rate (percent)

| Variable | 1971–75 | | 1976–80 | | 1981–85 | | 1986–90 | | 1986 | | 1987 |
	FYP9 (1)	Actual (2)	FYP10 (3)	Actual (4)	FYP11 (5)	Actual (6)	FYP12p (7)	FYP12f (8)	Annual plan (9)	Actual (10)	Annual plan (11)
National income utilized	6.7	5.1	4.7	3.9	3.4	2.7[a]	3.5–4.1	4.1	3.8	3.9	n.a.
Industrial production	8.0	7.4	6.3	4.5	4.7	3.7	3.9–4.4	4.6	4.3	4.9	4.4
Machinebuilding and metalworking	11.4	11.6	n.a.	8.2	7.0	6.2	7.0–7.7	7.4	6.6	7.3	7.3
Agricultural production	4.0	0.6	3.0	1.5	2.5	2.1	2.7–3.0	2.7	4.4	5.1	7.6
Labor productivity in industry	6.8	6.0	5.5	3.1	3.6	3.2	4.2–4.6	4.6	4.1	4.6	4.4
Gross state investment[b]	6.2[c]	7.1	2.8	3.7	1.1	3.5	3.4–3.8	2.9[d]	8.2	8.8	5.1
Real per capita income	5.5	4.4	3.9	3.3	3.1	2.1	2.5–2.8	2.7	2.5	2.3	2.6

Sources: Data for 1971–80, plan data for 1981–85, and the preliminary draft targets for the Twelfth Five Year Plan (1986–1990) (FYP12p) are taken from Ed A. Hewett, "Gorbachev's Economic Strategy: A Preliminary Assessment," *Soviet Economy*, vol. 1 (October–December 1985), p. 289. Data for 1981–85 performance are from Tsentral'noe statisticheskoe upravlenie SSSR, *Narodnoe khoziaistvo SSSR v 1985 g.: statisticheskii ezhegodnik* (Moscow: "Finansy i statistika," 1986). (Hereafter *Narkhoz*.) Data for 1986 are from Tsentral'noe statisticheskoe upravlenie SSSR, *SSSR v tsifrakh v 1986 godu* (The USSR in figures in 1986) (Moscow: "Finansy i statistika," 1987). The final Twelfth FYP targets (FYP12f) are from N. I. Ryzhkov's speech, "O gosudarstvennom plane ekonomicheskogo i sotsial'nogo razvitiia SSSR na 1986–1990 gody" (On the state plan of economic and social development of the USSR for 1986–1990), *Pravda*, June 19, 1986. The annual plan data for 1985 and 1986 are from speeches of the chairmen of Gosplan (N.K. Baibakov and N. V. Talyzin, respectively) on the respective plans. See "O gosudarstvennom plane ekonomicheskogo i sotsial'nogo razvitiia SSSR na 1985 god i vypolnenii plana v 1984 godu" (On the state plan of economic and social development of the USSR in 1985 and fulfillment of the plan in 1984), *Ekon. gaz.*, no. 49 (December 1984), insert; and "O gosudarstvennom plane ekonomicheskogo i sotsial'nogo razvitiia SSSR na 1986 god i vypolnenii plana v 1985 godu" (On the state plan of economic and social development of the USSR in 1986 and fulfillment of the plan in 1985), *Ekon. gaz.*, no. 48 (November 1985), insert. Data for 1987 are from "Zakon Soiuza Sovetskikh Sotsialisticheskikh Respublik. O gosudarstvennom plane ekonomicheskogo i sotsial'nogo razvitiia SSSR na 1987 god" (A law of the Union of Soviet Socialist Republics. On the state plan of economic and social development of the USSR for 1987), *Pravda*, November 20, 1986; and "O gosudarstvennom plane ekonomicheskogo i sotsial'nogo razvitiia SSSR na 1987 god i o khode vypolneniia plana v 1986 godu" (On the state plan of economic and social development of the USSR for 1987 and the course of fulfillment of the plan in 1986), *Pravda*, November 18, 1986. Additional plan data for 1971–75 are from *Gosudarstvennyi piatiletnii plan razvitiia narodogo khoziaistva SSSR na 1971–75 gochy* (Moscow: Politizdat, 1972). (Hereafter *Gosplan 1971–1975*.) Additional plan data for 1976–80 are from *Ekon. gaz.*, no. 51 (December 1975); and *Ekon. gaz.*, no. 45 (November 1976). Additional data for 1981–85 are from *Pravda*, November 20, 1981. Additional data for 1981–85 performance, plan data for 1986–90, annual plan data for 1986 and 1987, and data for 1986 performance are from Ed A. Hewett, Bryan Roberts, and Jan Vanous, "On the Feasibility of Key Targets in the Soviet Twelfth Five Year Plan (1986–90)," in Joint Economic Committee, *Gorbachev's Economic Plans*, Joint Committee Print, 100 Cong. 1 sess., vol. 1 (GPO, forthcoming).

n.a. Not available.

a. *Narkhoz 1985* (p. 40) reports two figures for the growth of "National income utilized" in 1985: 3.1 percent and 0.8 percent (implied from p. 410 of *Narkhoz 1985* and p. 425 of *Narkhoz 1984*). The higher figure yields a growth rate for 1981–85 of 3.1 percent (*Narkhoz 1985*, p. 41). The lower figure yields a growth rate for 1981–85 of 2.7 percent (*Narkhoz 1984*, p. 425). The problem appears to be in the treatment of alcohol production. See "1987 Panel on the Soviet Economic Outlook: Perceptions on a Confusing Set of Statistics," *Soviet Economy*, vol. 3 (January–March 1987), pp. 3–39. I have tentatively accepted the lower figure as the best indicator of performance over that period.

b. Excludes investments by collective farms and private individuals.

c. See *Gosplan 1971–1975*, p. 352; and *Narkhoz 1922–1972*, p. 321.

d. State "centralized" investment, which presumably excludes investments by state enterprises financed from their own funds.

immediately. Then, in the 1990s—when reforms are in place—the *uskorenie* will be in full swing.

Second, the turnaround Gorbachev seeks is qualitative as well as quantitative. He does not simply want increased production of the goods the economy now produces. He wants Soviet products to be at least up to world standards, if not actually setting those standards. The desire to accelerate growth rates, given the secular decline in capital and labor inputs, is in itself ambitious for this economy. But to also hope for a qualitative change across the board, and in a very short time, borders on fantasy.

One should hasten to add, however, that the quantitative targets should probably be regarded as conscious political hyperbole designed to convey to the society the enormous magnitude of Soviet backwardness. It is unlikely that Gorbachev believes that by 1990 Soviet enterprises will be capable of matching the best world standards in almost all of the machinery and equipment they produce. But the important issue is not his ability to predict what is possible, nor his willingness to discuss it publicly. Rather, the issue is whether, in the design and implementation of a reform, he will be sufficiently ruthless (economically) to institutionalize genuine pressure for high-quality output in the Soviet civilian economy. The answer to that question will determine the ultimate fate of this reform; and it is deeds, not speeches or reform decrees, that will provide the answer.

Overview of Gorbachev's Economic Strategy

From the very beginning Gorbachev has indicated that his economic strategy consists of roughly two stages.[8] The first, or pre-reform, stage, which runs approximately until the end of the decade, relies heavily on a myriad of economic and social policy changes, personnel shifts, and some partial reforms to turn around economic performance and start the *uskorenie*. During this period, economic reforms are prepared and introduced as soon as they are ready.

8. For an early discussion of the strategy in essentially these terms from one of Gorbachev's closest academic economic advisers, see Abel Aganbegian, "Strategiia uskoreniia sotsial'no ekonomicheskogo razvitiia" (The strategy of acceleration of social-economic development), *Problemy mira i sotsializma*, no. 9 (September 1985), pp. 13–18.

By 1991, when the Thirteenth Five-Year Plan is to begin, the economic reforms will be in place for the second stage of the strategy. Here the *uskorenie* begins in full force, with dramatic improvements in quality and a national income growth rate in the range of 5 percent per annum.

The pre-reform stage of Gorbachev's strategy began formally on the day he became general secretary, but in fact it was before that, as his power grew in the position of second secretary under Chernenko. That part of the strategy is now clear, and so far it is working fairly well.

Both the timing and character of the second stage are still uncertain. Until the June 1987 plenum there was considerable reason to doubt that Gorbachev even understood the need to articulate in some detail a well-designed, radical reform to guide the decrees that had already begun emerging in 1985–86. The June plenum speech and the accompanying document outlining reform principles essentially removed that doubt. But important issues remain on the actual design of the reform and the drafting and implementation of its provisions.

I turn now to a discussion of the two stages of Gorbachev's strategy. Many specific measures are examined, but many more are omitted. A somewhat more detailed, but still selective, chronology of measures, with full references, is provided in appendix table 7A-1.

The Pre-Reform Stage

Gorbachev's approach in this first stage is not easily defined in terms of simple categories. He is doing what one would expect of a good politician: using whatever instruments are available to turn the economy around. Rousing speeches to various audiences, summary dismissals of recalcitrant officials, quick promotions of others, shifts in investment priorities, and overtures to international economic organizations are a sampling of the eclectic foundation on which Gorbachev's economic strategy currently rests. At the same time, he has encouraged and participated in a debate on the reform. This stage is intended to last only for the remainder of this decade; by 1991 the new reformed system is to be up and running.

It is possible to cut through much of the chaos of these first few years by focusing on the two most important aspects of Gorbachev's approach: changes under the general heading of the "human factor" and changes in economic policy. Discussion of the third important aspect of this period, the economic reforms already introduced in 1985–86, is post-poned to the next section, which is devoted to the emerging reform strategy for the 1990s.

The Human Factor

Gorbachev has consistently emphasized the importance of the human factor (*chelovecheskii faktor*) in the revitalization of the Soviet economic system. The ultimate success of his efforts turns on his ability to improve discipline and create enthusiasm, which is now lacking in this system. Economic reform is an effort to institutionalize the pressure for greater economic discipline, but in a broader sense Gorbachev is attempting to address a more fundamental problem—the fact that self-discipline has not been the hallmark of the system up to now. To the extent he succeeds, economic performance could benefit even without further economic reforms; in addition, success here is a necessary prerequisite to the proper functioning of a reformed system.

Gorbachev's anti-alcohol campaign constituted his most important early measure in this realm. The laws and decrees of May 1985 restricted the production, sale, and consumption of alcohol, while instituting new penalties for drunkenness in public or on the job.[9] There are good economic reasons for the anti-alcohol campaign, which could contribute to increased labor productivity. But there are many other reasons to pursue such a course, including general considerations of quality of life, and in particular an effort to reverse the decline in male life expectancy.[10]

Gorbachev's effort to mobilize the human factor has also led to rapid personnel changes in the party and the government. By the fall of 1985 the two key central planning bodies—Gosplan and Gossnab—were under the new leadership of L. A. Voronin and N. V. Talyzin, respectively. Both men had a history linked to the defense industries. These are but two examples of Gorbachev's resort to those cadres in an effort to

9. The drinking age was raised to twenty-one years; alcohol sales were limited to a relatively few stores, none of them near factories; stores were to be open only from 2:00 p.m. to 7:00 p.m.; the price of alcohol was raised; and plans were announced to shift production from alcoholic to nonalcoholic beverages.

10. Murray Feshbach, "The Age Structure of Soviet Population: Preliminary Analysis of Unpublished Data," *Soviet Economy*, vol. 1 (April–June, 1985), p. 187. Feshbach estimates—using unpublished, but nevertheless purportedly Soviet, census data for 1979—that the life expectancy of Soviet males at birth is fifty-six years, compared with more than sixty-six years for males in the United States.

reinvigorate the civilian economy. By November, Nikolai I. Ryzhkov, who had been with Gosplan and before that was the general director of Uralmash, was the new chairman of the Council of Ministers; and by December of that year Gorbachev had already replaced approximately one-third of the men heading the approximately fifty branch ministries.[11] The new appointments continued throughout 1986, so that by early 1987 all leading institutions in the economic hierarchy, and a good portion of the ministries, were headed by new appointees.

Another aspect of the human factor campaign is a general emphasis on discipline throughout the hierarchy, combined with an enhanced emphasis on the need for individuals to take responsibility for decisions taken by them, or under their leadership. This approach is closely linked to that part of the *glasnost'* campaign emphasizing the right and duty of citizens to criticize their leadership (although not the top leadership). Gorbachev's rapid replacement of top leaders is in itself an important manifestation of his intention to increase discipline. Most of those leaders have left quietly, and many with full honors befitting their years of service to the state or party. However, others have been publicly castigated before their departure, with implicit and specific charges of failure to carry out their responsibilities.[12]

Glasnost' is being used to support the discipline campaign in a number of ways. For example, authorities are promoting increased public accountability of ministers through televised call-in shows, are sending local leaders similar messages through town meetings, and are encouraging a more lively and critical local press. Gorbachev has also empha-

11. Fourteen of the forty-nine branch ministries in existence at the end of 1985 had come under new leadership that year (a few during Chernenko's last months in office, but presumably with Gorbachev's approval), including virtually the entire leadership of the fuel and energy sectors.

12. The obvious case here is in the aftermath of Chernobyl', where Gorbachev ordered a full investigation. On the strength of that, he systematically fired the leaders most directly responsible for design and procedural flaws leading to the Chernobyl' accident, including the head of the State Committee for Safety in the Nuclear Power Industry, and deputy ministers in Minenergo (Electric Power), and Minsredmash (Medium Machinebuilding, supplying reactors). See "Special Politburo Meeting on Chernobyl'," *Soviet Economy,* vol. 2 (April–June 1986), p. 181.

Other, less dramatic, examples are more common. For instance, I. P. Kazanets, the head of Minchermet (Ferrous Metallurgy) when Gorbachev came to power, was severely criticized at the April 18, 1985, Politburo meeting, along with his counterpart in the Ukraine, for persistent problems in the steel industry. See "V Politbiuro TsK KPSS" (In the Politburo of the CC of the CPSU), *Pravda,* April 19, 1985. Soon thereafter he was replaced by S. V. Kolpakov.

sized the necessity of listening to and responding to criticism and complaints from below, including what in the United States are referred to as "whistle-blowers."[13]

The diverse elements of the human factor approach are bound together by an underlying hypothesis that much can be done in this system simply by forcing individuals to live up to their responsibilities. The device is discipline reinforced by limited accountability from below, along with new people in leadership positions who are ready to enforce the new discipline and accept the new accountability.

In this first, pre-reform, stage, the pressure for increased discipline comes primarily from above. The purpose of the reforms will be to institutionalize that pressure in two ways. The economic system itself will introduce clear rules for winners and losers and clear limits on exceptions; by definition, that is an increase in discipline. The democratization reforms, which will introduce limited candidate selection procedures into economic and political institutions, represent an institutionalization of pressures from below.

Economic Policy Changes

To realize the ambitious Twelfth FYP goals, Soviet planners must devise an investment policy that will generate new capital resources and channel them into machinebuilding and metalworking (MBMW). Planners can accomplish that through a combination of three strategies. First, they can pursue a "foreign borrowing" strategy. New foreign loans would permit a trade deficit that supports an increase in the share of investment in national income, channeled primarily to MBMW. This tactic has the double advantage of postponing the costs of the modernization program to the future (when the loans must be serviced, and finally repaid) while financing the purchase of advanced capital equipment from the West. The major disadvantage is that a trade surplus would be required down the road to service and repay the new debt.

A second possible strategy might be called "domestic borrowing." In

13. See, for example, the account of the July 18, 1985, Politburo meeting. One of the major topics reportedly discussed was the need to encourage and give fair consideration to suggestions and complaints to party and government officials by citizens. It specifically ordered party authorities to protect individuals who uncover problems whether or not they are party members. See "V Politbiuro TsK KPSS," *Pravda,* July 18, 1985.

Table 7-2. *Investments, 1976–90, by Quinquennia*
1984 prices; billions of rubles

Category	1976–80 (1)	1981–85 (2)	Col. 2/ col. 1 (3)	1986–90 (4)	Col. 4/ col. 2 (5)
Total investment	**717.7**	**843.2**	**1.175**	**1,033**	**1.225**
Machinery and					
equipment	243.2	311.2	1.280	444	1.430
Other	474.5	532.0	1.121	589	1.107
Investment by sector					
Industry	251.4	300.7	1.196	n.a.	n.a.
Energy and electricity	74.9	108.4	1.447	n.a.	n.a.
MBMW	60.9	73.0	1.199	131.4	1.800
Chemicals	24.8	22.6	0.911	33.9	1.500
Light	9.6	11.0	1.146	13.8	1.25
Food	16.3	18.3	1.123	n.a.	n.a.
Other	64.9	67.4	1.039	n.a.	n.a.
Agriculture	143.2	156.2	1.091	(160)	(1.024)
Transport and commu-					
nications	85.0	104.3	1.227	n.a.	n.a.
Housing	101.9	127.7	1.253	n.a.	n.a.
Construction and other	136.2	154.3	1.133	n.a.	n.a.
Investment by complex					
Agro-industrial	240.0	269	1.121	331	1.230
Fuel-energy	99.4	144	1.45	180	1.25
Transport	n.a.	n.a.	n.a.	62	n.a.

Sources: Data for 1976–85 (with the exception of the fuel-energy complex figures) are taken from *Narkhoz 1985:* total investment data from p. 364; sectorial investment data from pp. 366–68; the agro-industrial data from p. 259. The fuel-energy complex data are from Ed A. Hewett, *Energy, Economics, and Foreign Policy in the Soviet Union* (Brookings, 1984), p. 176. They have been converted to 1984 prices using the implied inflator from the overlapping years of 1.13.

Data for 1986–90 are based on Ryzhkov's statement on the Twelfth FYP, "O gosudarstvennom plane ekonomicheskogo i sotsial'nogo razvitiia SSSR na 1986–1990 gody" (On the state plan of economic and social development of the USSR for 1986–1990), *Pravda,* June 19, 1986, and on guesses by the author. The figure for total investment is not the figure Ryzhkov gave in the speech (994 billion rubles), but is consistent with the real increment he gave for total investment (190 billion rubles). There was even a third figure of 1,042 implied by the growth rate he gave; I have chosen 1,033 as a best guess.

The growth rate for investment in equipment is a guess based on the assumption that the share of investment in equipment will rise approximately as the share of renovation and reequipping is planned to rise (from 38.5 percent in 1985 to 50.5 percent in 1990). I have assumed that when Ryzhkov said investment in "machinebuilding" would be 1.8 times what it was in 1981–85, he meant all machinebuilding, though that is not certain by any means. The figure for light industry accepts Ryzhkov's statement that investment there will grow by 25 percent, but ignores the fact that he says investment will equal 11 billion rubles, since that is what it was in 1981–85.

The figure for the agro-industrial complex is quite rough. It comes from Ryzhkov's statement that this sector's investment share will be one-third of the total. I assume here that he was using the 994 for that figure, since that was the only level figure he cited for total investment. Also, that figure yields an increment to investment, which, with the increments to investment in the fuel-energy complex (36 billion rubles), chemicals (11.3 rubles), and machinebuilding (58.4 rubles), totals 167.5 billion rubles. This is 88 percent of the 190-billion-ruble increment Ryzhkov has announced for 1986–90, and is consistent with his statement that 90 percent of the increment would go to increases in precisely these areas.

Finally, the fuel-energy complex figure is Ryzhkov's, but is not consistent with the 35 percent growth rate he also gives for investment in the fuel-energy complex in 1986–90 relative to 1981–85. (Note 15 explains why I chose the 180-billion-ruble figure.)

this case, investment's share in national income, channeled to MBMW, would be increased by "borrowing" from consumers and government, which means decreasing the growth rate of consumption and government spending. The implication is that the new investments will allow higher levels of consumption and government spending in the future. On the plus side, this strategy would not incur new foreign economic liabilities. On the minus side, it would impose a heavy burden on Soviet industry to produce all the technically advanced machinery and equipment needed to support the modernization program. Moreover, should the growth rate of consumption fall off, there could be political repercussions.

A third possible strategy is "domestic restructuring." That is, instead of increasing the share of investment in national income, authorities could shift investment toward MBMW and away from other sectors. This would have no immediate impact on consumption or government spending. However, the sectors called upon to give up capital resources to support the modernization program would have to dramatically improve the efficiency with which they use their now reduced investment capital, or the growth rates of goods and services they supply would begin to fall off.

These three strategies are not mutually exclusive. Each is likely to play some role in Gorbachev's investment strategy. The question is which strategy will receive the greatest emphasis.

There are two primary sources of information on that. First, the targets for the Twelfth FYP provide the most detailed, albeit rather sketchy, picture of the weights Soviet planners intended to place on these three strategies on the eve of the Twelfth FYP. Second, the actual and plan data for 1986–87 provide a preliminary view of actual investment policy, which seems to differ in significant ways from the intentions signaled in the targets for the Twelfth FYP.

INVESTMENT POLICY IN THE TWELFTH FYP: THE FIVE-YEAR PLAN TARGETS. It is not an easy matter to piece together a complete picture of Gorbachev's new investment policy. The published documents for the Twelfth FYP leave many important numbers out. Furthermore, the presentation of data in terms of ill-defined complexes (machinebuilding, agro-industrial, transportation, and so on), with only sparse historical data, makes it extremely difficult to compare the past and the future.[14] Table 7-2 seems to be the best that can be done with the available information.

14. One of the most difficult issues in this regard is the increasing reference in Soviet

The high priority for MBMW is clearly indicated by the 80 percent increase in investment during 1986–90 in that sector, relative to 1981–85. Total investment is to grow by 22.5 percent over the same period. Chemicals are also receiving a relatively large infusion of new investment, after an absolute decline in the first half of the 1980s, in order to support the development of new products for the construction materials industry and MBMW. The precise planned increments for energy and electric power are not given, but the entire fuel-energy complex is probably scheduled for only a 25 percent increase, which is considerably less than in the last plan, and suggests that this sector is to pay part of the bill for the ambitious modernization program.[15]

In order to finance this dramatic shift in investment priorities, the policy relies almost totally on a "domestic restructuring" strategy. Foreign borrowing is given a minor role, if any, in the modernization program. Most indications point to a heavy reliance on Soviet industry

---

writings to the "machinebuilding complex." That term means different things to different people: for some it just refers to the output of the twenty machinebuilding ministries; to others it means only the output of machinery and equipment (excluding nonmachine output in the twenty ministries, but including machinery output elsewhere); and to still others it means output in the twenty ministries plus machinery plants in other ministries. As chapter 4 indicated, the latter two categories include important components of Soviet machinebuilding capacity. Unfortunately, many Soviet sources simply refer to the machinebuilding complex without specifying which definition they are using.

A further complication comes from the treatment of defense. Separate data for the nine defense machinebuilding ministries are not public, but some data for machinebuilding include those ministries (for example, in the *Narkhoz),* and some do not (for example, in some statements from Soviet leaders).

These two considerations lead to important ambiguities in Soviet leaders' statements on the priority given to machinebuilding and the investment resources devoted to that part of the economy. For an excellent discussion on the problems here, see Robert W. Campbell, mimeo, Fall 1986 (prepared for a Center for Strategic and International Studies project on civil-military relations).

15. I say "probably scheduled for a 25 percent increase" because this is one point of many on which Ryzhkov contradicts himself, saying that investment in the fuel-energy complex will be 180 billion rubles, which—he says—is 35 percent above 1981–85. It is only 25 percent above 1986–90, and I have taken the level to be the actual figure. My reasoning here is just a feeling from reading the text carefully that Ryzhkov mistakenly linked some of his figures to investment figures for 1981–85 in 1973, not 1984, prices. In 1973 prices the investment in the fuel-energy complex was scheduled to be 132 billion rubles, which, when multiplied by 1.35, yields 178 billion rubles, a figure quite close to Ryzhkov's 180 billion rubles. "O gosudarstvennom plane ekonomicheskogo i sotsial'nogo razvitiia SSR na 1986–1990 gody. Doklad Predsedatelia Soveta ministrov SSSR deputata Ryzhkova N.I." (On the state plan for the economic and social development of the USSR during 1986–1990. The report of the chairman of the USSR Council of Ministers, N. I. Ryzhkov), *Pravda,* June 19, 1986.

for products embodying the new technologies, with some contribution from Eastern Europe through shipments of higher-quality machinery and equipment.[16] There are no signals of an intention to rely on domestic borrowing by increasing investment's share in national income. The growth rate of total investment (22.5 percent) is virtually identical to the planned growth rate for national income during 1986–90. Clearly, planners entered the Twelfth FYP with the intention of managing the modernization by shifting the composition of investment, and thereby avoiding significant impacts on consumption or on the trade balance.

The domestic restructuring strategy has two parts. First, as can be seen from the second and third rows of table 7-2, the emphasis in the Twelfth FYP is on renovating and reequipping (hereafter: re & re) existing enterprises, rather than building new ones. Thus the growth of the machinery and equipment component of total investment is quadruple that of other (primarily buildings) components of total investment. Re & re is expected to increase the increments to productive capacity per ruble of new investment, which Soviet planners hope will allow them to accelerate the growth rate of national income with only a modest increase in the growth rate of total investment.

Second, the Twelfth FYP proposes a shift in investment resources toward MBMW and away from other sectors. The available data do not indicate precisely where the sacrifices are to be made, but probable targets are housing, the construction industry, and a broad category of "other," in which most social infrastructure investment can be found. It is quite likely that the Twelfth FYP calls for a relatively low growth rate in investment in these three areas. In particular, housing investment in the Twelfth FYP is probably not scheduled to rise more than about 13 percent, which is almost certainly not sufficient to meet the hoped-for 7.8 percent increase in the square meterage of housing completions in 1986–90 relative to 1981–85.[17]

16. The issue of plans for machinery and equipment imports from the West is a difficult one because Soviet leaders are so secretive about their intentions in this area. Neither the five-year plans nor the annual plans provide any useful information on plans for foreign trade. Leadership statements on the issue tend to be few and vague. But according to what Gorbachev has said about the economy (particularly about Soviet machinebuilding) and the statements of other Soviet leaders and officials, it seems clear that there is no intention to dramatically increase Soviet hard-currency debt in order to finance an expansion in imports of machinery and equipment from the West.

17. My rough calculations are as follows. Assume investment in energy and electric power will grow at 25 percent, the same rate assumed for the fuel-energy complex; that

Aside from these quantitative indicators, there are other signals of a major change in investment policy. Most notable is the apparent decision to review all ongoing investment projects. This could be a way of forcing ministries to discontinue some and to redesign many others in order to update the technology built into each project.[18]

---

investment in the food industry will grow 40 percent (consistent with Gorbachev's many statements, a pure guess); that investment in other industrial sectors (ferrous metallurgy, wood and woodworking, paper products, and construction materials) does not grow at all—a very conservative assumption—and that investment in agriculture totals 160 million rubles for 1986–90 (consistent with many statements suggesting that agriculture's share of investment would not change, although the complex's share could rise). Then the three remaining sectors, which had 386.3 billion rubles in 1981–85, are left with 436 billion rubles during 1986–90, an increase of 12.9 percent. Within that total, investment in construction is presumably stagnant or falling, as a result of the shift away from new structures. Transport is probably growing at least as rapidly as the average for this group since an acceleration in growth should imply an acceleration in the demands on transport (depending on what assumptions have been made on how the planned-for rationalization of interministerial specialization and trade will affect this).

That suggests that investment in housing will not amount to much more than 13 percent above what it was in 1981–85. At the same time, the plan calls for an increase in new apartment completions of 7.8 percent to 595 million square meters, and for an increase in the quality of housing, which will probably be very difficult to carry off with only a 13 percent increase in housing investment. For example, during 1981–85 the square meterage of housing completions increased by only 4.7 percent, whereas investment in housing increased 25.3 percent, which was not accompanied by any widespread accolades for higher-quality housing. Figures are from Tsentral'noe statisticheskoe upravlenie SSSR, *Narodnoe khoziaistvo SSSR v 1985 g: Statisticheskii ezhegodnik* (Moscow: "Finansy i statistika," 1986), p. 424 and table 7.2. (Hereafter *Narkhoz.*)

18. Ryzhkov in his June speech on the Twelfth FYP stated that a sample survey, apparently in selected MBMW ministries, showed that 10 percent of the investment projects under way were not worth continuing, and that in Minstankoprom (Machine Tool and Tool Building) and Minstroimaterialov (Construction Materials) 60 to 80 percent of the projects approved by those ministries were in fact unacceptable. "O gosudarstvennom plane." Gorbachev, in his speech to the Central Committee Plenum in June 1986, stated that the ministries had temporarily halted more than 100 investment projects in order to speed up completion on the remaining projects. "O piatiletnem plane ekonomicheskogo i sotsial'nogo razvitiia SSSR na 1986–1990 gody i zadachakh partiinykh organizatsii po ego realizatsii. Doklad General'nogo sekretariia TsK KPSS M. S. Gorbacheva" (On the five-year plan of economic and social development of the USSR during 1986–1990 and the tasks of party organizations for its realization. Report of the general secretary of the CC of the CPSU, M. S. Gorbachev), *Pravda*, June 17, 1986.

The problem the leadership is addressing here is a difficult one as it represents one of the most stubborn legacies of the old system. One survey by *Stroibank* of projects under way or proposed in the Twelfth FYP indicated that 25 percent were designed ten to twenty years ago, which virtually guarantees that the technology embodied in them was far from what the leadership had in mind. Some individual ministries came in with

At the same time, ministries are under pressure to dramatically increase scrapping rates on existing capital stock. Ryzhkov is calling on MBMW to double their scrapping rates on machinery and equipment, which averaged 3.2 percent in 1985, to 6.2 percent per annum. To some extent the new machinery coming out of MBMW is to sustain that higher scrapping rate. But in addition, the leadership is pushing enterprises to scrap old equipment and move to double or triple shifts on the newer equipment in an effort to get a one-time boost in productivity out of the existing capital stock.[19]

This amounts to an expectation that Soviet industry can, essentially on its own, modernize by replacing old equipment at an accelerated rate with new equipment of Soviet origin. That very tight circle is implicit in the goal that calls on Soviet industry to introduce new products in 13 percent of its product line every year, so that new products will be up to 60 percent by 1990, a considerable leap from the 3 percent per annum product replacement rates of the early 1980s.[20]

INVESTMENT POLICY IN THE TWELFTH FYP: THE ANNUAL PLANS. As chapter 2 indicated, five-year plans are notoriously poor predictors of actual investment policy. A careful study of annual plans and actual investment figures will provide a better indication of actual policy. The data available

---

particularly egregious results. Mintsvetmet (Nonferrous Metallurgy) had certified sixty-nine projects as being at the high technical levels required for the Twelfth FYP, even though the initial design phase began anywhere from the mid-1960s to the mid-1970s. Minavtoprom (Automobiles) had approved twenty projects in which the average time from the initial project design work to final completion was two decades. See "Ob osnovnykh napravleniiakh ekonomicheskogo i sotsial'nogo razvitiia SSSR na 1986–1990 gody i na period do 2000. Doklad Predsedatelia Soveta Ministrov SSSR tovarishcha N. I. Ryzhkova XXVII s"ezdu Kommunisticheskoi partii Sovetskogo Soiuza" (On the basic guidelines of economic and social development of the USSR during 1986–1990 and in the period until the year 2000. Report of the chairman of the Council of Ministers of the USSR, Comrade N. I. Ryzhkov to the XXVII Congress of the Communist Party of the Soviet Union), *Materialy XXVII s"ezda kommunisticheskoi partii Sovetskogo Soiuza* (Materials of the XXVII Congress of the Communist Party of the Soviet Union) (Moscow: Politizdat, 1986), pp. 243–44.

19. In theory, the boost could be large. Gorbachev notes that there are already about 700,000 "empty" workers' places—in effect, unemployed machines. If, he contends, the shift coefficient in industry were raised to 1.7 (70 percent of employees working a second shift), that could be raised to 4 million workers, which would allow a considerable amount of scrapping of old equipment. "O plutiletnem plane." Of course, the problem is that the new machinery may not be of the right kind. It would also require a considerable change in life-styles for the labor force, and not a very popular one.

20. Ryzhkov, "O gosudarstvennom plane."

for 1986–87 strongly suggest that, once again, actual investment policy differs significantly from the intentions signaled in the five-year plan.

Planners are clearly under enormous pressure to permit investment's share in national income to increase. Although the targeted growth rate for total investment in the Twelfth FYP was set at 4.3 percent, the target for 1986 was 8.2 percent, a rate reminiscent of the 1960s. Actual investment was 8.8 percent and so was even higher. The plan for 1987 calls for a more modest 5.1 percent growth in total investment, but the continued pressure of the modernization program will probably lead to an overfulfillment of that plan again in 1987.

The source of the pressure is difficult to pinpoint given the scarcity of actual data on the structure of investment during 1986–87.[21] It is clear from plan data that MBMW has received the extraordinarily high priority it was promised. Investment in MBMW in 1986 was scheduled to grow at 30 percent, which is well above the planned five-year rate of 12.5 percent and probably well above what it could absorb. But that was anticipated in the Twelfth FYP. Much more surprising are the investment growth rates in the energy sector, which range from 24 percent to 31 percent for 1986 alone.[22] That suggests a very traditional supply-side approach to energy. In contrast, Gorbachev's rhetoric has been favoring demand-side solutions to the energy problem, and the Twelfth FYP targets imply a relatively modest commitment to expanding energy supplies. Furthermore, there are clear indications that housing investment is being given substantially higher priority in the annual plans than in the Twelfth FYP.[23]

These preliminary bits and pieces of information suggest that the leadership remains committed to channeling new resources into MBMW, but is abandoning the plan to draw these resources from other sectors.

21. Statistics on the structure of investment are only published in *Narkhoz,* which traditionally appears about fifteen to eighteen months after the end of the year to which it applies. Therefore data on the structure of investment in 1986 will not appear—if the traditional schedule applies—until spring 1988.

22. The plan calls for investment in the oil industry to grow 31 percent; coal, 27 percent; and electric power, 24 percent. The latter figure was, of course, pre-Chernobyl'. Ryzhkov, "O gosudarstvennom plane."

23. The originally proposed targets for housing construction during the Twelfth FYP called for construction of 565–70 million square meters (msm), a modest increase from the 552.2 msm constructed in 1981–85 (*Narkhoz 1985*, p. 420). By the final draft of the Twelfth FYP, the target had been increased to 595 msm. In 1987 the Politburo once again raised the target, to 630 msm. "V Politbiuro TsK KPSS," *Pravda,* March 27, 1987.

Instead, the growth rate of total investment is well above that for national income. The high priority for housing and energy, for example, could raise the average growth rate for total investment during 1986–90 from 4.3 percent to 5 percent. Other factors yet to emerge will also push the figure upward, so that Twelfth FYP state investment could easily average 6 percent during this period.[24]

That suggests either a foreign or domestic borrowing strategy for investment in 1986–90. As of yet there is no strong indication of heavy reliance on foreign borrowing associated with significant increases in imports of machinery and equipment.[25] The only remaining option is the domestic borrowing strategy, and there the key question is whether consumers or government will end up financing the planned investment growth rates. It is too soon to answer that question, or even to be sure

24. The increase from 4.3 percent to 5 percent is a very rough estimate. The final version of the Twelfth FYP called for a 7.8 percent increase in housing construction over the five years, for which I assume (see note 17) that planners allocated a 13 percent increment in Twelfth FYP housing investment, relative to Eleventh FYP, an annual growth rate of approximately 2.5 percent. The shift to a 14.1 percent housing target would presumably raise the investment target up in the range of 25 percent, or about 4.6 percent a year. That increment to the growth of housing investment of 2.1 percent a year would, given housing's 15 percent share in total investment in 1981–85, add about 0.3 percent to total investment growth during 1986–90. For energy, I have guessed (see text) that the planned investment growth rate was no more than 25 percent (total investment in 1986–90 compared with 1981–85), or 4.6 percent a year. But the high growth rates in 1986 and the well-known problems in that sector suggest that a more reasonable figure would, at a minimum, be 50 percent (slightly above actual for 1981–85 compared with 1976–80), or 8.4 percent a year. The additional growth of 3.8 percent, multiplied by energy's 13 percent share of total investment in 1981–85, yields an addition to total investment growth of about 0.5 percent.

If one adds in the presumably higher-than-planned investment growth rates for raw materials—for which data are not available—and the spillover investment requirements coming out of the modernization program, then the 6 percent investment figure for 1986–90 begins to look plausible.

25. Soviet foreign borrowing in 1986 was high—approximately 6 billion U.S dollars. But much of that is attributable to the decline in oil prices that year. In any event, a foreign borrowing strategy would require a far higher level of borrowing than even that. If, for example, Soviet investment were to grow at 6 percent a year, rather than the planned 4.1 percent, that would imply an additional 95 billion rubles in investment expenditures (in 1984 rubles) over 1986–90 (the difference between 1,033 billion rubles planned for total investment in 1986–90 and the 1,128 billion rubles that would result if the investment growth rate were 6 percent). Assuming, conservatively, that 45 percent of that incremental demand was for machinery and equipment, that implies an additional demand for machinery and equipment of approximately 43 billion rubles over 1986–90, or an average of 8.5 billion rubles a year. Assuming for this very rough calculation that the conversion rate between the domestic ruble and the dollar is approximately unity, that implies net new demands for Western loans of $8.5 billion a year.

that in fact the high investment growth rates will continue throughout this decade. But it seems plausible to suppose that the costs will fall primarily on consumption, but in areas other than housing—possibly through implicit or actual price increases for goods and services. That suggests an impending political problem for Gorbachev, which he seems to be attempting to avoid by encouraging the rapid expansion of privately and cooperatively supplied goods and services. The private investments that would accompany those new activities would be "off-budget" for Gorbachev, as they would draw on the population's financial balances, and on real resources both inside and outside the Gossnab system.

Economic Reforms

For all of the energy Mikhail Gorbachev has put into the human factor and economic policy measures of his first two years, he shows no signs of deluding himself that those measures will be sufficient in and of themselves to realize his ambitious aspirations for the economy. He seems truly convinced that his economic goals can be achieved only through a radical economic reform. "We cannot," he told the delegates to an April 1985 Central Committee meeting on the economy, "as they say, count on manna from heaven.[26]

Gorbachev's approach to economic reforms has operated on both a practical and a conceptual level. On the practical level, reform decrees and related policy decisions have been coming out since spring 1985 in a fairly constant stream. Some of the measures are direct descendants of measures from the Chernenko, Andropov, and Brezhnev eras—for example, a July 1985 decree extended the Andropov experiments to all Soviet industry by January 1, 1987.[27] Other measures in 1985–86 represented the first components of the Gorbachev reforms—for example, a series of decrees in 1985–86 created the various Council of Minister bodies needed to supervise the economic complexes (such as the MBMW *biuro* and Gosagroprom), which play a prominent role in the administration of Gorbachev's reformed economic system.

On the conceptual level, reforms have emerged more slowly. Gor-

---

26. "Initsiativa, organizovannost', effektivnost' " (Initiative, organization, and efficiency), *Sots. ind.*, April 12, 1985.

27. For the reference on this decree, and those referred to in the remainder of this chapter for which a specific reference is not provided, see table 7A-1.

bachev began to sketch out his views on the overall nature of the reform soon after he assumed the post of general secretary.[28] He envisions an economic system in which enterprises and local authorities have much more decisionmaking authority than they now enjoy, and much greater responsibility to use that authority wisely. Good decisions and errors in judgment will generate, respectively, rewards and penalties, according to rules determined ahead of time and strictly enforced. Increased responsibility and the associated penalties and rewards apply also to each worker: individuals who work hard will receive much higher incomes than those who do not. Central authorities, freed of any operational role, will focus on improving the general economic environment and directing the basic steps of economic development. Central control over the economy will be enhanced, while local autonomy is preserved, by relying primarily on economic instruments (taxes, subsidies, interest rates, and so on), rather than on direct administrative orders, to exert control.

These were the general principles that Gorbachev enunciated by the summer of 1985. They clearly indicated his intention to radically reform the system, but they were far too vague to guide the actual implementation of that reform. Issues of fundamental importance, such as the nature of the price and financial reforms, were accorded little or no attention. Statements on other issues—for example, the role of branch ministries—were open to differing interpretations, with different implications for the character of the reform itself.

Throughout 1985–86 the Gorbachev reforms began to unfold in a vacuum. There was no overarching conceptual document guiding the reform; the Economics Department of the Central Committee staff—the

28. Gorbachev's most important early statements on the economy can be found in "Zhivoe tvorchestvo naroda" (The living creativity of the people), *Pravda*, December 11, 1984; "Kursom edinstva i splochennosti" (The course of unity and firmness), *Pravda*, February 21, 1985; "Rech' General'nogo sekretaria TsK KPSS tovarishcha M. C. Gorbacheva na Plenume TsK KPSS 11 Marta 1985 goda" (Speech of the general secretary of the CC of the CPSU, Comrade M. S. Gorbachev, at the plenum of the CC of the CPSU on 11 March 1985), *Pravda*, March 12, 1985; "Rech' M. S. Gorbacheva" (Speech of M. S. Gorbachev), *Sots. ind.*, April 12, 1985; "O sozyve ocherednogo XXVII s"ezda KPSS i zadachakh, sviazannykh s ego podgotovkoi i provedeniem. Doklad General'nogo sekretaria TsK KPSS M. S. Gorbacheva" (On the convening of the regular XXVII Congress of the CPSU, and the tasks connected with its preparation and conduct), *Pravda*, April 24, 1985; "Korennoi vopros ekonomicheskoi politiki partii. Doklad tovarishcha M. S. Gorbacheva" (The fundamental issue of the economic policy of the party), *Pravda*, June 12, 1985; and "Politicheskii doklad tsentral'nogo komiteta" (see note 4).

party's instrument for shaping the reform—operated without a head
after Ryzhkov was elevated to chairman of the Council of Ministers. A
complex system of committees brought together academics and government officials to debate various aspects of the reform, but without the
clear central guidance needed to decide issues of principle.[29] As a result,
the measures introduced began to define the reform. Because some of
those measures were modest and others seemed to contradict Gorbachev's general reform principles, there was room for confusion on
precisely what Gorbachev had in mind when he talked of a "radical"
reform.

In 1987 the conceptual side finally received the attention it deserved.
At the January party plenum Gorbachev received approval for his
democratization reforms. Although their primary significance lay in the
political and social spheres, they nevertheless set the foundation for the
self-management component of his reforms. Nikolai Slyun'kov, formerly
first secretary of the Belorussian Communist Party, took over as head
of the Economic Department of the Central Committee in January 1987.
The draft law on enterprises published in February contained, directly
or by implication, many of the important components of the reform.[30] It
also revealed many important contradictions remaining in the basic
conceptual framework. These contradictions fueled a debate. Simultaneously the system of committees working on the various elements of
the reform, under Abel Aganbegian's leadership, moved ahead in seeking
a consensus on the most important details of the reform.[31] Throughout

29. From the beginning of Gorbachev's reform, the *Komissiia po sovershenstvovaniiu
upravleniia, planirovaniia i khoziaistvennogo mekhanizma* (Commission on the Improvement of the Management, Planning, and Economic Mechanism), under the general
authority of the Council of Ministers, and chaired by Gosplan's chairman, N. V. Talyzin,
has been charged with overseeing the process of designing and implementing the reform.
On the conceptual side, the important body in the commission has been its Scientific
Council, chaired since the summer of 1986 by Abel Aganbegian, and before that by G.
Gvishiani. The Scientific Council, through its twenty-six working groups, has brought
together academics and government officials to work on the key aspects of the reform.
By the summer of 1985, the twenty-six working groups together had produced a set of
documents outlining a reform which amounted, in total, to 300–400 pages. But the
proposals contradicted each other in important ways, and they lay dormant throughout
the fall of 1986, a sign of the lack of guidance for the conceptual side of the reform
process.

30. "Proekt zakon Soiuza Sovetskikh Sotsialisticheskikh Respublik. O gosudarstvennom predpriatii (ob"edinenii)" (Draft law of the Union of Soviet Socialist Republics.
On the state enterprise [association]), *Pravda*, February 8, 1987.

31. Slyunkov reportedly provided the leadership necessary to move toward consen-

the spring, the Politburo debated key components of the reform in preparation for the June 1987 plenum.[32] The public debate operated in close parallel, partly because the proposals being argued in the Aganbegian Scientific Council served as a foundation for many articles in the economic press.

In June 1987 the Central Committee Plenum approved the *Osnovnye polozheniia*, a document that specifies the guiding principles and basic outline of the Gorbachev reforms, and is designed to set the agenda for reform in this decade.[33] The Politburo then moved quickly to approve the basic documents implementing the reform, which are to be issued during the fall of 1987 as a series of decrees.[34]

The Design

The reform consists of an interrelated set of changes in all of the key mechanisms operating the system.[35] Therefore, by definition, it is intended as a comprehensive reform. It is also clearly emerging as a radical reform, at least in its intentions. Centrally determined annual plans are eliminated; private and cooperative economic activity is being encouraged in some sectors; enterprises can go bankrupt, and workers can lose their jobs; prices are to take on a flexibility they have not had since the New Economic Policy (NEP); money is to develop as a true medium of exchange, replacing the *zakazy nariady*. The reform does not copy any other reform, but elements of Eastern European and Chinese reforms are easily recognizable in some of the provisions.

---

sus, the result being a draft of what became the *Osnovnye polozheniia*, based upon the work of many of the twenty-six committees, in the spring of 1987.

32. The most important Politburo meetings were on April 23 (price and finance reform), April 30 (planning and material-technical supply), and May 14 (the law on enterprises), and May 22 (reforms of central administration). See "V Politbiuro TsK KPSS," *Pravda,* April 24, May 1, May 15, May 22, 1987.

33. "Osnovnye polozheniia korennoi perestroiki upravleniia ekonomikoi" (Basic theses for the radical restructuring of the management of the economy), *Pravda,* June 27, 1987. (Hereafter "Osnovnye polozheniia.")

34. "V Politbiuro TsK KPSS," *Pravda,* July 18, 1987.

35. Unless otherwise indicated, this section is based on the *Osnovnye polozheniia* of June 1987 (see table 7A-1; the text published in *Pravda* is used in the references below), and Gorbachev's accompanying speech, "O zadachakh partii po korennoi perestroike upravleniia ekonomikoi. Doklad General'nogo sekretaria TsK KPSS M. S. Gorbacheva na Plenume TsK KPSS 25 Iiunia 1987 goda" (On the tasks of the party for the radical restructuring of the management of the economy. Report of the General Secretary of the CC of the CPSU M. S. Gorbachev to the Plenum of the CC of the CPSU, June 25, 1987), *Pravda,* June 26, 1987.

Gorbachev's complicated and fairly rich reform agenda can best be understood in the framework of the categories used in chapters 3 and 4: the decisionmaking hierarchy, the information system, and the incentive system. Because the actual decrees implementing the *Osnovnye polozheniia* have not yet been published, some of the details of changes in each of these areas are not yet publicly known. But the basic approach is clear.

THE DECISIONMAKING HIERARCHY. The Gorbachev reforms are the first serious attempt since the *sovnarkhoz* reforms (1950s) to radically redistribute rights and responsibilities between the ministries and lower levels of the economic hierarchy. They also have potentially radical implications for the distribution of rights and responsibilities within the central hierarchy.

New authority for the enterprise. The logic of the changes is driven by a new approach to the state enterprise, which gives it far more economic autonomy than it has enjoyed in the past. Output and input mix, customers and suppliers, the structure of wages and bonuses, and the magnitude of capital investments—matters hitherto handled in detailed directives from the central apparatus through the ministries—are now in large measure decided by enterprises themselves. At the same time, enterprises face a new potentially hostile economic environment in which their ability to produce salable output directly and unambiguously determines funds available for wages, bonuses, and new capital projects. This is *samofinansirovanie* (self-financing), the embodiment of Gorbachev's new emphasis on responsibility at the enterprise level: the enterprise is responsible for the economical use of its own assets, and it will receive rewards, or incur costs, depending on how cleverly it shepherds those assets.[36]

That unforgiving economic environment implies that the enterprise should be able to function unconstrained by operational interference by

---

36. As a general rule, large investments will be financed through long-term credits that the enterprises will have to repay in full. Investments directly financed by the state are to be limited primarily to new enterprises or plants in high-priority sectors.

A second related requirement for all Soviet enterprises operating in the new system will be *samookupaemost'*, which has no simple English translation. It means that all enterprises, whatever the sources of their investment funds—their own funds, state funds, or long-term loans—must ensure that the resulting profit at least satisfies a minimum rate of return requirement. See P. Bunich and V. Moskalenko, "Samofinansirovanie: rezul'taty i problemy" (Self-financing: results and problems), *Kommunist*, no. 14 (September 1986), p. 30.

outside authorities, and that is the subject of several basic guarantees in the *Osnovnye polozheniia*, and in the enterprise law. The ministries are still responsible for the general performance of their sector, but are now to use primarily economic instruments (norms, taxes, prices, various charges) to influence enterprises. Direct, detailed management through an annual plan is eliminated. Enterprises are also to be freed from local interference in their operations. Most notably, the *shefstvo* system, as it currently operates in the form of a tax in kind on enterprise labor and capital (see chapter 4), is to be eliminated; in the future local authorities can call on enterprises for capital and labor only in the most exceptional circumstances, according to a signed contract, and for full costs.[37]

The removal of these constraints so prominent in the state enterprise's current relationship to the center is attenuated somewhat from enterprise management's point of view by the addition of a potentially powerful constraint in the form of self-management (*samoupravlenie*), procedures for which are fully specified in the enterprise law passed in June 1987. Top enterprise management is now to be periodically elected for a five-year term, by a workers' conference, in multicandidate elections, confirmed by superior organs. Management has control over the enterprise, but it is to work closely with a workers' council in devising ways to improve enterprise performance. (The council is chosen by the workers' conference and is to exercise the workers' rights between meetings of the workers' conference.)

The expanded role for private and cooperative economic activity. An additional and important change under the reform is the new role for private and cooperative economic activity. The basic notion here is that the supply of consumer goods and services, as well as possibly some industrial goods, can be substantially improved by encouraging individuals and small cooperative enterprises to devote their after-hours to working for additional incomes. The result is an expansion of the possible forms of business, and in some carefully controlled cases implies competition between state enterprises and cooperatives or individuals engaged in legally sanctioned private economic activity.

The new autonomy for enterprises in operational decisions means the elimination of that aspect of the work of the central apparatus. With the exception of a limited number of first-priority products, Gosplan and Gossnab will no longer be involved in constructing the detailed balances

37. "Osnovnye polozheniia."

that the central authorities used to determine the output and distribution of key products. Most of the approximately 2,000 products centrally allocated by Gosplan and Gossnab will shift to the wholesale trade system. That in turn eliminates the need for ministries to disaggregate centrally determined production plans for most products, or to reaggregate information used in the process of arriving at those obligatory plans. The implication is that the All-Union Industrial Associations (VPOs) can be eliminated, leaving essentially a direct link between the enterprise and the ministry.

The distribution of rights and responsibilities in the central hierarchy. Rights and responsibilities within the various levels of the hierarchy are also slated for several important changes. Most important, the branch ministries are to be controlled by ministerial-level bodies charged with coordinating the development of the complex as a whole. The basic idea here is to eliminate duplication and to harness the potential of the various ministries for addressing the challenge of technological change at a level of complexity similar to that in capitalist countries. If, for example, numerically controlled machines are being developed—something that requires the cooperation of many machinebuilding ministries—the MBMW *biuro* will directly supervise the cooperation to make sure that each part of the project goes to the right ministry and that all ministries do their part to ensure that the new product line is successfully developed. Eventually the ministries may be absorbed into the new complexes, along the lines of Gosagroprom, which now controls much of the agro-industrial complex.[38]

Other changes in the system, particularly the increased role for a flexible price system and the increased importance of money, imply a shift in power from Gosplan to financial authorities. There are plans to develop a system of specialized banks to handle finance in their particular complexes, under the general control of Gosbank. The Minfin (finance) and Gosbank will be much more deeply involved in enforcing limits on the growth of the money supply. This is an important part of the commitment to enforce the rules in the new system and means that poor economic decisions can no longer be ratified through ex post subsidies.

THE INFORMATION SYSTEM. The reform will replace the current infor-

38. As of now, it would appear that the remainder of the economy will be divided into the following, somewhat overlapping, complexes: machinebuilding, transportation, construction, fuel and energy, metallurgical, chemicals and timber, foreign economic relations, and consumer goods.

mation system with one that relies primarily on indirect economic instruments and flexible prices working together to control economic activity.

The shift from obligatory targets to norms and other indirect instruments. The goal for the planning system is a familiar one, with clear links to the July 1979 decree: a shift to five-year plans, in which the most important decision variables for planners are norms, fixed for five years and linking enterprise accounts (and state tax receipts) to enterprise performance. This is one way in which planners will convey to enterprises (through ministries) state preferences concerning their economic activity. But there are two other routes for conveying central desires to the enterprise.

Gosplan, the branch ministries, and republican authorities will have the right to issue orders (*goszakazy*) for the fulfillment of the state's highest-priority needs (for example, defense), and for supplies for investment projects financed through centralized state capital expenditures. *Goszakazy*, which will in some cases be issued competitively, will probably be more profitable for enterprises than other orders, and will come with guarantees for key inputs.[39] Obviously one of the key indicators of the depth of change in this reform will be the share of industrial output subject to state orders; if it is very high, then this system approaches the old material-balance system by another name.

Aside from *goszakazy*, central planners will also be able to convey a considerable amount of information to enterprises through control figures (*kontrolnyie tsifry*), which will be sent to them as part of each five-year planning cycle. These figures will include a few basic indicators on productive activity and efficiency, none of which are intended to be obligatory.[40] This is one of the most striking ways in which the Soviet reform proposals differ from those of Hungary, and is obviously one of the greatest potential dangers to the new reform.[41]

---

39. The concern among some of the economists who have worked on this reform is not how enterprises can avoid *goszakazy*, but rather how those that do not win them can get along.

40. The five basic indicators will be for the value of enterprise output, profits, foreign exchange receipts, selected indicators for scientific-technical progress, and indicators of development in social services through the enterprise (housing and day care, for example). During the transition to the new system, indicators of labor productivity and materials use may also be included.

41. The natural fear among the academic economists who worked on the reform, and who generally opposed the use of control figures, is that the ministries and central

Price reform. To the extent that *goszakazy* take up only a modest share of total output and control figures are truly no more than information for the enterprise, the role of the price system looms large in determining the success of the reform. Mikhail Gorbachev has only recently emphasized (and appeared to recognize) how important price reform is to the fate of the entire reform.[42]

Price reform will most likely come in two stages. A revision of prices is to be completed some time in 1988, in time for the preparation of the Thirteenth FYP, where the most important change will be a substantial increase in the price of fuels and raw materials relative to that of manufactured products.[43] A reform of the price-setting mechanism itself will begin at the same time, but will not be completed before the end of the decade.

In the new price system, only a few key products (probably raw materials, fuels, and scarce, nationally important products) will have centrally set prices. The bulk of interenterprise trade will occur at contractual prices (*dogovornye tseny*) negotiated between buyer and seller, following rules established by Goskomtsen. The general rule will be that new products used as inputs in other industries will be priced to divide up the actual (not the projected) productivity gains between buyer and seller. The prices of older, outmoded products will fall over time.[44]

Retail prices will certainly change as part of this reform. For example, food prices are likely to rise sharply, in order to reduce food subsidies. The goal in the new system will be to create a close link between wholesale prices and agricultural procurement prices, on the one hand,

planners will use them to retain control over the basic operation of enterprises. That the ministries will make such an effort seems highly likely, given the experience as recent as the Andropov experiments, when ministries persisted in treating nonobligatory indicators (gross output) as effectively obligatory.

42. As late as the Twenty-seventh Party Congress speech, Gorbachev was engaging in brief and very vague generalities on the need for a much more flexible price system capable of supporting the expansion of *khozraschet*. However, by June 1987 the radical price reform had become the "most important component" of the *perestroika*. Gorbachev, "O zadachakh partii."

43. Interview material. See also Nikolai Ia. Petrakov, "Prospects for Change in the System of Price Formation and Finance-Credit Policy in the USSR," *Soviet Economy*, vol. 3 (April–June 1987), pp. 135–44.

44. These rules are similar to those for new product pricing discussed in chapter 6. Note, however, that the old rules were based on an estimate of the productivity gains, whereas the new rules will be geared to actual productivity gains, specified, presumably, according to rules set by Goskomtsen. For details see N. Petrakov, "Prospects for Change."

and retail prices on the other, in order to avoid an uncontrolled growth of subsidies.

Because economic power is highly concentrated in this system—it might become even more concentrated once the reforms are introduced[45]— and competition from imports is virtually absent, price control in this new system could be problematic. The *Osnovnye polozheniia* and Gorbachev emphasize the importance of economic competition. But they do not link it directly to control over price levels, and the general impression is that Goskomstsen's rules are to be the major source of control over the level of prices, not competition among Soviet enterprises, nor competition via imports. If that is indeed so, then this is one of the most important potential conceptual weaknesses in the reform.

THE INCENTIVE SYSTEM. If fully adopted, this system would create fundamentally different incentives for enterprises and their workers, and even for the ministries that supervise them all. By far the most radical changes would take place in the enterprises.

The reform would have all enterprises operating according to the principles of complete *khozraschet* and *samofinasirovanie*, which, in practical terms, means that they should earn sufficient funds to cover current labor and material costs and have an investable surplus (to be supplemented, for large projects, by loans). Although this gives enterprises two basic options to choose from, either way they are on their own financially.[46] Thus there are provisions for identifying insolvent enterprises and for beginning bankruptcy procedures. The traditional avenues open to enterprise management to protect jobs—such as making special deals with the ministry—are formally precluded by the reforms.

This move will substantially increase the interest of workers in the management of their enterprise. The reform could have the immediate effect of creating labor income differentials among enterprises in the

45. The *Osnovnye polozheniia* portray the future industrial structure as one in which a few thousand large, vertically integrated, national-level enterprises would handle national-level markets, while local and regional markets, as well as some of the needs of these national-level enterprises, would be handled by enterprises founded and operating under republican and local authorities. Depending on how that is managed, the result could be near monopolies in many product groups.

46. There are two basic models from which the enterprise can choose. In the first model, the wage account is linked directly to normative net output (NNO, see chapter 5), and the residual is left for interest payments and taxes (first claims), the remainder of that going to enterprise accounts for development, science and technology, social development, and bonuses. In the second model, wages are the final residual after payments for taxes, interest, and the other enterprise accounts according to norms.

same sector, even for people with the same jobs, all related to differences in enterprise performance. It is in this sense that *samoupravlenie* is intended to play an important role in the reform: Gorbachev is threatening the workers of poorly managed enterprises with lower income, and even the loss of their jobs, but at the same time is giving them a role in choosing and controlling enterprise management.

The reforms go one step further in their effort to link personal performance with incomes as closely as possible by pushing for wide-spread adoption of brigade systems for compensating labor. In these systems, which can take various forms, groups of workers in a factory form a brigade, which is compensated as a whole for its work, according to what is in effect an internal contract with the enterprise management. The brigade itself then has considerable control over the compensation of its members. Those systems, to the extent that they are introduced, would lead to income dispersion even within the enterprise and would further enhance workers' interest in the management of the enterprise.

For ministries, the new system represents a complicated mix of new and old incentives. They are still held responsible in general, and even in some specific ways, for the performance of "their" enterprises.[47] On the other hand, ministries are to be put on full *khozraschet*, which means that the value of enterprise sales may take on more importance than it had for ministries in the old system.

For both ministries and enterprises, one of the most important goals of the reform is to impose self-control in the demands for capital and materials through the mechanism of *samofinansirovanie*. But a price system relatively free of distortions, providing acceptably accurate information on supply and demand, is indispensable to the successful operation of *samofinansirovanie*.

The Timetable for Implementation

The deadline for the implementation of the entire reform is the beginning of the Thirteenth FYP, January 1, 1991. But within that overall goal, there are separate timetables for some of the components. Because the Thirteenth FYP, for which work begins in 1988, will have to be

47. Although the *Osnovnye polozheniia* free the ministries from operational respon-sibilities, the latter are still responsible for satisfying demands for products in their sector, removing disproportions, achieving world technological levels in their sectors, and implementing sector-side scientific-technical programs.

constructed according to the new procedures and focused on a full new set of norms, new planning prices must be introduced by the end of 1988.[48] The reform of the price mechanism itself, which involves the transition to contract pricing and changes in price formation in the retail and agricultural sectors, will presumably move more slowly.

The switch to wholesale trade must be implemented in three to four years, which presumably means 1990–91. It is to be done in steps, beginning with those inputs used in the production of consumer goods, agricultural products, construction and machinebuilding, and in cooperative and individual economic activity.

The enterprise law, already passed, is to be implemented by 1989, although that will depend in part on the companion laws outlining the operation of the central organs. Those decrees are to be published in the fall of 1987 and will presumably include specific deadlines. They are likely to call for a gradual transition to a system in which *goszakazy* account for a decreasing share of industrial output, but there is as yet no official estimate of what that share might be.

The Reforms of 1985–86 and Their Relationship to the *Osnovnye Polozheniia*

Although the principles guiding Gorbachev's reforms were only fully articulated and approved by the party in June 1987, reform decrees have been emerging since 1985 at an impressive pace. In July of 1985 a decree announced measures to extend the Andropov experiments to all industry in 1986–87. An effort to reorganize the economic hierarchy began in the fall of 1985 with the formation of the MBMW *biuro* and Gosagroprom, followed in 1986 by the establishment of similar organs controlling fuel and energy, construction, and foreign economic relations. In March 1986 a reform of the agricultural sector was introduced. In July 1986 a totally new quality-control procedure was introduced experimentally in parts of industry (Gospriemka), then extended to more enterprises in 1987. During the fall of 1986 the new laws on individual economic activity and reforms of the apparatus governing Soviet foreign economic relations were in place. In September 1986, in the midst of this activity, the official

48. The *Osnovnye polozheniia* simply say that work on the price system must go quickly so that the Thirteenth FYP can be done in the new prices.

legal gazette of the Supreme Soviet published a long list of reform decrees to be enacted, with a precise timetable, indicating a commitment to further reforms. By the end of 1986 this initial surge of reforms wound down as the debate surrounding the *Osnovnye polozheniia* began in earnest.

These reforms, enacted roughly between the summer of 1985 and the end of 1986, consisted of a melange of measures, some of which were clearly related to reforms and experiments of the 1970s and early 1980s, whereas others previewed elements of the *Osnovnye polozheniia*. The July 1985 decree extending the Andropov experiments to all of Soviet industry during 1986–87 preserves major components of the traditional central planning system, including the apparatus of obligatory plans, and it makes no mention of workers' management. Just two years later, in July 1987, a dramatically different approach emerged in the *Osnovnye polozheniia*, codified in a new enterprise law that eliminates obligatory central plans and gives a prominent place to workers' management.

In other ways the reforms of 1985–86 and the *Osnovnye polozheniia* are in basic agreement. The new laws on cooperative and individual economic activity are an obvious example. The reorganization of the economic hierarchy into economic complexes represents a clear effort to simplify and rationalize the extraordinarily complex web of ministries that supervise economic activity, an important component of the *Osnovnye polozheniia*.

This complicated and contradictory relationship between the economic reforms introduced in the first two years under Gorbachev and those enacted by the June 1987 plenum suggests that the *Osnovnye polozheniia* are best viewed as a very important milepost in the midst of the reform process. They represent, in effect, an ex post rationalization of some of the reforms already under way, an ex post critique of others, and a framework for future reform decrees. In their totality, they depart from the first two years in the direction of a more radical reform.

However, the prospects for the successful implementation of a reform consistent with the principles espoused at the June 1987 plenum cannot be evaluated without reference to the 1985–86 period. As mentioned earlier, some of the measures introduced in 1985–86 are consistent with the *Osnovnye polozheniia,* which means that reforms consistent with those principles are already being implemented.

Another reason to look at 1985–86 carefully is that the contradictions emerging in that period are likely previews of contradictions that will persist as reform decrees are introduced and implemented in the remainder of the decade. The culture of central planning—more accurately, micromanagement of economic affairs—is deeply rooted in the psyche of Soviet society. No matter how compelling the case for decentralization and a disengagement of central authorities from the management of the minute details of economic affairs, there is still every reason to expect the culture of central planning to persist, and to reemerge periodically under the guise of "reform." That is precisely what happened in 1985–86, and it is important to understand that background in analyzing the prospects for future reforms.

The Period 1985–86 as a Preview of the Osnovnye Polozheniia

Most of the principles of the *Osnovnye polozheniia* will require new decrees if they are to be implemented; the activities of 1985–86 did little to lay the preparatory ground. This is particularly true in the area of price reform, where virtually nothing was accomplished during 1985–86. It is also essentially true for changes in the incentive system, which are only now promised under the July 1987 enterprise law.

It was only in the area of decisionmaking hierarchy that some progress was made in directions generally consistent with the *Osnovnye polozheniia*. The administrative streamlining of the system began in late 1985, although the start was slow and uncertain. The laws on individual and cooperative economic activity open up new possibilities outside the tight control of the ministerial system for individuals to supply consumer goods and services. The reform in foreign economic relations has begun to modernize the antiquated system heretofore used to manage Soviet foreign economic relations.

STREAMLINING THE MINISTERIAL SYSTEM. Gorbachev moved quickly in 1985–86 to begin reorganizing the hierarchy around the concept of economic complexes. The general strategy is to divide the economic hierarchy into ministries in closely related complexes, placing over them a supraministerial body headed by a deputy prime minister and charged with coordinating and rationalizing the operation of the ministries.[49]

49. The idea behind this draws on, but does not fully imitate, the model of the Military-Industrial Commission, which oversees the nine military machinebuilding ministries, and several other ministries in addition to selected activities of Minkhimprom (Chemicals), Minelektrotekhprom (Electrical Equipment), and Minneftekhimprom (Pe-

Table 7-3. *The Ministerial Hierarchy by Complex, November 1986*

Supraministerial organ	Number of ministries	Date created[a]	Head[b]
Military-Industrial Commission	9	...	Y. D. Masliukov
Machinebuilding Bureau	11	October 17, 1985	I. S. Silaev
State Agro-Industrial Committee	1[c]	November 23, 1985	V. S. Murakhovsky[d]
Fuel-Energy Bureau	6	March 14, 1986	B. E. Shcherbina
State Construction Committee	4[e]	September 13, 1986	Y. P. Batalin
Commission on Foreign Economic Relations	2	August 19, 1986	V. M. Kamentsev
Bureau for Social Development	...	...	G. A. Aliev

a. Table 7A-1 lists the decrees with references. The dates given here are the dates the decrees were published, which is not necessarily the actual date on which the body was created.

b. Unless otherwise indicated, the rank of the head is deputy prime minister.

c. Combines five former ministries and a state committee into one body with the powers of a ministry.

d. Murakhovsky is one of four first-deputy prime ministers.

e. Takes over the functions of the now-eliminated Minstroi (Construction) as an upgraded state committee, supervising newly formed, regionally oriented, ministries.

The definition of the complexes and boundaries between them began to emerge in the fall of 1985 and winter of 1986. The results—seven complexes, each headed by at least a deputy chairman of the Council of Ministers—are summarized in table 7-3. In addition, recent plan documents indicate that planners are working with three other complexes: metallurgical, chemical and woodworking, and transport and communications.

At least during the first year or so of the complexes, it was not clear if they would really have an impact on the planning process, or if they were simply another effort to change formal responsibilities in the hope that something might come of it. There is no fixed pattern to even the name, let alone the apparent duties, of the bodies, although by the end of 1986 two types seemed to be emerging, as illustrated by the differences between Gosagroprom and the MBMW *biuro*.

---

troleum Refining and Petrochemicals). U.S. Central Intelligence Agency, *Soviet Acquisition of Militarily Significant Western Technology: An Update* (Washington, D.C.: Department of Defense, 1985). It is chaired by Deputy Prime Minister Y. D. Masliukov. It also generally resembles an intended organizational structure that General Secretary Leonid I. Brezhnev called for in the Twenty-fifth (1976) Party Congress when he advocated the formation of superministries. Paul Cocks, "Administrative Reform and Soviet Politics," in U.S. Congress Joint Economic Committee, *Soviet Economy in the 1980s: Problems and Prospects*, Joint Committee Print, 97 Cong. 2 sess. (GPO, 1982), pt. 1, p. 58.

Gosagroprom represents the most powerful of the new supraminis-terial organs created under Mikhail Gorbachev. The idea of treating agro-industry as a whole goes back to the 1970s, and is the centerpiece of Brezhnev's Food Program (developed when Gorbachev was party secretary for agriculture). But until the creation of Gosagroprom the supervision of the agro-industrial complex had been scattered among a number of ministries.

As head of Gosagroprom, V. S. Murakhovsky enjoys, it would appear, full control over the core of Soviet agro-industry: fruit and vegetable farming, meat and dairy production, the food industry, rural construc-tion, and agro-technology. Because Gosagroprom absorbed five former ministries, including the Minsel'khoz (Agriculture), and Sel'khoztekhnika (the organization charged with purchasing machinery and equipment for agriculture), by implication Murakhovsky has formal control over the formation of plan targets, and in particular the allocation of investment, within the areas of responsibility for his committee.[50] Yet, even with these considerable powers, Murakhovsky does not formally control the entire agro-industrial complex.[51]

One of the purposes of forming Gosagroprom, and all the supramin-isterial bodies, is to reduce staffs through efficiency savings, which will be made possible by changes in the work load of the ministerial system. It will not be evident for some time whether anything of this sort is going to stick, let alone occur. But it is interesting that, in the case of Gosagroprom, the Central Committee and Council of Ministers author-ized leaders at all levels in agro-industry to release workers and give them three months' severance pay while they search for another job.[52]

The Machinebuilding *biuro* is at the other end of the spectrum. The decree establishing the *biuro* some time in October 1985 has not been published. Nevertheless, various sources clearly indicate that its head, Deputy Prime Minister I. S. Silaev, has limited power.[53] The *biuro*'s

---

50. See, for example, an interview with Murakhovsky in Foreign Broadcast Infor-mation Service, *Daily Report: Soviet Union*, February 4, 1986, pp. T1–5. (Hereafter *FBIS-SU.*)

51. Five ministries controlling grain procurement, fishing, fertilizer production, land reclamation and irrigation, and timber retain separate identity. Nevertheless, Murak-hovsky, as a first deputy prime minister, presumably carries considerable influence over their operation.

52. V. Kostakov, "One for Seven," *FBIS-SU*, January 13, 1986, p. S3.

53. I base the discussion here on the summary of the October 17, 1985, Politburo meeting ("V Politibiuro TsK KPSS," *Pravda*, October 18, 1985); on an interview with

main tasks seem to be to (1) coordinate specialization and trade among the eleven machinebuilding ministries, and thus reduce autarky and the inefficiencies that flow from it; (2) stimulate innovation throughout the system; and (3) push for a general increase in output quality.

The most important evidence on the limited powers of this *biuro* is indirect: no ministries were absorbed in its creation. Those eleven ministries remain intact; their heads retain positions on the Council of Ministers; the annual plans presumably are addressed to each of the eleven ministries individually. This already suggests that Silaev's power is limited, at least in the critical areas of investment and mobilizing productive capacity to fulfill plans. If the ministries still face individual plan targets, they have a powerful excuse to ignore the instructions from the *biuro* with which they disagree, since they can cite plan fulfillment as the highest priority.

In the end, how much power this *biuro* actually has will probably depend more on Silaev and the backing he receives from the Politburo, than on the regulations themselves.[54]

These supraministerial organs will eventually assume important planning functions for their complexes, as Gosplan takes on the more general role of focusing on the entire economy, which includes coordinating relations among the complexes.[55] Presumably this will involve constructing balances for the key products in the complex, allocating investment, reorganizing the sector, and so on. But those are the functions of a *super*ministry, such as Gosagroprom, and the much weaker supraministerial *biuros* will need new powers if they are to fulfill them. At the June 1987 plenum Gorbachev indicated that he was dissatisfied with the initial experiences with the *biuros*—especially the MBMW *biuro*—and he seemed to be clearly signaling an intention to expand their powers by reducing the powers of the constituent ministries and of Gosplan.[56]

In the context of the current system, these changes amount to a recentralization of economic power in a new, supraministerial, level of the hierarchy. As long as the center is still constructing material balances,

Silaev ("Zadachi biuro po mashinostroeniiu" [Tasks of the biuro on machinebuilding], *Izvestiia*, March 11, 1986); and on personal interviews.

54. During a visit to Moscow in June–July 1986, I encountered several different versions of Silaev's powers, but with a general tone suggesting that he would have to fight for whatever true power he might have over the activities of the eleven ministries under him.

55. See Ryzhkov, "O gosudarstvennom plane."

56. Gorbachev, "O zadachakh partii."

the supraministerial bodies at least coordinate—and in the case of Gosagroprom actually construct and enforce—sectorally based balances that generate obligatory plans for individual enterprises. But if, and when, the reforms embodied in the *Osnovnye polozheniia* are introduced, this administrative recentralization should logically move ahead and allow ministries to be absorbed into these bodies at the same time that they are being disengaged from micromanagement of the system. In the new system, the *biuros*, operating with considerably reduced staffs, would serve as the locus of sectorally based policies and would use norms, taxes, and other indirect instruments to regulate enterprises.

The second major thrust of the reorganization is to eliminate the VPOs and convert to a system in which the ministry and the enterprise are directly linked, without any intermediate authority. At the same time, enterprises are to be merged into stronger *ob"edinenie*, to which will be added previously independent research institutes and construction organizations in order to focus productive activity in large, conglomerate-like associations. The purpose is to eliminate the hard-core resistance to reforms in VPOs; reduce within-ministry autarkic tendencies between VPOs, and thereby increase efficiency; and to streamline the entire system by merging enterprises into larger units that the ministry can deal with directly. This is in part a move away from the thrust of the 1972 mergers, which created the VPOs, but at the same time represents yet another attempt to devolve to *khozraschet* bodies below the ministry some of the functions hitherto performed by the ministry.

Minpribor (Instrument-making, Automation Equipment, and Control Systems), a veteran of experiments and reforms, led the way from an experiment begun in 1985,[57] to the measures introduced in 1986 that have eliminated sixteen VPOs (it is not clear if this is all of them) and merged all research and design organizations, except a main research institute for the branch as a whole, with individual enterprises (which were merged into about half of their previous number). In the process, the staff at the ministry was reduced; some were pensioned off, and others (170 persons) moved to enterprises.[58] Subsequently, the remaining ten

57. Minpribor has a long history as a test bed for reforms, and as a leader. It was the first ministry to have almost all of its plants operating on the new system in 1966; its *glavki* were put on a *khozraschet* basis in 1968; and in 1970 it was reorganized into a Ministry-VPO-*ob"edinenie* arrangement presaging the 1972 merger decree. See William J. Conyngham, *The Modernization of Soviet Industrial Management: Socioeconomic Development and the Search for Viability* (Cambridge University Press, 1982), p. 216.

58. M. Shkabardnia, "Logika razvitiia" (The logic of development), *Sots. ind.*, July

civilian machinebuilding ministries were moved to the new system, and the VPOs were "basically" eliminated.[59] But, ironically, indications are that the "elimination" has in effect resurrected the old *glavki,* which the VPOs replaced.[60]

LEGALIZATION OF PRIVATE ECONOMIC ACTIVITY. The measures of the 1985–86 period with the closest links to the *Osnovnye polozheniia* are those legalizing private and cooperative economic activity. These measures were introduced in the fall of 1986 and early in 1987. They clearly indicate the willingness of Soviet authorities to allow productive activities to expand outside the framework of the state enterprise, and therefore the ministerial system, with little interference from government or the party. These new laws are mainly designed to expand the supply of consumer goods and services without any significant drain on state capital, material, or labor resources.

The law on private economic activity, passed in November 1986 but put into effect in May 1987, allows individuals to engage in a broad range of hitherto illegal productive activities, including most services and handicrafts. The main restriction on eligibility is that workers employed in state industry can only do this in their off-hours. But members of their immediate family over the age of sixteen and living with them can work in the business full time. In addition, students, housewives, and pensioners can work full time in such businesses. Any individual engaged in such activity must be licensed by local governmental authorities *(ispol'komy)* and must pay either an annual income tax or an up-front fee *(patent).* The *patent* applies to those activities where it is difficult to monitor the income and determine the tax (private taxis, for example). The taxes and the *patenty* are high, but not exorbitant.[61]

19, 1985; and M. Shkabardnia, "Rezhim perestroiki" (We are resolving the restructuring), *Sots. ind.,* February 22, 1986.

59. Ryzhkov, "O gosudarstvennom plane."

60. D. Levchuk, "Na osnove novykh general'nykh skhem" (On the basis of new general schemes), *Khoziaistvo i pravo,* no. 2 (1987), pp. 54–58, reports that, though 108 VPOs were eliminated in the eleven civilian machinebuilding ministries in 1986, the smaller enterprises in each ministry are now being managed by *glavki,* which are serving essentially the same functions as the old VPOs. In addition, many of the operations of the old functional VPOs are now being carried out by functional *glavki.*

61. The marginal tax rates range from 15 percent for incomes up to 3,000 rubles a year to 65 percent on incomes above 6,000 rubles. The average money wage in the USSR in 1986 was 2,340 rubles a year, so this tax allows fairly high incomes with no danger of confiscation. On the other hand, these incomes will essentially come from "moonlighting," so it may be quite difficult to reach the higher income levels legally.

The *patenty* prices are set by region and are generally rather high. For example, in

The regulations on cooperative economic activity issued in the fall of 1986 and early 1987, and effective immediately, differ somewhat in details, but share a common general approach. They authorize house-wives, pensioners, students (above the age of sixteen), and state em-ployees (in their free time) to form cooperatives for the production of various consumer goods and services, for example, restaurants, auto repair services, or small manufacturing operations that would use industrial by-products to produce consumer goods and other inputs for industry. The co-ops are licensed by different local authorities, depend-ing on their area of operation, but are subject to only a few regulations, which govern procedures for adding or subtracting members, voting procedures, and rules for hiring wage labor. Their income net of material costs and wages for contracted labor goes first to payments for state income tax, and the remainder is at the disposal of the cooperative.[62]

The expansion of rights for individual and cooperative economic activity represents an effort to expand the supply of consumer goods and services rapidly. In part, this involves legalizing some of the activities now occurring in the second economy, but it also means that those who are not active members of the labor force will have more opportunities to go to work without having to seek employment in a state enterprise. This expansion will result in some competition for state enterprises, but for the most part—because the supply of goods and services is so inadequate—the output of these new businesses will at first simply fill a large gap. That is clearly the hope of Soviet leaders. All of the laws in this area promise such businesses state assistance in finding facilities for their operations and some materials.

Nevertheless, these new opportunities for individuals, alone or in cooperatives, to engage in economic activity are carefully constrained to limit the impact on the state sector. Most important is the prohibition against full-time employment for those now employed in the state sector. This provision, which evidently was not in earlier drafts of the law on individual economic activity, protects state enterprises from "raids" on already scarce labor.[63] That provision limits considerably the possibility that privately produced goods and services will play an important role

---

the RFSFR the *patent* for a private taxi costs 560 rubles, which means that the worker must—on his off-hours—earn at least the equivalent of three months' wages before he can clear any net revenues after taxes. For the data on taxes and patents, see A. Cherniak, "Pol'za dlia vsekh" (Of use to all), *Pravda*, April 24, 1987.

62. See the February 1987 regulations for additional details in table 7A-1.

63. Interview material.

soon in the USSR. But even within current restrictions, the possibilities are considerably expanded over those of the past.

These decrees from the 1985–86 period are clearly in the spirit of the *Osnovnye polozheniia*, and if national and local authorities encourage this activity, then the state of the consumer goods market in the USSR could improve dramatically in a relatively short period of time, with very little new commitment of state capital, labor, or material resources. That is clearly part of Gorbachev's strategy. If he succeeds, it will mean that even without success in those reforms aimed at heavy industry, consumers will see a substantial improvement in the supply of goods and services.

THE NEW APPROACH TO FOREIGN ECONOMIC RELATIONS. The most interesting development in the creation of complexes, which was virtually unheralded by prior debate, was the formation in August 1986 of the State Commission for Foreign Economic Relations (*Gosudarstvennyi vneshneekonomicheskaia komissiia,* or GVEK) under the leadership of V. M. Kamentsev, a deputy chairman of the Council of Ministers. This and subsequent decrees and regulations issued in January 1987 authorizing joint ventures with enterprises in socialist and nonsocialist countries represent a major change in the practical definition of the monopoly of foreign trade. These decrees are an attempt to introduce much-needed decentralization in some areas of foreign trade decisionmaking and a renewed effort to coordinate overall foreign economic policy. Although the *Osnovnye polozheniia* say very little about foreign economic relations, these measures are unambiguously in the spirit of the June 1987 plenum.[64]

The formation of GVEK was accompanied by a major redistribution of decisionmaking rights over foreign trade within the economic hierarchy. Foreign trade organizations (FTOs), which used to be almost exclusively under the supervision of the Ministry of Foreign Trade, have now, in large measure, shifted to twenty domestic ministries; in addition, about seventy enterprises have been given the right to direct export and import operations.[65] The ministries with their own FTOs and the enter-

64. In addition to the decrees of August 18, 1986, and the regulations of January 13, 1987, see V. Shemiatenkov, "Perestroika vneshneekonomicheskoi deiatel'nosti" (The restructuring of foreign economic activities), *Ekon. gaz.*, no. 46 (November 1986); and "Sovershenstvovanie vneshneekonomicheskoi deiatel'nosti" (The improvement of foreign economic activities), an interview with V. M. Kamentsev, *Ekon. gaz.*, no. 3 (January 1987).

65. The MFT retained only FTOs that are handling fuels, raw materials, and food trade, all of which will remain under central controls.

prises with direct foreign trade rights will be operating on a self-financing basis, meaning that they can retain a portion of their export proceeds (determined by centrally set norms) and can use those to purchase imports. Special exchange rates are being introduced to link the domestic ruble with foreign currencies, which will make it possible to include foreign trade results directly in the sales figures for the enterprise.

There are many important impediments to the full realization of this aspect of the Gorbachev reforms. Simply finding and training personnel capable of operating this new system in various ministries and enterprises will take time, and the Ministry of Foreign Trade—which lost out in the internal debate over this part of the reform—is unlikely to offer much assistance during the transition. In addition, a thorough reform of domestic prices is a critical precondition to any significant increase in enterprise rights to export or import products directly. There are many other roadblocks ahead. But the important point here is that these measures represent a clear effort to decentralize control over the operation of the system in an area that in the past has virtually suffocated from the conservative restraints imposed by the Ministry of Foreign Trade.

The Period 1985–86 as a Preview of the Tensions between Old and New Approaches

Other measures in 1985–86, far from preparing the ground for the *Osnovnye polozheniia*, instead signal the almost unconscious tendency for Soviet leaders to rely on traditional administrative methods, even while talking convincingly of their commitment to radical reforms. The two most notable illustrations of that tendency are the continued reliance on new plan targets and central directives in an effort to achieve what, in principle, the reform itself should automatically achieve; and the schizophrenic double message that Soviet leaders impress upon the ministries and local party officials.

THE PERSISTENCE OF ADMINISTRATIVE METHODS IN THE MIDST OF "REFORM." A glance at table 7A-1 shows a series of measures stretching from 1985 to the present in which Soviet leaders, while talking of decreased interference in the operational decisions of enterprises, nevertheless issue orders that directly interfere in those operations. The July 1985 decree extending the Andropov experiments actually added to the number of obligatory indicators that ministries could pass on to enterprises (relative to those authorized in the 1985 version of the Andropov experiments).[66]

After the July 1985 decree was issued, new regulations were introduced, adding even more indicators. An August 21, 1985, decree added new bonuses linked to consumer goods production targets for enterprises whose primary (greater than 50 percent) output was not consumer goods; it also provided new bonuses for consumer goods enterprises producing higher-quality goods and services. On September 12, 1986, a decree was issued calling for the general application, on a regular basis, of work place "certification" (*attestatsiia*), a procedure whereby enterprises and other institutions take a census of the jobs in their organizations, whether filled or not, and eliminate the unneeded jobs, or those violating health and safety regulations.[67]

A May 15, 1986, decree on energy and raw material conservation introduced specific targets for ministries and union republics and new penalties for enterprises that violate energy conservation targets. A June 5, 1986, decree sought to strengthen the rights of the consumer in contract formation and disputes and to increase the interest of enterprises fulfilling contracts. A February 27, 1987, decree ordered all enterprises to move to double-shift, and in some cases triple-shift, work on their new machinery and equipment.

Taken together, the July 1985 and subsequent decrees speak rather clearly of Soviet leaders' approach to the enterprise in the new system. The message is a familiar one, namely, that enterprises cannot be trusted—whatever the incentive system—to do what is in the interest of the state unless the state specifies precisely what it wants to have happen. The charitable interpretation of this is a variant of the notion that "one can never be too careful." By sending two or three strong signals on product quality, innovation, contract fulfillment, and so on, planners are making double or triple sure that enterprises get the message. But the more plausible interpretation is that old habits are asserting themselves, that old assumptions are still accepted (that everything can be quantified; and that multiple targets are required to obtain the desired results). The potential casualty in all of this, already clear at this early formative stage in the reforms, is enterprise independence.

66. In addition to targets for output in physical units, the new law allowed for targets for the output of experimental products and the introduction of new products in serial production.

67. When individuals are in those job slots, they are to be moved within the organization if possible.

The mirror image of this revealed distrust of enterprises is an implicit trust in bureaucratic procedures to simulate market pressures. Even though Gorbachev's vision seems to imply a willingness to place greater trust in markets to induce enterprises to produce higher-quality output more efficiently, the decrees suggest a far more conservative approach. This is abundantly clear in the quality control legislation passed on July 2, 1986, introducing *gospriemka* (state acceptance).

As chapter 4 indicated, the existing quality control procedures in Soviet industry are flawed. This is clear not only in the final result—the persistently low quality of output—but also in the procedures themselves. In the past, enterprises have found it too easy to circumvent the spirit of quality targets while formally fulfilling them, and ministries have succumbed to an irresistible temptation to go along with that because they, themselves, are judged in part by the quality indicators.

The root of the problem is the absence of incentives to truly attempt to increase quality, incentives that are an automatic by-product of competitive mechanisms. Bureaucratic procedures can never simulate the intense concentration fostered in the mind of an enterprise manager who knows that if he does not meet the actual quality demands of the real customer, he will go out of business. At best, they can provide a faint imitation of that effect. Gorbachev's vision for the economy, based in part on the notion that enterprises should face hard budget constraints and be compelled to satisfy consumers, seemed to be an attempt to address that issue.

Nevertheless, Gorbachev still apparently entertains a strong faith in bureaucratic quality control procedures, a point emphasized by the July 2, 1986, quality control law. That law shifts from the ministries to Gosstandardt (State Standards), the primary responsibility for overseeing the quality control process. It establishes within selected factories a new quality control section, which duplicates the factory's quality control department (OTK, see chapter 4), but which, unlike the OTK, is under the direct control of Gosstandardt. It gives to consumers the right to reject products not meeting contractually specified quality standards and holds the enterprise's ministry responsible for somehow satisfying the contract on schedule. In addition, it specifies that penalties for nondelivery or low-quality output come out of the Material Incentive Account.

The quality control system apparently had some effect on industrial performance in industry in early 1987; at least, Soviet leaders are using that as a reason for the underfulfillment of plans for industrial performance in that year. But from the point of view of the reforms, whether this or the other administrative regulations work is not the point. They are all manifestations of the mentality according to which nothing happens unless the center orders it. Such measures are contrary to the reform; indeed they undermine it. Yet they are likely to continue throughout the remainder of this decade, leading to a tension between the reform and the mentality it is trying to change.

THE SCHIZOPHRENIC MESSAGE TO MINISTRIES AND LOCAL PARTY OFFI-CIALS. One of the clear implications of the *Osnovnye polozheniia* is that ministries and local party officials, because they can no longer interfere directly in the operational decisions of enterprises, will see a reduction in their ability to control the operations of those enterprises. The logical conclusion is that the leadership shall have to accept a situation such that if, for example, there are shortages of particular products, or a certain industry lags in technological progress, the minister involved, and local party officials, cannot be held fully accountable for the problems. The reform desocializes responsibility for mistakes on the part of enterprises.

Yet the leadership and Gorbachev himself have actually increased the pressure on ministries and local party officials to take responsibility for the quality of goods and services produced in "their" enterprises, and for the rate at which "their" enterprises modernize. When the Central Committee *apparat* looked into why the "Ekran" *ob"edinenie* of Minradioprom (Radio Industry) persisted in producing low-quality, unreliable televisions, it blamed not only the leadership of the enterprise, but also the ministry and the party committee of the *ob"edinenie* for putting up with these problems and not forcing a "restructuring" of work along the lines suggested at the Twenty-seventh Party Congress. The general director of the *ob"edinenie* was fired, and reprimands were given to the head of the party committee and P. S. Pleshakov, head of Minradioprom. Pleshakov was admonished to pay greater attention to the production of consumer goods and their quality in enterprises under his control.[68]

68. "V Tsentral'nom Komitete KPSS" (In the Central Committee of the CPSU), *Pravda*, June 3, 1986. The additional significance of this is the fact that Minradioprom is one of the nine defense ministries. In this decree three other defense industry ministries—Minsviaz (Communications), Minelektronprom (Electronics), and Minob-shchemash (General Machinebuilding)—were admonished to do their part to contribute to an improvement in television and radio technology.

Similar examples can be cited from the short period under Gorbachev. B. N. Yeltsin, first secretary of the Moscow *gorkom*, has admonished the first secretaries under him to be tough with their enterprises on issues of efficient operation and product quality. "All newly introduced manufactured goods must be produced only with the mark of quality (*znak kachestva*)," Yeltsin told party leaders in late 1985, "the party organization must head a constant struggle for the honor of the capital's [quality] mark."[69] The Khar'kovskii *gorkom* was publicly castigated in the summer of 1985 for putting up with the tendency of its enterprises to submit unambitious plans for output and labor productivity growth, and for tolerating the very modest rates of modernization. The Central Committee decree on this *gorkom*, obviously meant as a warning to all local party leaders, orders them to work to guarantee the unquestioning fulfillment of plans and delivery commitments by every enterprise.[70]

For ministers who, despite these multiple messages, were in doubt as to the magnitude of their responsibilities, Nikolai Ryzhkov spoke plainly at the Twenty-seventh Party Congress:[71]

We should decisively restructure the economic mechanism in order to accelerate scientific-technical progress in every sector of the economy. But we need to take account of the fact that this mechanism cannot in itself give results if simultaneously there is no increase in the responsibility of economic leaders, primarily ministers. They must carry full responsibility for the technical level of production in the sectors.

At the June 1987 plenum Mikhail Gorbachev conveyed a similar message castigating several ministers by name for failing in their responsibility to guarantee sufficient material inputs to the economy during early 1987.[72] Later he leaves no doubt that ministers will be personally

69. B. N. Yeltsin, "Accountability Report of the Moscow CPSU Gorkom," *FBIS-SU*, January 31, 1986, pp. 01–012; quotation on p. 04.

70. The decree, issued under the heading "V Tsentral'nom Komitete KPSS," was titled "O rabote Khar'kovskogo gorkoma Kompartii Ukrainy po mobilizatsii trudovykh kollektivov na vypolnenie plana 1985 goda i sotsialisticheskikh obiazatel'stv prorabotat' ne menee dvukh dnei na sekonomlennykh material'nykh resursakh" (On the work of the Kharkovsk gorkom of the Communist party of the Ukraine on the mobilization of labor collectives for the fulfillment of the plan for 1985 and the socialist duty to work not less than two days on economized material resources), *Ekon. gaz.*, no. 28 (July 1985).

71. Ryzhkov, "Ob osnovnykh napravlenniiakh," in *Materialy*, p. 239.

72. Gorbachev, "O zadachakh partii."

responsible for the quality and technical level of production in their sectors.

For a party leader, or a minister, the message of these and similar decrees and declarations is clear: "these are *your* enterprises, and you will be held responsible for the quality of the goods they produce, and for the rate at which they modernize." That tends to reinforce behavior patterns long ingrained in this system tending toward central intervention in the daily affairs of enterprises. If reforms are to truly change the distribution of power among the party, the central government, and enterprises, that will require not only new decrees outlining the duties of each actor, but also clear signals delineating new responsibilities for each of them. A system designed to change the powers of various actors without changing their responsibilities invites internal opposition.

Guideposts to the Future

For the rest of this decade, the June 1987 plenum, particularly the *Osnovnye polozheniia*, will set the agenda for economic reforms. It is too soon to judge how strong the legacy of the conservative mentality of the past will prove to be or, conversely, how powerful the influence of the new reform campaign will be. But it is possible even now to identify the most difficult issues that will arise to test the relative strength of the two forces. As noted in the discussion in chapter 1 on the normal course of reforms, the first and most important threat to the reform is its design, or its internal logic. Problems there lead inevitably to serious difficulties with economic performance and a predictable pressure to respond with old administrative methods. Enough is now known about the general design of this reform to identify potential weak spots that will cause trouble down the road if they are not fixed.

It is also possible now to identify at least a few of the most important issues that will arise during the implementation of the reform, in part because the principles of this reform differ so dramatically from those of the existing system. If the reforms of the second half of this decade are true to the principles embodied in the *Osnovnye polozheniia,* then the result will be a true economic revolution involving economic and political issues sufficient to test the resolve of even the most dedicated reformers.

The sum of these considerations will be a set of guideposts for the future, useful for judging the progress, or the lack thereof, in the effort to implement reforms. In arriving at those guideposts, the starting point must be the few key principles underlying the reform. Those determine the design, and they underlie the agenda for the implementation of the reforms.

The Principles Guiding the Reform

The *Osnovnye polozheniia* and the accompanying speech at the June 1987 plenum are the culmination of the search by Gorbachev and his advisers for a set of principles to guide the reform. Despite all the remaining ambiguities, these principles are expressed with a clarity and consistency that can be attained only in the early stages of a reform, before the actual legislation that makes up the reform is crafted, with all the inevitable compromises, and before the implementation of the reform forces even more, possibly fatal, compromises. These *Osnovnye polozheniia* constitute a target for the ultimate effect of the myriad of reform decrees that will eventually make up the actual reform.

Stripped to their barest essentials, the *Osnovnye polozheniia* rest on four principles. First, and most important, the Soviet economy will still be a centrally planned economy. But planning will focus on only the most important variables of national importance, leaving all operational decisions to lower levels. Planners will use economic instruments to control economic activity, eschewing any resort to micromanagement through direct commands to individual enterprises.

Second, it will be a system in which success and failure for enterprises and for individuals will be determined impersonally, according to publicly specified, and inviolable, rules based on economic—not political—criteria. In the old Soviet socialism, economic failure and economic success were socialized; in the new Soviet socialism, they will be individualized. That, inevitably, will lead to greater inequality and a reduction in economic security. To be sure, the resulting inequality and increase in economic insecurity will never be allowed to approach levels characteristic of Western capitalist countries; but they will both reach levels unattained in the USSR since Stalin. In the new system, in theory, it will now be possible to lose one's job, but easy to find another, and to be retrained for the new job, if that is required.

The third principle follows from the first two: enterprises in the new system have the right to their autonomy in operational decisions. In part this is the obverse of the prohibition against micromanagement by the center. But far more important is the fact that if enterprises are to be held responsible for their success and failure, they must be able to make their own decisions without the interference of any outside authority, whether it be party or government, local or national. Outside interference provides the enterprise with the justification to argue for exceptions.

That leads to the fourth, and final principle: individual workers will exercise control over management so that they can participate in the decisions that lead to the success or failure of the enterprise. Without that right, the failure of the enterprise is only a failure of the state-appointed management, which provides the workers with the excuse they need to argue for exceptions.

As the reform decrees emerge, these four interrelated principles will provide the litmus test by which to determine how closely the actual decrees correspond to the reforms outlined in the *Osnovnye polozheniia*. Of all the many measures required to realize these four principles, none is more important than a radical reform of the price system. Central authorities cannot and should not give up micromanagement of resource allocation until they have a price system that is capable of taking on the job. The rules for winners and losers will not work and will carry no moral force unless the price system is working well. Enterprises cannot be trusted with their autonomy unless the price system provides accurate and fair judgments on the economic contribution each enterprise is making to total economic welfare. Workers will find little comfort in their control over management if the enterprise is faced with a price system full of distortions and rigidities that lead to artificial losses for some and artificial profits for others. Without a carefully constructed, fully implemented price reform, economic reform cannot work.

The Design of the Reform

Although the *Osnovnye polozheniia* offer the most detailed statement yet outlined by the Gorbachev reform, they are only a sketch of what that reform will eventually look like. The decrees implementing basic elements of the reform will provide the first good look at the details of the design. But even now the overall architecture of the reform is apparent. In general, it is not a badly designed system; the basic components of a comprehensive reform are at least mentioned, and their interconnections seem—at this level of generality—plausible. As the decrees emerge, many specific design issues will surely arise, but for now the three most important areas of concern are the price system, the de facto change in enterprise autonomy, and the mechanism for allocating capital investments.

THE PRICE REFORM. This is the most important part of the reform, and the most difficult. The economic case for a retail price reform is undeniable, but the political dangers in such a reform are enormous, vividly illustrated by the Polish experience. The case is equally compelling for a simultaneous overhaul of the entire wholesale price system—in part to bring retail and wholesale prices into harmony—but the economic challenges there are also formidable.

For retail prices the major changes will be in the relative prices, as prices of essentials—most notably food and housing, hitherto heavily subsidized—will have to rise; other products currently in excess supply will have their prices reduced. This adjustment in relative prices need not technically increase the general level of prices, but consumers will most likely perceive that to be the case, since prices will rise for products in demand, and fall for those products currently piling up in inventory because of low demand. Even if income supplements are granted to compensate for increased prices for food and other essentials, people will probably perceive a drop in their living standards.

Although political leaders will seek to allay such concerns, the only effective antidote will be an expansion in the supply of goods in demand, and a gradual decline in their relative prices, which can occur only with time, if the reform begins to have an effect on Soviet industry and agriculture. Furthermore, this system will work best if retail prices are decontrolled so that the system can respond quickly to changes in supply and demand. But that, too, will be difficult for political leaders and the population to accept in light of the many years of fixed prices.

To some degree the issues here turn on the equity-efficiency trade-off. The current price system is responsible for long lines for many products; a more flexible price system would shorten those lines. But long lines are egalitarian: they distribute products not according to income so much as according to the willingness to wait. A more flexible price system would ration according to income, which, combined with a wage and salary system tightly linking income to worker productivity, would enhance rewards for hard work. It would be a more efficient system, consistent with the socialist notion that each is paid according to his contribution. But many Soviet citizens may prefer to stick with the socialism they are used to, characterized by low prices and long lines.

A smoothly functioning retail price system will, in turn, depend in part on the reform in the wholesale price system, and how effectively that system works with the other components of the reform to compel Soviet producers to identify and satisfy consumer demands. In addition the reform of the wholesale price system will be fundamentally important to the quality and reliability of goods moving in interenterprise trade, which determines the quality of all final goods in the system and the efficiency with which they are produced.

The major innovation in interenterprise transactions is contract pricing according to which the bulk of prices of manufactured goods will be set in bilateral agreements between producer and user. The primary function of Goskomtsen will be to set and enforce the rules, leaving to the two sides the issue of the particular price. That is a dramatic departure from the formal system, and even significant in terms of the de facto system. In the reformed system, the two sides in a contract will be much more on their own than in the past in determining a fair price.

The clear danger here—for both wholesale and retail prices—is that the concentration of economic power in the hands of a few enterprises will create a fertile environment for open inflation, particularly for advanced technologies. The standard ways to counteract that—conditions encouraging entry into industry and import competition—receive little if any attention in the *Osnovnye polozheniia* or the June 1987 plenum speech. Virtually all of the statements of the leadership, the most important being the statements of V. M. Kamentsev (the head of GVEK), indicate no inclination to rely heavily on competitive imports to pressure industry either to keep down costs or to develop new technologies.[73] The conditions for entry still seem to be tightly controlled by the ministries. There is, for example, no sign of a willingness to encourage enterprises that produce a broad range of products outside their formally specified product mix to begin expanding production for customers other than themselves. More disturbing is the emphasis the *Osnovnye polozheniia* place on the desirability of moving toward an economic system dominated by several thousand large, vertically integrated mega-enterprises at the all-union level, supplemented by thousands of republican and locally based enterprises.

That increase in economic concentration behind what will presumably continue to be enormous protective barriers is an invitation for high rates of open inflation. In addition, the enormous pressure throughout the

73. See, for example, "Sovershenstvovanie vneshneekonomicheskoi deiatel' nosti."

system for new products, combined with a high concentration of economic power, will encourage hidden inflation.

This appears to be the weakest link in the design of the reform, and it is a critical one. Unless far more attention is given to the use of competitive pressures to automatically control the natural inflationary pressures during the transition, the resulting inflation will create enormous pressures for retrenchment that will not be without justification. It will be important to follow very closely the decrees on price formation, but also those on imports and the conditions for entry into industry, to see if this aspect of the reform design is improved.

ENTERPRISE AUTONOMY IN THE NEW SYSTEM. Workers' participation plays a crucial role in this reform, primarily from the political point of view. The enterprise will be under far more pressure than it has experienced heretofore to operate efficiently and to produce goods in demand. Failure on either front will directly affect wages. Workers' participation is an attempt to legitimize those potential penalties by giving workers themselves a major role in the choice of enterprise management and the operation of the enterprise. But it is not at all clear how workers are to be treated in the new system relative to the traditional outside forces with influence on the enterprise, most notably the local party and the ministry.

The July 1987 enterprise law that outlines the rights of workers and managers is at best obscure on the nature of the relationship between the enterprise management and the ministry, and even less forthcoming on how the enterprise will relate to the local party organization. In the de facto system, both of these relationships are complex and have mutual benefits and obligations. The party and the ministry aid the enterprise in acquiring capital funds and materials; the ministry, working closely with the party, appoints management and determines the salaries and bonuses of top management. The enterprise, for its part, assists both the party and the ministry in fulfilling the most important part of the plan and in providing resources for local social welfare projects.

The new reform implies a revolution in those long-standing relations whereby the ministry and the party will lose all operational roles and the enterprise will be much more on its own than in the past. Many enterprises will try on their own to retain the close links with the party and government in order to lobby for special regulations favoring them.[74]

---

74. In Hungary, the reform has resulted in a shift from what used to be called "plan-

But those enterprises that really are ready to operate more independently than in the past may find their ministries and local party organs loath to give up their influence.

This will be a very complex aspect of the reform, which will require careful scrutiny as it unfolds. Since the real problems are in the de facto system and how it will evolve in response to the reform, a clear idea of how these important interrelationships are changing will take some years to emerge.

Even if the new system works out in such a way that the party and the government leave the enterprise to operate on its own and the enterprise accepts that, the assumption underlying the reform is that workers' participation will facilitate workers' concurrence with a system that takes away their job guarantee. There may be some truth to that, but obviously there will still be some very difficult political issues associated with the transition from total job security on an enterprise basis to a more general full-employment regime in which workers can lose the particular job they now have, but can find another.

THE MOVEMENT OF CAPITAL. One of the critical issues in any society is how the investable surplus is distributed. An effective mechanism for directing the surplus to investments with the highest social payoff will support the satisfaction of changing consumer needs and minimize the potential for imbalances arising over time. On the other hand, a system insensitive to relative rates of return can misallocate capital, and thereby make way for slower growth and persistent imbalances.

The *Osnovnye polozheniia* address the issue of capital mobility in two ways. First, enterprises are required to finance their own investments, either with their own funds, or with borrowed funds. Second, the reform slated for the banking system will establish a set of sectorally specialized banks to distribute loans in their areas of competence.

However, the most important issues here are given little or no attention in the *Osnovnye polozheniia*. How, for example, will capital be allocated among sectors (or among the specialized banks)? If, as is likely, the center retains control over this area—traditionally one of the most tightly controlled elements of resource allocation in a centrally planned economy—then, even after the reform, enterprises in some sectors enjoying central favor may find a surfeit of capital, whereas those in other sectors with potentially high rates of return will starve for capital.

---

bargaining" to "regulation-bargaining," in which enterprises seek regulations specially favorable to their situation, much as firms in the West seek special tax treatment.

The corollary to this is that self-finance will not allow for the possibility of transferring funds among enterprises, for the center would lose control over the allocation of capital. Enterprises that are profitable can invest only in themselves, whereas those that are not profitable cannot. But that will make sense only if the price system is working extremely well so that profits provide a true reading on the efficiency with which a product is produced, or the demand for the product. Price distortions stemming from monopoly profits, for example, will mean that self-finance will open the door to self-perpetuating monopolies.

In this sense self-finance should come only at the same time as, or after, the full price reform. But that is an implementation issue to be discussed in the next section.

The Implementation

The implementation of the reform will be extremely tricky from the economic point of view, and sensitive from the political point of view. These challenges will provide a severe test for Soviet leaders, particularly for Mikhail Gorbachev. There will be powerful and frequent temptations to retreat from the principles of the reform.

None of the problems of transition are purely economic or purely political, but most fall primarily in one category or the other. The most important economic problems relate to the timing of the transition: can any components of the reform lead the transition? Or must all be introduced more or less simultaneously? The question of how to treat the legacies of the old system fairly introduces further problems with both political and economic dimensions: how can enterprises built under the old system and unviable in the new system be treated fairly while preserving the integrity of the new rules of the economic game?

The most important political question is how to ameliorate the effects of the transition, and of the operation of the new system, in a way that will preserve some minimum amount of legitimacy for the system. Temporary unemployment, bankruptcies, rising prices for the products in greatest demand, and an increasing spread in the income distribution are all inevitable consequences of a successful reform. But how they are handled, particularly during the transition, when the potential for chaos will be highest, will determine what political support the reform will receive.

Aside from the political and economic problems, or possibly related to them, is the frame of mind with which the leadership approaches the implementation phase. The temptation will be to reach for administrative means when something goes wrong; to blame ministries when their enterprises perform poorly; to blame Goskomtsen when inflation rates rise; and to blame Gosplan for imbalances. Yet the philosophy of the reform is precisely the opposite. And unless leaders can keep the basic principles of the reform uppermost in their minds, they will drift into retreat, possibly with the best of intentions. As we saw in 1985–86, these tendencies are still quite alive, and the danger here is real.

THE ECONOMICS OF IMPLEMENTATION. The issue of timing is a difficult one. In theory, some parts of the system should be in place before others, the new price system being one of the most obvious examples. On the other hand, not everything needs to be done at once. The administrative consolidation now under way could easily be completed before the remainder of the reform, by postponing the changes in functions linked to reforming the remainder of the system. The critical issue here is that the most closely interconnected components of the system should be introduced as close together as possible.

So far, Soviet leaders under Gorbachev have approached the issue of timing rather cavalierly. The problem is that the price reform will probably be the last element to be fully implemented—some time in 1990–91, although changes in some prices will come much sooner—as a consequence of the extraordinary amount of time it took Gorbachev to recognize how important this part of the reform is. As indicated earlier, the design does not seem to take into account the new tasks that prices are expected to perform.

Yet the enterprise law, including the provisions for self-finance and operation according to economic norms, is slated for implementation in 1988–89. That gives enterprises several years to operate with distorted prices that will arbitrarily give profits to some enterprises and losses to others. That, in turn, gives enterprise directors ample ammunition to argue for exceptions (special subsidies or tax breaks), which could set the tone for the next decade or so. The delay in price reform will give rise to similar distortions and games between central authorities and enterprises because of the early introduction of decentralized decision-making in foreign trade.

This delay in the price reform is by far the most serious threat to the entire implementation process, and a good case could be made for delaying much of the rest of the reform until the price reform has been thoroughly thought out and is ready for implementation. That does not seem to be the inclination of Soviet leaders at present, and therefore the distortions arising from the tension between components of the new system and the old and the reaction of central authorities to those distortions should be watched carefully.

The treatment of the economic legacies of the old system is another major issue.[75] The enterprises being subjected to reform are all composed of human and physical capital from the old system. Many of them could not possibly be profitable in a new price system that reflects true demand and full input costs, and many workers in these enterprises have skills that will be much less valued in the new system than in the old system.[76] Aside from the obvious political problems associated with the virtual overnight declaration of obsolescence for many factories and their workers, there are some difficult economic issues to be resolved. Presumably some enterprises can be saved if their management truly believes that the only two options are to operate more profitably or go under. Old capital combined with a generous dose of ingenuity can, in some circumstances, keep an enterprise economically viable. On the other hand, some subsidies during a transition period might well increase the number of survivors substantially, as long as they are convinced that the subsidies are truly temporary and will disappear. The economic issue is how large those subsidies should be and where they should go.[77] The political issue is whether the leadership will be able to stick to the criteria for distributing subsidies and the schedule for reducing them in the face of tremendous political pressure arguing for exceptions.

A third issue with interconnected political and economic dimensions concerns the treatment of unemployment and retraining. It is now commonplace among Soviet economists involved in designing the reform to discuss the inevitability of unemployment in the new system, as was

75. As mentioned in chapter 5, this phrase was coined by Egon Neuberger. See "Central Planning and Its Legacies: Implications for Foreign Trade," in Alan A. Brown and Egon Neuberger, eds., *International Trade and Central Planning: An Analysis of Economic Interactions* (University of California Press, 1968), p. 349.

76. For example, unskilled workers in relatively high demand in the Soviet economy today, owing to low levels of mechanization in the handling of materials at factories, will be in less demand in the new system as enterprises mechanize in order to economize on labor costs.

77. The information problem for planners, discussed in detail in chapter 4, means that they cannot possibly know enough to say for sure where the subsidies should go. But it may be possible to devise some general criteria that favor industries and enterprises that appear to have decent chances of survival, while cutting off others.

noted in chapter 6. Some have even extolled the virtues of unemployment as a stimulus for labor productivity. The economic issue here is particularly difficult in a socialist society. If unemployment benefits are too high or retraining programs too generous in their wages, then those programs will take over the job guarantee function that the enterprise serves in the old system. Underemployment will be converted to open unemployment without a concomitant increase in the stimulus for high labor productivity. As a consequence, pure economic considerations dictate fairly harsh conditions for able-bodied individuals who cannot hold a job; yet political considerations, particularly in a socialist society, suggest a much more generous approach.

Finally, there is the closely related issue of the income distribution. The economics of the situation suggest a strong bias favoring wide income dispersion as a stimulus for higher productivity on the part of individuals and higher efficiency on the part of enterprises. Monopoly profits, or individual economic rents, should be taxed away to the extent they can be identified; but the economist would tend to favor erring on the side of missing a few of those to ensure that taxes do not reduce the incentive for efficient performance. But, again, the politics in this socialist society are pushing in the opposite direction; the income distribution has been, and will continue to be, a neuralgic issue for socialists.

THE POLITICS OF IMPLEMENTATION. The political dilemmas associated with handling legacies, the income distribution, price reform, and unemployment are a few of the many challenges that will test the wisdom of leaders and their dedication to economic reforms during the implementation. There are no ready-made, easy, solutions to these problems. These issues are at the core of the trade-off between efficiency and equity. During the implementation of reforms, as Soviet leaders are beset with pleas for exceptions, they will, through their response, decide whether that trade-off is indeed changing in the USSR.

The information problem makes their task almost impossible to resolve with any certainty. They can never know which of the many requests for special treatment will in fact aid the transition and lead to a more efficient system. If they had enough information to make those choices, they wouldn't need reform; they could manage all enterprises from the center. It is precisely because they cannot know enough to decide on issues such as requests for subsidies that they are being forced into reform. Inevitably, any subsidies they grant will be based on only partial information; and some will be a pure shot in the dark.

On the other hand, it would be political suicide for a Soviet leader to exclude the possibility of exceptions in a reform; and it might do serious damage to the economy. The real issue will be whether this leadership, and Gorbachev in particular, can make enough of the right decisions during the next few chaotic years to preserve the essence of the reform, while retreating wherever it is economically or politically necessary.

Other important considerations relate to bureaucratic politics. Ministries are bad for the health of reforms; that is the lesson of 1965, and one that Gorbachev has fully absorbed. But it is not clear that he understands yet that the ministries' view of a reform is directly linked to the pressures they are under to oversee the operation of the system. The chances for a successful implementation of this reform will be significantly increased if ministerial staffs are reduced and combined, possibly into the current complexes, and ministries are truly freed of those responsibilities that induce them to interfere in enterprise affairs. The latter means that the leadership must learn to expect less of ministers in terms of rectifying imbalances or inducing enterprises to follow certain specific courses. Unless those expectations change, the ministries will, for wholly predictable reasons, continue to be a serious problem for the reform during the implementation stage.

THE APPROACH OF THE LEADERSHIP TO THE IMPLEMENTATION. The need for leaders to change their expectations regarding ministries is one example of how their approach to the transition will be critical to its outcome. If Soviet leaders are prepared for mistakes, performance problems, and some chaos and if they are firm in their determination to make the reform work, then the reform will eventually be implemented. But their instincts, both political and economic, will be just the opposite. Planners who see steel shortages will automatically reach for the phone to call the Minchermet and order increased output. When they see low-quality products, their first reaction will be to impose a requirement on the offending enterprise to produce higher-quality products. When they see individual high incomes, their inclination will be to tax them away.

The political signals will be pushing in the same direction as politicians' instincts. The opponents of reform will be waiting for performance problems, so they can exploit the natural anxieties that will surround them. Layoffs, bankruptcies, and spurts of price inflation will all provide fertile ground for opponents anxious to prove that the reform will lead to economic anarchy.

These pressures have led to retreat during previous reform efforts, both in Eastern Europe and in the Soviet Union. Mikhail Gorbachev brings to the current effort a degree of political skill and growing political power that are impressive by past Soviet or Eastern European standards; and he has outlined a comprehensive reform that is superior to the 1965 reforms despite all its flaws. But even Mikhail Gorbachev's skills may not be up to negotiating the minefield that lies ahead. All that can be said for sure at this early stage is that he is clearly going to give it a serious try.

Table 7A-1. *Selected and Annotated Listing of Major Decrees and Associated Policy Measures in the USSR, April 1985–July 1987*

Date announced[a]	Subject and brief summary of main points	Date in effect
1985		
April 14	Introduces measures to improve construction and repair services available to the population for their housing needs and for their garden plots. (Portion of the Consumer Goods and Services Program.)[b]	1986
April 18	Orders local governments to take measures that will encourage local industry to expand its output of high-quality goods and services.[c]	1986
May 17	Contains comprehensive measures controlling the production, sale, and consumption of alcohol, with strict penalties for drunkenness.[d]	Immediately
July 12	Extends the Andropov experiments, strongly asserting new expanded decisionmaking powers for enterprises and limiting the powers of ministries. Establishes new planning procedures consistent with those measures.[e]	1986–87
August 21	Introduces a new bonus-forming indicator for the production of consumer goods in enterprises that now produce primarily other goods, and new bonuses for increases in the quality of goods produced in light industry.[f]	Not available
September 12	Orders all government bodies down to local levels to institute and supervise workplace certification and to eliminate unneeded workplace slots.[g]	1985–87
October	Completes a program that (along with the April 14 and 18, 1985, decrees) is designed to guide development of the production of consumer goods and services for the remainder of the decade. The few quantitative targets given are generally modest.[h]	1986
October 17	Establishes a *biuro,* headed by a deputy prime minister, to coordinate the activities of the eleven civilian machinebuilding ministries.[i]	Immediately
November 23	Consolidates the agro-industrial complex. Five former ministries and a state committee are combined into the Gosagroprom (Agro-Industrial Committee), headed by a first deputy prime minister, with similar organizations to be created down to local levels.[j]	Immediately

Table 7A-1 (continued)

Date announced[a]	Subject and brief summary of main points	Date in effect
December 12	Creates intersectoral complexes combining research and design organizations with factories from multiple sectors and charged with producing prototypes. Complexes are to operate under a single plan, supervised by GKNT.[k]	Not available
1986		
March 14	Establishes a *biuro*, headed by a deputy prime minister, to coordinate the activities of the ministries supervising the fuel and energy industries.[l]	Immediately
March 29	Extends to the agricultural sector reforms similar in spirit to the July 1985 decree on industry, increasing the reliance on norms and reducing tautness in the plans for agricultural output. *Kolkhozy* and *sovkhozy* are given the right to sell all above-plan output, and much of the planned output for some products, through the cooperative network and on *kolkhoz* markets.[m]	1987
May 6	Places all of light industry on self-financing, making profits on sales the main performance indicator, and allowing buyers and sellers to determine prices bilaterally.[n]	1987
May 15	Calls for the conservation of fuels, energy, and other materials, with specific targets for ministries and the Union Republics. New penalties for enterprises that violate the targets.[o]	Immediately
May 28	Tightens the laws concerning unearned income (incomes from speculation, theft, and other illegal sources), and calls on enterprises to redouble their efforts to expand the supply of those consumer goods and services in short supply.[p]	Immediately
April	Creates a State Committee for Computer Technology and Informatics to coordinate the production and use of computers.[q]	Immediately
June 5	Changes the incentive system, strengthening the rights of customers and increasing the interest of enterprises in fulfilling contracts.[r]	1987
June 19	As the law for the Twelfth FYP, outlines economic targets and policy during 1986–90.[s]	1986–90
July 2	New law on quality control. Introduces in selected enterprises new bonus-forming targets on quality, new penalties for low-quality output, and new quality control procedures administered by Gosstandardt.[t]	1987
July 30	Increases the authority, but also the responsibility, of local governments for increasing locally produced food and consumer goods to better satisfy consumer demands.[u]	Immediately
August 5	Links reforms in retail trade and consumer cooperatives to May 6 reforms in light industry. Places orga-	1987

Table 7A-1 *(continued)*

Date announced[a]	Subject and brief summary of main points	Date in effect
	nizations in these sectors on full self-finance, reduces centrally set indicators, and makes sales the most important indicators.[v]	
August 19	Significantly increases the rights of Soviet enterprises to enter into cooperation agreements with their socialist counterparts, including joint ventures, without interference from the supervising ministry.[w]	Not available
August 19	Reorganizes the foreign sector, creating a Commission on Foreign Economic Relations supervised by a deputy prime minister, and selectively decentralizes export-import decisions of more than twenty ministries and seventy major associations. Allows joint ventures with Western firms.[x]	1987
August 28	Reforms the wage system, raising wage and salary rates, especially for highly qualified and productive workers; at the same time closely links those rates to individual productivity.[y]	Not available
August 28	Contains plans for various economic reform measures to be introduced in 1986–90, including a law on individual economic activity (1986), a law on the socialist enterprise (1986), a proposal to reform Gossnab, a proposal for a price reform (1986), a law on ministries (1986) and state committees (1987), and a decree on the GKNT (1986).[z]	Not available
September 13	Consolidates the construction complex under the leadership of an enhanced Gosstroi, directed by a deputy prime minister; abolishes Minstroi (Construction); and divides authority between new regionally based all-union construction ministries and the republics.[aa]	1986–87
October 16	Contains Model Statute for the Establishment of Cooperatives consisting of five to sixty persons manufacturing products from by-products for sale to the population and to enterprises.[bb]	Immediately
November 21	Sets forth law authorizing a significant expansion in the scope of individual economic activity under the regulation of local *sovety*.[cc]	May 1, 1987
1987		
January 13	Provides separate, but very similar, regulations governing the formation of joint ventures with enterprises in CMEA and enterprises in developed or developing capitalist countries.[dd]	Immediately
February 12	Authorizes the formation of cooperatives for the production of consumer goods and services, licensed and controlled by local *ispolkomy*.[ee]	Immediately
February 27	Orders enterprises to implement double-shift, and—in the case of unique equipment—triple-shift work, and	1987–88

Table 7A-1 *(continued)*

Date announced[a]	Subject and brief summary of main points	Date in effect
	discusses issues relating to work organization and supporting social services.[ff]	
June 27	Embodies official approval by the CC Plenum of the *Osnovnye polozheniia* as the guiding document for the Gorbachev reforms during 1987–91.[gg]	. . .
July 1	Replaces the 1965 statute with a new law expanding the economic autonomy of the socialist enterprise, enhancing protections from outside interference, and mandating self-management by the enterprise's workers.[hh]	1988–89

a. With very few exceptions, Soviet authorities publish only summaries of decrees, which are what are referenced here. Because the dates for many decrees are not given when their summaries are published in the press, I am only able to indicate the date of publication, unless otherwise specified. All decrees, except those indicated, are issued jointly by the Central Committee and the Council of Ministers.

b. "O merakh po razvitiiu uslug po remontu i stroitel'stvu zhilishch, postroek dlia sadovodcheskikh tovarishchestv, garazhei i drugikh stroenii po zakazam naseleniia v 1986–1990 godakh i v period do 2000 goda" (On measures concerning the development of services for the repair and construction of housing, structures for horticulturist associations, garages, and other structures on order of the population during 1986–90, and in the period to the year 2000), *Sots. ind.*, April 14, 1985. (Decree approved March 7, 1985.)

c. "O merakh po dal'neishemu razvitiiu mestnoi promyshlennosti v 1986–1990 godakh i v period do 2000 goda" (On measures for the further development of local industry in 1986–1990, and in the period to the year 2000), *Sots. ind.*, April 30, 1985. (April 18 is the date the measure was actually approved.)

d. Separate decrees by the Central Committee, "O merakh po preodoleniiu p"ianstva i alkogolizma" (On measures for overcoming drunkenness and alcoholism), by the Council of Ministers, "O merakh po preodoleniiu p"ianstva i alkogolizma, iskoreneniiu samogonovareniia" (On measures for overcoming drunkenness and alcoholism, eliminating illegal distillation of alcohol), and by the Supreme Soviet (untitled), all published in *Sots. ind.*, May 17, 1985.

e. "O shirokom rasprostranenii novykh metodov khoziaistvovaniia i usilenii ikh vozdeistviia na uskorenie nauchno-tekhnicheskogo progressa. Postanovlenie Tsentral'nogo Komiteta KPSS i Soveta Ministrov SSSR ot 12 Iulia 1985 g. no. 669" (On the broad diffusion of new methods of economic management and the strengthening of their effect on the acceleration of scientific-technical progress. Decree no. 669 of the Central Committee of the CPSU and the USSR Council of Ministers of July 12, 1985), *Ekon. gaz.*, no. 32 (August 1985), insert. This appears to be the complete text of the decree.

f. "Polozhenie o stimulirovanii proizvodstva tovarov narodnogo potrebleniia, vypolneniia ustanovlennykh zadanii po proizvodstvu etikh tovarov na rubl' fonda zarabotnoi platu i povysheniia ikh kachestva" (Regulation on the stimulation of production of consumer goods, the fulfillment of established targets for the production of these goods per ruble of wages, and the increase in their quality), *Ekon. gaz.*, no. 40 (October 1985). Regulation issued by four all-union bodies: Gosplan, Goskomtrud, Minfin (Finance), and VTsSPS (Trade Union Council).

g. "O shirokom provedenii attestatsii rabochikh mest i ikh ratsionalizatsii v promyshlennosti i drugikh otrasliakh narodnogo khoziaistva" (On the broad introduction of workplace certification and rationalization in industry and other sectors of the economy), *Sots. ind.*, September 12, 1985. This is only a decree of the Council of Ministers and the Trade Union Council.

h. "Kompleksnaia programma razvitiia proizvodstva tovarov narodnogo potrebleniia i sfery uslug na 1986–2000" (A comprehensive program for the development of the production of consumer goods and services during 1986–2000), *Ekon. gaz.*, no. 41 (October 1985).

i. "O merakh po sovershenstvovaniiu rukovodstva otrasliami mashinostroeniia" (On measures for improving the management of the machinebuilding sectors), unpublished, but named and discussed at the October 17, 1985, Politboro meeting. "V Politbiuro TsK KPSS," *Pravda*, October 18, 1985.

j. "O dal'neishem sovershenstvovanii upravleniia agropromyshlennym kompleksom" (On the further improvement of the management of the agro-industrial complex), *Pravda*, November 23, 1985.

k. "O sozdanii mezhotraslevykh nauchno-tekhnicheskikh kompleksov i merakh po obespecheniiu ikh deiatel'nosti" (On the creation of intersectoral scientific-technical complexes, and measures for supporting their activities). Discussed at Politboro meeting on December 12, 1985. See "V Politbiuro TsK KPSS," *Pravda*, December 13, 1985.

l. "Mery po dal'neishemu sovershenstvovaniiu upravleniia otrasliami toplivno-energeticheskogo kompleksa strany" (Measures for the further improvement of the management of the fuel-energy complex of the country), unpublished (and this is only a probable title), but discussed at the March 13, 1986, Politboro meeting. "V Politbiuro TsK KPSS," *Pravda*, March 14, 1986.

m. "O dal'neishem sovershenstvovanii ekonomicheskogo mekhanizma khoziaistvovanie v agropromyshlennom komplekse strany" (On the further improvement of the economic mechanism in the agro-industrial complex of the country), *Pravda*, March 29, 1986.

n. "Ob uluchshenii planirovaniia, ekonomicheskogo stimulirovaniia i sovershenstvovanii upravleniia proizvodstvom tovarov narodnogo potrebleniia v legkoi promyshlennosti" (On the improvement of planning, economic simulation, and the improvement of the management of the production of consumer goods in light industry), *Sots. ind.*, May 6, 1986.

o. "O korennom uluchshenii ispol'zovaniia syr'evykh, toplivno-energeticheskikh i drugikh material'nykh resursov v usloviiakh intensivnogo razvitiia ekonomiki SSSR v 1986–1990 godakh i na period do 2000" (On radical improvements in the utilization of raw material, fuel-energy, and other material resources in conditions of intensive development of the economy of the USSR during 1986–90, and in the period to 2000), not published, but discussed in the May 15, 1986, meeting of the Politburo. "V Politbiuro TsK KPSS," *Pravda*, May 16, 1986.

p. "O merakh po usileniiu bor'by s netrudovymi dokhodami" (On measures for strengthening the battle against nonlabor incomes), *Pravda*, May 28, 1986.

q. "Ob uluchshenii koordinatsii rabot v oblasti vychislitel'noi tekhyniki i o povyshenii effektivnosti ee ispol'zovaniia" (On the improvement of coordination of the work of computer technology and on increasing the effectiveness of its utilization), discussed in the March 20, 1986, Politburo meeting. "V Politbiuro TsK KPSS," *Pravda*, March 21, 1986.

r. "O merakh po povysheniiu otvetstvennosti ob"edinenii, predpriatii i organizatsii za vypolnenie dogovorov postavki produktsii" (On measures for increasing the responsibility of associations, enterprises, and organizations for the fulfillment of contracts for the delivery of products), not published, but discussed in the report on the June 5, 1986, Politburo meeting. "V Politbiuro TsK KPSS," *Pravda*, June 6, 1986.

s. "Zakon Soiuza Sovetskikh Sotsialisticheskikh Respublik. O Gosudarstvennom plane ekonomicheskogo i sotsial'nogo razvitiia SSSR na 1986–1990" (A law of the Union of Soviet Socialist Republics. On the state plan of economic and social development of the USSR during 1986–1990), *Ekon. gaz.*, no. 26 (June 1986). The actual legal act placing the Twelfth FYP into force, enacted by the Supreme Soviet.

t. "O merakh po korennomu povysheniiu kachestva produktsii" (On measures for a radical improvement in the quality of production), *Pravda*, July 2, 1986.

u. "O merakh po dal'neishemu povysheniiu roli i usileniiu otvetstvennosti Sovetov narodnykh deputatov za uskorennie sotsial'no-ekonomicheskogo razvitiia v svete reshenii XXVII s"ezda KPSS" (On measures on the further increase in the role and strengthening the responsibility of Soviets of the people's deputies for the acceleration of social-economic development in light of the decisions of the Twenty-seventh Congress of the CPSU), *Izvestiia*, July 30, 1986.

v. "O sovershenstvovanii planirovaniia, ekonomicheskogo stimulirovaniia i upravleniia v gosudarstvennoi torgovle i potrebitel'skoi kooperatsii" (On the improvement of planning, economic stimulation and management in state trade and consumer cooperatives), *Pravda*, August 5, 1986.

w. "O merakh po sovershenstvovaniiu upravleniia ekonomicheskim i nauchno-tekhnicheskim sotrudnichestvom s sotsialisticheskimi stranami" (On measures to improve the management of economic and scientific-technical cooperation with the socialist countries), *Vneshniaia torgovlia*, no. 3 (March 1987), insert, pp. 4–8.

x. "O merakh po sovershenstvovaniiu upravleniia vneshneekonomicheskim sviaziami" (On measures for improving the management of foreign economic relations), *Vneshniaia torgovlia*, no. 3 (March 1987), insert, pp. 1–4.

y. "Mery po sovershenstvovaniiu organizatsii zarabotnoi platy i vvedeniiu novykh tarifnykh stavok i dolzhnostnykh okladov rabotnikov proizvodstvennykh otraslei narodnogo khoziaistva" (Measures for the improvement of the organization of wages and the introduction of new salary scales for workers of the productive sectors of the economy), unpublished, but briefly discussed in the August 28, 1986, Politburo meeting. "V TsK KPSS," *Pravda*, August 29, 1986.

z. "O plane podgotovki zakonodatel'nykh aktov SSSR, postanovlenii Pravitel'stva SSSR i predlozhenii po sovershenstvovaniiu zakonodatel'stva SSSR na 1986–1990 gody" (On the plan for the preparation of legal acts of the USSR, decrees of the government of the USSR, and proposals for improving the laws of the USSR during 1986–1990), *Vedomsti Verkhonogo Soveta Soiuza Sovetskikh Sotsialisticheskikh Respublik* (Gazette of the Supreme Soviet of the Union of Soviet Socialist Republics), no. 37 (September 10, 1986), pp. 729–36.

aa. "O dal'neishem sovershenstvovanii upravleniia stroitel'nym kompleksom strany" (On the further improvement of the management of the construction complex of the country), *Sots. ind.*, September 13, 1986.

bb. "Primernyi ustav kooperativa po zagotovke i pererabotke vtorichnogo syr'ia pri territorial'nykh organakh Gossnaba SSSR" (Model statute of cooperatives for the procurement and processing of secondary raw materials under the territorial organs of Gossnab), *Ekon. gaz.*, no. 43 (October 1986).

cc. "Zakon Soiuza Sovetskikh Sotsialisticheskikh Respublik. Ob individual'noi trudovoi deiatel'nosti" (A law of the Union of Soviet Socialist Republics. On individual labor activity), *Pravda*, November 21, 1986.

dd. "O sozdanii sovmestnykh predpriatii v SSSR" (On the creation of joint ventures in the USSR), *Vneshniaia torgovlia*, no. 3 (March 1987), insert.

ee. "V Sovete Ministrov SSSR" (In the Council of Ministers of the USSR), *Sots. ind.*, February 12, 1987. See also the model charters for cooperatives supplying food, services, and consumer goods (separate model charters) in *Ekon. gaz.*, no. 9 (February 1987).

ff. "V TsK KPSS, Sovete Ministrov SSSR i VTsSPS" (In the CC of the CPSU, the USSR Council of Ministers, and the VTsSPS), *Sots. ind.*, February 27, 1987.

gg. "Osnovnye polozheniia korennoi perestroiki upravleniia ekonomikoi" (Basic theses for the radical restructuring of the management of the economy), *Pravda*, June 27, 1987.

hh. "Zakon Soiuza Sovetskikh Sotsialisticheskikh Respublik. O gosudarstvennom predpriatii (ob"edinenii)" (A law of the Union of Soviet Socialist Republics. On state enterprises [associations]), *Pravda*, July 1, 1987.

CHAPTER EIGHT

The USSR on the Eve of the Twenty-first Century

The course of intensification is dictated by objective conditions, by the entire course of development of the country. There are no alternatives. Only an intensive economy, developing on the basis of a state-of-the-art scientific-technical base, can serve as a reliable material base for increasing the welfare of workers, guaranteeing the strengthening of the position of the country on the international arena, ensuring that it will deservingly enter the new century as a great and prospering power

—Mikhail S. Gorbachev, 1984[1]

THREE main concerns underlie Gorbachev's approach to the Soviet economy: the USSR's position in the world economy, Soviet national security, and domestic support for the party. Each is important to Gorbachev and to those who chose him.

The USSR's position in the world economy is far more important to Gorbachev than it was to any of his predecessors, with the possible exception of Iurii V. Andropov. To some extent this simply represents a recognition that Soviet citizens know more about the world's economies than they did twenty years ago. That knowledge implicitly sets a standard for the Soviet economy to match. Gorbachev accepts that standard as a challenge, understanding that when Soviets can genuinely feel pride in their economic system, even knowing full well the advan-

---

1. "Zhivoe tvorchestvo naroda. Doklad tovarishcha M. S. Gorbacheva" (The Living Creativity of the People. Report of Comrade M. S. Gorbachev), *Pravda,* December 11, 1984.

tages and disadvantages of other economic systems, then his cause—
and the party's cause—will be well served.

On a more practical plane, Gorbachev wishes to realize a long-held
Soviet goal to become a major exporter of manufactured goods, shifting
out of fuels and raw materials. In part this is a matter of pride. The most
developed Western countries are competitors in world markets for
manufactured goods; therefore, in Gorbachev's judgment, the Soviet
Union will not have successfully developed until it too can compete on
those markets. Good economic arguments can also be cited for such a
goal, although it is dangerous to be dogmatic in them.[2] Certainly the
success of economic reforms will depend in part on whether the Soviets
develop markets for their manufactured goods.

Concern about Soviet national security also points toward the need
for economic reform. So far the Soviets have managed to keep pace
with, some would say outpace, the United States in the arms race. Until
recently that race involved conventional arms and strategic weapons
embodying technology that the Soviets could manage. Now much greater
emphasis is on state-of-the-art technologies, a shift symbolized by
President Reagan's Strategic Defense Initiative. For the United States
this is a shift toward a strength of its economic system; but for the Soviet
Union this is a shift toward its greatest weakness.

The third and by far the most complicated concern is domestic support
for the party. The performance of the system constitutes an important
component of that support, or lack of it. The Soviet population wants
better supplies of consumer goods and services, better housing, and
better social infrastructure. Economic reforms are designed to bring
improvements in all of those areas; hence the domestic political logic
supports economic reforms.

The problem, to return to the argument put forth in chapter 2, is that
the strengths of the Soviet economy are also a source of support among
the population. The economic security that the population now enjoys
undoubtedly contributes to problems in economic performance, and a
radical economic reform will almost certainly have to reduce that
economic security. What the population would like, understandably, is
to retain the economic security characteristic of this system, yet enjoy
the benefits of improved economic performance. That presumably is

2. Comparative advantage does, after all, still ultimately determine the profitability
of exports. The United States, although a major competitor on world markets for
manufactured goods, is also a major exporter of grains.

impossible. However, the inconsistency in popular preferences is real and must somehow be addressed. That is Gorbachev's dilemma, and the dilemma for any leader who aspires to improve the performance of the economic system through reforms. He must somehow reduce economic security—albeit still retaining a far greater degree of economic security than is now available in most developed countries—in order to improve performance and gain popular support, or at least acquiescence, for doing so.

These three considerations add up to an agenda for transforming the USSR into a "great and prospering power," based on political and economic, as well as military, might. Gorbachev chose the eve of the twenty-first century as a convenient rhetorical benchmark for that achievement, even though he must surely know that the USSR will enter the next century—a mere dozen years from now—about as prosperous and as great as it is now.

The important issue for the USSR in the remainder of this century will be the direction of change and its momentum. If economic reforms gather momentum in the 1990s, the USSR could well enter the twenty-first century a great military power in the midst of an economic and political revolution. If economic reforms lose momentum, the USSR could find itself a great military power struggling with the consequences of economic and political stagnation. Mikhail Gorbachev is doing his utmost to achieve the first of those two outcomes.

Western countries share the Soviet leadership's interest in how economic reforms and the other components of overall Soviet economic strategy will affect the USSR's position in the world economy, its national security, and the economic foundations of support for the party. Major political and economic reforms in the USSR will inevitably transform the global political and economic landscape, presenting Western governments with a number of important policy decisions, some of which are already on the horizon. If, on the other hand, this new reform movement should lose momentum, the results could be equally profound as a militarily strong, but economically and politically weak, USSR seeks to maximize its position by relying primarily on military power.

Measuring the Impact of Gorbachev's Economic Strategy

It will not be easy for outsiders, let alone the Soviets themselves, to judge the success of Gorbachev's strategy for the economy as his reforms are implemented in the future. The main reason Gorbachev is attempting to accelerate social-economic development is that he wants to see a qualitative improvement in economic performance: stepped-up technological innovation in the processes used to produce output and vastly better goods and services produced for all markets—military and civilian, domestic and foreign. It would be difficult to measure such things directly in any system. The consequences once removed—higher growth, improved export performance, fewer consumer complaints—are what provide the first tangible signs of such changes. Soviet statistics, with their many peculiarities and weaknesses, will complicate the interpretation of even those indexes.

Nevertheless, it is important to try to develop a set of quantitative and qualitative criteria that will serve as independent measures of the impact of Gorbachev's economic strategy on the performance of the system. Without such measures we must fall back on official statements and official data, neither of which should be treated as any more than hypotheses to be tested by independent means.

National Income Growth: A Problematic Measure

Inevitably, the national income growth rate will remain an important measure of the impact of the reforms on the system, and rightfully so. Innovations in production processes that increase factor efficiency will raise factor productivities, and therefore measured economic growth. With improvements in the quality of machinery and equipment, Soviet industry should be able to improve its returns to investments, which will also help to accelerate growth. If the reform succeeds in shortening gestation periods for new investments, new plants could be commissioned at a faster pace without having to accelerate investment, and this too would increase the growth rate.

Nevertheless, Soviet national income statistics should not be the sole measure of the degree of success of Gorbachev's economic strategy. Because these statistics only apply to material production and exclude "nonproductive services" (those not contributing to material production), they fail to monitor consumer services, which may improve dramatically under Gorbachev. Until, and if, the Soviets switch to the concept of gross national product, their national income measures will underestimate, possibly severely, any expansion in productive activity.

However, as part of the reform of the statistical system, the Central

Statistical Administration may well switch to GNP accounts to measure aggregate economic activity. Even so, in view of the probable difficulties in developing a system to gather the underlying data and process them, Soviet GNP data would have to be handled with great care. If, on the one hand, the cooperative and individual economic activity laws were to succeed in drawing a significant portion of the second economy into the legal sphere, official accounts would show an increase in GNP, which, in reality, would partly be the consequence of the legalization of hitherto illegal activity. This would have the effect of overstating GNP growth.[3]

On the other hand, official GNP accounts would tend to understate the growth of consumer satisfaction associated with the production of GNP, owing to the difficulties of capturing qualitative improvements in final output. No country's statistical system is very good at distinguishing between qualitative and quantitative changes in final products, but an additional problem here is the lack of Soviet experience in this regard. A dramatically improved line of television sets—which work well and require only modest service over the years—could well show up in the Soviet GNP accounts (or, for that matter, the Marxian national income accounts) as an unchanged quantity, possibly with a higher price. Consumer satisfaction might be substantially higher, but the national income accounts cannot, and will not, pick that up. This is a particularly important consideration for services, where a successful economic reform would virtually revolutionize the quality of services, which official Soviet GNP accounts—if and when they are published—would be able to reflect only in part.

Aside from all of these considerations, it is important to keep in mind that the tremendous pressure for high profits and new products, in the context of highly protected markets, invites hidden inflation, which will show up in aggregate statistics as "real" growth.[4]

The national income growth rate is therefore not the best measure of the success of these reforms. The counteracting biases may cancel out

3. The only way this could be avoided would be if Soviet statisticians would construct a historical series for GNP, including an estimate of value-added in the second economy over that historical period. The data may exist for such a task, but it would be difficult, and the Central Statistical Administration is not likely to undertake it.

4. Soviet statisticians, if they are very careful, may be able to filter out some of that hidden inflation. But they have shown no inclination whatsoever to attempt to do so in the past, and even if they begin in earnest to try now, they could expect only limited success.

on average, but it would be risky to count on that. In any event, these aggregate data may be the least satisfactory way to measure the achievements of these reforms in any of the three areas of concern to Gorbachev and the West. If, for example, the target for national income growth of 5 percent in the 1990s is not met but the quality of goods and services improves at that rate, the Soviet population would be much happier; the military would find it could rely on the civilian economy for some of its inputs more heavily than in the past; and the Soviets might begin to see some success in their efforts to sell manufactured goods in the West.

The conclusion is that national income growth rates are only one of several considerations behind a judgment on the degree of success of Gorbachev's economic strategy. There are limits to what they can tell us, and other measures must also be used to capture qualitative change in the system.

Measures of Qualitative Change

As the Gorbachev reforms progress, Soviet leaders will undoubtedly try to measure qualitative change through familiar techniques developed over the years: the proportion of industry's output awarded *znak kachestvo* status, or—more recently—the proportion of output passing *gospriemka* (state acceptance) procedures; the proportion of contracts fulfilled to customer satisfaction; the number of new products introduced in a year; savings in energy and raw material inputs relative to what the use would have been without new measures on the part of an enterprise; and the decline in production costs that customers will experience when they buy a new machine. These indicators will provide Soviet leaders with the raw material for their pronouncements on qualitative improvements attributable to the Gorbachev reforms, or the lack thereof.

These measures should not be dismissed out of hand. In some cases, possibly many, they contain useful information for supplementing aggregate data. A rise in the proportion of products passing *gospriemka* may truly signal an increase in quality. But, in general, one cannot be sure. The major source of information must be the Soviet producer, or— at best—Gosstandardt employees, neither of whom may have actually seen the products with which they are comparing their own. Furthermore, *znak kachestvo* and *gospriemka* are at best measures of quality in the abstract, without any reading on how the world market actually values the particular quality of the Soviet product. High or rapidly increasing quality measures based on such data must be treated with skepticism. They may say something about how closely serially produced goods approach their original specifications, but they say little about actual consumer evaluations and are essentially useless in capturing the world market's evaluation of the product.

Measures of actual costs compared with some hypothetical measure of what costs would have otherwise been are obviously treacherous. Soviet enterprises excel in proving they conserve energy when in fact the savings are probably nil.[5] Soviet producers can be counted on to supply spectacular documentation on the cost savings associated with their new machinery and equipment, and their customers are likely to go along as long as the sellers' market persists.

These reservations suggest that alternative measures are needed to supplement, if not supplant, the traditional measures that Soviet leaders have relied on in the past. Given the importance Gorbachev attaches to the impact of his reforms on Soviet exports, various measures of Soviet exports of machinery and equipment to the West are obvious candidates. These might include Soviet market shares in European countries belonging to the Organization for Economic Cooperation and Development (OECD), changes in the relative technological sophistication of the machinery and equipment sold, and the share of Soviet hard-currency earnings from machinery and equipment. The advantage of such measures is that they provide objective information on the world market's evaluation of Soviet industrial output. The main disadvantage is that they provide overly demanding criteria. In the current international economic environment it is difficult to penetrate OECD markets with new products, and it will prove particularly difficult for the USSR. One possibility, then, is that the general quality of Soviet manufactured goods, including exportables, will rise substantially, but Soviet abilities to export their manufactures will remain modest.

That suggests a need for direct indicators of change in the quality of final products sold in the USSR since improvements there—even if they had no tangible impact on Soviet exports of manufactured goods—would affect both the domestic economic situation and the ability of civilian industry to meet military demands. Beyond the problematic measures discussed above, the only two likely sources of additional information

5. See Ed A. Hewett, *Energy, Economics, and Foreign Policy in the Soviet Union* (Brookings, 1984), pp. 122–27.

will be anecdotes and surveys. It may be possible, through a careful reading of the press, to form an impression about the general rate of improvement in the quality of manufactured goods, particularly consumer goods. In addition, for some highly visible products such as consumer durables or computers, it is conceivable that technical information will provide more objective measures of quality to supplement the anecdotal evidence. Although evidence of this sort is at best fragmentary (see chapter 1), it can be useful.

Surveys conducted by Soviet scholars are another potential source of information. I am not aware of published data on what Soviet consumers or manufacturers think about product quality, but it would be surprising if such data did not exist. If *glasnost'* continues to expand, we will quite possibly have access to more economic information, which will substantially improve the quality of our information about the impact of Gorbachev's reforms on the economy.

Among the other potentially useful measures of qualitative changes in economic performance is the growth rate of key inputs, since one of the major goals of the reforms is to compel enterprises to economize on the material and labor inputs they use. For example, the growth rate of energy consumption, linked to some measure of economic activity, provides a useful summary of progress in this area. The Soviet energy-to-GNP elasticity has remained above unity since the early 1970s[6] — despite numerous efforts by Soviet leaders to encourage energy conservation—whereas it has fallen far below unity in the OECD countries in response to price changes by the Organization of Petroleum Exporting Countries (OPEC).[7] A significant and sustained reduction in the energy-to-GNP elasticity would be a clear signal of the reform's success. Measures of consumption of other key raw materials and intermediates are also useful. If, for example, they all show similar behavior—say, a dramatic reduction in growth relative to the past—the change is a major one and is most likely the result of the reforms. These changes should make their way into the national income accounts as an increase in value-added, but by following them directly one can monitor a major success indicator for the reforms.

Similarly, an increase in labor dismissals, and therefore an increase in transitory unemployment, will indicate that the reform is having an

6. The percentage growth in energy consumption divided by the percentage growth in GNP.

7. See Hewett, *Energy, Economics, and Foreign Policy in the Soviet Union,* chap. 3.

effect on enterprises. There may be no aggregate data on these variables, but anecdotal evidence will prove quite useful.

Using Multiple Indicators to Form a Single Judgment

As the discussion indicates, a certain degree of uncertainty about the consequences of these reforms is inevitable. If qualitative variables were as easy to measure as tons of steel, planners would have done so a long time ago and built them into the annual plans. Gorbachev's reforms are a tacit admission of the intractability of that measurement task.

Another problem in judging the success of these reforms is that the various measures of performance are likely to differ. Assume, for example, that productivity growth accelerates primarily in response to greater discipline, improvements in the utilization of existing capital, and the imposition of different investment priorities. Growth rates would then accelerate without any dramatic improvement in the quality of goods and services. On the other hand, it could be that quality is improving, but primarily in consumer goods, rather than capital goods. In that case, consumer satisfaction would rise, but productivity growth rates, and therefore aggregate growth, would remain low. Even if qualitative improvements (through capital and other channels) began to increase factor productivities, there could be a considerable lag before these results would occur, so that for a while qualitative improvements might show up alongside poor growth statistics.

These and other possibilities serve to emphasize the quite likely prospect that the consequences of these reforms will not lend themselves to a simple judgment of success or failure. For Gorbachev, for the Soviet population, and for the West, different combinations of outcomes will have different consequences.

It is too early to attempt to predict the outcomes of the Gorbachev reforms in terms of these indicators. Too much remains to be decided, and the possibilities, depending on what is decided, span an enormous range. But it is helpful to sketch a few scenarios and to identify their implications for the USSR and for the West.

Alternative Scenarios for the Gorbachev Reforms

The purpose here is to explore in a general sense several plausible scenarios. They do not exhaust what is possible; things could be even worse or even better than any of the following four scenarios suggest. But they do, in my judgment, encompass the most likely possibilities.

An Outline of Four Scenarios

The four scenarios presented here are named "success," "high growth," "high quality," and "failure." The time horizon is the remainder of the century. The three variables of interest in each scenario are national income growth rates, improvements in output quality, and improvements in input efficiency; the last two represent the qualitative improvements Gorbachev seeks through his reforms.

It is important to note how these three sets of variables are interconnected. The labor force that will be available to the Soviet economy for the rest of this century is already born. The capital stock currently on the books will form the foundation for economic performance over the next dozen years. Increases in growth rates will have to come through increases in input efficiency—through the conservation of energy and raw material, and economies in the use of labor and capital.

In part those efficiency gains can be achieved through more careful management of existing resources, without the aid of new capital or labor. But new, higher-quality machinery and equipment will greatly facilitate the task. Furthermore, higher-quality consumer goods, although they will not directly affect the efficiency of the production process, may nevertheless stimulate Soviet workers to work harder in order to earn the wages needed to buy the goods, and that will contribute to higher productivity.

Thus, although the quantitative and qualitative effects of Gorbachev's reforms can be measured separately, they are intertwined in important ways. The scenarios turn on how those interactions operate.

SUCCESS. In this scenario, everything works as planned. The reforms take hold quickly, and output quality improves by leaps and bounds, as does the efficiency of the system. In turn, national income growth accelerates in immediate response to increases in efficiency as enterprises squeeze waste out of existing facilities, and because investments have installed new high-quality machinery and equipment in Soviet enterprises that have raised their efficiency.

In this scenario, the USSR may not be entering the twenty-first century successfully competing head to head with Japan for U.S. automobile and electronic markets, but it is a much more formidable competitor on world markets than at present. Certainly the transformation on the domestic economic landscape in a dozen years could be impressive, with many new shops offering goods and services heretofore available only in the *Beriozka* (hard currency) stores. Food supplies will be improved; and the housing situation will begin to loosen up somewhat.

HIGH GROWTH. In the high growth scenario, national income growth rates are approximately those announced for the remainder of the century, say 4 percent in the second half of the 1980s and 5 percent in the 1990s.[8] But there is only a modest improvement, if that, in the quality of goods and services. Factor productivities grow rapidly—that is implicit in the high national income growth rates, since presumably there will be no new influx of labor and capital. But the resulting products are not a major improvement over what is currently being produced; there is simply more of the traditional output. New shops are still an exception, their shelves sparsely supplied with a mixture of imports (primarily from Eastern Europe) and some new Soviet goods. In some areas—for example, housing— things are improving; this reflects the investment dividends of high growth.

HIGH QUALITY. The third scenario is the mirror image of the second. Growth performance is lackluster, say, an average of 3 percent in the remainder of this century. But the quality indicators tell a generally positive story: various measures point to a significant and sustained improvement in product quality.

Even here the picture is mixed, however, since the qualitative improvements are not accompanied by substantial improvements in efficiency (in the use of material inputs and labor). This explains the slow national income growth rates. In a way, the situation could be regarded as the "militarization" of the civilian economy, as civilian industry comes to more closely resemble the Soviet military by producing higher-quality output, but at a high cost. This change will partly be the result of the lags between improvements in the quality of capital and other inputs and efficiency gains. It could also be the result of first focusing on the quality of consumer goods, which would improve consumer welfare, and not on efficiency. Barriers to import competition would also contribute to continued inefficiencies.

In this case, new shops are around, and services and inventories are

8. Whether or not the Soviets switch to GNP accounts is not important for these scenarios, given the level of generality. Here, if numbers are used for national income growth rates, they refer to current Soviet concepts that exclude services.

greatly improved over those of the 1980s. However, the prices are quite high—owing to modest productivity gains—with the result that the population has limited access to the new goods. Food supplies are much improved, but, again, the prices are high. Those who earn high incomes in the new system can afford new and much better housing, but the majority must rely on state housing.

FAILURE. In this scenario, nothing works; either the reforms are a facade behind which the old system remains intact, or they are introduced and then retracted. The growth decline, temporarily interrupted in the mid-1980s, resumes as the productivity "dividend" associated with the influx of new personnel under Gorbachev dissipates. There is no noticeable improvement in the quality of goods and services, except in the traditional measures that show such improvements irrespective of underlying reality.

There are few or no new shops and only a modest expansion in the supply of new goods. Prices are high and rising because of the low productivity gains. For some segments of the population, living standards may be falling.

The Likelihood of the Four Scenarios

None of these scenarios is out of the question; however, they are not all equally likely. The extremes seem least likely. Everything could go very well for Gorbachev, and the reform could be a complete success. However, Gorbachev would have to do everything just right—the reform's design would have to be perfect, the implementation strategy flawless—and a virtual quality explosion would have to occur immediately. There are already signs that the economy is not so prone to shift to a totally new economic paradigm, and common sense suggests that is to be expected. The USSR could be another Japan, ready to surprise the world with a miraculous turnaround; but if it has the potential for such a transformation buried in its social fabric, the seeds are buried very deep. What we know of this society suggests that, even with an energetic and determined general secretary, neither the work force nor industrial management will respond instantaneously to a new reform in a way that will bring about a quality revolution. In any event, the chances that the reform's design and implementation strategy will be perfect, or even close to that, seem remote at present.

A complete failure is also not excluded, although at this point it would be a great surprise. It would require some dramatic turnaround in the current situation: Gorbachev's removal and replacement by a conservative group intent on restoring the old centralized system or a totally inept handling by Gorbachev of the entire reform process. Neither of these outcomes is likely at present. Gorbachev's position appears to be politically secure; his reform program is emerging as a serious effort to change the system. If the conservatives have an alternative program, it is a well-kept secret. This worst case, at least from the current vantage point, seems no more than remotely possible.

The two middle scenarios are the ones that represent the more likely outcomes, although the actual situation—aside from being far more complicated than the abstract picture here—will surely be some combination of both. As in the high-growth and high-quality scenarios, the strong likelihood is that this reform will have some successes and some failures. In fact as the reform unfolds, Gorbachev will quite probably be forced into choosing between these two scenarios, as he must decide whether to push for high growth or allow that part of his goals to slide and push for high quality.

HIGH GROWTH. The high-growth scenario is, in some ways, an anti-reform scenario. It could come about if, as the reforms were being implemented, growth rates began to falter as enterprises struggled to absorb the new higher-quality requirements.

This scenario might begin with shortages, already a constant in the system, growing worse in some sectors. Fears of a downward spiral increase. Gorbachev and the leadership respond by reminding central ministries of their responsibilities for guaranteeing supplies of "their" products on markets. Ministries respond by pressuring enterprises to expand supplies. The signal, and the accompanying pressures, are strong: enterprises face the possibility of bankruptcy if their ministries think they are doing poorly; the workers are operating in a wage system with strong penalties for shirking.

These are familiar pressures for enterprise directors, although they are more intense than under Brezhnev. Directors respond with expanded supplies, but quickly, and quality standards stagnate or fall.

An informal deal emerges, of the sort familiar to the de facto system of the past. The leadership tacitly allows a "temporary" reduction in the pressure for high quality in order to expand product supplies and break bottlenecks, although the rhetoric supporting quality improvements continues unabated. Growth rates begin to rise, but quality does not. Therefore new central targets are designed to force higher quality while retaining high growth. All of this takes on a familiar cast as the system slips into traditional habits.

In the system that emerges the central authorities remain strong and are still able—whether formally or informally—to micro-manage the economy. It is a leaner central management, focused on complexes, and it is managed more efficiently than in the past by the new Gorbachev appointees. Much of the rhetoric of the reform remains, but behind that facade stands the old system, somewhat more efficient and therefore capable of squeezing out higher growth rates.

HIGH QUALITY. The high-quality scenario implies a different mindset for the leadership, particularly for Gorbachev. When growth rates begin to falter, and when, nevertheless, quality proves disappointing in comparison with the goals of the reform, attention focuses on product quality. The leadership, and Gorbachev personally, inform the ministries and the enterprises that growth rates, although important, are a second-order concern, the prime concern being the quality of enterprise output, and its saleability to consumers, domestic and foreign. High growth, they will argue, will follow if they handle the quality issue correctly.

To make its point, the leadership aggressively increases competitive pressures on state industry, allowing individual state enterprises to compete with each other by developing whatever new products they wish, encouraging cooperative enterprises to compete with state enterprise where possible, liberalizing import controls in selective areas, and using joint ventures to compete with state enterprises in some branches. The deemphasis on growth for its own sake inevitably comes through as a deemphasis on increased efficiency, so that the enterprise feels the strongest pressure to increase output quality, even if the costs are high. And the protective barriers remain sufficiently high to support that.

Like the high-growth scenario, this one involves compromises, but they tilt strongly toward the new system, in the process redefining what the leadership calls success. The assumption is that, for political reasons, Gorbachev has decided that he would rather explain slow growth to the population and the military in the context of visible improvements in the quality of what they can purchase than to explain a continued stagnation in the quality of goods and services. It is also assumed that Gorbachev and the entire leadership will be willing to accept shortages in some products for some period as the system adjusts to a drastically different mode of operation.

The trade-off between quality improvements and growth assumed in this scenario does not last forever; gradually, over time, the emphasis on quality will have an impact on growth, as competitive pressures among enterprises lead to improvements in efficiency. But in this century, given the tremendous amount that must be done to turn the Soviet economy around, the choice will probably be necessary. It will be similar to a choice between investment and consumption, the question being whether it is prudent to push for high growth immediately or wait, and "invest" in future high growth by focusing on quality.

The West and the Reform Process

The consequences of economic reform for the Soviet Union are also consequences for the rest of the world. A successful reform and a revitalization of the Soviet economy could drastically change the economic relationship between the Soviet Union and the West, with benefits to both sides. A successful reform process combined with a new approach to Soviet foreign economic policy would eventually allow the USSR to join the major international economic institutions and assume a far more influential position than it has hitherto enjoyed in international economic affairs.

Soviet foreign and defense policy would thus come to rest on a stronger economic foundation and therefore might also pose a formidable challenge to U.S. influence in world affairs. What motives might drive the foreign and defense policies of this newly reformed system—a matter of vital interest to the West—would depend heavily on the political changes that accompanied the reforms.

The more far-reaching the changes, the longer it will take to see them happen. Such developments could no more than begin toward the end of this century. But faint glimmerings of what is possible have appeared under Gorbachev—in his new and much more vigorous pursuit of Soviet foreign policy goals, in the suggestion of membership or some special relationship with the General Agreement on Tariffs and Trade (GATT) and the International Monetary Fund (IMF), and in a formidable arms control offensive.

It is the West's interest in these matters that dictates an interest in the reform process itself and in its consequences. To the extent that Western policy on relations with the Soviet Union could have even a marginal impact on that process, either speeding it up or slowing it down, the West becomes part of the process. Therefore the important questions to consider are what outcome is most consistent with Western interests and what policies that may imply on issues such as Soviet membership in IMF, or even on the far more complex issue of arms control agreements with the USSR.

The answers to both questions depend largely on the success of Soviet reform. For the purposes of this discussion I collapse the scenarios of the previous section into two categories. I place the "success" and "high-quality" scenarios into one category of generally successful outcomes for the reform. They differ primarily in terms of efficiency gains, but share qualitative improvements that would have similar implications for the West. On the other hand, the "failure" and the "high-growth" scenarios, which I characterize as generally unsuccessful outcomes for the reform, share a lackluster qualitative performance that would have considerably different implications for the West.

Consequences of a Generally Successful Reform Process

A reform process that spurs technological innovation and brings about a significant improvement in the quality of goods and services produced in the system will cause a dramatic change in Soviet economic relations with the West. What that would imply for Soviet foreign and defense policy and for Soviet society as a whole is far less easy to say.

IMPLICATIONS FOR EAST-WEST ECONOMIC RELATIONS. A successful reform process would most likely involve an opening to the West at an early stage, through a reduction of import barriers, with the goal of increasing competitive pressures on Soviet enterprises. This could be accomplished through joint venture arrangements, such as those made possible by the January 1987 law on ventures (see table 7A-1). But it would also involve a conscious decision to expose Soviet enterprises to increased competition from abroad, forcing them to be much more aggressive than heretofore in upgrading their products to world standards, either to retain domestic customers or to replace lost domestic orders with foreign orders. This would imply a move toward a unified and meaningful exchange rate as part of a full-scale price reform. This process would logically lead to convertibility of the ruble, but that is some time away, because a considerable qualitative improvement in Soviet productive capacity would be required to successfully market manufactured goods.

A successful reform would also probably involve a substantial increase in Soviet utilization of world capital markets to finance the modernization program. The expanded industrial capacity would be expected to represent a quantum leap in the supply of salable exportables capable of servicing the resulting debt. The logical consequence of that development would be increased Soviet involvement in world financial markets, and, eventually, Soviet membership in the IMF.

The consequences of such a reform and the way it would unfold would be an increased, and increasingly successful, Soviet effort to export manufactured goods to the West. Presumably, Soviet exports would initially compete primarily with those from the newly industrializing countries and Eastern Europe. But eventually, particularly if the Soviets mobilized the defense industries in the export drive, they could prove formidable competitors to industrialized countries in selected product groups. Depending on how skillfully and expeditiously the joint venture laws were handled, Soviet enterprises with significant Western ownership could also play a significant role in the export drive. A logical accompaniment to this policy would be membership in GATT in order to break down barriers to Western imports of Soviet goods. Some sort of special accommodation with the European Community, possibly through the Council for Mutual Economic Assistance (CMEA), would also be sensible.

Furthermore, as the reform began to take hold, the domestic demand for fuels, raw materials, and intermediates would fall, as would the demand for labor. In the short run that would have the effect of increasing net Soviet exports of a wide range of raw materials and fuels, most notably fuels. In the medium-to-longer term the effects might dissipate as Soviet planners, or Soviet banks—as the case may be—shifted capital away from the production of fuels and raw materials into manufacturing, thereby decreasing the supply of those products. The reduced demand for labor would cheapen that factor of production, at least in the short run, and enhance the appeal of the USSR as a joint venture partner.

Soviet leaders have apparently thought through some of these consequences. A Soviet request for observer status leading to membership in GATT was submitted in the summer of 1986. It was rejected, but presumably the Soviets will come back again. Also during the summer of 1986 some Soviet officials hinted at an interest in some sort of special relationship with, not necessarily membership in, the IMF.[9] Through

9. Paul Marer, "Growing Soviet International Economic Isolation and Severe Problems Ahead in the Foreign Trade Sector Prompt Top Soviet Economists to Advocate

CMEA the Soviet Union is negotiating for a long sought special relationship with the European Community under an umbrella agreement permitting a range of special agreements between CMEA and EC members.

The U.S. government has opposed Soviet efforts to join GATT and has generally discouraged broader Soviet involvement in international economic organizations. But that position is based on very little consultation within the U.S. government or with other Western governments. However, if Gorbachev continues to push hard for reform, then the issues will arise again and will deserve somewhat more serious deliberation.

IMPLICATIONS FOR THE GENERAL STATE OF EAST-WEST RELATIONS. It is difficult to predict how a fairly successful economic reform would affect Soviet foreign and defense policy. One does not know, for example, whether a successful reform presupposes a change in Soviet foreign and defense policy in the direction of accommodation (in order to create "breathing space" for the reforms to work) and an environment conducive to arranging the financing and improved foreign economic relations needed to support the reform. In any case, successful reforms would provide Soviet leaders with greater resources to pursue their policy goals, which would give them the *capability*, although not necessarily the inclination, to follow a more aggressive foreign policy and to finance a military buildup that would pose an even greater threat to U.S. national security. How Soviet leaders would use those enhanced capabilities would depend heavily on whether successful reforms were accompanied by, or even required, changes in the Soviet political system. In that case, the complexion of Soviet society could undergo a tremendous change, which could, but need not, have a profound effect on Soviet foreign and defense policies.

The breathing space. Reform would clearly be easier to achieve if tensions with the West were under better control than they have been during the Reagan period. An arms control agreement, particularly one that constrained U.S. military programs, could allow Soviet leaders more time to devote resources to the civilian economy in order to strengthen it, possibly in preparation for a new high-tech round of the arms race in the 1990s. For Soviet planners, reduced U.S.-Soviet tensions would ease the task of seeking finance and Western direct

Membership in the IMF, World Bank, and GATT," *PlanEcon Report*, vol. 2 (July 31, 1986).

investment in the Soviet economy. Presumably that consideration, along with some others, stimulated Gorbachev in 1986 to go on the offensive in searching for a broad accommodation with the United States on arms control issues.

But this incentive should not be interpreted as an imperative. The Soviet Union could construct a reform program almost exclusively on domestic capital and on domestically generated competitive pressures, supplemented by reduced import barriers and increased trade primarily with Europe and Japan. This would require a highly aggressive antimonopoly, deconcentration strategy in Soviet industry and careful shepherding of foreign exchange reserves; and it probably could be managed along with a judicious investment in new military technologies that have a decent chance of reducing significantly, but in a cost-effective way, the reliability of U.S. military programs.

This is not Gorbachev's preferred path, as is evident from his determined pursuit of a different path. But his enthusiasm should not be mistaken for desperation. There are other alternatives, even if Gorbachev persists in pushing for a radical reform; and even if Gorbachev has not yet thought through those possibilities, the logic of the situation will suggest them.

The increased resources available for foreign policy and defense goals. Successful reforms will provide the Soviet leadership with increased resources to serve its foreign policy and defense goals. Increased support for liberation movements in developing countries, increased economic involvement in these countries in general, and a still more ambitious defense effort are all possibilities. In this sense a successful economic reform in the USSR is a potential threat to U.S. interests, although not automatically a real threat. The question is whether economic reform will induce political change, and if that change in turn will lead to changes in policy.

There is a good chance that successful economic reforms will be accompanied by increased popular participation in the decisionmaking process, first in the workplace, and then in society at large. The January 1987 plenum has already begun to set the process in motion. But it requires a big leap to believe that such change would come quickly or be profound, or that Soviet foreign and defense policy would be immediately affected. It seems more plausible to suppose that whatever political reforms transpire would first affect primarily domestic policy, the impact on foreign and defense policies coming much later, if at all.

For that reason, whatever political change occurs in the USSR, it is not likely to touch policies of most concern to the West, particularly the United States. The result, then, could be a USSR having more economic resources and pursuing with considerably more vigor than before its traditional foreign policy and defense agenda. Even if the domestic sources of Soviet foreign policy become more heavily democratized, it is not clear that the result will necessarily be a more benign outcome for the West. To accept such a link is to accept the proposition that the Soviet Union's aspirations to be a world power rest primarily on the logic of Soviet socialism. But is it not also plausible to suppose that Soviet socialism has simply adopted the aspirations of Russian nationalism, and that a revitalized Soviet system would pursue those goals even more aggressively than before?

Those who believe that economic reforms will change the Soviet foreign and defense policy agenda have a better case in the "breathing space" argument, which states that the reform process represents such a heavy drain on Soviet economic and political resources that Soviet leaders must seek at least a temporary reduction in tensions with the West if they hope to continue along this path. The argument of a long-term link between reform and democratization, or between democratization and changes in Soviet foreign policy, is a more tenuous one.

Even if there were no dramatic change in the thrust of Soviet foreign policy as an indirect consequence of successful reforms, changes in the domestic political situation in the USSR could improve the atmosphere of U.S.-Soviet relations. Presumably, improvements in Soviet human rights policy and a visible increase in political participation in the USSR would—even in the absence of changes in Soviet defense and foreign policies—remove one source of U.S.-Soviet tension.

Consequences of a Generally Unsuccessful Reform Process

If, throughout the 1990s, the Soviet economy follows either the high-growth or failure scenarios, the consequences for East-West economic relations would be much different, as would be the consequences for Soviet foreign and defense policy.

IMPLICATIONS FOR EAST-WEST ECONOMIC RELATIONS. If the reform process were to fail, the Soviet Union would have to continue depending on raw materials, fuels, and weapons to support the bulk of its hard-currency earnings. With respect to the price of oil and related commodities, that could represent any of a wide range of hard-currency scenarios, none of which would be easy for Soviet policymakers to handle. At best the real price of energy in the 1990s might move back to its level of the late 1970s, but by the 1990s the USSR would be facing marginal costs for energy production far higher than they were in the 1970s. Energy exports, although still probably profitable, would therefore be less appealing than they were in the 1970s.

These difficulties should not prove unmanageable barring some bad luck (a collapse in oil prices, for example). Historically, Soviet financial planners have managed Soviet foreign financial dealings in a conservative and quite effective way in the face of extreme difficulties during certain periods. Because they are likely to continue in that vein, economic difficulties resulting from the failed reform process would not spill over uncontrollably into the foreign sector.

Instead, the consequence would be a probable increase in indebtedness, but within manageable limits. There would be no significant progress on joint ventures and no dramatic change in the character of Soviet-Western economic relations. Talk of membership in the IMF and GATT would dwindle, and policymakers would come to recognize that the reforms were not living up to their promise. In short, East-West economic relations would continue much as they have in recent years—in limbo.

IMPLICATIONS FOR THE GENERAL STATE OF EAST-WEST RELATIONS. A general failure in economic reforms, whether accompanied by high or low growth, would create increasing difficulties by the end of the century. If the reforms follow the failure scenario, the growth decline will recur in the 1990s. That, combined with a probable need to sustain, possibly increase, the commitment to defense, will lead to a stagnation in living standards, and a resulting increase in domestic tensions. Even with high growth, the civilian population and the military would become increasingly dissatisfied with the ability of the system to meet their needs.

In international affairs, Soviet leaders could rely only on the military to support the Soviet superpower role, a dangerous outcome for the rest of the world. Foreign policy—after a brief, but not very successful, public relations effort by Gorbachev—would return to a defensive and fairly insecure position that would help prolong U.S.-Soviet tensions. It would not be that much different from the policy of the late Brezhnev years, except for an important twist: the USSR would be more obviously stagnating, a situation that both it and the West might find difficult to manage without risk.

Implications for Western Policy

Western interests in the outcome of Soviet reform are somewhat mixed. Successful reform could mean a Soviet Union better equipped to pursue its traditional foreign policy and defense goals and a new customer for Western goods, but also a new competitor on world markets. At the same time, it could also mean gradual political liberalization and consequences very much in keeping with long-term Western interests.

Unsuccessful reform efforts would mean a USSR in difficulty. Although in this case Soviet military capability would be less of a direct threat to the West, a Soviet Union in decline might respond with a more aggressive, less stable foreign and defense policy.

Whatever the nature of Western interests, Western policy will not greatly affect the outcome of the process. The dynamics of reform in the USSR are primarily internal; what happens is affected by, but hardly driven by, developments in the outside world. Western influence, through various policies, will at most be capable of forcing minor corrections in the course of reform. Western credits cannot dramatically speed the process, although they could help it along. Withholding those credits, an implausible assumption given the current state of the Western alliance, would do no more than slow the process. Membership in the IMF or GATT would not make or break the reform, but might help the process along.

Thus, however strong Western feelings may be about the possible outcomes of this reform effort, Western policymakers should see that their "influence" on this process can be no more than modest. We, the outsiders, are primarily observers, not participants.

However, to the extent that Western governments can, and must, make decisions, the question remains, what should they do? Because of the mixed feelings about the outcome of the reforms, the answer here must reflect a net judgment that may, owing to the uncertainties, meet with substantial disagreement. My own view is that Western governments should favor economic reforms in the USSR. The main argument for such a position is that a USSR which is improving its economic performance and widening the basis on which its superpower status rests may ultimately become a more responsible participant in international political and economic affairs. There are no guarantees here, and the changes would take time. But it seems a more reasonable risk than the opposite one, namely, hoping that a USSR in decline will eventually be forced to change its foreign and defense policies in a way more to Western liking.

It is also possible to be agnostic on the reform process, arguing that it is difficult to know whether it will be good or bad for the West, and therefore decide to do nothing to either hinder or encourage reform. Given the uncertainties on these matters, that is a defensible position, but not one that I would support.

The most dangerous move would be to actively oppose the reform process. This would amount to formal and open disapproval of any improvement in Soviet economic performance, and implies a policy of economic warfare against the USSR. It also implies that the USSR cannot sustain its status as a superpower. That assumption denies reality and increases tensions with the USSR, possibly in the context of a failure of economic reforms. In itself such a policy would not significantly worsen relations, but in some contexts it could do so, and the consequences could be dangerous.

Practically speaking, the stand that Western governments take on economic reforms requires policy decisions in three general areas: arms control, potential Soviet requests for membership in international economic organizations, and policy changes to accommodate improved East-West economic relations.

ARMS CONTROL NEGOTIATIONS AND SOVIET ECONOMIC REFORMS. The "breathing space" argument points to the only potential link between arms control negotiations and Soviet economic reform. That is, the United States could take advantage of Soviet desire for improved U.S.-Soviet relations to reach agreements on important arms control issues. One consequence of such agreements, so this argument goes, would be to allow the Soviets to proceed with economic reforms more quickly than they otherwise could; some would even argue that without an arms control agreement, economic reforms would be difficult to implement.

Although this may accurately represent Gorbachev's motives and a broad agreement on arms control issues might indeed accelerate the economic reform, these seem to be minor considerations in the matter of arms control. Our interests in Soviet economic reform are so ambiguous, the links of reforms to foreign and defense policy so tenuous, that, on vital issues involving U.S. national security, the possible impact on Soviet economic reforms should be regarded as a possible small bonus, but no more. There are fundamentally sound, and very important, reasons to reach arms control agreements with the USSR that are directly linked to U.S. national security goals; encouraging economic reforms in the USSR is not one of those important reasons.

POSSIBLE SOVIET MEMBERSHIP IN INTERNATIONAL ECONOMIC ORGANIZA-TIONS. For some time, CMEA countries such as Romania, Poland, and Hungary have been members of GATT, the World Bank, and IMF; some have enjoyed that status for over a decade. In general, they have worked well in those organizations, conforming to the rules as well as many developing countries do, and participating responsibly in decisions. Although the Soviet Union belongs to none of those organizations, it participated in the Bretton Woods talks that led to the formation of the IMF and the World Bank, but dropped out at the end, apparently over the issue of being required to reveal the size of its gold reserves.[10]

However, the case of the USSR today is obviously a different one. As one of the world's largest economies, it would exert significant influence in each of these organizations. Unless the reforms were unexpectedly successful, the USSR would enter the organizations as a centrally planned economy, operating according to principles inconsistent with the free-trade goals of GATT and the convertible currency goals of the IMF. Moreover, barring a dramatic improvement in U.S.-Soviet relations, USSR membership would inevitably politicize the deliberations of organizations that aspire to be apolitical and objective in their decisions.

If there are good reasons to be skeptical of the workability, let alone the advisability, of Soviet membership in these organizations, there are also sound reasons to explore the possibility of some sort of relationship. Membership by a superpower in an international economic organization brings with it responsibilities to think about, and seek solutions for, some of the most troubling economic problems facing the world economy. The Soviet Union has managed, because of its detachment from world economic organizations, to avoid many of the issues involved here

10. On socialist countries in international economic organizations, see Paul Marer, "Centrally Planned Economies in the IMF, the World Bank, and GATT," in Josef C. Brada, Ed A. Hewett, and Thomas A. Wolf, eds., *Economic Adjustment and Reform in Eastern Europe and the Soviet Union: Essays in Honor of Franklyn D. Holzman* (forthcoming).

or to take relatively easy positions chosen mainly for their propaganda value. Membership in the IMF, the World Bank, and GATT would make that approach more difficult. Furthermore, the Soviet Union would be drawn directly into discussions with the West on its economic policy toward those Eastern European countries that are members.

Also, membership in these organizations could be used by Western countries to gain a better understanding of the Soviet economy and of Soviet economic policy. The data requirements associated with membership in these organizations and the right of IMF and World Bank delegations to regularly visit the USSR and interview top economic officials would give the West a new window on the Soviet economy. The information gained would significantly improve our understanding of how the Soviet system operates.

Finally, Soviet membership in these organizations would serve to broaden somewhat and stabilize the basis of the East-West relationship. An East-West relationship built solely on arms-control negotiations is, both sides agree, a fragile relationship.

If to all these considerations one adds a desire to see economic reforms move forward, the logic is compelling for at least discussing with the USSR the possibility of membership in these organizations. There is no need to assume that such discussions would lead to membership; it might prove impossible to work anything out in the current political climate. Moreover, if Soviet economic reforms soon begin to experience significant difficulties, that could reduce Soviet enthusiasm for membership in these organizations. But, from the Western point of view, it seems advisable not to reject Soviet expressions of interest in these international economic organizations out of hand, but rather to keep the option open through discussions in which the United States would have to take the lead.

POLICY CHANGES TO ACCOMMODATE IMPROVED EAST-WEST ECONOMIC RELATIONS. A number of trade and financial issues, most of which involve individual Western countries, will arise as the Soviets move to improve their economic relations with the West. U.S. export controls are bound to be an issue, as are U.S. restrictions on financing exports to the USSR, most-favored-nation (MFN) treatment, and antidumping legislation relating to trade with the USSR. Without going into detail on these issues, I mention several general considerations that should guide policies in these areas.

First, if there is a consensus in the U.S. government that we would be better off seeing reforms succeed in the USSR, controls on exports and financial flows should be pared down to the minimum consistent with basic national security interests. With regard to financial flows, that would mean reopening Soviet access to Export-Import Bank credits on terms available to other countries. It would also generally mean reducing U.S. export controls to a level conforming with those of other industrialized countries, following a narrow definition of dual-use (civilian-defense) commodities. This will undoubtedly be an even more controversial issue than it has been, since successful economic reform in the USSR would involve a considerable expansion in its demands for fairly advanced technology from the West.

The other important issue has to do with barriers to imports of manufactured goods from the USSR. A general policy supporting the reform process in the USSR would suggest that MFN status should be granted without links to human rights issues. How the Soviets could reciprocate with an equivalent to MFN treatment in their own system is an issue requiring careful attention.[11] But the general principle should be that no special barriers are erected to discriminate against the USSR in its efforts to expand exports of manufactured goods. The United States can, and should, continue its pressure on the USSR in the area of human rights, in the process broadening the agenda beyond a focus on the right to free immigration. But our most effective tool there is surely the moral force of our arguments. It is hard to see how a continuation of discriminatory tariffs on Soviet imports advances the cause of human rights in the USSR, and easy to see how the lack of MFN treatment is a highly visible roadblock to a normalization of economic relations.

In all of these policies, U.S. and Western measures should be carefully drawn and modest. It would be unwise to fall into the trap of offering special credits or other subsidies to the Soviet Union in support of economic reforms. Western interest is not so strong, nor are the consequences of reform so certain, to dictate such a policy.

The USSR in the Twenty-first Century

The reform of the Soviet economy has been a more or less constant goal of Soviet leaders since the death of Stalin. Every Soviet leader has

11. See, for example, Edward A. Hewett, "Most-Favored Nation Treatment under Central Planning," *Slavic Review,* vol. 37 (March 1978), pp. 25–39.

tried in his own way to push that agenda forward, and none before Gorbachev has enjoyed notable success. That uninspired record serves as a cautionary note to any tendency toward inflated claims of what Gorbachev can accomplish in this, the latest, effort to reform the Soviet economy.

Mikhail Sergeevich Gorbachev seems to be a different kind of leader; he is more internationally minded and tougher in pushing his policies, yet more flexible in what those policies are, and acts with a greater sense of urgency than previous Soviet leaders did.

But he is also a product of the old system. He has been educated by it and is a politician who has succeeded by working the system. His approach reflects the continuity of his background: in part it is a refutation of the past, and in part it is a recasting of past policies. Those links to the past bring with them the weaknesses of past approaches.

It will be some time before it is clear how this tension between the old and the new—between Gorbachev the product of the system and Gorbachev the transformer of the system—will be resolved. He could fail. But much that he has done suggests that failure would come only after a very determined struggle to succeed. And that suggests we should be cautious about being too impressed by the failures of the past. Mikhail Gorbachev just may be the first leader in the post-Stalin era to succeed in beginning the long, arduous task of transforming the Soviet economy and Soviet society.

Index

Abalkin, Leonid, 266n, 274n, 278n, 292n, 294
Adam, Jan, 141n, 206n, 207n, 243n
Adams, Arthur E., 5n
Afonin, Veniamin G., 104n
Aganbegian, Abel G., 69, 70, 71, 73, 267n, 309n, 324
Agriculture: enterprise food-production requirements, 175; investment policy changes, 19; output growth rates, 52, 54, 60–61; party intervention in, 166–67; plans for, 128–29; private plots, 117; procurement prices, 131; short-comings of, 32; subsidies in, 133; urban labor requisitioned for, 166–67; weather factors, 95
Agro-industrial complex, 109, 328, 337
Aliev, Geidar A., 107
All-union industrial associations (VPOs): Andropov experiment, interference with, 264, 266; creation of, 246–47; elimination under Gorbachev, 328, 339–40; function of, 116
Amann, Ronald, 146n, 174n, 204n, 217n, 219n
Ambartsumov, E. A., 288
Andreev, V., 173n
Andrienko, G. N., 180n
Andropov, Iurii V., 162; on corrections of plans, 208; debates on the economy, encouragement of, 21, 274, 288; on incentive system, 211; on innovation, 216; last speech, 273n; on need for economic reform, 31, 32, 257–58, 259; on quality problem, 78, 81; reform philosophy, 259–60; on Soviet position in world economy, 365

Andropov experiment, 260–61; contract fulfillment indicator, 261–62, 269–70; design flaws, 270–71; as detail-oriented reform, 272; discipline in the economy, emphasis on, 259, 261–62; extension of, 267, 322, 334, 343–44; implementation of, 263–66; incentive system reform, 260, 261–62, 267–68n, 270–71; independence for enterprises, 263; limits to, 271–73; ministerial interference, 264–66; ministries, impact on, 271; moderates' views on, 284; new technology introduced to the workplace, 263; *1965* reforms, similarity to, 272; output performance measures, 262–63; plan indicators, 261; "ratchet" principle and, 263, 268–69; results of, 266–70; successes of, 266–67
Annual plans, 58, 124–29; in Gorbachev investment policy, 319–22
Antonov, Alexei, 261n
Aranovskii, V. A., 42n
Arms control, 382–83, 387–88
Autarky of ministries and enterprises, 170–76, 227
Avdeenko, Aleksandr, 201

Baibakov, Nikolai, 112n, 260, 281–82, 283n, 308n
Baibakov Commission, 260, 300
Baily, Martin Neil, 77n
Balan, V., 76n
Banking system: reform of, 299; supervision of, 114
Bankruptcy, 16; equality-efficiency trade-off and, 295–96; radicals' views on, 295

393